WILLIAM MORRIS

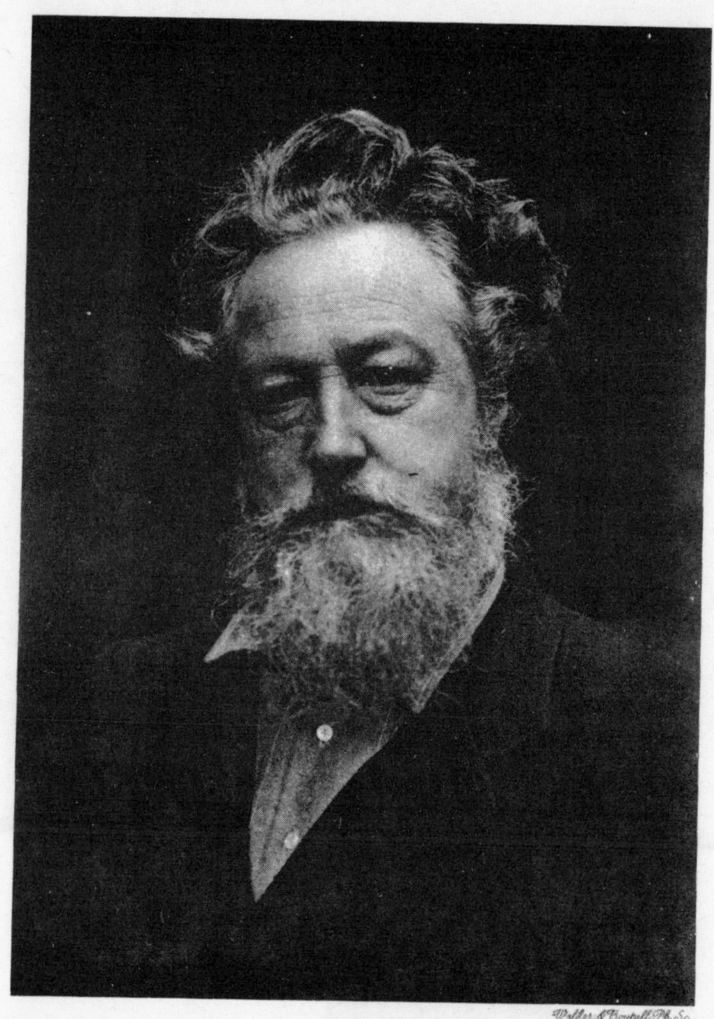

Walker & Boutall Ph. Sc.

William Morris

WILLIAM MORRIS
HIS ART HIS WRITINGS AND HIS PUBLIC LIFE

A RECORD BY

AYMER VALLANCE

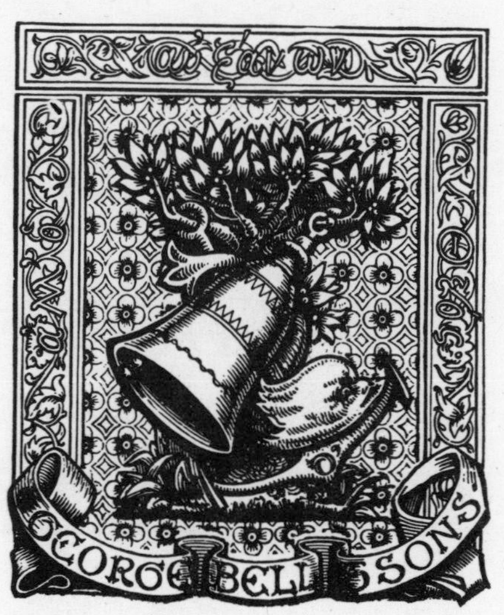

The Life and Work of William Morris

First published in 1897 by George Bell & Sons

This edition published in 1995 by Studio Editions,
an imprint of Studio Editions Ltd, Princess House,
50 Eastcastle Street, London W1N 7AP, England

ISBN 1 85891 287 3

Printed at Thomson Press (India) Ltd.

PREFACE

THOUGH it was not my intention to conform to the convention of writing a preface, circumstances have made it necessary that I should do so. In the first place I may draw attention to the fact that I chose purposely to name my book as I have done, so as to show that it makes no claim to be a biography or a record of Mr. Morris's private and family affairs. Such a work I was neither asked nor authorized to write. It is true, of course, that I had the privilege of knowing the late Mr. Morris personally—from the year 1883 onwards until his death. At the same time I submit that, with a few trifling exceptions, I have not introduced into the book any details of his life which were not already common property—which could not just as well have been strung together by any-one who knew where to find the scattered references in Mr. Morris's own writings, and in various other publications, without ever having met Mr. Morris face to face; nor more than such as were necessary to link together the contents of the book in some sort of consecutive order.

I am bound to state that when, having been commissioned to do so, I first approached Mr. Morris, in the autumn of 1894, on the question of the proposed book, he told me frankly that he did not want it done either by myself or anybody else so long as he was alive, but that if I would only wait until his death I might do it. Thus I am now in the position of having Mr. Morris's express sanction to bring out a work upon himself; nor need I point out that he could have stopped its preparation at the outset, had he chosen to withhold permission to reproduce his designs. Whereas, on the contrary, he insisted that, if the work came out at all, it must be illustrated; he gave me then and there a general permission to reproduce a selection from the property of the firm of Morris and Co., provided I obtained the consent of his partners. He wrote to them himself, as I afterwards learned, to let them know that he, for his part, had given his consent, and left the matter thenceforward to their discretion to accord me such facilities as they pleased (which I am bound to say they did with a courtesy coupled with the kindest assistance, for which I do not know how to express all the thanks that are due); he gave me specific authority to reproduce a number of ornaments of the Kelmscott Press, some of which he suggested and chose for me himself, only stipulating that the blocks for this purpose should be prepared by Mr. Emery Walker; he referred me to Mr. Fairfax Murray, the owner of some early cartoons of great value from the artist's hand; and lastly, when he lay on his deathbed, Lady Burne-Jones having asked him, on my application to be shown the books illuminated by him in her possession, whether he approved of her doing so, he replied that it was quite right, and himself told her of the forthcoming book I had in preparation. Accordingly, Lady Burne-Jones was good enough to let me see all the books I desired, and moreover allowed me the opportunity of making what notes of them I pleased for publication. For the rest, except for a number of necessary corrections and useful suggestions, kindly offered me by Mr. F. S. Ellis and Mr. S. C. Cockerell, most of which are incorporated into the chapter on the Kelmscott Press, neither the members of Mr. Morris's family nor his friends have made themselves responsible for what I have written.

I was compelled, for reasons explained in the preface to "The Art of William Morris,"[1] to confine myself then to a portion only of the work I had intended to publish. At the same time I hinted at the possibility of issuing at some future date all the matter I had in hand relating to the subject. This I am glad to be able now to do. The present volume comprises fifteen, whereas the former consisted of only eight chapters, and represents my work in a complete form. As in the case of the former book the chapter on the firm of Morris and Co., Decorators, remains perhaps the distinctive feature, treating as it does connectedly of what is, I believe, so far fresh ground, nothing beyond incidental notices or short articles having been written by previous writers on the history of this

[1] "The Art of William Morris." By Aymer Vallance; and Bibliography by Temple Scott. Imperial 4to. London, 1897.

most important factor in the progress of modern art. Added to the above I may venture to name the twelfth chapter, the compilation of which cost me more anxious care and research than almost any other portion of my book. Here, again, more exhaustively and in greater detail than anybody has done hitherto, I have traced the course of Mr. Morris's connection with a movement which, whether one sympathizes with it or not, has been described as "the vital force in contemporary society and politics."

In conclusion I have to acknowledge my indebtedness to Mr. Temple Scott for allowing me to base upon his bibliography my chronological list of Mr. Morris's printed works and of the Kelmscott publications; to Mr. Fairfax Murray for much information, and for permission to reproduce some beautiful works of art in his collection; to Sir Edward Burne-Jones for helping me to select for reproduction certain typical details of tapestry from his design; and, lastly, to the many others, especially Mr. Gleeson White, Mr. Emery Walker, Mr. Frederick H. Evans, and Miss Gertrude Anderson, who, in various ways, have contributed to lighten the responsibilities of my task.

AYMER VALLANCE.

LONDON, *August*, 1897.

CONTENTS

destined to have an extraordinary influence upon him and his circle, the 'Morte d'Arthur' of Malory. The copy, in two volumes, of Southey's edition of 1817, is still in existence, which Morris bought and had bound in white vellum, while he was still an undergraduate at Exeter, and in which he and his friends became acquainted with the Arthurian legend."

But that was not all. The Pre-Raphaelite movement, which was by this time steadily making its way, was not wholly unrepresented in the city of Oxford, where Mr. Combe, the director of the Clarendon Press and a liberal art patron, had already gathered together the nucleus of a Pre-Raphaelite collection. Amongst other works of which he acquired possession were Holman Hunt's famous "Light of the World," and his less known picture "A family of Converted Britons succouring Christian priests," and also Dante Gabriel Rossetti's beautiful water colour, "Dante celebrating the anniversary of Beatrice's death." The work of the latter artist only needed to become known to Morris and Burne-Jones to find at once a responsive chord in the breasts of the two friends; for them to recognize in him the truest exponent living of their own high ideals. It is difficult to say which of them conceived the more passionate admiration for the great Pre-Raphaelite master. In the mind of either no doubt remained as to his proper vocation, and both decided to devote themselves to an artistic calling; and that notwithstanding the prevailing bias of University opinion was decidedly adverse to such a course, if we may accept what one of their friends wrote in the "Oxford and Cambridge Magazine" in an essay entitled "Oxford." "The Fine Arts," the writer remarks, "wherein Truth appears in its most lovable aspect, where are they? Mr. Ruskin says bitterly, that only they who have had the blessing of a bad education can be expected to know anything of painting. Certainly Oxford must bear a large share of the shame that in England the Fine Arts are considered only as 'accomplishments' for ladies, and artists are held to follow only a superior trade."

It was some time about Christmas 1855, that Burne-Jones, abandoning his idea of entering the ministry, first sought out Rossetti in London with the intention of becoming his pupil. Nor did long time elapse before he introduced his friend Morris to his new-found master, whom he then described as "the greatest man in Europe." Following the latter's advice, Burne-Jones went down from Oxford instead of waiting to take his degree, in order to begin the systematic study and practice of art without loss of time. William Morris, on the contrary, in no hurry to leave Oxford, preferred to complete his University course, and took his B.A. degree in 1856.

CHAPTER TWO: FROM OXFORD TO LONDON.

MORRIS was, as has been stated, only a boy at Marlborough College at the date of the original formation of the Pre-Raphaelite Brotherhood, nor was he at any time later on enrolled formally in their ranks. Yet he did not hold himself so far aloof but that he became associated, like Ford Madox Brown, who neither belonged to the Brotherhood, with the most prominent members of the school in more than one early enterprise. In fact, to so large an extent was he influenced by them, that, if not in absolute accord with their aims and theories in every detail, it cannot be said that the standpoint from which he started differed in any material degree from theirs. A year or two before his death Rossetti is stated to have spoken with some amount of contempt of the movement and of "the visionary vanities of half a dozen boys," adding "we've all grown out of them, I hope, by now." Anyhow, the members of the school were very much in earnest at the beginning, and it does not appear that Morris ever referred to them otherwise than in the highest terms. "You know well," said he, in a lecture delivered at Birmingham in 1880, "that one of the master arts, the art of painting, has been revolutionized. I have a genuine difficulty in speaking to you of men who are my own personal friends, nay, my masters. Still, since I cannot quite say nothing of them, I must say the plain truth, which is this: never in the whole history of art did any set of men come nearer to the feat of making something out of nothing than that little knot of painters who have raised English art from what it was when as a boy I used to go to the Royal Academy Exhibition, to what it is now." The principles of the Brotherhood, as understood by Mr. Morris, and as set forth by him in the already referred to address at Birmingham in 1891, are, briefly, as follows: firstly, "the root doctrine, Naturalism," by no means to be confounded with Realism in the modern sense, for "pictures painted with that end in view will be scarcely works of Art." The Naturalism of the Pre-

Raphaelites meant the deriving inspiration direct from Nature, instead of allowing themselves to be fettered by the lifeless conventions of Academical tradition. In the second place, their work must have an epical quality; in other words, they "aimed, some of them no doubt much more than others, at the conscientious presentment of incident." The third necessity is the ornamental quality. "No picture, it seems to me," says Mr. Morris, "is complete unless it is something more than a representation of nature and the teller of a tale. It ought also to have a definite, harmonious, conscious beauty. It ought to be ornamental. It ought to be possible for it to be part of a beautiful whole in a room, or church, or hall. Now, of the original Pre-Raphaelites, Rossetti was the man who mostly felt that side of the art of painting; all his pictures have a decorative quality as an essential, and not as a mere accident of them." But to add, for the fuller development of the school, what was lacking of "the element of *perfect* ornamentation," to vindicate its position as representing "a branch of the great Gothic art which once pervaded all Europe," one other distinguishing feature was necessary, viz., Romance; "and this quality is eminently characteristic of both Rossetti and Burne-Jones, but especially of the latter."

Is it permissible to go a step further and to affirm that all these excellent qualities were yet inadequate, so long as the consummating quality, too apt to be overlooked just because of its very humbleness, was lacking? that one which, in default of a better name, may be called the domestic element? Perhaps the difference it made was not so much one of kind as of degree, of the extent to which Pre-Raphaelite principles were capable of application, or ought properly to be applied, to other arts beside painting. It is due to William Morris that all arts were brought within the comprehension of one and the same organic scheme; and herein he proved himself in advance of the Pre-Raphaelites, that he did succeed in giving the revival of art a wider and profounder scope than they. True, one of them was a sculptor, others men of letters;

but excepting the production of the short-lived magazine "The Germ," until Mr. Morris joined the movement, the function of art in their hands had been confined practically to the making of pictures; and thus the best of their works, in the nature of the case, could affect the public taste but indirectly and to a limited degree. For a number of years such pictures as were exhibited by the painters of the Pre-Raphaelite school were to be found, as a rule, only in obscure galleries; many were not shown to the public at all, but passed direct from the artists' studios into the hands of private purchasers. In any event, not the many but the few could possibly become the fortunate possessors of original paintings. It is, therefore, a supreme achievement of William Morris's to have brought Art, through the medium of the handicrafts, within reach of thousands who could never hope to obtain but a transitory view of Pre-Raphaelite pictures; his distinction, by decorating the less pretending but not less necessary articles of household furnishing, to have done more than any man in the present century to beautify the plain, everyday home-life of the people.

That was a fitting tribute, paid in his official capacity of Vice-President of the Society of Arts, when, taking the chair at the reading of Mr. Morris's paper on the Woodcuts of Gothic Books, Sir George Birdwood thus introduced the lecturer:—"It is not only as a poet and an art critic that he is one of the first Englishmen of the Victorian age. When the decorative arts of this country had, about the middle of the present century, become denationalised, it was Mr. William Morris 'who stemmed the torrent of a downward age,' and, by the vigour of his characteristic English genius, upraised those household arts again from the degradation of nearly two generations, and carried them to a perfection never before reached by them. . . . A born decorator, he knew that it is decoration that animates architecture, and all form, with life and beauty, But being also a trained architect, he from the first recognized that ornament was but an accessory to construction of every kind, from the vessels turned on a potter's wheel to the grandest creations of the builder's master art. Thus, and by his commanding intellectual and moral personal influence with his contemporaries, the future of English decorative design, in all its applications, was redeemed by Mr. Morris."

But, not to anticipate, the various stages by which this came about must be traced step by step. Referring to the time when Mr. Morris found himself at the outset of his artistic career, the late Mr. William Bell Scott wrote: "Morris's first step in this direction was to article himself to George Edmund Street, then located in the University town as architect to the diocese" of Oxford. The very fact of his electing an architect's training proves how thoroughly William Morris, as compared with the others of the movement, had grasped the fundamental idea of the the nature and essence of Art. If not the first of them to recognize in theory, he was at any rate the first to act logically upon what is involved by the principle that all true ornament must be derived from and allied to some archetypal form of architecture, not necessarily in so pronounced a manner as to be obvious at first sight, yet always in such a way as may be disclosed on analysis. To William Morris architecture is at once the basis and crowning-point of every other art, the standard by which all the rest must be dominated and appraised: again and again has he insisted that no sound art can exist as the common practice and possession of a nation which has lost its architectural traditions. Thus he himself puts the case:—"I have spoken of the popular arts, but they might all be summed up in that one word Architecture; they are all parts of that great whole, and the art of house-building begins it all: if we did not know how to dye or to weave; if we had neither gold, nor silver, nor silk; and no pigments to paint with, but half a dozen ochres and umbers, we might yet frame a worthy art that would lead to everything, if we had but timber, stone and lime, and a few cutting tools to make these common things not only shelter us from wind and weather, but also express the thoughts and aspirations that stir in us. Architecture would lead us to all the arts, as it did with earlier men: but if we despise it and take no note of how we are housed, the other arts will have a hard time of it indeed." Architecture, therefore, in the wider sense of the term, he considers "to mean the art of creating a building with all the appliances fit for carrying on a dignified and happy life." Again, "A true architectural work is a building duly provided with all the necessary furniture, decorated with all due ornament, according to the use, quality and dignity of the building, from mere mouldings or abstract lines, to the great epical works of sculpture and painting, which, except as decorations of the nobler form of such buildings, cannot be produced at all. So looked on, a work of architecture is a harmonious, co-operative work of art, inclusive of all the serious arts, all those which are not engaged in the production of mere toys, or of ephemeral prettinesses."

This is the keynote of Morris's art doctrine, this the secret of his own masterful power of constructive ornament. Whether or not he intend to devote his life to an architect's profession, no better education for an artist can be desired than that he should be strengthened at the beginning with an architectural back-bone. Consider, for instance, the one continental decorator who, beside the honourable exception of M. Serrurier of Liège, may be said to share in any notable degree the æsthetic qualities of the English school, that is, of the school of Morris. Although it is true that neither does Eugène Grasset any longer practise as an architect, still, when one contrasts his work with that which generally passes for decoration in the modern French school, the remarkable breadth and versatility of his designs must be attributed to the early discipline of his architectural training.

Judged by the standard of the present day, Mr. Morris's choice of a master may be indeed not a little surprising. Nay, in view of Mr. Street's neo-thirteenth century platitudes, more particularly in view of his largest and most conspicuous performance, the Courts of Justice in Fleet Street, it is hard to imagine how, save by way of warning what at all hazards to avoid, there could have been anything to impart by such a teacher to the pupil so gifted. Mr. Morris, with generous loyalty, has indeed written: "As to public buildings, Mr. Street's Law Courts are the last attempt we are likely to see of producing anything reasonable or beautiful for that use." And in addition it is only fair to recall the fact that time was when in cases of proposed "restorations" of ancient churches, &c., cautious and discriminating judges of these matters used to consider Street, among the contemporary architects, the most capable and the safest man to be entrusted with the responsibility of dealing with the precious handiworks that our fathers have bequeathed to us. Moreover, for upwards of five years, from May, 1852, the date when, by the advice of Mr. J. H. Parker, he migrated from Wantage, Mr. Street had been quartered in Oxford. Thence he eventually moved to Montague Place, Bloomsbury. But his residence in the University city coincided exactly with the space of Morris's undergraduate period, and during that time and onwards Mr. Street continued to maintain the kindliest attitude towards the leaders of the æsthetic revival. "The Pre-Raphaelite movement," to quote the memoir written by his son, Arthur Edmund Street, "found in him a hearty and earnest adherent, and one who on many occasions, by writing and speaking, impressed on his brethren the importance and propriety of their giving it all the moral support in their power. He felt truly that the aim of the young enthusiasts, who were striving for truth before everything, was, in their particular field, identical with the aim of the leaders of the Gothic revival in the field of architecture. His known views speedily brought him into relations of friendship with many of those who belonged to the Pre-Raphaelite group, or were in sympathy with it." So after all it is not difficult to account for the fact of Mr. Morris having been drawn to look for the realization of his hopes under Mr. Street's tuition. For a time, at least, he entered with enthusiasm into his master's projects. For instance, there happened an open competition of designs for a Cathedral to be erected at Lille. The announcement had been made in the previous year, 1855. The chief condition stipulated on was that the building must be in the French Gothic style. Morris's principal was one of the English architects who prepared and sent in designs. Contrary to usual custom, the several drawings were shown to the public before being submitted to the jury for selection. Mr. Street, accompanied by William Morris, took the occasion to run over to Lille for a few days' visit, and wrote home thence with reference to the designs. "We have had about three hours at the Exhibition. We are agreed naturally that I ought to have place No. 1. . . . . I really think I shall have one of the prizes. Morris says the first." The pupil's over sanguine, yet pardonable, expectations, were not destined to be fulfilled; for as a matter of fact Street's design, though not passed over altogether, was awarded only the second prize.

It was a comparatively short time that Morris continued under Street's tuition. Not the least of Morris's characteristics was his remarkable gift of concentration; and this, together with the astounding rapidity with which he was wont to go straight to the root of a matter and to master in the space of a few months, or even weeks, that of which it would take an ordinary mortal as many years of laborious application to learn maybe the bare rudiments, fortunately made it unnecessary for him to submit to be hampered for any length of time by the irksome routine of office work. After nine months had expired Morris threw up his articles with Mr. Street; for the premium he had paid he preferred to sacrifice if by so doing he might only be set free to strike out an independent line of action for himself. He never qualified nor entered the formal profession of architect.

One circumstance of no small importance in his subsequent career Mr. Morris owed to the brief period of his discipleship, namely, his becoming acquainted with his loyal and intimate friend Mr. Philip Webb, who at that time was employed as chief assistant to Mr. Street, and is well known at the present day as an architect in practice in Raymond Buildings, Gray's Inn. The other advantage that had resulted, says Mr. Herbert Horne (who, however, takes perhaps rather a cynical view of the case), was that "Morris soon discovered that the modern architect is concerned not with the production of architecture, but with the conduct of business." Unquestionably Morris conceived a strong aversion to the mechanical office-plan system of neat and elaborately laboured drawings on paper for the art of architecture. No permanent or vital good could result from such a system, he was convinced,—a system belonging to the period when the accepted teaching was "that nothing could be art that was not done by a named man under academical rules." But, further, Mr. Street, in his capacity of official architect of the diocese of Oxford, was engaged, at the very time of Mr. Morris's articles, "in the wholesale 'restoration' of Gothic buildings, as their destruction is still euphemistically called for the purposes of the profession." It was therefore impossible but that the pupil should have an opportunity of gaining "that insight into the ways of the 'restorer' which afterwards caused" him and his companion Webb "to found and carry on, with so much influence for good, . . . the Society for the Protection of Ancient Buildings."

On going down from Oxford in 1856, Mr. Morris settled in lodgings, with his friend Burne-Jones, at 17, Red Lion Square, where they shared a studio in common. There was, indeed, at the beginning of the next year, some idea of extending the *ménage* so as to form a sort of college of artists working together with kindred tastes and aims, but, for some reason or other, the plan was not found to be practicable, and so nothing came of it.

Another event of 1856 was the appearance of "The Oxford and Cambridge Magazine," in the preparation of which, under the direction of Rev. Canon R. W. Dixon and Rev. William Fulford, Mr. Morris took a prominent part. Conducted by members of the two Universities, the magazine was issued in London from the house of Messrs. Bell and Daldy. This serial lasted exactly a year, being published in monthly numbers from January to December inclusive. Originally sold at one shilling per part, it has now become both scarce and valuable. Mr. Morris's own copy was guarded with the utmost care; while that in the British Museum is to be seen only by the reader who, passing through a barrier into an inner room, remains under the immediate observation of one of the library officials. The contents of the magazine comprise essays, tales, poems, and notices of books, all the matter, except the verse, being printed in double columns. One or two contributions are initialled, but not one appears with the full signature of its author. Dante Gabriel Rossetti, who, however, was not connected with the "Oxford and Cambridge Magazine" for the first half year of its existence, contributed "The Burden of Nineveh" to the August part, "The Blessed Damozel," a version of which had already appeared in "The Germ," to the November part, and "The Staff and Scrip" in December. Among other writers were Vernon Lushington, Jex-Blake and Burne-Jones. But the largest contributor was William Morris, who furnished a series of short prose romances, and a small number of poems, which immediately signalized their author as a man of extraordinary talents, on the strength of which it was not rash for his friends and others to whom his identity was known to augur that a brilliant future in the world of letters awaited him. It was evident that Ruskin had influenced him to no small extent, and also that he was imbued very deeply, with the spirit of mediæval romance.

The following, as far as can be ascertained, is a complete list of William Morris's contributions to "The Oxford and Cambridge Magazine," in the order of publication:

The Story of the Unknown Church. A tale	January.
Winter Weather. A poem	"
The Churches of North France. I. Shadows of Amiens. An essay	February.
A Dream. A tale	March.

"Men and Women" by Robert Browning. Critical notice	March.
Frank's Sealed Letter. A tale . .	April.
A Night in a Cathedral. A tale . .	May.
Riding Together. A poem	,,
Ruskin and the Quarterly. An essay .	June.
Gertha's Lovers. A tale. Part I. Chapters 1-3	July.
Hands. A poem	,,
"Death the Avenger" and "Death the Friend." Critical notice . .	August.
Svend and his Brethren. A tale . .	,,
Gertha's Lovers. Part II. Chapters 4 and 5	,,
Lindenborg Pool. A tale	September.
The Hollow Land. A tale. Part I. Chapters 1 and 2	,,
The Chapel in Lyoness. A poem . .	,,
The Hollow Land. Part II. Chapter 3.	October.
Pray but one Prayer for us, &c. A poem.	,,
Golden Wings. A tale	December.

"Perhaps the best of Morris's tales in the 'Oxford and Cambridge Magazine,'" says the late William Bell Scott, "were 'Gertha's Lovers' and the 'Hollow Land,' but all of his contributions were unmistakable in imaginative beauty, and will some day be re-published." The poems which first saw the light in the magazine, with the exception of that entitled "Winter Weather," did in fact appear in the volume which Mr. Morris published two years later. But as regards the prose writings, unhappily the day for the fulfilment of Bell Scott's prediction has not yet arrived. Nor, seeing how severe a critic Mr. Morris was of his own work, and how sensitive he was on the subject of whatever he deemed immature experiments of his, was it probable that he ever would have consented to reprint any of his early writings in prose that were included in the "Oxford and Cambridge Magazine." And so they still lie buried, these "wonderful prose fantasies" of Mr.

Morris's, "these strangely coloured and magical dreams," as Mr. Andrew Lang not inaptly calls them. If "Lindenborg Pool" may not be accounted among the best or the most original of Morris's tales, nevertheless there attaches to it a peculiar interest, because of its opening passage: "I read once in lazy humour Thorpe's 'Northern Mythology' on a cold May night when the north wind was blowing; in lazy humour, but when I came to the tale that is here amplified, there was something in the tale that fixed my attention and made me think of it; and whether I would or no, my thoughts ran in this way, as here follows. So I felt obliged to write, and wrote accordingly, and by the time I had done the grey light filled all my room; so I put out my candles, and went to bed, not without fear and trembling, for the morning twilight is so strange and lonely." The above should not fail to be noted as the earliest published reference to its author's being attracted to a branch of study—Norse folk-lore and language, to wit—the knowledge of which he has done so much to extend amongst us that he may be said to have imparted additional distinction to the olden literature, and to have given it a fresh lease of life that shall endure, coupled henceforward with his own illustrious name, as long as the English tongue is spoken.

CHAPTER THREE: EARLY ART AND POETRY.

ESTABLISHED in town with his friend Edward Burne-Jones, at an age when, on looking back after ten or eleven years, he deemed himself as having been "pretty much a boy," it was only natural that Morris should begin to enlarge his circle of literary and artistic acquaintances. In a letter to William Bell Scott in 1875, acknowledging the gift of a book of verse by that writer, Morris refers to these early days and thanks him for "the poems that I first found so sympathetic when I came up to London years ago."

Rossetti, who was the means of introducing Morris to Ruskin and other well-known artists and literary men, writes thus to Bell Scott in the spring of the year 1857: "Two young men, projectors of 'The Oxford and Cambridge Magazine,' have recently come to town from Oxford, and are now very intimate friends of mine. Their names are Morris and Jones." (How commonplace a sound has this introductory mention, and how little suggestive of the celebrity they were ultimately to attain!) "They have turned artists instead of taking up any other career to which the University generally leads, and both are men of real genius. Jones's designs are marvels of finish and imaginative detail, unequalled by anything unless perhaps Albert Dürer's finest works; and Morris, though without practice as yet, has no less power, I fancy. He has written some really wonderful poetry too." That "the powers of the two men were very distinct" is the judgment which, when Bell Scott came to know them, himself formed and left on record in his "Autobiographical Notes."

Morris now set to work in real earnest, the preparation of his first volume of poems occupying no small portion of his time and attention. Nevertheless, he did not devote his energies exclusively to literature. In June, 1857, Rossetti writes again to Bell Scott, "Morris has as yet done nothing in art, but is now busily painting his first picture, 'Sir Tristram after his illness, in the garden of King Mark's Palace, recognized by the dog he had given to Iseult,' from the 'Morte d'Arthur.' It is being done all from nature of course, and I believe will turn out capitally." The picture was ordered by Mr. Plint who, growing impatient, it would appear, at the artist's delay in finishing it, wrote to Morris's friend, Madox Brown, to find out how the work was progressing, and when he should receive it. In reply Madox Brown writes as follows on April 23rd, 1861 :—"Morris I have spoken to. His picture is now in my house, and at my suggestion he has so altered it that it is quite a fresh work. There is still a figure in the foreground to be scraped out and another put in its place. It is this sort of work which makes it so difficult for a real artist to say when a painting will be finished. I take as much interest in Morris's picture turning out good as though it were my own, for, though it was not commissioned at my recommendation, I have repeatedly since told you that Morris is a man of real genius."

Rossetti was mainly instrumental, with others of Morris's friends, in founding the Club known as the "Hogarth," a name of evil promise—so one might have supposed—to any who seriously entertained hopes of the regeneration of English art. Mr. William Michael Rossetti is the authority for saying that "the original Hogarth Club was so named on the ground that Hogarth was the first great figure in British art, and still remains one of the greatest. Madox Brown (not to speak of other projectors of the Club) entertained this view very strongly, and I think it probable that *he* was the proposer of the name." But for this statement one would have believed that the choice of style could only have been one of those audacious whims wheretoward youthfulness, prone to paradox, will sometimes be drawn. Be that as it may, from its foundation and first meeting in July, 1858, down to April, 1861, when it was dissolved, the Hogarth Club proved a select resort of many distinguished men of the advanced artists and litterateurs of the time. It counted among its members, beside William Morris and the two brothers Rossetti, Mr. F. G. Stephens, who was Honorary Secretary, Lord Houghton, Sir Frederic Leighton, Sir Edward Burne-Jones, Col. Gillum, and Messrs. J. Ruskin, Ford Madox Brown, Spencer Stanhope, G. F. Watts, Arthur Hughes, Thomas Woolner, Hungerford Pollen, A. C. Swinburne, the Lushingtons, R. B. Martineau, Henry Wallis, P. A. Daniell, G. F. Bodley, John Brett, Eyre Crowe, jun., Michael F. Halliday, W. Holman Hunt, Edward Lear, Val. Prinsep, W. Bell Scott, George Edmund Street, Philip Webb, Benjamin Woodward, and various other men of mark. At the picture exhibitions held under its auspices from time to time, works of the Pre-Raphaelite school were sure of finding a welcome. Moving, after no long while, from its original premises at 178, Piccadilly, the Hogarth then continued for the remainder of its existence at 6, Waterloo Place. It had no connection of any sort—it may be observed—with the Club which but lately bore the same name, in Dover Street.

The year 1858 was one "which seems," says Mr. George Saintsbury in "Corrected Impressions," "to have exercised a very remarkable influence on the books and persons born in it," since "the books (as biographers and bibliographers have before noticed) were unusually epoch-making." It was in this year that Morris published his first book. To be quite accurate one must not omit to record that the earliest work to bear the name of William Morris for author was a short poem, "Sir Galahad: a Christmas mystery" (Messrs. Bell and Daldy); but seeing that it only preceded "The Defence of Guenevere and other Poems" by a few months, and was incorporated in that volume, there is no need here to treat of it as a separate work. The significance of "The Defence of Guenevere," all things considered, has never perhaps been appreciated as was due. A young man, but twenty-four years old, Morris must be regarded, for all intents and purposes, as a pioneer in his kind. Tennyson's "Idylls of the King" had not as yet appeared; nor ought it to be forgotten that at this date the published poems of Rossetti, who is generally accredited as standing to Morris in the relationship of master to disciple, did not consist of above a few occasional pieces contributed to periodicals. One has no desire, of course, to deny that the elder poet had already written a number of poems that Morris must have heard or read privately. Indeed, he himself was only too ready to acknowledge his indebtedness to Rossetti ; whereof the dedication of "The Defence of Guenevere," "to my friend, Dante Gabriel Rossetti, painter," is evidence enough and to spare, if such were wanted. But at the same time it must be borne in mind that Morris was before him in making the venture of publishing a collection of poems that should court success or failure openly in the world of book-buyers and critics. "This book was and is," says William Bell Scott, "the most notable first volume of any poet ; many of the poems represent the mediæval spirit in a new way, not by a sentimental-nineteenth-century-revival-mediævalism, but they give a poetical sense of a barbaric age strongly and sharply real. Woolner wrote to me at the time of publication, 'I believe they are exciting a good deal of attention among the intelligent on the outlook for something new.'" So recently, however, as 1895, Mr. Saintsbury could write on the subject of Mr. Morris, "It has always seemed to me that not merely the general, but even the critical public, ranks him far below his proper station as a poet." An appreciative writer, the late Mr. Walter Pater, in an essay on "Æsthetic Poetry" (1868), while as yet only the first part of "The Earthly Paradise" had appeared, accounts Morris as the type and personification of the poetry of the revived romantic school. This new poetry, according to him, takes possession of a transfigured world, "and sublimates beyond it another still fainter and more spectral, which is literally an artificial or 'Earthly Paradise.' It is a finer ideal, extracted from what, in relation to any actual world, is already an ideal. Like some strange, second flowering after date, it renews on a more delicate type the poetry of a past age, but must not be confounded with it." The earliest of the modern romanticists, as represented by Scott and Goethe, had dealt with but one, and that the most superficial, aspect of mediæval poetry, viz., its purely adventurous side. Later on the elements of mediæval passion and mysticism were embodied in the works of Victor Hugo in France and of Heine in Germany.

But in "The Defence of Guenevere" Mr. Pater discerns "a refinement upon this later, profounder mediævalism" and "the first typical specimen of æsthetic poetry." The book was in truth phenomenal. Its like had not before been known in England; where hitherto, as Mr. George Saintsbury rightly remarks, "only one or two snatches of Coleridge and Keats had caught the peculiar mediæval tone which the Pre-Raphaelites in poetry, following the Pre-Raphaelites in art, were now about to sound. Even 'La Belle Dame sans Merci,' that wonderful divination, in which Keats hit upon the true and very mediæval, . . . is an exception, a casual inspiration rather than a full reflection." The strange gift of insight displayed in the just named poem of Keats, and less fully in Coleridge's "Christabel," has perhaps no parallel in history, nor one in fiction, save in Rudyard Kipling's "Finest Story in the World." Even in the case of the two poets in whom it was manifested it was, as it were, an inspiration vouchsafed for the occasion only, to be immediately afterwards withdrawn. Neither of them was able to follow it up consistently: and Coleridge wittingly left "Christabel" a fragment. But with Morris the exact opposite was the case. His "Defence of Guenevere" and the three poems next in order in the volume were saturated through and through with the true and vital essence of Arthurian romance; while the remaining poems savoured not less thoroughly of the very atmosphere of the Middle Ages. There was nothing that had found its way into these pages by haphazard, nothing sporadic; but the whole book from end to end was alive with the antique spirit of the days of chivalry, recreated and quickened by the hand of genius. Withal there was some indefinable quality superadded of the poet's very own. And so, possessing as they did "the bizarrerie of a new thing in beauty," the "imperishable fantasies" of "The Defence of Guenevere" "did fill a fresh page in English poetry." Mr. Arthur Symons writes of Mr. Morris's "Guenevere" thus: "His first book—which invented a new movement, doing easily, with a certain appropriate quaintness, what Tennyson all his life had been trying to do—has all the exquisite trouble of his first awakening to the love of Romance." Nor was Morris yet, it has been observed, under the influence of Chaucer, whose narrative manner was to inspire the poems he published later.

Of the poems contained in "The Defence of Guenevere," &c., the following had appeared previously in "The Oxford and Cambridge Magazine," viz., "The Chapel in Lyoness;" the concluding part of "Rapunzel," under the title "Hands;" "Riding Together," and "Summer Dawn." This last, in its original form, lacked a title; while the first line of it, "Pray but one prayer for us 'twixt thy closed lips," was now altered to "Pray but one prayer for me," &c. The poem "Golden Wings" is not to be confounded with the prose tale which Morris contributed, with the same title, to the magazine.

It is interesting, moreover, to note the interchange of ideas consequent on the intimacy of the group of artist friends; their common studies acting and reacting upon them, and supplying some with themes for verses, some for pictures. Often it is a problem to determine whether it was the poem of one that suggested the painting of the other or *vice versâ*. Thus the Arthurian legend, rhymed by Morris in "The Defence of Guenevere," was with Rossetti and his friends at this time a favourite for illustration. Not only are the wall paintings in the Debating Hall, the present Library, of the Union Society at Oxford, a case in point; but a certain number also of sketches and water-colours of Rossetti's, belonging to this period, bear the identical titles borne by poems of Morris's, *e.g.*, "King Arthur's Tomb," or the last meeting of Lancelot and Guenevere; "Sir Galahad;" "The Blue Closet," and "The Tune of Seven Towers;" while other drawings, such as that of "Lancelot in the Chamber of Guenevere," are obvious representations of incidents described in the poetry of Morris. Some of these works of Rossetti's were actual commissions executed by him for Morris, from whom afterwards they were purchased by Mr. George Rae. Again, "Burd Ellayne," the central figure in Morris's spirited ballad of "Welland River," was pictured by Rossetti and became the property of the late Mr. J. Leathart of Gateshead on Tyne. In the way of reading, Pastor William Meinhold's wonderful romance of "Sidonia the Sorceress" was, to use Morris's own words, "a great favourite with the more literary part of the Pre-Raphaelite artists in the earlier days of that movement." Their common delight in it produced, for immediate result, "two beautiful water-colour pictures of Sidonia and Clara von Dewitz," by Sir Edward Burne-Jones; while on Morris's imagination it took powerful hold, as no one could fail to be assured who had once had the privilege of hearing him read aloud a passage such, for instance, as that which relates how Lord Otto von Bork received the homage of Vidante von Meseritz and his feudal vassals. Morris simply revelled in the description of the knights riding into the hall, each with his blazoned banner displayed; and one can imagine how he would have relished giving the order, "the kinsman in full armour shall ride into the hall upon his war-horse, bearing the banner of his house in his hand, and all my retainers shall follow on horses, each bearing his banner also, and shall range themselves by the great window of the hall; and let the windows be open, that the wind may play through the banners and make the spectacle yet grander." This final direction was one which Morris knew how to appreciate to the full. Nor did the deep impression fade from his mind with the lapse of time, but was destined to take practical form years afterwards in a reprint of the book at the Kelmscott Press. Indeed, throughout the career of the two friends nothing is more striking than the close parallel presented in the subjects chosen by them for treatment in their several ways, by Morris for poetry, by Burne-Jones for pictorial illustration. But these are points which will have to be referred to again presently.

Meanwhile, to resume the consideration of "The Defence of Guenevere and other Poems." Strong as is the temptation to quote largely, one must be content with a verse or two to demonstrate certain charming characteristics of the poet. "The Eve of Crecy" contains two magnificent examples of that mode of poetic expression, dubbed "echolalia" by Max Nordau, and as such condemned by him; a mode which, if few may attempt it with safety, is yet, in the hands of so consummate a master as Morris, unsurpassed for the peculiarly soothing and satisfying sense of beauty it produces.

> "Gold on her head, and gold on her feet,
> And gold where the hems of her kirtle meet,
> And a golden girdle round my sweet;—
> *Ah! qu'elle est belle La Marguerite.*"

And again, a few stanzas lower down we read:

> "Yet even now it is good to think
> * * * * *
> Of Margaret sitting glorious there,
> In glory of gold and glory of hair,
> And glory of glorious face most fair;
> *Ah! qu'elle est belle La Marguerite.*"

The refrains are always melodious and grateful, whether, as in the case of "Two red roses across the moon," they seem to have no necessary connection with the body of the poem, or whether, as in the case of "The Sailing of the Sword," on the other hand, they form, with slight variations from verse to verse, an integral part in the progress of the ballad-story. The same poem may illustrate Morris's gift of conveying, and that too from a point of view as fresh as it is convincing, the most graphic impression in the shortest number of words: *e.g.*,

> "The hot sun bit the garden beds,"

and

> "Grey gleamed the thirsty castle-leads;"

or this night-scene:

> "The while the moon did watch the wood,"

from "Riding Together;" or this:

> "After these years the flowers forget their blood,"

from the poem "Concerning Geffray Teste Noire." Yet again take the refrain of the poem called "The Wind:"

> "Wind, wind! thou art sad, art thou kind?
> Wind, wind, unhappy! thou art blind,
> Yet still thou wanderest the lily-seed to find."

What an exquisite thought is enshrined in the last line! Here is a picture from "King Arthur's Tomb:"

> "I gazed upon the arras giddily,
> Where the wind set the silken kings a-sway."

And, once more, how perfect a description is the following, from "Golden Wings:"

> "No answer through the moonlit night;
> No answer in the cold grey dawn;
> No answer when the shaven lawn
> Grew green, and all the roses bright."

Nothing is wanting here. No paraphrasing of words, no further detail could express the sense more vividly or more completely than the poet has done in these four short, simple lines.

It may not be amiss, before leaving the subject of "The Defence of Guenevere" to gather from the writings of some competent critics a few judgments concerning the work; dismissing, before the rest, that estimate which is the least favourable. Mr. Henry G. Hewlett, in the "Contemporary Review" for December, 1874, is of opinion that "Quaint archaisms of diction, forced and bald rhymes, wilful obscurity, harshness, not to say ugliness of metaphor, disfigure nearly every page." Having said this much, however, the very worst that anyone with any show of fairness could possibly say, he continues: "But a just and careful critic could not fail to discern that the singer was worthier than his song. He had so saturated his imagination with the glow of chivalric romance and Catholic mythology as to be incapable for the moment of anything beyond reproduction. But the receptive and assimilative power which enabled him to apprehend thus intimately the spirit of so remote an age, and imitate thus faithfully the relics of its living literature, required only time and training to mature into one of the richest of poetic faculties. No sign of this power is more marked in the volume than the tone of *naïf* unconsciousness which the writer has caught from his models. His personality is never visible; he never preaches; dispenses praise and blame but rarely, and then in accordance with a standard not of his own raising. With calm impartiality he sets forth in successive pictures the double aspect in which the love of Guenevere for Lancelot seems to have presented itself to mediæval imagination,—the view adopted by Chivalry, and the view sanctioned by the Church. In 'The Defence of Guenevere' she is a Phryne, voluptuous, imperial, irresistible; in 'King Arthur's Tomb,' a Magdalen, tortured by remorse and tempted by passion, but sustained by penitence and faith unto the end. In 'Sir Galahad' the portrait of the saint-knight is painted with a truthfulness that atones for whatever clumsiness of handling may at first repel us. He is represented as setting out in his quest of the San-Greal with sharp misgivings of spirit as to the career of chastity to which he must vow himself. He witnesses the tender leave-taking of a lady and her knight, and thinks sorrowfully that for him no maiden will mourn if he falls. He recalls the loves of Lancelot and Guenevere, of Tristram and Iseult, and is tempted to envy their happiness and forget their sin. But in the chapel where he passes his first vigil, he has a vision of

"'One sitting on the altar as a throne,
 Whose face no man could say he did not know,
And though the bell still rang, He sat alone,
 With raiment half blood-red, half white as snow.'

"Overpowered with shame, he sinks nerveless on the floor." Then are heard the tender accents of the Divine Wisdom condescending to reason with His wavering servant. "The struggle in the youth's soul ceases ere the voice dies into silence, and the vision of the San-Greal is then revealed to eyes fitted to perceive it.

"The minor poems, of which the greater number are ballads, bear the same marks of the writer's thorough sympathy with a particular era of history and type of literature. . . . His attempts seem to us as successful as any that have since been made. 'The Sailing of the Sword,' which is the least imitative, and therefore the freest from affectations, approaches, perhaps, as nearly as a modern ballad can hope to do, the genuine simplicity of the antique."

Of the latter portion of the work Mr. Andrew Lang writes, "Leaving the Arthurian cycle Mr. Morris entered on his specially sympathetic period—the gloom and sad sunset glory of the late fourteenth century, the age of Froissart, and wicked wasteful wars. To Froissart it all seemed one magnificent pageant of knightly and kingly fortunes; he only murmurs 'a great pity' for the death of a knight or the massacre of a town. It is rather the pity of it that Mr. Morris sees, hearts broken in a corner, as in 'Sir Peter Harpdon's End,' or beside 'The Haystack in the Floods.' . . . The astonishing vividness, again, of the tragedy told in 'Geffray Teste Noire' is like that of a vision in a magic mirror or crystal ball, rather than like a picture suggested by printed words. 'Shameful Death' has the same enchanted kind of presentment. We look through a 'magic casement opening on the foam' of the old waves of war. Poems of a pure fantasy, unequalled out of Coleridge and Poe, are 'The Wind' and 'The Blue Closet.' Each only lives in fantasy. Motives and facts and story are unimportant and out of view. The pictures arise distinct, unsummoned, spontaneous, like the faces and places which are flashed on our eyes between sleeping and waking. Fantastic too, but with more of recognizable human setting, is 'Golden Wings.'"

Another critic, Mr. Buxton Forman, in "Our Living Poets" (1871), says of "The Defence of Guenevere and other Poems," the "volume has very striking affinities with the poetry of more than one contemporary writer. Mr. Rossetti's influence is the easiest to discern; but there are also several attempts at psychological art, clearly indicating Browning's influence. . . . Connected mainly with the age of Chivalry in subject, every page is full of an exquisite tender feeling; and in many instances there is great splendour of imagination. . . . Several small poems are masterpieces in their way; and every poem in the book is full of beauties. But such pieces as 'Shameful Death,' 'The Judgment of God,' and 'Old Love,' monologues dealing subtly with the soul, have more real analogy with ballad poetry than with monologue poetry of the modern type, and would probably have been more perfect had they been executed in ballad form. In 'The Judgment of God' in particular, the actual point of time whereat the monologue is spoken is anything but clearly distinguished from points of past time referred to. It is interesting to compare this piece with 'The Haystack in the Floods,' which is admirably graphic in narration, and as complete and excellent in its degree as are some later higher flights of Mr. Morris. 'The Judgment of God' is spoken by an evil-hearted knight about to engage in single combat with a good knight, who, as he fears, is to overcome him; the mental material is the series of thoughts passing through the false knight's mind immediately before engaging in the combat; and so mistily are some of the verses framed, that it is hard to know whether the facts referred to in them have just taken place or are from the storehouse of old memories. . . . With Mr. Morris this want of perspicuity finds its preventive in direct narration, as in 'The Haystack in the Floods.' The subject of the poem is not in itself so simple as the other; but, instead of either of the principal actors being commissioned with the narrative, the whole is given to us in Mr. Morris's own clear objective style. . . . The physiology and psychology in the sketch of Jehane are alike excellent. . . . It is probable that, were Mr. Morris treating a similar subject to this now, we should miss a certain fierceness that exists in it as matters stand. . . . 'Sir Peter Harpdon's End' is an excessively clever little play in five scenes; but it falls as far short of dramatic excellence as the monologues fall short of technical excellence in their kind."

"Over the first fortunes of a newly-born work of art," writes Mr. Algernon Charles Swinburne, who, as an undergraduate at Balliol, had made Mr. Morris's acquaintance at Oxford in 1857, "accident must usually preside for good or for evil. Over the earliest work of the artist . . . that purblind leader of the blind, accident, presided on the whole for evil. Here and there it met with eager recognition and earnest applause; nowhere, if I err not, with just praise or blame worth heeding. It seems to have been now lauded and now decried as the result and expression of a school rather than a man, of a theory or tradition rather than a poet or student. . . . Such things as were in the book are taught and learnt in no school but that of instinct. Upon no piece of work in the world was the impress of native character ever more distinctly stamped, more deeply branded. . . . In form, in structure, in composition, few poems can be . . . faultier than those of Mr. Morris which deal with the legend of Arthur and Guenevere. . . . I do not speak here of form in the abstract and absolute sense. . . . I speak of that secondary excellence always necessary to perfection but not always indispensable to the existence of art. These first poems of Mr. Morris are not malformed; . . . but they are not well-clad; . . . they have need sometimes of combing and trimming. Take that one for example called 'King Arthur's Tomb.' It has not been constructed at all; the parts hardly hold together. . . . There is scarcely any connection here, and scarcely composition. . . . But where, among other and older poets of his time and country, is there one comparable for perception and expression of tragic truth, of subtle and noble, terrible and piteous things? Where a touch of passion at once so broad and so sure? The figures here given have the blood and breath, the shape and step of life; they can move and suffer; their repentance is as real as their desire; their shame lies as deep as their love. They are at once remorseful for the sin and regretful of the pleasure that is past. The retrospective vision of Lancelot and of Guenevere is as passionate and profound as life. Riding towards her without hope, in the darkness and heat of the way, he can but divert and sustain his spirit by the recollection of her loveliness and her love, seen long since asleep and waking, in another place than this, on a distant night. . . . Retrospect and vision, natural memories and spiritual, here coalesce; and how exquisite is the retrospect, and how passionate the vision, of past light and colour in the sky, past emotion and conception in the soul! Not in the idyllic school is a chord ever struck, a note ever sounded, so tender and subtle as this. Again, when Guenevere has maddened herself and him with wild words of reproach and remorse, abhorrence and attraction, her sharp and sudden memory of old sights and sounds and splendid irrevocable days finds word and form not less noble and faithful to fact and life. . . . Such verses are not forgetable. They are not, indeed,—as are the 'Idylls of the King,'—the work of a dexterous craftsman in full practice. Little beyond dexterity, a rare eloquence, and a laborious patience of hand, has been given to the one or denied to the other. These are good gifts and great; but it is better to want clothes than limbs."

Mr. Pater, in the work already quoted, says: "The poem which gives its name to the volume is a thing tormented and awry with passion, like the body of Guenevere defending herself from the charge of adultery, and the accent falls in strange, unwonted places with the effect of a great cry. . . . Reverie, illusion, delirium: they are the three stages of a fatal descent both in the religion and the loves of the Middle Ages. . . . The English poet, too, has learned the secret. He has diffused through 'King Arthur's Tomb' the maddening white glare of the sun, the tyranny of the moon, not tender and far-off, but close down—the sorcerer's moon, large and feverish. The colouring is intricate and delirious, as of 'scarlet lilies.' The influence of summer is like a poison in one's blood, with a sudden bewildered sickening of life and all things. In 'Galahad: a Mystery,' the frost of Christmas night on the chapel stones acts as a strong narcotic: a sudden shrill ringing pierces through the numbness: a voice proclaims that the Grail has gone forth through the great forest. It is in the 'Blue Closet' that this delirium reaches its height with a singular beauty, reserved perhaps for the enjoyment of the few. . . . Those in whom what Rousseau calls *les frayeurs noctUrnes* are constitutional, know what splendour they give to the things of the morning. . . . The crown of the English poet's book is one of these appreciations of the dawn: ' Pray but one prayer for me 'twixt thy closed lips,' &c. It is the very soul of the bridegroom which goes forth to the bride: inanimate things are longing with him: all the sweetness of the imaginative loves of the Middle Age, with a superadded spirituality of touch all its own, is in that!"

Lastly, in "The Academy," just a week after William Morris's death, Mr. Robert Steele wrote: "Living as we do in surroundings so modified by the efforts of its author, we cannot fully estimate the worth of this little volume. It is totally unlike any other of his works." This is perfectly true. "The Defence of Guenevere and other Poems" is but a small book, and were its bulk alone to be the measure of value, the amount of space devoted to it in these pages might well seem disproportionate. It is, on the contrary, altogether inadequate. For this remarkable collection of poems stands alone not only in the literature of our age and of our country, but, what is more to the present purpose, alone also among its author's own productions.

CHAPTER FOUR: IN BETWEEN-WHILES: THE RED HOUSE.

HIS "Defence of Guenevere" finished and sent to press, William Morris did not rest idly. Before the work was yet issued he had applied himself, with his wonted industry, it must not be said to the composing—for the very idea of anything forced and artificial was foreign to the spontaneity of his nature—but to the inditing of more poetry; the greater part of which, however, was suffered to remain unpublished. Nor would a large portion of it, maybe, have survived at all, but for the friendly intervention of Mr. Charles Fairfax Murray, who preserves the manuscript among the most valued of his treasures. Of the number of Morris's poems that belong to this early period, nothing has appeared beside "The God of the Poor," printed in "The Fortnightly," 1868, and the song, "In the white-flowered hawthorn brake," which was introduced into the story of "Ogier the Dane" in "The Earthly Paradise." According to the author's original plan, this lyric was to have formed part of a long poem entitled "Scenes from the Fall of Troy," of which, as projected, not more than about a third was ever written. Among the other unpublished MSS. in the possession of Mr. Murray is an additional scene to "Sir Peter Harpdon's End." Morris's old friend, Mr. Theodore Watts-Dunton, in an obituary notice in "The Athenæum," says, "Morris could and did write humorous poetry, and then withheld it from publication. For the splendid poem of 'Sir Peter Harpdon's End,' printed in his first volume, Morris wrote a humorous scene of the highest order, in which the hero said to his faithful fellow-captive and follower, John Curzon, that, as their deaths were so near, he felt a sudden interest in what had never interested him before—the story of John's life before they had been brought so close to each other. The heroic but dull-witted soldier acceded to his master's request, and the incoherent, muddle-headed way in which he gave his autobiography was full of a dramatic and subtle humour. . . . This he refused to print, in deference, I suspect, to a theory of poetic art."

And, moreover, Mr. Edmund Gosse writes in the "St. James's Gazette," within a few days after Morris's death: "It is said that vast sections of 'The Earthly Paradise' remain unpublished; and I can vouch for it that more than twenty years ago I heard the poet read, in his full, slightly monotonous voice, a long story of 'Amis and Amylion' (I think these were the names), which has never, to my knowledge, appeared in print. Rossetti used to declare that there was a room, a 'blue closet,' in the Queen's-square house, entirely crammed with Morris's poetry from floor to ceiling. This was a humorous exaggeration of that wonderful fluency which was a characteristic of Morris's genius."

But the fact of the existence of certain unpublished verse-writings of Morris's, if not indeed known widely, was by no means a secret confined to the circle of his personal friends. Thus Mr. George Saintsbury, while avowing himself an absolute stranger to William Morris, declares that he has "been told that all the defaulting poems exist;" and, in addition, a writer in "The Sunday Times," on the day following the poet's death, understands "that there is a large mass of unpublished material which may be found more or less available for future issue." This, no doubt, has reference to prose writings of Morris's as well as poetry; but Mr. Saintsbury is clearly alluding to those poems which were advertised shortly beforehand but did not eventually make their appearance in "The Earthly Paradise."

Further MS. poetry, owned by Mr. Fairfax Murray, comprises a prologue to "The Earthly Paradise" in four-line stanzas, and a set of verses for the months of the year. All these portions of the work were re-written and other passages substituted in their room when the poem assumed its final state. From the MS. it would appear that even the very name was changed, the author having at one period an idea of calling it "The Fools' Paradise."

Another unpublished fragment is extant, being part of a poem "The Romance of the Wooers;" and yet another work, in this case completed, a version of one of the most beautiful legends of Christian martyrology, viz., "The Story of Dorothea," dating from the time when Mr. Morris began to write again after the space of seven silent years or more that ensued upon the appearance of "The Defence of Guenevere." For so discouraging to the young author was the reception accorded to his first work that he had little enough heart to keep up his writing continuously, but turned his hand to other and more grateful occupations. His poems had, it is true, "found a few staunch friends," but, for the rest, "were absolutely neglected by the 'reading public.'" It is on record that only some 250 copies of the first issue of the work were sold. Therefore in stating, as he does in his "Reminiscences," that the publication of "The Defence of Guenevere" was "what gave Morris his proper position," Bell Scott must be taken as referring to the judgment of their own limited set. For he has to admit that, in spite of everything, "the book was still-born. The considerable body of perfectly-informed but unsympathetic professional critics are, strange to say, so useless as directors of public taste that they have never yet lifted the right man into his right place at once. After repeated volumes had attracted public favour," but not till then, a demand arose for Morris's earliest volume, and it had to be reprinted, the stock of "the original impression having been returned to the paper-mill."

"At one time," says a writer who is described by Max Nordau as "an Anglo-German critic of repute," Dr. Francis Hueffer, the author of the memoir prefixed to the Tauchnitz selection from Morris's poems, "little was wanting to make Morris follow his friend Burne-Jones's example, and leave the pen for the brush. There is indeed still extant from his hand an unfinished picture evincing a remarkable sense of colour." The work referred to, which is a portrait study, depicts a lady in the act of unfastening her girdle. It is a wonder that this painting is yet intact, for its history, a somewhat curious one, is as follows. Left at Ford Madox Brown's, it was conveyed thence by his son, Oliver Madox Brown, and given to Rossetti, who kept it by him with the view of repainting it, because he was not satisfied that it did justice to the lady it portrayed. However, he never carried out his intention, and, after his death, the picture passed, with other property of the deceased painter, into the hands of his brother, William Michael. In this gentleman's possession it might possibly have still remained, but that he, being informed of its rightful ownership within a few months of the death of Dante Gabriel Rossetti, took steps to have the painting returned to Mr. Morris.

While staying temporarily in Oxford in the autumn of 1857 William Morris met the lady who, two years later, became his wife; the marriage, appropriately enough in the case of so eminent a scholar of English as the bridegroom, taking place in the old Saxon-towered Church of St. Michael in the Corn. There is no need to attempt any description of Mrs. Morris, since her features have been immortalized in numerous drawings and paintings from the hand of Dante Gabriel Rossetti.

Morris's engagement necessitated the providing a suitable home, with the preparation of which he was now busily occupying himself. The house was not got ready in time for him to take up his residence there at his marriage, so he had to wait awhile, and moved in shortly after. In the meantime, a company of ladies, friends of Mr. Morris, used to meet at the studio in Red Lion Square, and, while he himself was doing decoration in oil colour, they, under his superintendence, embroidered hangings, &c., for the adornment of his future home. One of these pieces of needlework was taken eventually to Kelmscott Manor and hung there. It was powdered all over with a repeated pattern, a design of Morris's of the quaintest description,—birds, for all the world like those in a Noah's ark, trees as stiff-looking as the clipped trees in a Dutch garden or a child's toy-box, and scrolls inscribed with the motto "If I can." The whole of it was executed in Berlin wool (the only medium available, except silk, in those days before crewels and Tussore-silks had been introduced), not of course in the fashion which then pre-

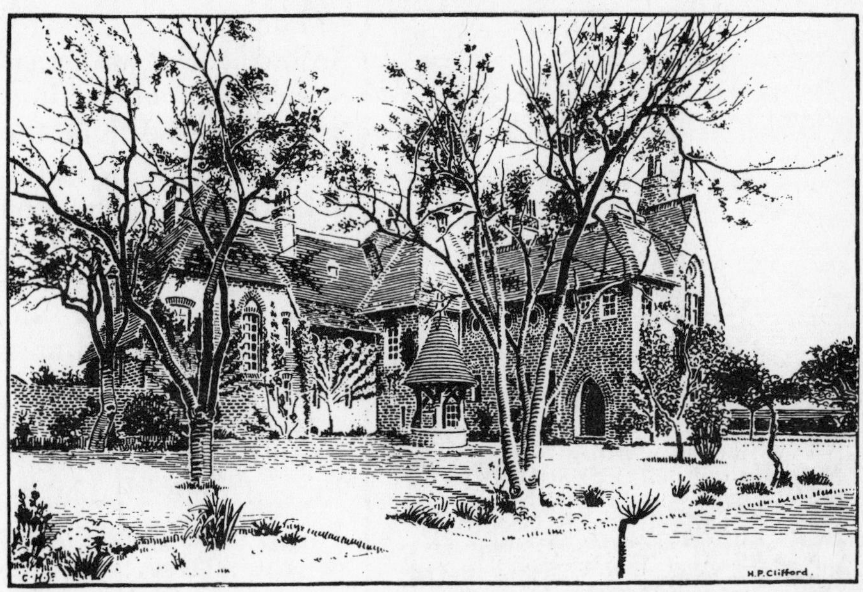

THE RED HOUSE. FROM THE GARDEN.

vailed and, it is to be feared, is not yet extinct, to wit, cross stitches on a canvas foundation; but with a very different manner of working, in long and coarse stitches, as bold as effective. Another strip of embroidery executed for the same purpose, of a floral pattern, drawn likewise by Mr. Morris, was given by him, after its removal from its original position, to Sir Edward Burne-Jones, and is now at his house at Rottingdean.

The site Morris chose for his new house was an orchard at Upton, near Bexley Heath, amid "the rose-hung lanes of woody Kent." The highways of the county were dear to the poet through their having been trodden by the feet of Chaucer's Canterbury pilgrims; while its historic memories were illustrious in his eyes, because it was there had sprung up and spread among carles and yeomen the popular movement led by valorous John Ball.

Morris was not his own architect, but he employed his friend Philip Webb; who, however, in effect was merely carrying out Morris's directions, more particularly in the design of the internal fixtures. The building was given the appropriate name of "The Red House." A writer in

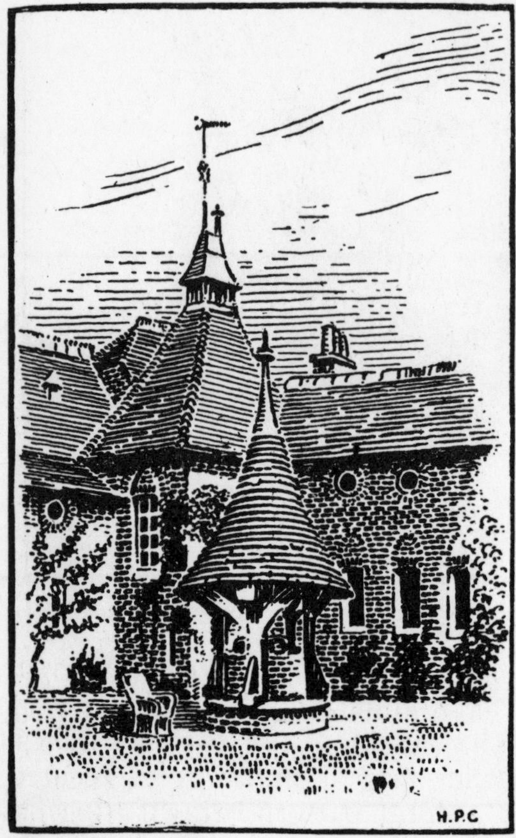

THE RED HOUSE. THE WELL.

"The Studio" has referred to it as "that wonderful red building which proved to be the prototype of all the beautiful houses of the so-called 'Queen Anne' revival; although that house, it may be said in passing, is almost entirely Gothic, with strong French influence apparent." It is indeed remarkable as being the first example of the artistic use revived of red brick for domestic purposes. Picturesque and irregular of construction, it has an architectural character that distinguished it among its contemporaries of the ugly, square-box order which at that date seemed to be accepted almost universally. It was, for its time, a bold innovation, which cannot be said to have been without extraordinary results for good. Nay, as an experiment on the part of a man who had both the hopefulness and the dauntless will necessary to enable him to make a stand against the tyranny of custom, to William Morris is owing the credit of having initiated, with his Red House, a new era in house-building.

Morris set forth his views on the subject of architecture in a paper he contributed to "The Fortnightly Review" in May, 1888. "The revival of the art of architecture in Great Britain," he says, "may be said to have been a natural consequence of the rise of the romantic school in literature, although it lagged some way behind it. . . . Up

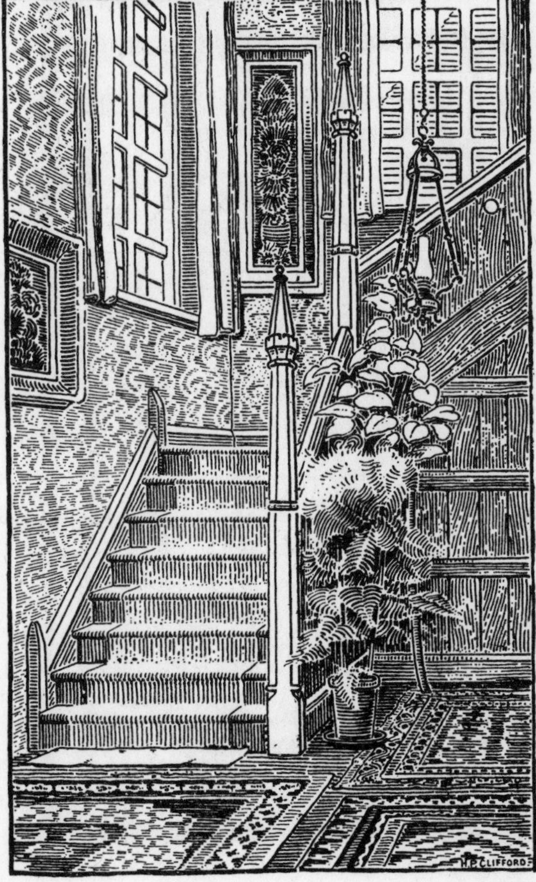

THE RED HOUSE. STAIRCASE.

to a period long after the death of Shelley and Keats and Scott, architecture could do nothing but produce on the one hand pedantic imitations of classical architecture of the most revolting ugliness, and ridiculous travesties of Gothic buildings, not quite so ugly, but meaner and sillier; and on the other hand, the utilitarian brick-box with a slate lid which the Anglo-Saxon generally in modern times considers as a good sensible house with no nonsense about it." But, he continues further on, "Were the rows of square brown brick boxes which Keats and Shelley had to look on, or the stuccoed villa which enshrined Tennyson's genius, to be the perpetual concomitants of such masters of verbal beauty; was no beauty but the beauty of words to be produced by man in our times; was the intelligence of the age to be for ever so preposterously lop-sided? We could see no reason for it and accordingly our hope was strong; for though we had learned something of the art and history of the Middle Ages we had not learned enough. . . . Anyhow, this period of fresh hope and partial insight produced many interesting buildings and other works of art, and afforded a pleasant time indeed to the hopeful but very small minority engaged in it, in spite of

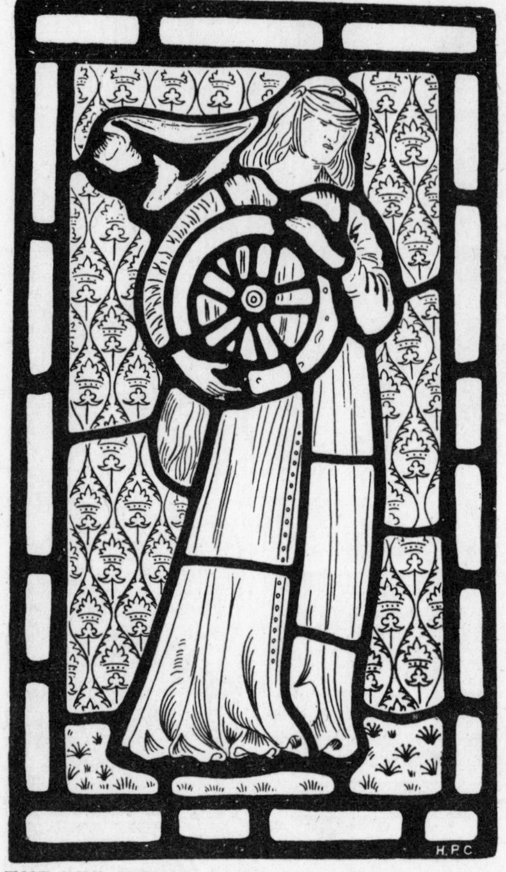

THE RED HOUSE. EARLY MORRIS GLASS.

all vexations and disappointments." How that hope was dissipated he goes on to show: "At last one man, who had done more than any one else to make this hopeful time possible, drew a line sternly through these hopes founded on imperfect knowledge. This man was John Ruskin. By a marvellous inspiration of genius (I can call it nothing else) he attained at one leap to a true conception of mediæval art, which years of minute study had not gained for others. In his chapter in 'The Stones of Venice,' entitled 'On the Nature of Gothic and the Function of the Workman therein,' he showed us the gulf which lay between us and the Middle Ages. From that time all was changed. . . . I do not say that the change in the Gothic revivalists produced by this discovery was sudden, but it was effective. It has gradually sunk deep into the intelligence of the art and literature of to-day."

The above passages were written, it is important to note, some thirty-five years after the appearance of "The Stones of Venice." In the interval Morris had had time to recover from the shock of disillusionment. It had become evident to him that the splendid monuments of architecture of the Middle Ages, as well as all the minor arts, had been produced under, and owed their very existence to, circumstances totally different from our own—to

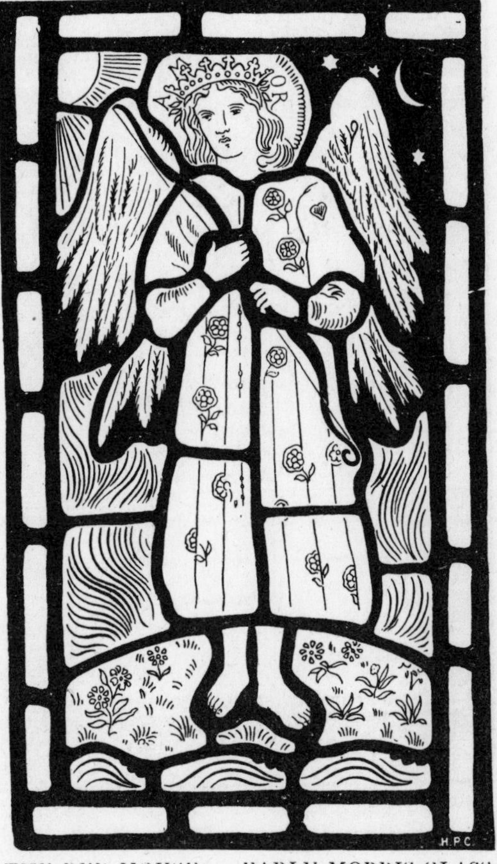

THE RED HOUSE. EARLY MORRIS GLASS.

a set of traditions and a concurrence of forces, such that, if one or more of them could conceivably be resuscitated, would yet assuredly never again be found together in the same proportions and the same combinations as of old. However unwelcome the truth, the logic of facts and of history was not to be gainsaid save by "those who wilfully shut their eyes." To abandon oneself, nevertheless, to unprofitable bewailings for a vanished past that could not be recalled were sheer cowardice, as Morris perceived. So, once convinced that the causes of the dearth of sound art amongst us lay deeper than he had at first suspected, viz., in the very conditions of our modern social and industrial system, he determined to think the matter out and to devise, if it might be, a remedy for existing evils. Hence he learned to look for the fulfilment of his aspirations in the ideal of a future, wherein a reconstructed society should even surpass anything hitherto achieved in the most glorious of days bygone. "The hope of our ignorance has passed away," he wrote, "but it has given place to the hope born of fresh knowledge." Experts indeed were slow to grasp the full significance of the teaching of Ruskin, as Morris did not fail to record. And he himself, young and ardent as he was at the time, would naturally be as loth as any among them to accept

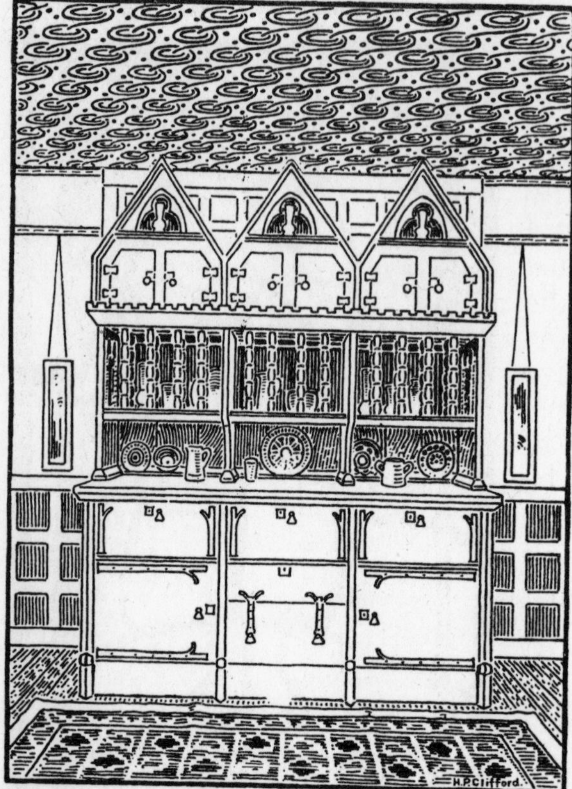

THE RED HOUSE. DINING-ROOM BUFFET.

conclusions so tremendous. Had the consequent lesson come home to him, and had his reluctance given way earlier than it did, it is scarcely too much to assert that the Red House might not have existed at all. At any rate, Morris built but that once only, and never afterwards.

The date of the Red House, as the vane on the top of the roof shows, is 1859. "The only thing you saw from a distance," says Bell Scott in his "Reminiscences," "was an immense red-tiled, steep and high roof; and the only room I remember was the dining-room or hall, which seemed to occupy the whole area of the mansion. It had a fixed settle all round the walls, a curious music-gallery entered by a stair outside the room, breaking out high upon the gable, and no furniture but a long table of oak reaching nearly from end to end. This vast, empty hall was painted coarsely in bands of wild foliage over both wall and ceiling, which was open-timber and lofty." (There are some obvious mistakes here. Bell Scott, though right enough in his impression of the general effect of the furnishing and so on, is decidedly wrong in detail. In fact, he confounds the features of two separate rooms, and would lead one to suppose, from the way he speaks of them, that all were to be found together in one apartment.) "The adornment," he continues, "had a novel, not to say striking, character. . . . Morris did whatever seemed good to him unhesitatingly, and it has been very good."

The following account is based on notes supplied by one who used to know the house in the old days. "The first sight of the Red House in 1863," says this writer, "gave me an astonished pleasure. The deep red colour, the great sloping, tiled roofs; the small-paned windows; the low, wide porch and massive door; the surrounding garden divided into many squares, hedged by sweetbriar or wild rose, each enclosure with its own particular show of flowers; on this side a green alley with a bowling green, on that orchard walks amid gnarled old fruit-trees;—all struck me as vividly picturesque and uniquely original." In the grass-plot at the back of the house is a covered well, with a quaint conical roof. "Upon entering the porch, the hall appeared to one accustomed to the narrow ugliness of the usual middle-class dwelling of those days as being grand and severely simple. A solid oak table with trestle-like legs stood in the middle of the red-tiled floor, while a fireplace gave a hospitable look to the hall place." To the left, close to the foot of the stairs, is a wooden partition, panelled with leaded panes of plain glass of antique quality. This screen divides the main hall from a lesser hall or corridor, which leads, at right angles, into the garden and is lighted by windows of glass quarries decorated with various kinds of birds and other devices. In the centre of two of these windows are single figure panels; the one representing Love, in a rich red tunic, flames of fire at his back, and a stream of water traversing the flowery sward at his feet; the other, Fate, robed to the feet in green, with a wheel of fortune in her hand.

Immediately to the right as one enters the hall is a wooden structure, the lower part projecting to form a bench seat; the upper part being a press or cupboard, with unfinished colour decorations. On the outside of the two doors of it are figure compositions, sketched in, and begun in oils, but left incomplete: while inside are some interesting experiments in diapering in black on a gold ground,

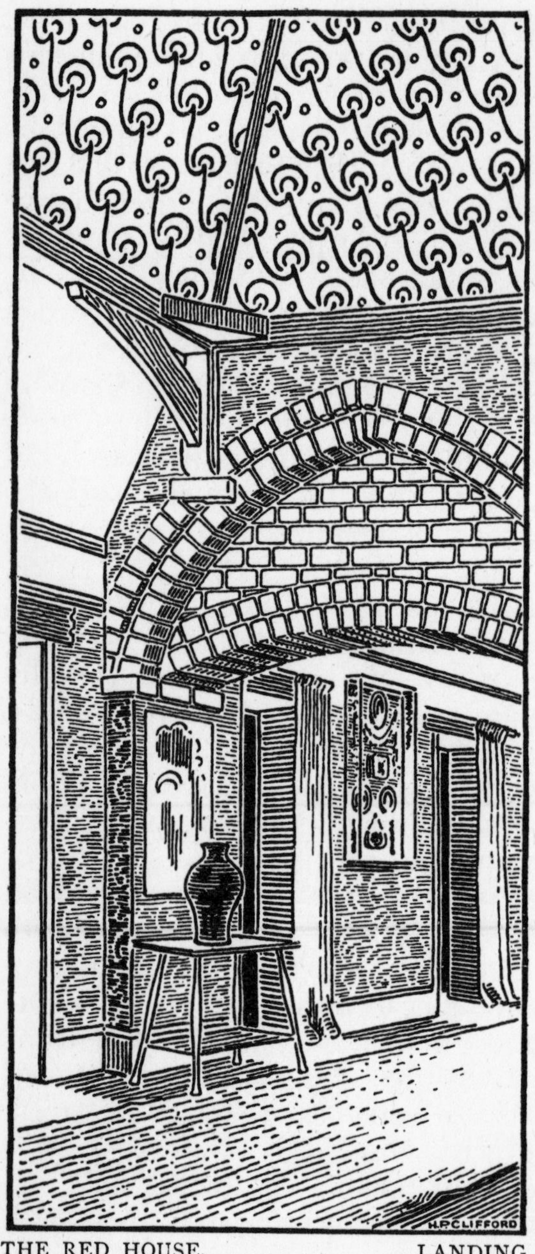

THE RED HOUSE. LANDING.

by Mr. Morris's hand. Beyond this press is "the door of the dining-room, the living room in fact. This is a long room and lies parallel to the hall. The fire-place stands out in the middle of the wall facing the entrance." It is of brick and, like the rest of the fire-places in the house, is not provided with a mantelshelf, the chimney-breast of brick going straight up to within a short distance of the ceiling, where it finishes off with a coved top. Near the door, and occupying the greater part of the wall space to the left as one enters the room, a prominent feature "was a wide dresser which reached to the ceiling and was ornamented richly with painted decoration. By the fireplace stood a movable settle, with high back, the panels of it filled with leather, gilt and coloured. The chairs were plain black, with rush seats." Commonly accepted as is the use of this simple and picturesque form of chair at the present day, its revival is due to Mr. Morris's example.

"The walls were tinted with pale distemper, and the ceiling ornamented by hand in yellow on white." The manner in which the ceiling decoration is carried out in this room and other parts of the house is most ingenious and effective. The pattern, a conventional repeat of the simplest form, was pricked upon the plaster, while yet moist and unhardened, the spaces between the pricked outlines being afterwards filled in with a flat tint of distemper colour, bright, but not so strongly pronounced as to be staring, or in any degree disagreeable.

Opposite to the front door, beneath an open pyramidal sort of lantern roof, rises the wide oaken staircase, with Gothic newel-posts at the angles; the underneath part of it not boxed in, as the ordinary custom is to conceal the construction, but left open and showing the form of the steps from below. "Upstairs—only one floor—above the dining-room is the drawing-room, with a decorated, open roof." The fireplace of brick with an open hearth, is provided with a brick hood, which slopes narrowing to the roof. "To the left of the fireplace was a daïs alcove with windows and window-seats. But the chief means of lighting was a large window at the end of the room furthest from the door. Facing the window was the most important feature of the room, viz., a painted bookcase or cabinet, —one scarcely knows how to describe it correctly. This great cabinet, of which the effect was gorgeous, nearly filled the end of the room. At one side was a wooden ladder stairway by which one could mount to the upper part of it and find room to sit or move about on the top, as on a balcony. From this stage another short ladder led into a storage-loft in the roof beyond."

"The walls of the principal bedroom were hung with embroidered serge. Here also stood a splendid wardrobe," decorated all over with gilding and colour, a wedding present painted and given by Burne-Jones. Morris himself executed part of the decoration on the inner folds of the doors. The subject which covers the front of this wardrobe is "The Prioress's Tale" from Chaucer; perhaps to the modern reader the most familiar of all the "Canterbury Tales," through Wordsworth's popularized version of it. The legend is not to be confounded with that of Little St. Hugh of Lincoln, though there are certain points in common. The various scenes of the story are all represented, as was customary with mediæval artists, in the same picture, the principal subject being on a larger scale than the rest and occupying the foremost place in the composition. It depicts the Blessed Virgin stooping over the pit which contains the body of the murdered boy who in life had always been devout towards her, and placing on his tongue a grain which should enable him in death to continue singing "Alma Redemptoris Mater" to her praise.

Towards the end of the year 1860 Burne-Jones, while on a visit at the Red House, commenced a series of paintings in tempera upon the end wall of the large drawing-room there; Morris also himself contributing somewhat to the decorative work, of which, however, the more important share was necessarily that undertaken by Burne-Jones. The subject was the mediæval story of Sir Degravaunt, another of those romances which, like "Sidonia the Sorceress," had begun to exercise a powerful charm upon both the painter and his host. The charm, indeed, survived to the end, as was testified by the fact that a Kelmscott Press edition of "Sire Degravaunt," with a woodcut frontispiece designed by Burne-Jones, had for some time past been in preparation, although unhappily Mr. Morris did not live to see it issued, dying as he did before it was ready. Only three panels, and these forming the last out of the set, were ever painted at the Red House. In one of them Burne-Jones introduced the portraits of Mr. and Mrs. Morris, seated side by side, in robes of state and crowned with coronets, in the characters of Sir Degravaunt and his bride in the scene of the wedding banquet. These paintings are in a bad position for light, but they are in good hands and well cared for, having been covered with glass to insure their thorough preservation.

Nearabout the same time, *i.e.* the latter part of 1860, in a letter to Bell Scott, Rossetti writes to say that his wife has "gone for a few days to stay with the Morrises at their Red House at Upton, and I am to join her there to-morrow, but shall probably return before her, as I am full of things to do, and could not go there at all, but that I have a panel to paint there." The work was in oils, and it is said that one week sufficed for its execution. The subject of one of Rossetti's compositions for the Red House was the Garden of Eden. He also painted the first meeting and the last meeting of Dante and Beatrice; in the middle, between the two scenes, being an allegorical figure of Love, holding a dial-plate in his hands. These panels were eventually removed when Morris parted with the Red House, and were framed in the form of a diptych. Morris did not occupy the Red House above six years. He gave it up at the end of that space and came back to live in London in 1865.

CHAPTER FIVE: OF THE FIRM OF MORRIS AND CO., DECORATORS.

"EVERYONE interested in the decoration of houses," said the chairman in introducing Morris before the lecture on "Textile Fabrics" at the Health Exhibition in 1884, "knew something of the good work which Mr. Morris had been doing during the last twenty years, and some day the history of what at one time appeared a mad enough venture, would not only be profitable, but amusing. In our days when young men left Oxford and Cambridge, they took to" one or other of the recognized professions; "but twenty years ago Mr. Morris entered upon a venture which seemed likely to end in loss of money and discomfiture, although, fortunately, it proved not to be the case." It was remarked by Mr. William Michael Rossetti, in the work containing his brother's life and letters, that a "detailed history of the firm of Morris, Marshall and Faulkner, or Morris and Co., would by this time" (1895) "be an interesting thing," but that such a record had "not yet been written." Nor maybe among those that now survive, except to Sir Edward Burne-Jones and Mr. Philip Webb, who, if any, should be in possession of the necessary particulars, can it be looked to furnish a full account; especially of facts and incidents relating to the earlier days, when the firm was more of the nature of an informal association of friends working together than a business partnership in the ordinary sense of the term.

To whom belongs the credit of having been the first to conceive the idea of the artistic venture that has developed since into the business of Messrs. Morris and Co., may not now perhaps be determined with absolute certainty. The initiation of the project has been attributed at various times to various members of the original firm; but the balance seems rather to incline in favour of Ford Madox Brown as one of the patriarchs of the revival. However, one thing at any rate is beyond doubt, that the whole undertaking owes its success to the patience and energy, to the enthusiasm, the originality—in a word, to the genius of William Morris, whose name it bears.

It has been shown how the furnishing of his own house at Bexley Heath had been made by Morris the occasion for exercising his ingenuity in embroidery design, in ceiling and mural decoration, and in several other ways, and generally of acquiring practical experience in different branches of domestic art. But what he began by doing then on a small scale, was destined to engage him from that time forward for the remainder of his life.

There is but slight necessity to enumerate the horrors proper to the early Victorian period—the Berlin woolwork and the bead mats; the crochet antimacassars upon horsehair sofas; the wax flowers under glass shades; the monstrosities in stamped brass and gilded stucco; chairs, tables, and other furniture hideous with veneer and curly distortions; the would-be naturalistic vegetable-patterned carpets with false shadows and misplaced perspective; and all the despicable legion of mean shams and vulgarities which have been exposed and held up to ridicule times without number. The memory of them, associated as it is indissolubly with the geranium and the crinoline, must be only too painfully vivid to the minds of many of us. It is sufficient to say that love nor money could procure beautiful objects of contemporary manufacture for any purpose of household furnishing or adornment when William Morris undertook the Herculean and seemingly hopeless task of decorative reform, and wrought and brought deliverance from the thraldom of the ugly, which oppressed all the so-called arts of this country.

Two years and more elapsed from the time the proposition was first mooted; and during that interval not a few preliminary meetings were held, not a few times merely was the scheme discussed, before anything like a definite working plan was determined on. At one time two or three of those who originally constituted themselves members of the firm would assemble to discuss their plans at Madox Brown's house at 13, Fortess Terrace (now Junction Road), Kentish Town; at another time at Burne-Jones's rooms in Charlotte Street, Fitzroy Square; at another time again at Morris's own studio in Red Lion

Square. Morris is described by one, who met him first on one such occasion, as keenly alert and full of energy and movement,—altogether a most striking personality. There were other meetings, or, as they used to be called, "gatherings of the clans," at Madox Brown's house, for instance when himself took the chair and a larger number were present. Several ladies also who were interested as taking part in the work were present on certain occasions. At one of the general meetings, which took place about the middle of the year 1861, it was announced that rooms, for business premises, had been taken at No. 8, on the north side of Red Lion Square, W.C. "We had no idea whatever of commercial success," remarked Rossetti, ten years afterwards, in relating the circumstances to Mr. Theodore Watts, "but it succeeded in our own despite." "With a view," writes Mr. Ford Madox Hueffer, in his record of the life and works of Ford Madox Brown, "of starting a sort of co-operative agency for supplying artistic furniture and surroundings primarily to themselves, but also to the general public, each of those present," it was agreed, "should lay down a stipulated sum. . . . The rules of incorporation were briefly: that each member should contribute designs for the various articles of use and ornament for which demand arose, and should be paid for his work in the usual course of events, before the profits, if any, were shared." Moreover, at the same time, it was mentioned that Mr. Bodley, the architect, had promised to commit the execution of certain orders for stained glass and other decorations to the firm, provided they were organized so as to be able to undertake them. Proposals as to ways and means having thus already been formulated, the business, under the style of Messrs. Morris, Marshall, Faulkner and Co., was now definitely set on foot. A strangely assorted group were they who comprised the original members of the firm. Ford Madox Brown, Dante Gabriel Rossetti, Edward Burne-Jones and Arthur Hughes, painters, the last of whom shortly withdrew; Philip Webb, architect; Peter Paul Marshall, district surveyor at Tottenham and engineer; and Charles

Joseph Faulkner, an Oxford don—these were Morris's partners in the firm. He himself was to undertake the business management and general direction of the affair. His father, before him, had been a man of business, and William Morris had inherited presumably some measure of his father's capacity. "Mr. Morris," says Mr. W. M. Rossetti, "came much the foremost, not only by being constantly on the spot, to work, direct and to transact, but also by his abnormal and varied aptitude at all kinds of practical processes." Beside the partners, of whom all, as it has been stated above, were to give active assistance according to their ability, the staff at the outset was of the smallest. There was Mr. George F. Campfield, subsequently appointed foreman, whom Madox Brown and Burne-Jones had met some two years previously among the students in Ruskin's class at the Working Men's College in Great Ormond Street; and there was also a man engaged to do the rough work of packing and so on. He, by the way, is the same who figures as one of the labourers in Madox Brown's "Work" at the Corporation Art Gallery at Manchester. When the business of the firm began to expand, others were engaged, as required, through the means of advertisements in the Clerkenwell local paper, in "The Builder," &c. But the scheme indicated in the circular, as below, was so unusual from its utter disregard of established conventions, and had caused so much dismay among trade circles, that men on the look-out for employment were for a long time afraid to come forward in response, being wary of identifying themselves with an undertaking on the face of it so hazardous, and such that obviously was foredoomed to failure. The firm, on their part, were anxious to exclude the merely commercial element, and required of all who joined in their work fair evidence, at least, of artistic appreciation beyond the ordinary standard.

The first step the firm took to make their existence known to the public was to send forth a circular in which they explained their aims. The purport of this document was that "a company of historical artists had banded themselves together to execute work in a thoroughly artistic and inexpensive manner; and that they had determined to devote their spare time to designing for all kinds of manufactures of an artistic nature." In our days—so far have conditions been modified and views progressed—a notice of this sort would excite but little comment. Yet in the period when the decorative arts, as then practised, were understood to be a mere polite accomplishment for young ladies who had no better occupation to keep them amused; and when also the line of demarcation between the gentleman, the man, that is, who did nothing to earn his bread, and the business man was drawn with uncompromising sharpness, it was not to be wondered at if the announcement came with the provocation and force of a challenge, and dumbfounded those who read it at the audacity of the venture. The amount of prejudice it aroused would scarcely be believed at the present time. Professionals felt themselves aggrieved at the intrusion, as they regarded it, of a body of men whose training had not been strictly commercial into the close premises of their own peculiar domain; and, had it been possible to form a ring and to exclude Messrs. Morris, Marshall, Faulkner and Co. from the market, the thing would infallibly have been done. But if from without there was much bad blood to encounter and live down, the enthusiasm that reigned among themselves and inspired the courageous little band of pioneers—for they were indeed no less than that—was such that it is difficult to form any conception of it at this distance of time. Pioneers! Nay, Morris and his fellow-workers must have felt themselves to be something far exceeding that;—no mere Columbus was Morris, guiding the helm of his craft to the discovery and exploitation of some already existing land:—no, but since he and they that followed his leadership were actually constructing by their own efforts a new and unknown territory which before had had no being, theirs was rather the divine joy of creating, a joy that is given to none but to an artist, himself a creator, to appreciate. "Ah! but those were grand times," remarked one who has worked with the firm from the very commencement. Furthermore, a thing rarer then than nowadays, there was an all but unlimited freedom of criticism admitted on both sides, between employers and employed, a freedom that virtually amounted to equality of condition between them.

The approaching International Exhibition in London, 1862, and the prospect of being represented worthily thereat, gave the newly-founded firm a definite motive for rallying together and an extra incentive, if it were possible, to strenuous exertion. To meet the pressure of work thereby entailed, the staff of Messrs. Morris, Marshall, Faulkner and Co. was increased towards the end of 1861; the new-comers being Messrs. Albert and Harry Goodwin and Weigand. The latter assisted Rossetti in the decoration of Mr. Seddon's cabinet, and was taken on ultimately as a regular worker in the firm. Finding themselves in need of additional help also in preparing the glass in hand for exhibition, the firm advertised in "The Builder" of November 9th, 1861, for "a first-rate fret glazier wanted." This led to the engaging of Mr. Charles Holloway, who has since become a painter.

Practically no particulars of the exhibits of Messrs. Morris, Marshall, Faulkner and Co. are to be gathered from the Official Illustrated Catalogue of the Exhibition of 1862, printed for her Majesty's Commissioners. It contains but two meagre entries of objects shown by the firm, viz., "Exhibit No. 5783: Decorated furniture, tapestries, &c.," and "Exhibit No. 6734: Stained glass windows." The report of the juries and list of awards witnesses that a medal (United Kingdom) was bestowed on the firm for their work in either class. In the case of the stained glass the award was given "for artistic qualities of colour and design," while in the case of their contributions to the class for furniture and upholstery, paper-hangings, &c., the record runs: "Messrs. Morris and Co. have exhibited several pieces of furniture, tapestries, &c., in the style of the Middle Ages. The general forms of the furniture, the arrangement of the tapestry, and the character of the details are satisfactory to the archæologist from the exactness of the imitation, at the same time that the general effect is excellent."

This recognition, scanty and inadequate as it was, from the authorities, was not allowed to pass unchallenged. The hostility displayed in certain quarters was of the most determined character. Opponents of the firm even went the length of starting a petition to get the work disqualified, on the ground that it was other than it professed to be. In particular they maintained, and that with a dogged obstinacy which did little credit to their own acquaintance with technique, that Morris, Marshall, Faulkner and Co.'s stained glass was not new work or new material at all, but in reality old glass touched up for the occasion—that it was, in plain language, a fraud. But misunderstandings on the part of brother-artists and more bitter jealousy on the part of the trade were of little avail. The awards of the official judges were upheld. And perhaps, after all, the animosity of rivals afforded really testimony the strongest and the most valuable, just because it was involuntary, to the very remarkable qualities of the work which the firm, during so brief a period of existence, had succeeded in producing. At least one expert, Mr. Clayton, of the firm of Clayton and Bell, and formerly a fellow-student with Rossetti at the Royal Academy Schools, when he came to adjudicate, pronounced the work of Messrs. Morris and Co. to be the finest of its kind in the Exhibition.

Before the close of the Exhibition orders were received through Mr. Bodley, then a generous friend and supporter of the firm, for glass for St. Michael's, Brighton, and also for another new church, built in 1862, viz., All Saints', Selsley, a fresh district formed out of the parish of King Stanley in Gloucestershire. The design for the latter church comprises some square quarries with fine circular ornament and delicate yellow stain, in the execution of which quarries Morris personally bore a share. To help in this work an ordinary glazier was engaged to cut and glaze the glass. Another order that followed shortly after was for glass for Bradford, Yorkshire.

During their first year Mr. J. P. Seddon, the architect, had commissioned Messrs. Morris, Marshall, Faulkner and Co. to decorate a cabinet made from his own design.

This was one of the earliest works undertaken by the firm, and was included among the furniture shown at the Exhibition of 1862. It is still in Mr. Seddon's possession. "The subjects proposed for the decoration of this cabinet," says a note by the editor of "The Century Guild Hobby Horse," October, 1888, "being Architecture, Painting, Sculpture and Music, Mr. Ford Madox Brown suggested a series of imaginary incidents in the 'Honeymoon' of King René by which to express them, that king having been skilled in all these arts; Mr. Madox Brown himself designing the 'Architecture,' while the other subjects were invented by Dante Gabriel Rossetti and Mr. Burne-Jones. . . . The cabinet . . . is Gothic in character, and made of oak, polished and inlaid with woods of various colours; the hinges being of metal, painted. The face of the lower portion, which rests immediately upon the ground and forms the greater bulk of the cabinet, contains four panelled doors, the central two of which project slightly beyond those which are at either end. On the panel of the door to the extreme left is painted in oils the design significant of Architecture. . . . Upon the gold background is a pattern of lines and dots, and above the figures is set the kind of canopy represented in mediæval manuscripts," a trefoiled arch, the spandrels of which contain, within circles, shields with the arms of King René, &c. "This background and canopy is repeated in the three other panels. The dress of the king is of a purplish red, lined with blue, his shoes of scarlet; while the white dress of the queen is edged with dark fur, and embroidered with red and blue flowers done in outline. The two panels of the projecting central portion of the cabinet were painted by Mr. Burne-Jones. In the first of these, the king is shown drawing the figure of a woman, as his queen stands over him; in the third panel he is at work carving a statue, while the attitude of the queen would seem to express astonishment at his art. The remaining panel on the right, representing 'Music,' was designed by Rossetti. Here the queen is seated, playing at a kind of regal, or chamber organ, the bellows of which are blown by King René. She is in a dress of green; and, as she is playing, a cloak of fur, lined with orange, falls from her shoulders, as the king bends over the instrument to kiss her." The six small panels in the upper part contain half-length single figures painted, representing various arts and professions:—iron-smelting, horticulture, embroidery, pottery-making, weaving, and glass-making. "One of them is at a frame, embroidering; another, wearing a wimple, weaves a chequered cloth." The first and last are male figures. Part of the decoration was done also by Mr. Val. Prinsep. Yet another cabinet, produced later, should be mentioned; a high one, for the design and execution of which the firm was responsible; the subject of the panel decoration, "Green Summer," being the work of Burne-Jones.

But of Messrs. Morris, Marshall, Faulkner and Co.'s exhibits at the Exhibition of 1862 neither the least interesting nor the least beautiful was a piece of furniture, now in private ownership, a cabinet, raised on a stand and furnished with doors, both the designing and the painting of the four panels being the work of William Morris's own hand. His original pen-and-ink studies belong to Mr. Fairfax Murray. The subject is the legend of St. George, the series beginning with the royal proclamation and surrender of the victim to the dragon, and ending with the triumphal return of St. George with the rescued maiden; it does not, however, include the oft-repeated subject of the combat with the dragon. While Morris was engaged upon this work at Red Lion Square, he received a visit from the master of his old school at Walthamstow, Mr. Guy, who was not only delighted but astonished at the work offered for the inspection of himself and the friends who accompanied him; a fact which goes to prove what has already been stated, viz., that there was no tradition of the extraordinary artistic powers Morris developed when he grew up having been manifested or even suspected in him in boyhood.

If Morris's position at the head of affairs at Messrs. Morris, Marshall, Faulkner and Co.'s had hitherto not been appreciated, the mark that, owing to his guiding genius, the firm made at the Exhibition left no doubt as to his real importance. At a social gathering at the Red House, to which, after the close of the Exhibition, Morris invited all the members of the firm, partners and staff in a body, he seemed instinctively to be acknowledged with one accord as occupying the leading place. The entire direction thenceforward was virtually in his hands, and he applied himself unremittingly to the task. When, in 1865, the firm removed from their original quarters to No. 26, Queen Square, Bloomsbury, Mr. Morris left Upton and took up his residence under the same roof. The house being a large one, the accommodation was sufficient, and, by living thus on the spot, he was enabled to devote still more of his time to superintending the industries carried on by the firm. But although he was, for all intents and purposes, in command of the whole business, he did not become the formal and official head until 1874. In the summer of that year, the original partnership was dissolved, Mr. Theodore Watts taking an active part in the arrangement of the affair. Mr. Morris then bought out the other partners and himself remained as sole representative of the Company, styled thenceforward simply Morris and Co. A fresh notice was issued to announce the change in the firm and to explain that the character of its work would remain unchanged, Burne-Jones continuing as before to furnish cartoons for stained glass. But one must not anticipate. Towards the beginning of 1865 Mr. Warrington Taylor came into the business, in the capacity of acting manager under Mr. Morris, and was of great service to the firm, while he lived; for, unhappily, in a few years' time he was carried off by consumption. He was succeeded by Mr. George Wardle, who had formerly acted as his assistant, and who remained in conduct of affairs from the death of Mr. Taylor for a considerable time—in fact, until within about six or seven years ago, when he resigned and went abroad. The names of some others who have, in the past, been workers on behalf of the firm may be mentioned: Messrs. Fairfax Murray, Charles Napier Hemy, James Egan, Fletcher, Wilday, and the Misses Faulkner.

With reference to the remarks in the official report of the Exhibition of 1862, it should be observed that in the early days of Messrs. Morris, Marshall, Faulkner and Co., their productions, though far from being merely imitative, presented a greater degree of resemblance to mediæval work than they came to have in later times, when Morris's distinctly characteristic style had matured. Thus, in the powderings and diaperings of draperies, backgrounds, &c., for stained glass, the firm, about the middle of the sixties, made some use of a collection of ancient examples of decorations copied from different churches in Norfolk and Suffolk. These patterns and details of ornaments from paintings on walls and roofs, mouldings and carved woodwork, &c., including a series of figures of the angelic hierarchy from the rood-screen of St. Michael's Church, Barton Turf, Norfolk (date c. 1430), and some figures of saints, also of the fifteenth century, from Cawston Church in the same county, were selected and drawn by Mr. G. Wardle. Executed in pencil, and in many instances coloured, with a rare mastery of draughtsmanship, upon tracing paper, mounted on cards and enclosed in three portfolios, this valuable set of designs was acquired in the years 1866 and 1867 for the National Art Library at the South Kensington Museum.

When first the firm started to execute stained glass, Mr. Morris himself had no practical experience of the technicalities of the art. Madox Brown had previously made one design for the purpose, viz., the Transfiguration, for Messrs. Powell and Sons; while Burne-Jones, it is true, had already projected a course of instructions on the subject at the Working Men's College in Great Ormond Street, and had even designed a small quantity of glass, *e.g.*, for Waltham Abbey Church, as well as the St. Frideswide window in the Latin Chapel at Christ Church. To the lot of neither of these, however, did it fall, but to another member of the firm, Mr. Webb, to test the proficiency of their foreman, Mr. Campfield, who, having been employed for a short time by a firm of stained glass manufacturers, was entrusted with the getting together the necessary plant and with the arranging of the working details at the commencement. A small kiln for firing the glass was constructed in the basement of the premises at Red Lion Square, and they set to work. Of course Mr. Morris was not content to stand by and watch other people engaged in a craft in which himself had no part. So he took up the work, and practised painting glass quarries, with the rest. It came to be the custom for the choice of the particular diapers and borders for draperies, &c., to be left to the artist who actually executed the glass-painting, but it was reserved for Morris to determine the scheme of colouring in each case. And when also it is remembered that Burne-Jones was not in the habit of inserting the lead-lines in his cartoons, and that Madox Brown did so only occasionally, one can understand how much remained over and above for Morris and his assistants to do to adapt the designers' monochrome drawings for practical execution.

The stained glass shown by the firm at the Exhibition consisted of some few pieces for domestic purposes, ornamental quarries, and a set of seven panels, designed by Rossetti, to illustrate the parable of the Wicked Husbandmen in the Vineyard. This series was erected eventually in the east window of St. Martin's on the Hill, Scarborough, through the recommendation of Mr. G. F. Bodley, who built the church, and entrusted a considerable part of the internal decoration to Messrs. Morris, Marshall, Faulkner and Co. The pulpit was decorated by the firm, two panels in it being painted by Rossetti himself. The mural painting above the altar was also, in its original state, the work of the firm, but having fallen into a ruinous condition, it has since been completely repainted by local painters. "The first impression," says M. Olivier Georges Destrée, a Belgian writer, in "The Savoy" of October, 1896, "given by the window of the Parable of the Vineyard, which lights the choir, is an impression of colour, dazzling and magnificent, velvety and harmonious, resembling the Flemish stained glass windows decorating the Gothic cathedrals. From the point of view of stained glass, this is the one I consider to be the most perfect. It has all the qualities which . . . were considered essential by Madox Brown, . . . and all these qualities are united in a high degree of perfection. In fact, when we approach this window and examine it in detail, we perceive that it is no less remarkable for its ingenious and original composition than for the sensation of opulent colour which it at first gave us. . . . Sumptuous in colour, ingenious in composition, the window of the Parable appears to be of a design more entirely and peculiarly Rossetti's than that of Adam and Eve, of which certain details seem to show the influence of Madox Brown." The subject of the "most beautiful and impressive" lancets, which are situated at the west end of the church, should be described more correctly as Adam and Eve in Paradise before the Fall. The date of them is 1862. "One is struck by the ingenious arrangement of the branches and leaves by which Rossetti veils the nudity of the bodies of Adam and Eve, for the rosy colours of the flesh look brighter in the violent contrast with the uniform blue of the sky seen behind them; and these ingenious contrasts give to these two nude bodies a vividness of life which is rendered by no other stained glass window which I have ever seen. These resplendent bodies of Adam and Eve illuminate the church, and seem to give it some of their own life. The composition is no less original and new in its details than in the beauty of its colouring. Adam is depicted standing, picturesquely leaning on a branch of a tree with large sombre leaves, a fig-tree I think; with the tip of his foot he amuses himself by tickling a small bear curled up at his feet; the blue sky is seen behind him, and sunflowers, flowering at the end of their long stems, expand at his right hand; in the branches of the tree above him a curious and familiar squirrel watches him. Standing also, Eve has stopped in the middle of a field richly studded with small flowers and red poppies; of the same fairness as the hair and beard of Adam, her unbound hair falls in an opulent stream over her shoulders. In her arms she holds, tenderly pressed to her bosom, a white dove, and in the sombre tree above, his eyes fixed

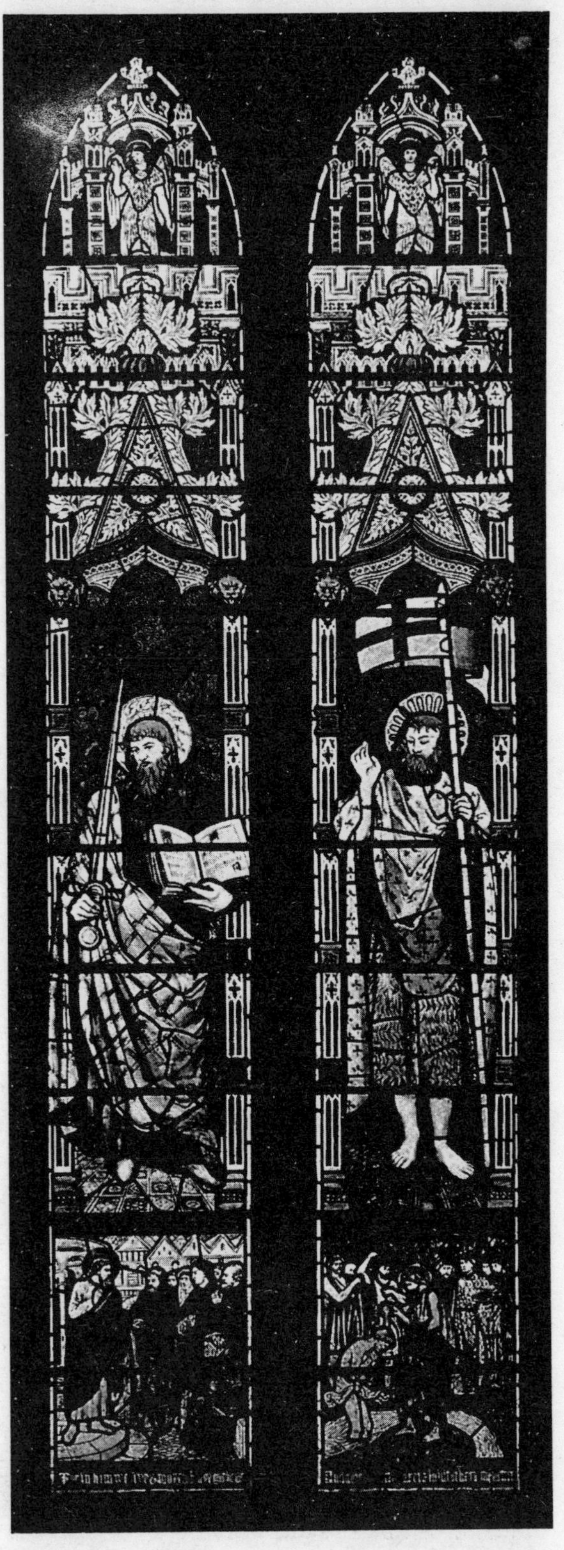

WINDOW IN ST. GILES' CHURCH, CAMBERWELL.

FIGURE OF ST. PAUL DESIGNED BY WILLIAM MORRIS.

EXECUTED BY MORRIS AND CO.

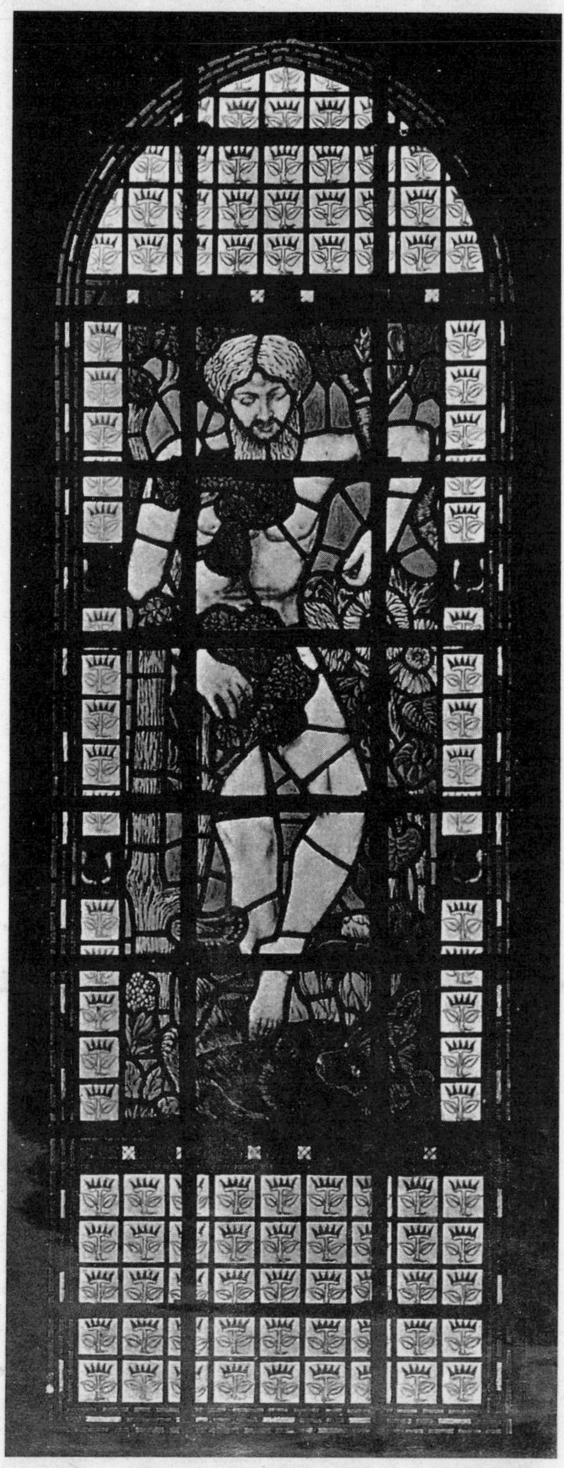

FIGURE OF ADAM (FROM WINDOW BY MORRIS AND CO.), ST. MARTIN'S, SCARBOROUGH.

DESIGNED BY FORD MADOX BROWN.

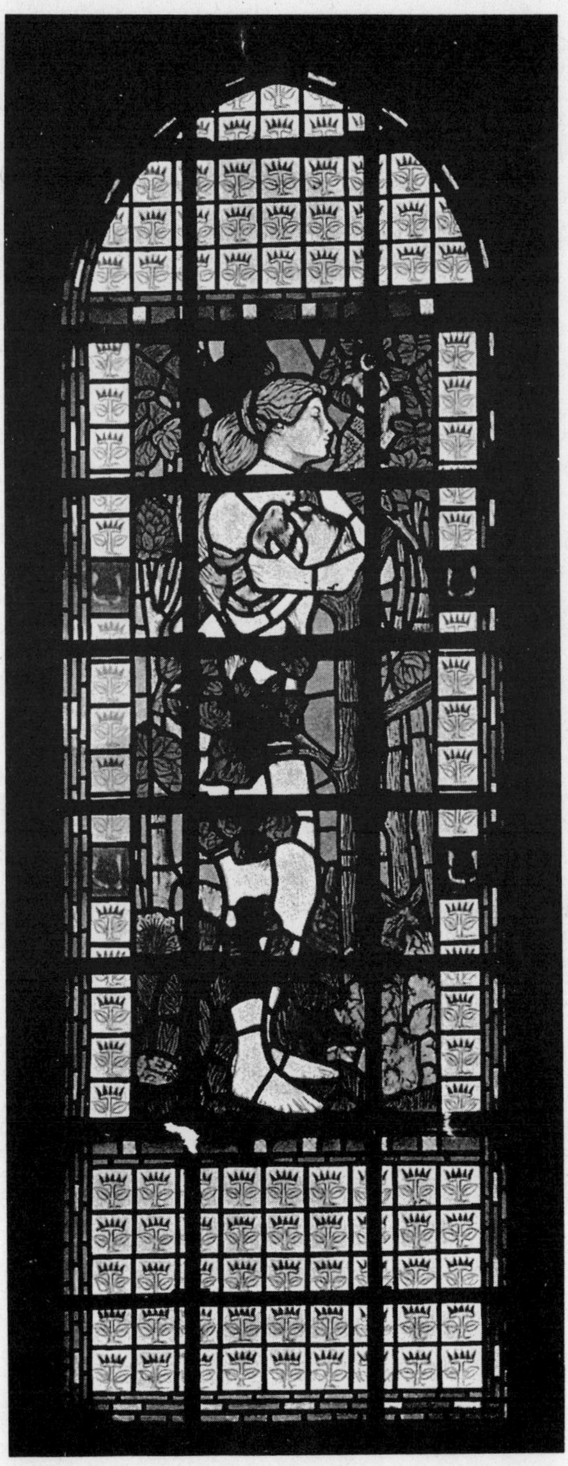

FIGURE OF EVE (FROM WINDOW BY MORRIS AND CO.), ST. MARTIN'S, SCARBOROUGH.

DESIGNED BY FORD MADOX BROWN.

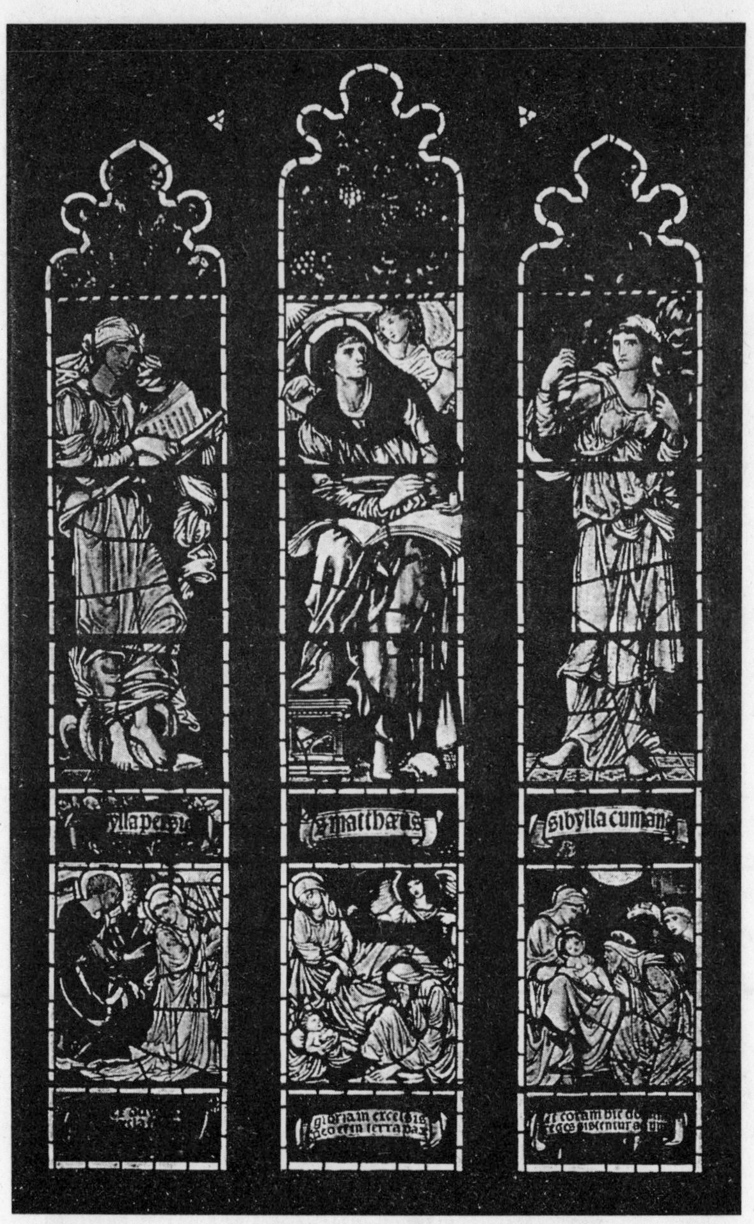

WINDOW IN JESUS COLLEGE, CAMBRIDGE.

DESIGNED BY SIR E. BURNE-JONES, BART.

EXECUTED BY MORRIS AND CO.

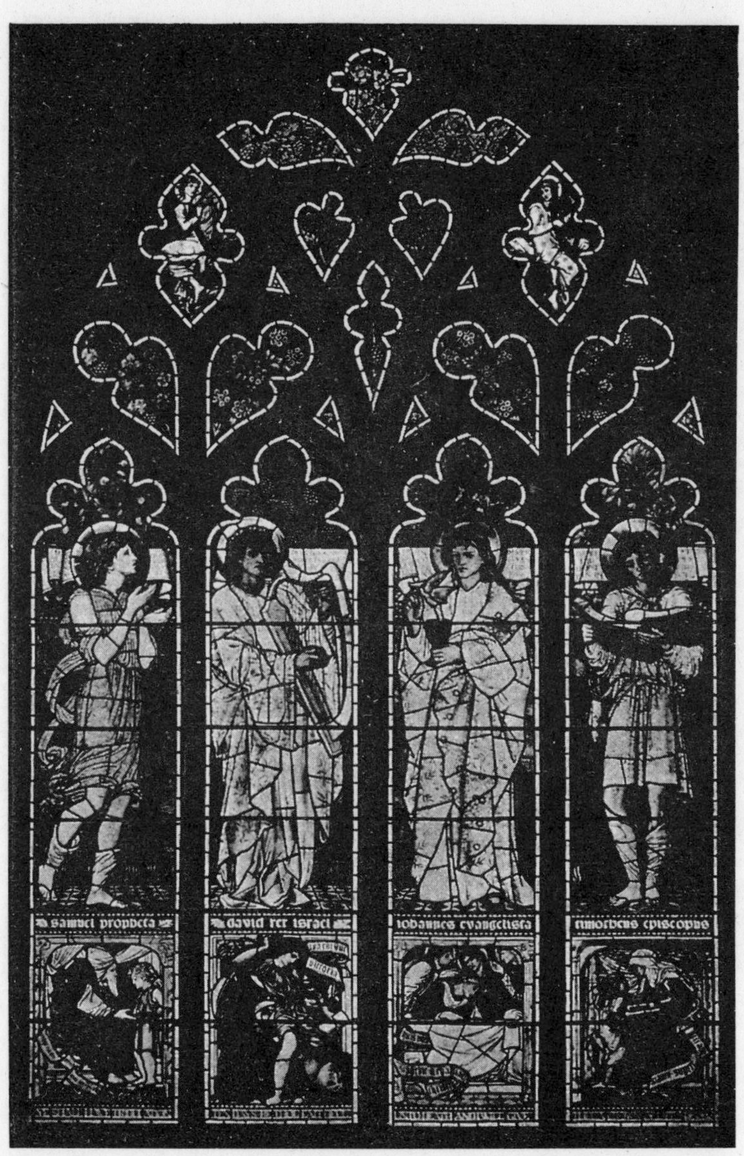

VYNER MEMORIAL WINDOW,
CHRIST CHURCH, OXFORD.

DESIGNED BY SIR E.
BURNE-JONES, BART.

EXECUTED BY MORRIS AND CO.

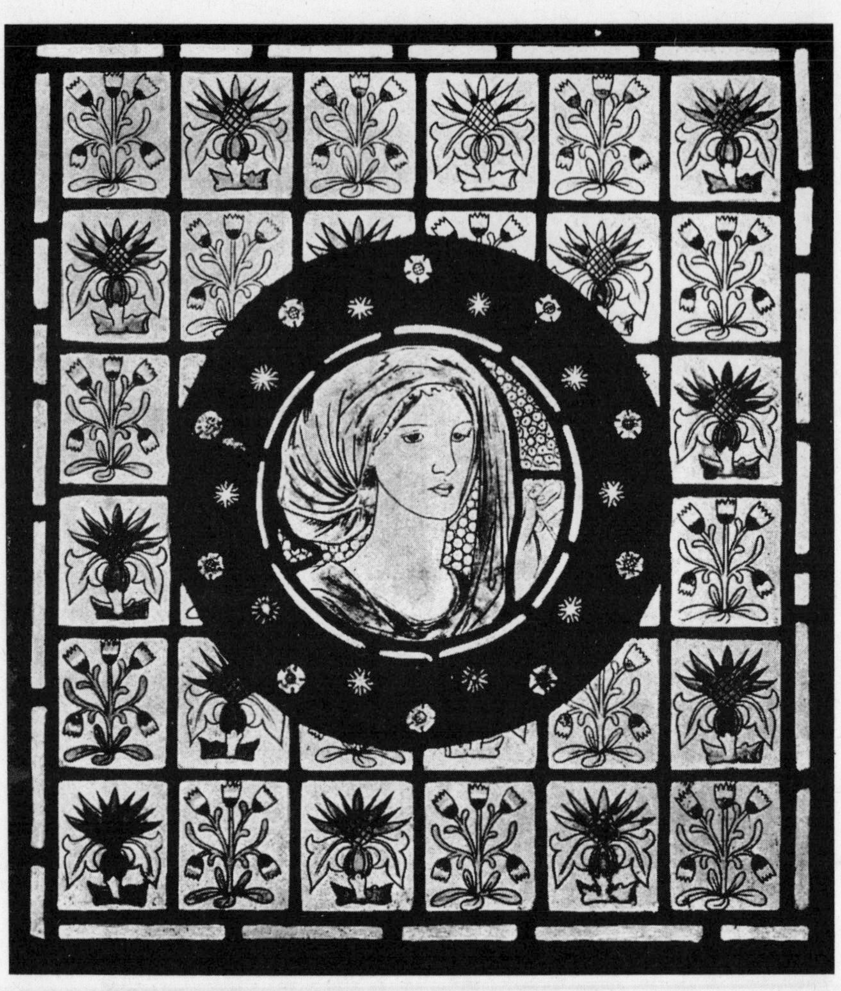

PAINTED GLASS, "PENELOPE"
(SOUTH KENSINGTON MUSEUM).

THE MEDALLION DESIGNED BY
SIR E. BURNE-JONES, BART.

EXECUTED BY MORRIS AND CO.

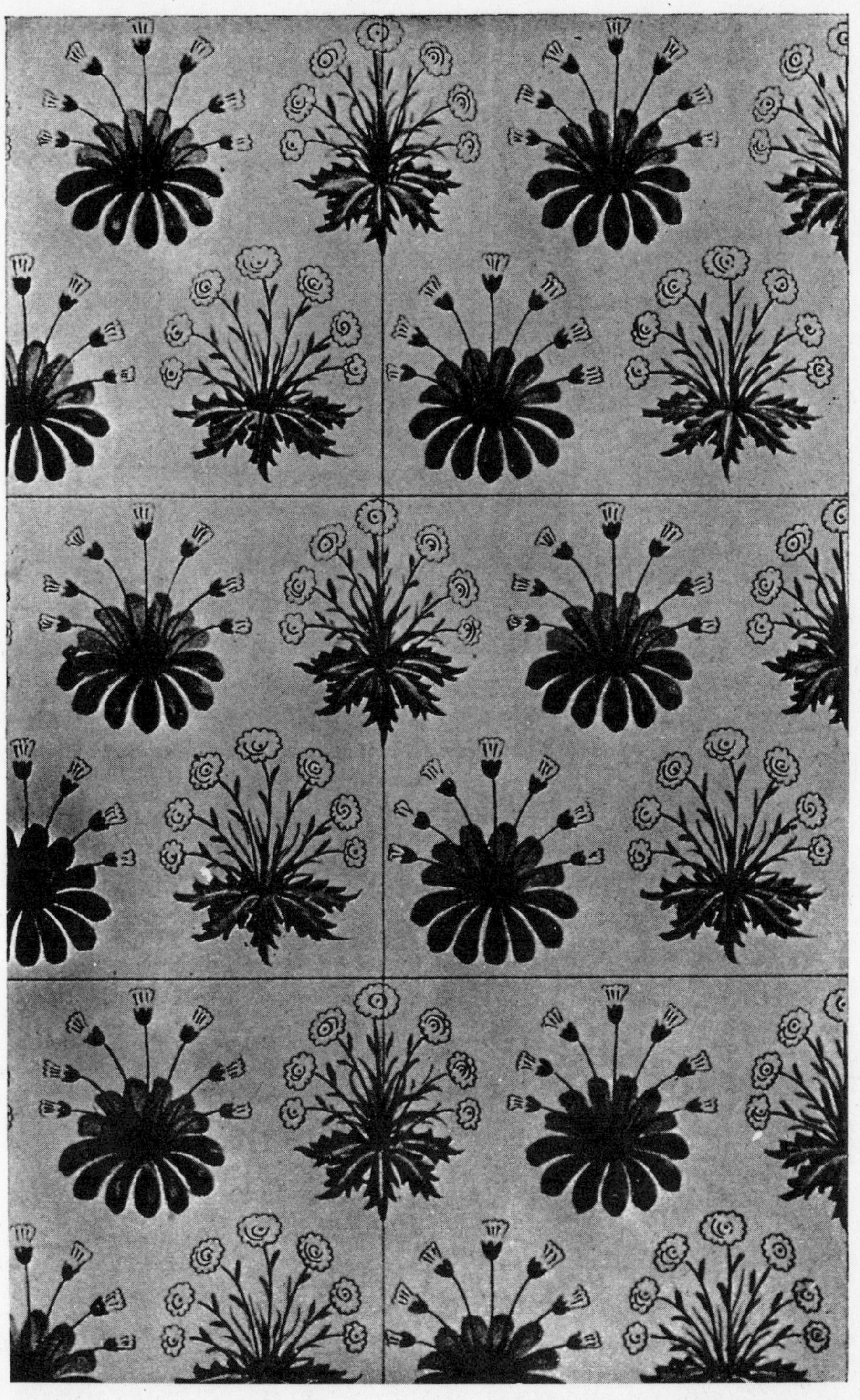

HAND-PAINTED TILES, THE "DAISY" PATTERN. DESIGNED BY WILLIAM MORRIS.

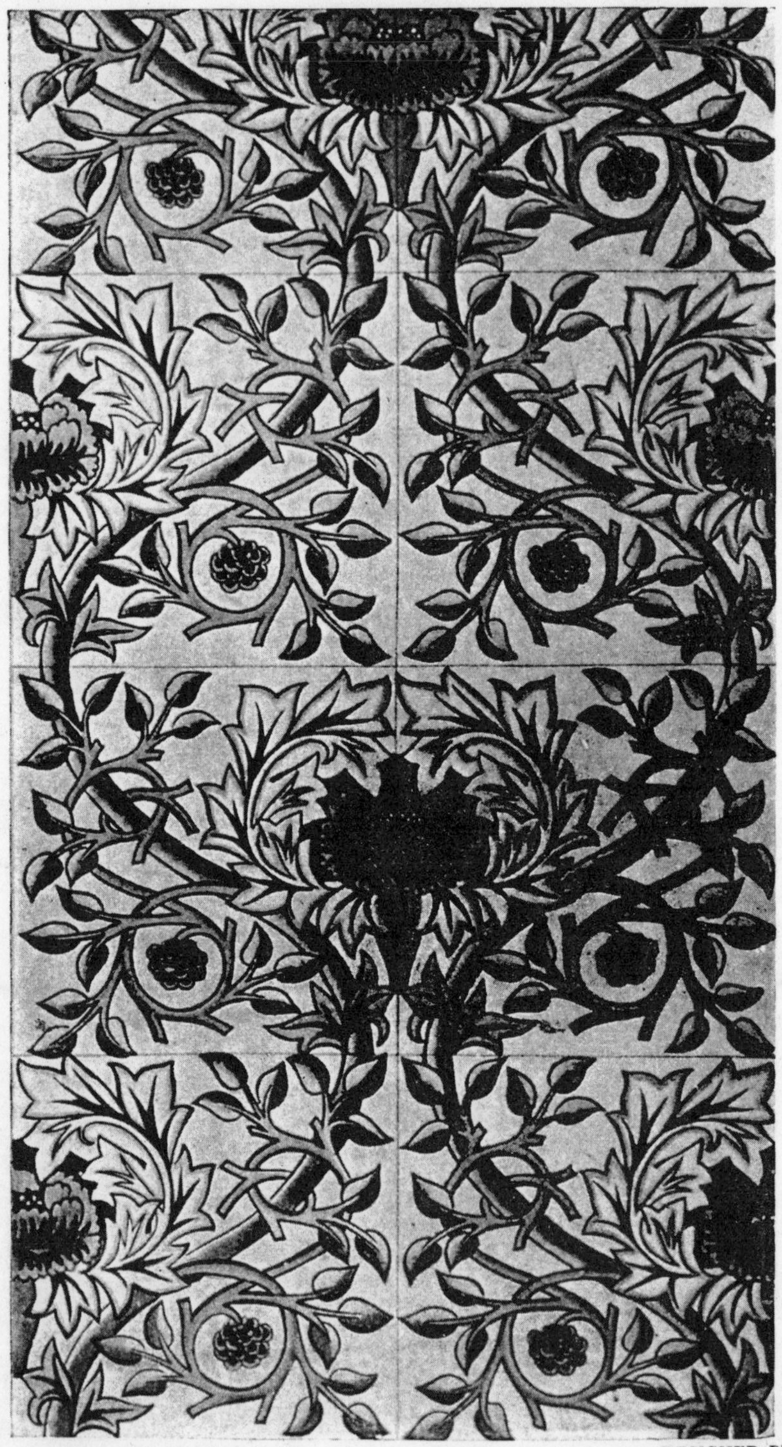

HAND-PAINTED TILES, THE "ROSE" PATTERN. DESIGNED BY WILLIAM MORRIS.

and shining, an owl surveys her. The predominant colours of this admirable window are flesh colour, dark green and light gold." Mr. William Sharp, describing the same windows, says, "A strict harmony of colour is maintained between the rich brown of the bear and squirrel, the varying green of the trees and foliage, the light golden hair and the flesh tints of Adam, the yellow sunflower, &c.; the same being observed in the Eve picture, where also one or two red flowers give a deeper contrast." On the ground, close behind Eve, crouches a tawny brown rabbit. "Above the windows of Adam and Eve," says M. Destrée, "the Annunciation, by Burne-Jones, which decorates the large rose-window, and the 'Angels playing musical instruments' of the nine smaller roses which surround it, form with the windows of Rossetti a remarkable and charming contrast. . . . White, azure blue and ruby are the colours principally and almost exclusively used" in this group of ten openings which form the rose. There is altogether an abundance of Morris glass in St. Martin's, including, on the north side, figures of characters of the Old Testament, and, on the south, of saints of the Christian dispensation.

Rossetti's designs for stained glass, however, were not very numerous. He produced a specially fine cartoon, which was executed by the firm, the subject being Christ in majesty, surrounded by angels; but "his last composition of this class," writes Mr. William Sharp, was a memorial to his aunt, Miss M. M. Polidori, who died in 1867. It was erected in Christ Church, Albany Street, Regent's Park, and is the second window from the bottom of the nave on the right as one faces altarwards, "the colouring throughout being rich and harmonious." The subject is the Sermon on the Mount. It is divided into three compartments, each panel being surrounded by small square panes of white glass, ornamented uniformly with a many-petalled rose, painted with great delicacy in sepia, with yellow stain introduced here and there to heighten the effect of leaves and stalks.

In the north transept of St. Giles's Church, Camberwell, is a two-light window, erected in December, 1864. An early example, it is of unusual interest, not only because of the introduction of canopies, a feature not too common in the glass of the firm, but also because, what is more important, the figure on the left was designed by Mr. Morris himself. It represents St. Paul, clothed in a blue robe, with white cloak, lined with green; the diapered background being of rich red glass. The figure of St. John Baptist on the right, against a blue background, diapered in similar manner, has a red-lined white cloak over his camel-hair vest. The small groups below represent severally St. Paul preaching and St. John baptizing. Besides ornamental quarries, of which he produced a great variety, Mr. Morris's own designs for stained glass were but few. One of his larger cartoons for this purpose is in the collection of Mr. Fairfax Murray. The subject is St. Mary Magdalene, the pattern upon her robe being remarkably elaborate and beautiful. Far more prolific as a designer of glass than either Rossetti or Morris was Ford Madox Brown, who between 1862 and 1875 must have supplied, according to Mr. F. M. Hueffer's estimate, over 150 designs for the use of the firm. Among Madox Brown's cartoons for glass, beside two subjects from the Legend of St. Martin, for the church of that dedication at Scarborough, may be mentioned Christ blessing little Children (1862); Abraham and Isaac, Isaac blessing Esau, SS. Paul, Elizabeth, John, and Matthew (1863); a magnificent set of six scenes (designed in 1864 and 1865) from the life and death of St. Oswald, now occupying the west window of St. Oswald's Church, Durham; a series representing the Legend of St. Edith, for Tamworth Church (1873); and two more subjects, the Incredulity of St. Thomas (1874), and Christ appearing to St. Mary Magdalene in the Garden (1875).

The church of St. Michael at Brighton, the very first which Mr. Bodley ever built, contains, in his opinion, some of the finest specimens of early Morris glass, designed, with the exception named below, by Burne-Jones. By the font, at the west end of the south transept of the original church—that is, of the church as Mr. Bodley built it; for it has since been enlarged—is a two-light window, a memorial to Dr. Bodley, representing the Baptism of Christ. At the east end of the south transept is a small chapel containing two low windows of two lights each, the subject of the first being three Angels conducting Mary and Joseph and the Holy Child into Egypt; the subject of the other the Angel with the three Maries at the Sepulchre. Above is a small circle with the emblematic pelican. But the most interesting and important glass is that in the west wall of the nave. The upper part is a rose window, which comprises a seven-foiled circle, containing the Madonna and Child, surrounded by seven smaller circles, each with an angel, robed in dark green, striking a bell, upon a background of white quarries with yellow stained ornament. The lower part consists of two double lancets, each pair surmounted by a six-foiled circle, containing respectively St. Michael and the Dragon on the left, and the Annunciation on the right. The lancets represent four Archangels in the following order, reckoned from left to right: St. Michael, with shield and lance, St. Raphael, St. Uriel, and St. Gabriel holding a lily. The figures of these lights, which have, it has been observed, a "mysterious witch-like glamour" about them, were executed from designs by Ford Madox Brown in 1863. Other early Morris glass is at Coddington Church, Newark-on-Trent. The east window was erected in 1865, and one more at the same time; while others have been inserted at various subsequent dates. The figures are upon a quarried ground, without canopies.

Mr. Madox Brown, in the preface to a catalogue of his work entitled "Cartoons for Stained Glass" (1865), sets forth the general rules followed by the Pre-Raphaelite painters in the designing of stained glass and the customary method employed by Messrs. Morris, Marshall, Faulkner and Co. in the execution of the same. "With its heavy lead lines," he says, "surrounding every part (and no stained glass can be rational and good without strong lead lines),"—a fundamental condition, which, by the way, entails the condemnation of Sir Joshua Reynolds's glass pictures, howsoever admired by American visitors, in the west window of New College Chapel, Oxford,—"stained glass does not admit of refined drawing; or else it is thrown away upon it. What it does admit of, and what above all things it imperatively requires, is fine colour" (Sir Joshua Reynolds's glass, mentioned above, is mostly brown and drab): "and what it can admit of, and does very much require also, is invention, expression and good dramatic action. For this reason work by the greatest historical artists is not thrown away upon stained glass windows, because, though high finish of execution is superfluous, and against the spirit of this beautiful decorative art, yet, as expression and action can be conveyed in a few strokes equally as in the most elaborate art, on this side therefore stained glass rises to the epic height. . . . The cartoons of this firm are never coloured, that task devolving on Mr. Morris, the manager, who makes his colour (by selecting the glass) out of the very manufacture of the article. The revival of the mediæval art of stained glass dates back now some twenty years in the earliest established firms; nevertheless with the public it is still little understood; a general impression prevails that bright colouring is the one thing desirable. . . . The result of this is that the manufacturers, goaded on by their clients, and the fatal facility of the material (for all coloured glass is bright), produce too frequently kaleidoscopic effects of the most painful description."

In some interesting notes on "Stained Glass, Ancient and Modern," in the "Century Guild Hobby Horse" of October, 1887, Mr. John Aldam Heaton writes, "In Keble College the other day, a friend remarked, 'we shall soon want a fresh set of Church restorations—to get rid of modern stained glass;' and certainly the specimens before us justified the remark—a remark which brought to one's mind all the gross vulgarity of colour, feebleness of execution, poverty of design, and general inanity of scheme, all overshadowed by a strong tendency towards greenish-jaundice, which characterizes ninety per cent. of all the glass now being made for cathedrals, churches, and alas! also for houses."

"I am far indeed from wishing to include Mr. Morris's work in this condemnation, and as he doesn't make anything like a tenth of what is produced, I leave room for *some* respectable work by other makers: but this does not even veil the fact that the production of this splendid item of the decorator's art has fallen into *most* incompetent hands, and has become a prominent source of *de*-decoration to our buildings, and of annoyance and vexation to all men of cultivated taste. . . . The mere fact of modern glass being drawn on paper only, even by such accomplished designers as Mr. Burne-Jones, and then transferred to glass by copyists,—copyists whom one feels inclined to class as 'clerks,'—points at once to an inevitable and fatal element of inferiority. What would a man think, having given an order for a picture to an eminent artist, when he discovered that the eminent artist had only drawn it in chalk on paper, and then handed it over to his 'young man' to copy it in colours on canvas! Yet this is done universally in stained glass; whereby we at once lose 'touch,' sparkle, breadth and originality of handling, and get in exchange the mechanical monotony of the copyist; with this further mischief, that whereas the canvas or the panel may bear, and often with great advantage, the most minute detailing and stippling, as witness the work of Memling or Van Eyck, such work is fatal on glass, where translucency should be a prominent characteristic. . . . The copyist delights in a hard, wire-like, mechanical line, and is proud of it: the artist avoids it as he would a plague. The copyist, if he has projection to express, knows no way but stippling the whole surface—now light maybe, now dark, but everywhere stippled, suffering always from that most inartistic fault of not knowing where to stop: the mediæval artist, who always appears to have known and felt the qualities and capabilities of the material he was working in, saw at once that sparkle, translucency—*life*—disappear under excess of stippling, and so stopped very far short indeed of the whole surface—often didn't stipple at all.

Indeed, stained glass, theoretically, should be very much of the nature of a *sketch* by an able hand, vigorous in conception, strong in the handling of the principal forms, and slight as possible in mechanism of detail; practically, the glass should be variable in thickness, ribby, and full of air bubbles, so as to produce gradation of colour and enhance the jewel-like effect of its translucence: at least half of its surface should be left clean glass for the sun to shine through: no lines should be used and no 'matting' more than is absolutely necessary to express the intention; and the lead, broad and plentiful, should supply the place of darks."

Now, tested by these canons, the glass of the firm is pre-eminently satisfactory. It fulfils even that condition for which Mr. Heaton seems scarcely to recognize that credit is due to it. That Mr. Morris felt as keenly as any-one could feel the danger of glass executed by one man from the paper cartoon of another losing its spirit and finer qualities in the process of reproduction is a fact. And accordingly he made a special point of insisting on the literal preservation of every characteristic of the original design with the minutest fidelity possible. In every case for the faces and hands and the more important features, if not invariably for the remaining portions, he employed none but accomplished artists like Mr. Fairfax Murray, for example, or Mr. Campfield. It is not too much to assert that Mr. Murray's rendering of the Vyner memorial window at Christ Church, Oxford, from Sir Edward Burne-Jones's cartoons, could not have been surpassed had the execution of it been the actual work of the designer. If the system that prevailed at the time that Mr. Morris took the art in hand was that of mere dead copyism and obliteration of all character the originals might possess, he certainly was the leader to a more excellent way when he introduced the reform, now adopted, in theory at any rate, by all the best firms of stained glass manufacturers. The quality of the material employed was another important consideration with Morris, the pot metal being selected with the utmost care from the stock of Messrs. Powell and Sons, of Whitefriars. In the early days exception was taken frequently to the greenish hue of the white glass in the windows of the firm. Mr. Morris, however, was not to be persuaded to deviate from the course he had adopted. It was not his fault if the inartistic custom of modern glass-makers had used the public to prefer a cold and harsh white to the subtler-toned and mellower effects of the tinted glass he employed of deliberate purpose. He trusted that they would, in course of time, understand and approve what he did; as indeed it would seem that they have.

Another point to note in Morris glass is that, at the beginning, for faces, hands, &c., flesh-tint glass was used, a pale pot metal which would readily take yellow stain and could be modified with enamel colour when it was desired to depict hair, shading, and so on. The extreme delicacy of handling is indeed the reason why the finer details of some parts in early Morris glass have perished. A short period succeeded, in the early seventies, when white glass for flesh predominated; after which was resumed flesh-coloured metal again; stronger and darker, however, than formerly, and such that of late years, up to the present time, has continued deepening in intensity rather than the reverse. It is said that Morris was confirmed in his preference for this usage on seeing the large windows of the Nativity and Crucifixion, executed by the firm in 1888, from Sir Edward Burne-Jones's cartoons, for St. Philip's, Birmingham; for Morris was struck greatly with admiration for these splendid specimens of stained glass, held both by himself and by the designer for favourites among the many windows they had produced together. At St. Philip's the flesh tints are for the most part somewhat pronounced; those of the male figures in particular being of a dark brownish colour, strongly marked. It is not to be pretended that in the course of years there has been no change or development in the style of Morris glass. Nowhere perhaps is the contrast, both in scheme and colouring, illustrated more strikingly than in St. John's Church, Torquay, where the east and west windows are separated by an interval of many years. Nor to an unprejudiced mind can there be any question as to which of the two accords the better with the traditional character of stained glass, or which is the more appropriate for its ecclesiastical purpose: the east window, of early date, with its stately figures in rich-toned robes against a light background, or the recent west window, representing the nine choirs of Angels, crowded as it is with wings and draperies, of every gradation of colour from pink to lavender, a Burne-Jones picture every inch of it, albeit the material is glass. The same criticism applies, though perhaps in a lesser degree, to the glass at Morton Church, near Gainsborough, particularly to a window on the north side of the church, the subject being the stoning of St. Stephen, and to the east window, in which the pictorial rendering of sky and landscape might almost suggest a parallel to Munich glass. Moreover these windows tend to darken the church instead of admitting light. But happily this type is not the most general among the hundreds of windows produced by the firm from the designs of Sir Edward Burne-Jones, the artist who has supplied them with by far the largest proportion of cartoons for their stained glass.

Among the superb windows designed by Burne-Jones it seems invidious to single out any one as the best, in derogation, as it were, of the others. In 1866 he designed some splendid glass for the east window of All Saints' Church, built by Mr. Bodley at Cambridge. Afterwards there followed, in the seventies, a whole series of windows in the neighbouring Chapel of Jesus College. Of these the finest is undoubtedly the large window in the south wall of the south transept. The subject is the celestial hierarchy, of every grade, and, next after them, man made in the image of God, occupying the batement lights and two tiers of the five large lights above the transom. Below are five virgin saints, viz.: SS. Ursula, Dorothea, Radegund, Cecilia and Catherine; and below these again, Bishop Alcock, founder of the College, between the four Latin Fathers, SS. Jerome and Gregory on the left, and SS. Ambrose and Augustine on the right. No reproduction can convey the glorious effect of colour, more especially of the yellows, which range from palest amber to fiery orange in wings and other details of the composition. The south transept is lighted by two windows on either side, of three lights each; the scheme of subjects being the four Evangelists, one in the middle of each window, between two Sibyls, and smaller groups beneath from the life of our Lord. There are other fine windows by the firm in the nave—some half-hidden by the organ—and in the north transept: in all eleven Morris windows. It may be mentioned here that the firm was also employed under Mr. Bodley, to whose hands had been committed the restoration of the Chapel, to decorate the roof of the nave. For this purpose Morris himself designed a series of Angels holding scrolls inscribed with the *Vexilla Regis*. These were executed in tempera on either side of the coved roof.

Covering about the same period as the windows at Jesus College are four, also from Burne-Jones's designs, at Christ Church, Oxford; and it would be difficult to find more magnificent examples of Morris glass than three of the number. The earliest in date, a four-light window, contains large figures of Samuel, David, St. John, and Timothy. All in white vesture, relieved in parts with yellow diapering, they show up strikingly against a background of dark green foliage appearing over the top of a blue tapestry curtain. The pavement on which they stand is pale red, while the halos are of spoilt ruby glass, the effect of which, flecked with blood and flame colour, produced solely by the metal being coated without uniformity of surface, is remarkably rich and jewel-like. The flesh tints, perhaps by contrast to the white draperies, seem rather deep than otherwise. The colour scheme of the lower groups is mainly blue, bluish green, olive, amber and white. The next window, to the right of the last, is not less beautiful. It consists of three lights and represents St. Cecilia between two Angels. The red nimbuses, the light flesh tints, the draperies all white except for the brownish purple lining of the robe of the right-hand figure, and the Angels' wings of pale blue, splashed here and there with yellow stain, make an exquisite contrast to the rich green foliage and dark peacock-blue hangings draped in the background. The prevailing colours of the small groups below, from the life of the Saint, are blue, white and amber. At the east end of the south aisle of the choir is a window erected in 1877, representing St. Catherine between the Angel of Suffering and the Angel of Victory. Against a background of green foliage, of purple walls and dark blue curtains, the three figures stand all in white, the figure of the Saint peculiarly majestic. The Angels have spoilt ruby halos, the mutilated hands of the Angel on the left being veiled in a cloth of light cinnamon hue,—the same colour as the flames which the Angel on the opposite side is combating. Deeper tones prevail in the lower compartments, one of the floating Angels who carry the body of St. Catherine to her burial being of a ripe orange; while the glory of cherubim surrounding the Christ in the middle panel has an indescribable glow of ruby, purple and blue.

Among other windows of the firm may be named those in Peterhouse Combination Room at Cambridge, dating between 1869 and 1874. This room contains five windows of two lights each and a large bay window of six lights. The subject of the four windows on the north side is a series of poets from Homer to Milton, from designs by Madox Brown and Burne-Jones, upon a diamond quarried background. The two-light window on the south side represents King Edward I. and the founder, Hugh de Balsham, Bishop of Ely, designed by Madox Brown; while the bay window, on the same side of the room, illustrates Chaucer's "Legend of Good Women" from designs by Burne-Jones, the figures being portrayed in colours on a grisaille and yellow-stained background. In 1864 there were purchased for the South Kensington Museum four panels, by Messrs. Morris, Marshall, Faulkner and Co., three of them identical with the Peterhouse glass, viz., those which represent the poet Chaucer asleep, Dido and Cleopatra and the God of Love with Alceste. The fourth panel is a very beautiful head of Penelope, in the form of a medallion, within a wreath, upon a quarried ground of conventional floral pattern.

The west window of the Parish Church at Bishopsbourne, near Canterbury, is filled with Morris glass, designed by Burne-Jones, and erected in 1874. The three large lights are occupied by symbolical representations of Faith, Hope, and Charity, similar in drawing to those in the west window of the south aisle at Christ Church, only that the figures at Oxford are strong in colour, whereas at Bishopsbourne they are clothed entirely in white, which gives them a totally different effect. A richer colour tone is concentrated in the lower part of the window, which contains crouching figures symbolical of the vices opposed to the three theological virtues ; while in the two batement lights at the top are Angels playing on pipes. At St. Michael's, Torquay, is a fine east window designed by Burne-Jones ; an allegorical treatment of the Crucifixion, with full-size figures of Mary and John on either side, and square panels underneath with scenes from the life of our Lord.

Next may be mentioned the Morris glass, designed by Burne-Jones, at Paisley Abbey : and also the window, designed by the same hand and executed in 1879, in the south choir aisle of Salisbury Cathedral ;—the subject being two ministering and two praising Angels. In the early eighties Burne-Jones designed windows for the Savoy Chapel and for St. Peter's, Vere Street, and in 1885 for St. Giles's, Edinburgh. Thenceforward, nay, even before that date (for it is a fact that the late Dean Stanley was an admirer of the work of the firm and that Morris, had he chosen, might have obtained the order to execute stained glass for Westminster Abbey itself), it became a rare thing to find Morris glass inserted in any ancient building. There were of course special exceptions, as in places where glass of the firm existed already, and Mr. Morris was pressed to supply more *en suite* with the previous work ; or where personal claims seemed to justify such a proceeding, as in the case of the village church of Rottingdean, the country home of Burne-Jones. It was indeed a matter of principle with Morris, who, in order to be in a position to protest against the terrible disfiguring of old buildings by the introduction of wretched modern glass, &c., by others, had to set a consistent example and refrain himself. The pity of it was that this policy of his could not be guaranteed to effect the object he desired. For, given a person who has formed the generous determination to present a stained glass window—a memorial as often as not—to any particular church: suppose the capable firm has been offered and has refused the order, what is to hinder the intending donor from having recourse to some inferior firm of glass-makers, and thereby swelling the roll of deplorable defacements to ancient buildings? It is to be feared that Morris's conscientious scruples in this regard have made our land the poorer by the loss of many examples of stained glass which might else have been in existence. A Morris window of recent date, erected in 1895, and, from its dignified size, of no little importance (since it consists of as many as twelve lights), is the east window of Holy Trinity Church, Sloane Street. The glass was designed by Burne-Jones, but it must be confessed that, as a conception, it is far from deserving to rank among that great artist's most successful achievements. Here was a grand and, one may say, a unique opportunity; one of the largest window surfaces in London, and such that had the further advantage of Mr. Sedding's beautiful tracery to serve as a basis for the ornamental glass. But who is prepared to maintain that the glass bears any sort of relation to the tracery it fills? Does not it consist rather of a collection of figures, which, since they are designed by one and the same hand, have, indeed, a strong family likeness, but no homogeneity of plan beyond being all displayed similarly upon a background of tapestry-like foliage? What material difference would a dozen more or less of such figures have made to the work as an ordered and cohesive composition? Nay, a sampler, like this one, of sacred iconography, is capable of almost any number of additions or subtractions without increasing or impairing to an appreciable degree its completeness as an organic whole. It is scarcely necessary to observe that, regarded by itself, every single figure is beautiful, as whatever

Burne-Jones draws is bound to be; but, taken into account the position they occupy, their scale is too small to be proportionate to the great size of the window, in which, surely, if anywhere, a large and broad treatment is what was required. These remarks are not intended to reflect in any sense upon the execution or quality of the glass, which is as perfect as one would wish, and quite worthy of the renowned firm that produced it.

The ceramic art, or rather that branch of it represented by the ornamentation of tiles, is another industry which owes its rescue from degradation to William Morris. "All nations, however barbarous," said he, in his lecture on "The Lesser Arts of Life" (published in 1882), "have made pottery; . . . but none have ever failed to make it on true principles, none have made shapes ugly or base till quite modern times. I should say that the making of ugly pottery was one of the most remarkable inventions of our civilization." A little further on Morris states the main principles that should regulate the ornamentation of fictiles. "As to the surface decoration on pottery, it is clear it must never be printed; . . . one rule we have for a guide, and whatever we do if we abide by it, we are quite sure to go wrong if we neglect it: and it is common to all the lesser arts. Think of your material. Don't paint anything on pottery save what can be painted only on pottery; if you do it is clear that however good a draughtsman you may be, you do not care about that special art. You can't suppose that the Greek wall-painting was anything like their painting on pottery—there is plenty of evidence to show that it was not. Or, take another example from the Persian art; it is easy for those conversant with it to tell from an outline tracing of a design whether it was done for pottery painting or for other work."

It was at the beginning of 1862, and some tiles were required for use at the Red House. But at that time there simply were no hand-painted tiles produced in this country. So Morris had to begin from the very beginning. Plain white tiles were imported by the firm from Holland, and

Morris, Faulkner and others set about experimenting with various glazes, enamels, &c., until the desired results were obtained. The same kiln that was used for firing the stained glass was made to serve for the tiles also. An iron muffle with iron shelves carried the glass in the middle part, while the tiles were so placed as to be exposed to the greatest heat, at the top and bottom. A small wind-furnace was employed for slips and for colour-testing experiments. Burne-Jones furnished the figure designs that were painted on the earliest tiles of the firm. These figures having first been outlined by others, Mr. Morris, with Mr. Faulkner's help, tinted in the flat surfaces with enamel colour. After the first firing a soft glaze of the firm's own composition was applied to the surface of the tiles.

A set of tiles, with figures of Adam and Eve, was painted in readiness for the Exhibition of 1862, and was in fact delivered and unpacked with a view to being exhibited. But when Mr. William Burges, the architect, saw them, he failed to appreciate the decorative value of some scrolls, with verses by Morris, that had been introduced into the composition. Whereupon, in order to avoid misunderstandings, Morris had the tiles removed from among the exhibits, without submitting them to the inspection of the hanging committee as a body. He was, however, far from being deterred in any way by this incident, and the production of hand-painted tiles continued to be from thenceforward one of the regular crafts of the firm. Among Burne-Jones's designs for tiles were a series to illustrate Chaucer's "Good Women," the story of Cinderella, a favourite subject which was reproduced repeatedly, and the legend of the Sleeping Beauty. Rossetti and Madox Brown also designed tiles for the firm. There was one set of designs—a joint production—representing the several occupations of the months and seasons of the year. Of these Madox Brown designed the pictures of tree-felling, seed-sowing, and sheep-shearing, while Morris himself designed a mower whetting his scythe. Morris designed in addition a number of tiles of conventional floral and other diaper patterns to surround the figure subjects for fireplaces, &c. Of these one which was used frequently was known as the "Swan" pattern. It has been said above that at first Morris and Faulkner used to paint tiles themselves; later Miss Lucy Faulkner undertook this branch of the work in place of her brother and Mr. Morris. Miss Kate Faulkner also painted tiles for the firm, and continued to do so until within a few years ago. After Miss Lucy Faulkner's marriage the firm produced but few figure-subject tiles; one of the last of these being a medallion tile presented by Mr. Morris to Baron Leys.

Effective use of tiles was made by Messrs. Morris, Marshall, Faulkner and Co. for internal decorations. The firm supplied tiles of figure panels surrounded by diaper ornament for the fireplace in the hall of Sandroyd House, Cobham, Surrey, a house Mr. Webb built for Mr. Stanhope shortly after Morris's Red House at Upton. It so happened that both owners gave up their respective houses within a short period of one another.

The two fireplaces in Peterhouse Combination Room were fitted in 1870 with Morris tiles, in the shape of figure panels on a floral diaper ground. The larger of the fireplaces has representations of the four seasons, with verses by Morris—the same which he published in "The Academy" of February 1st, 1871; while the panels in the smaller fireplace have figures of SS. Peter and George. The chimney-breast of the Hall at Queen's College, Cambridge, is decorated by the firm with hand-painted tiles, consisting of figure subjects upon a ground-work of blue diaper ornament, within a conventional border of the same colour. The figures represent the two royal foundresses, Margaret of Anjou and Elizabeth Woodville, designed by Madox Brown in 1873; the tutelary saints of the college, SS. Bernard and Margaret, and allegorical figures of the twelve months of the year.

It was owing in great measure to Mr. Morris's initiative that Mr. William de Morgan, now of Chelsea and Great Marlborough Street, took up the art. He worked for a time in connection with Morris and Co., though his business was and is quite distinct from theirs. How he has revived and developed the exquisite Hispano-Moresque lustre for the painting of tiles and other fictile objects is well known to all artists and connoisseurs. Some early Morris tiles having suffered through the excess of borax in the ordinary enamels of commerce, the only colours available at the time that the industry was revived, it was decided to abandon them, and latterly the only colours used by Morris and Co. for the purpose have been those prepared and supplied by Mr. de Morgan.

The firm of Morris, Marshall, Faulkner and Co. had scarcely been in existence six years when they were commissioned to carry out the internal decorations of the Green Dining-Room at the South Kensington Museum. In this room are two windows, containing in all six panels, with figures, robed in white, designed by Burne-Jones in 1866 and 1867. These panels form a horizontal band across the windows, with roundels—another form of window decoration revived by Morris—above and below, of pale greenish white glass painted with a delicate pattern of conventional ornament. The walls of the dining-room are panelled with wood, painted green and rising from the floor to about half the height of the room. The upper panels are gilt, the majority of them being decorated with painted sprays of various trees and flowers, while at intervals are panels with decorative figures, in place of these floral designs, painted on them. It is characteristic of Mr. Morris's scrupulous thoroughness that, after the panels were finished, he came to the conclusion that the work, having been carried out by different painters, was not uniform enough in style to make a consecutive or harmonious scheme of decoration. Accordingly he insisted on having them all repainted almost afresh by the hand of Mr. Fairfax Murray. The wall-space above the panelling is covered with a conventional pattern of foliage in relief; and round the top runs a frieze with panels depicting a chase of animals.

From 1870 to 1873 Dr. Sandford, now Protestant titular

Bishop of Gibraltar, held the living of Bishopsbourne (a country parish the associations of which possess an interest for some, because Richard Hooker, called "the judicious," was a former rector; the yew-trees planted by him being shown in the garden to this day), and Mr. Morris, as a friend of Dr. Sandford's, visited him at the Rectory and decorated the dining-room there (the same room in which Hooker died). The decoration is of simple character, consisting of a delicate conventional pattern stencilled on the plaster between the moulded rafters; a narrow scroll painted round the top of the wall immediately below the roof-beams; and a Gothic pattern, brighter in colour and more solid than the rest, stencilled upon the panels of the dado.

Of the many industries connected with the name of Morris, none has more universal celebrity than that of wall-paper hangings; and rightly so. For it was Morris who made this a truly valuable branch of domestic ornamentation; Morris, who elevated it from the level of a temporary expedient of no great account to be a craft of the first rank. If in some other instances he was rather the restorer and infuser of fresh life into arts fallen into degeneracy, he was nothing short of a creator in the case of wall-paper design, which, as a serious decorative art, owes its existence to him before anyone else. The youngest in point of date, it is yet, of all the art industries of the present time, not far from being the most satisfactory, regarded from the standpoint of taste. It has commanded the services of the very foremost of decorative artists amongst us, of Messrs. Voysey and Butterfield, Walter Crane, Lewis Day, and Heywood Sumner, Mawson, the late Mr. A. Silver, and many more beside.

The importance of paying due regard to the artistic treatment of our wall spaces is a matter on which Morris has insisted in his lecture on "The Lesser Arts of Life," wherein he says, "Whatever you have in your rooms, think first of the walls; for they are that which makes your house and home; and if you don't make some sacrifice in their favour, you will find your chambers have a kind of makeshift, lodging-house look about them, however rich and handsome your movables may be." Thus much for the general principle. Coming to details, "I suppose I am bound," writes Morris, "to say something on the quite modern and very humble, but, as things go, useful art of printing patterns on paper for wall hangings. But really there is not much to be said about it, unless we were considering the arrangement and formation of its patterns; because it is so very free from those difficulties the meeting and conquering of which give character to the more intricate crafts. I think the real way to deal successfully with designing for paper-hangings is to accept their mechanical nature frankly, to avoid falling into the trap of trying to make your paper look as if it were painted by hand. Here is the place, if anywhere, for dots and lines and hatchings: mechanical enrichment is of the first necessity in it. After that you may be as intricate and elaborate in your pattern as you please; nay, the more and the more mysteriously you interweave your sprays and stems the better for your purpose, as the whole thing has to be pasted flat on a wall, and the cost of all this intricacy will but come out of your own brain and hand. For the rest, the fact that in this art we are so little helped by beautiful and varying material imposes on us the necessity for being specially thoughtful in our designs; every one of them must have a distinct idea in it; some beautiful piece of nature must have pressed itself on our notice so forcibly that we are quite full of it, and can, by submitting ourselves to the rules of art, express our pleasure to others, and give them some of the keen delight that we ourselves have felt. If we cannot do this in some measure our paper design will not be worth much; it will be but a makeshift expedient for covering a wall with something or other; and if we really care about art we shall not put up with 'something or other,' but shall choose honest whitewash instead, on which sun and shadow play so pleasantly, if only our room be well planned and well shaped, and look kindly on us." In the lecture, "Making the Best of it," with reference to the structure of patterns, Morris makes some general observations, which, however, apply in a peculiar degree to wall-paper design: "Whereas it has been said that a recurring pattern should be constructed on a geometrical basis, it is clear that it cannot be constructed otherwise; only the structure may be more or less masked, and some designers take a great deal of pains to do so. I cannot say that I think this always necessary. It may be so when the pattern is on a very small scale, and meant to attract but little attention. But it is sometimes the reverse of desirable in large and important patterns, and, to my mind, all noble patterns should at least *look* large. Some of the finest and pleasantest of these show their geometrical structure clearly enough; and if the lines of them grow strongly and flow gracefully, I think they are decidedly helped by their structure not being elaborately concealed. At the same time, in all patterns which are meant to fill the eye and satisfy the mind, there should be a certain mystery. We should not be able to read the whole thing at once, nor desire to do so, nor be impelled by that desire to go on tracing line after line to find out how the pattern is made, and I think that the obvious presence of a geometrical order, if it be, as it should be, beautiful, tends towards this end, and prevents our feeling restless over a pattern. That every line in a pattern should have its due growth, and be traceable to its beginning . . . is undoubtedly essential to the finest pattern work; equally so is it that no stem should be so far from its parent stock as to look weak or wavering. . . . Everyone who has practised the designing of patterns knows the necessity for covering the ground equably and richly. This is really to a great extent the secret of obtaining the look of satisfying mystery aforesaid, and it is the very test of capacity in a designer. Finally, no amount of delicacy is too great in drawing the curves of a pattern, no amount of care in getting the leading lines right from the first, can be thrown away, for beauty of detail cannot afterwards cure any shortcoming in this. Remember that a pattern is either right or wrong. It cannot be forgiven for blundering. . . . It is with a pattern as with a fortress, it is no stronger than its weakest point.

A failure for ever recurring torments the eye too much to allow the mind to take any pleasure in suggestion and intention."

"As to the second moral quality of design, meaning, I include in that the invention and imagination which forms the soul of this art, as of all others, and which, when submitted to the bonds of order, has a body and a visible existence. Now . . . form may be taught, but the spirit that breathes through it cannot be. So I will content myself with saying this on these qualities, that though a designer may put all manner of strangeness and surprise into his patterns, he must not do so at the expense of beauty. You will never find a case in this kind of work where ugliness and violence are not the result of barrenness, and not of fertility of invention. The fertile man, he of resource, has not to worry himself about invention. He need but think of beauty and simplicity of expression; his work will grow on and on, one thing leading to another, as it fares with a beautiful tree. . . . No pattern should be without some sort of meaning. True it is that that meaning may have come down to us traditionally, and not be our own invention, yet we must at heart understand it, or we can neither receive it, nor hand it down to our successors. It is no longer tradition if it is servilely copied, without change, the token of life. You may be sure that the softest and loveliest of patterns will weary the steadiest admirers of their school as soon as they see that there is no hope of growth in them. For you know all art is compact of effort, of failure and of hope, and we cannot but think that somewhere perfection lies ahead, as we look anxiously for the better thing that is to come from the good. Furthermore, you must not only mean something in your patterns, but must also be able to make others understand that meaning. . . . Now the only way in our craft of design for compelling people to understand you is to follow hard on Nature; for what else can you refer people to, or what else is there which everybody can understand? everybody that it is worth addressing yourself to, which includes all people who can feel and think."

In the manufacture of hand-printed wall-papers it was Morris's original intention to use zinc plates prepared by a method somewhat akin to process engraving at the present day, which however proved too slow and laborious to be practicable. Morris therefore had to have recourse to the ordinary mode of block-cutting; and the firm engaged the services of a block-cutter named Barrett of Bethnal Green, who undertook to execute the wood-blocks under the personal supervision of Mr. Morris. Again, in the matter of the printing, Morris's plan was to obtain more varied and artistic effects with transparent pigments instead of the solid body colours then in general use for the purpose. The production of paper-hangings has now reached so advanced a stage of development that there is not the smallest difficulty in the employment of wash tints, but in those early days the scheme could not be carried out. Indeed, but a brief period of trials on their own account convinced the firm of the expediency of transferring the manufacture of wall-papers bodily—the block-cutting as well as the printing—from their own premises to the experienced hands of Mr. Metford Warner, the acting principal of Messrs. Jeffrey and Co., Essex Road, Islington. The result was so satisfactory that the arrangement has been allowed to continue to this day. Messrs. Jeffrey and Co. have a separate department which they reserve exclusively for the carrying out of the work entrusted to them by Morris and Co., the paper-hangings so produced remaining, as it is perhaps scarcely necessary to say, the sole property of the latter.

The designs, with comparatively few exceptions, have always been drawn by William Morris himself. The first wall-paper to be designed, though it came third in order of production, consists of a trellis, which gives its name to the pattern, intertwining roses, somewhat stiff in growth, and brown birds here and there among the branches. Morris diffidently refrained from designing the bird forms with his own hand, preferring to have them drawn by Mr. Philip Webb. The earliest Morris wall-paper issued was the "Daisy," a quaint pattern consisting of plant-groups of daisies, columbines, &c., dotted at regular intervals on the field, in a manner so formal as none but a master of design could have ventured to do, nor certainly anyone else have achieved success in doing. Here then, with a frankness which in a designer less gifted must have produced inevitably results both harsh and crude, Morris has accepted the mechanical limitations of his craft and has triumphed in that accepting. The dexterity involved in a design like this is such that few perhaps would suspect. Yet if that saying be true, *Ars est celare artem*, then this is a consummate work of art. Some of Morris's patterns may possibly lend themselves to adaptation or—not to mince matters—to imitation, but this at least is out of reach, its virtues incommunicable. It has a delicacy of touch about it, a character all its own. The colours employed in it are neither few in number nor low in tone, and yet they are combined with such judgment that the harmony of the whole is perfect. There be Morris papers which, subordinate in scheme of colouring and undemonstrative of line, admit readily enough of accessory ornaments in the way of china, pictures, and so on. But the "Daisy" pattern is not of the number of these. It gives a room in which it may be hung an air of distinction and completeness that seems to deprecate any further embellishment. In a word, the "Daisy" is a marvel of supreme cleverness; and withal one of which the popularity declines no whit as time goes by. It is a startling evidence of the strength and enduring vitality of Morris's work that a design of his like this should have lost none of its charm and freshness after having been before the public for over thirty years. It is to this day among those most in demand, if not actually itself the most in demand of all his wall-papers. The second paper brought out by the firm was named the "Fruit," a design of stiff diagonal branches contrasting with the roundness of apples and pomegranates and the freer shapes of leaves and blossoms. After the "Trellis" Morris's next designs brought out were the "Diaper," the "Scroll," and the "Branch," of which none calls for any special remark. The "Larkspur" followed, in one print on a white ground, a very characteristic and beautiful pattern, with firmly-drawn leafage, the convolutions of which aptly illustrate Morris's remarks, quoted above, about the importance of getting one's curves true in a pattern. No more noble instance than this could be found of the value of careful draughtsmanship. The design contains also larkspur flowers and roses, not however very conspicuous. The name of the "Jasmine" indicates sufficiently the subject of the next design, which is in several colours. Then comes a peculiarly beautiful, if severe, design called the "Marigold," a single print, the pattern showing light upon a deeper toned ground. It has certain qualities of drawing in common with the "Larkspur," and yet set side by side, the two designs are quite distinct. Both, however, possess in a marked degree that indefinable sense of immortality which is the property of the best work in every age. Produced years ago they seem nevertheless as new as if they had been designed only yesterday. Though other designs should wax old and perish with the transient phases and fashions whose reflection they are, there is no danger of these at any rate ever becoming antiquated, or failing to fulfil the desire of human beings that crave for permanent beauty; and that just because they bear no label of place or period, but have in themselves a life that is free and independent of every change of time and circumstance. There is hardly need to say that it is not intended to limit the application of these remarks to the particular designs of Morris's which occasioned them. Only it happens that his wall-paper patterns, being both numerous and varied, furnish more typical instances than are to be met with in any one other branch of his art. After the "Marigold" came his "Lily" pattern, recalling in some sort the "Daisy;" then the "Powdered," and after that the "Willow." The last is a handsome design of willow-sprays upon an under-printed background of hawthorn blossoms. Next in order is the "Vine," a fine design which was reproduced later with bronze colouring. The "Acanthus" is a magnificent design. The grand sweep of the foliage, the rich and varied gradations of its colouring combine to produce a sumptuous effect which indicates the highest attainable point in paper staining, and such that could scarcely be surpassed even in tapestry-weaving. The pattern is so elaborate that it requires a double set of blocks and cannot be produced with less than thirty-two printings. It was made first in red, afterwards in a similar combination of green tones, and still more recently in yellowish browns. The "Pimpernel," the "Wreath," and the "Rose" preceded the "Chrysanthemum," a large and handsome pattern in many colours, and next, the "Apple." The last has a leaf which forms a prominent feature together with the fruit upon a background of willow leaves. There followed next a ceiling-paper in one print, consisting of floral forms, necessarily rigid in arrangement. Afterwards came the "Sunflower," the "Acorn," the "Poppy," and the "Carnation." Next an order for St. James's Palace evoked a very splendid wall-filling of conventional forms on a large scale and roses introduced in a less prominent manner, the whole printed in an elaborate scheme of colouring. The St. James's ceiling, designed to go with the last-named, is a large pattern, printed, however, in one colour only. The "Bird and Anemone" is a replica of a design for cretonne. The "Grafton" was succeeded by a ceiling-paper in which boldness of effect is in no way sacrificed, in spite of its being in several colours and altogether of a less simple character than the former ones. The "Wild Tulip" followed, a striking pattern with a large leaf, of which the form is emphasized by the ingenious use of dots; the background being also dotted. The composition includes a flower not unlike that in the above-mentioned "Poppy" pattern. Mr. Morris's next wall-paper was the "Fritillary," which has a very marked leaf and some points of resemblance to the "Wild Tulip design. Next is the "Garden Tulip" pattern, which consists of a tulip spray strongly accentuated by the slight and almost thin treatment of the background; next the "Lily and Pomegranate," a design which includes also marigolds—a stiff pattern in many colours with a dotted ground; next the "Willow Bough," a more naturalistic treatment than the earlier "Willow;" and next one named the "Merton," of no particular importance. The above were followed by the "Bruges," a superb design which it is impossible to praise in terms too high. Though entirely original in detail, its general aspect is more thoroughly Gothic and traditional than that of anything Morris ever produced in the way of repeated ornament. Conceived on broad mediæval lines, it forms a decoration which, upon the walls of a fifteenth century building, is in perfect accord with its surroundings. More in its favour could not well be said. Itself diagonal in plan, the "Bruges" was followed by a doubled pattern called "Autumn Flowers;" and then by the "Borage" ceiling-paper, a design in one print. The "Norwich" wall-paper is another instance of the effective use that may be made of dots in this class of design. Conventionalized peonies, roses, &c., are here rendered in an elaborate scheme of colouring. The "Wallflower" again is an example of dotted ornament. The "Hammersmith" has a large conventional form repeated in smaller compass than the "Norwich," which, however, in many ways it resembles. The "Pink and Rose," in one print, is an example of flat and decorative treatment for wall-surfaces; while the "Double Bough" introduces some familiar Morris forms and methods once more. The "Triple Net" is a light pattern on a coloured ground; while the "Flora," on the other hand, in colours on a white ground, is somewhat thin in effect. The "Bachelor's Button" design is yet another instance in which boldly-treated foliage and other well-known Morris forms appear; and the "Lechlade" is a large pattern in very light and delicate colouring, great concentric leaf-sprays and purely conventional flower forms being employed with admirable effect. The "Spring Thicket" is a large, set pattern with lilies, executed in soft and harmonious colouring. The "Compton," another very fine pattern in many colours upon a dark ground, has been reproduced also in the form of a cretonne. The "Net" ceiling-paper, in several colours, completes the list of Mr. Morris's designs for paper-hangings. Of the remaining patterns produced by the firm, amounting in all to no more than twenty, four were adaptations from various sources, while the rest were original designs by Miss Faulkner, Miss May Morris, and last, but not least, by Mr. H. Dearle, who has for some time past been resident manager of the works at Merton Abbey. It should be remarked that many of Messrs. Morris and Co.'s wall-papers have at different times been brought out by them in additional colourings, or with variations in their schemes of colouring subsequently to their original appearance; and also that by far the largest majority of the papers are printed from hand-blocks alone, but an insignificant proportion being machine-printed, *e.g.*, the "Loop Trail," "Merton," "Carnation," and the "Oak Tree." The latter, designed by Mr. Dearle, is the most recent of all Morris and Co.'s patterns in paper-hangings.

It was but two or three years after the firm of Morris, Marshall, Faulkner and Co. came into being that Mr. Morris formed the project of adding weaving to their other undertakings. What he has to say on the subject of this craft will be found in the address on "The Lesser Arts of Life," included in the volume of Lectures on Art by various authors, published in 1882; in the lecture entitled "Textile Fabrics" (in which the subject is treated mainly from the historical point of view), delivered in the Lecture Room of the International Health Exhibition in London on July 11th, 1884, and afterwards issued by authority as an official handbook; and lastly in the Essay prefixed to the Catalogue of the first Exhibition of the Arts and Crafts Society in the autumn of 1888, and republished in 1893 in the volume of collected Essays. In the first of these works, after referring briefly to the making of plain cloth which is "not susceptible of ornament," Morris says: "As the designing of woven stuffs fell into degradation in the latter days, the designers got fidgeting after trivial novelties; change for the sake of change; they must needs strive to make their woven flowers look as if they were painted with a brush, or even sometimes as if they were drawn by the engraver's burin. This gave them plenty of trouble and exercised their ingenuity in the tormenting of their web with spots and stripes and ribs and the rest of it, but quite destroyed the seriousness of the work and even its *raison d'être*. As of pottery-painting, so of figure-weaving: do nothing in it but that which only weaving can do: and to this end make your design as elaborate as you please in silhouette, but carry it out simply; you are not drawing lines freely with your shuttle, you are building up a pattern with a fine rectilinear mosaic. If this is kept well in mind by the designer, and he does not try to force his material into no-thoroughfares, he may have abundant pleasure in the making of woven stuffs, and he is perhaps less likely to go wrong (if he has a feeling for colour) in this art than in any other. I will say further that he should be careful to get due proportions between his warp and weft: not to starve the first, which is the body of the web so to say, for the sake of the second, which is its clothes: this is done now-a-days overmuch by ingenious designers who are trying to make their web look like non-mechanical stuffs, or who want to get a delusive show of solidity in a poor cloth, which is much to be avoided: a similar fault we are too likely to fall into is of a piece with what is done in all the lesser arts to-day; and which doubtless is much fostered by the ease given to our managers of works by the over-development of machinery: I am thinking of the weaving up of rubbish into apparently delicate and dainty wares. No man, with the true instinct of a workman, should have anything to do with this: it may not mean commercial dishonesty, though I suspect it sometimes does, but it must mean artistic dishonesty: poor materials in this craft, as in all others, should only be used in coarse work, where they are used without pretence for what they are: this we must agree to at once, or sink all art in commerce (so called) in these crafts." In the Arts and Crafts Essay Morris writes: "Mechanical weaving has to repeat the pattern on the cloth within comparatively narrow limits; the number of colours also is limited in most cases to four or five. In most cloths so woven, therefore, the best plan seems to be to choose a pleasant ground colour and to superimpose a pattern mainly composed of either a lighter shade of that colour, or a colour in no very strong contrast to the ground; and then, if you are using several colours, to light up this general arrangement either with a more forcible outline, or by spots of stronger colour carefully disposed. Often the lighter shade on the darker suffices, and hardly calls for anything else: some very beautiful cloths are merely damasks, in which the warp and weft are of the same colour, but a different tone is obtained by the figure and the ground being woven with a longer or shorter twill: the *tabby* being tied by the warp very often, the *satin* much more rarely. In any case, the patterned webs produced by mechanical weaving, if the ornament is to be effective and worth the doing, require the same Gothic crispness and clearness of detail which has been spoken of before: the geometrical structure of the pattern, which is a necessity in all recurring patterns, should be boldly insisted upon, so as to draw the eye from accidental figures, which the recurrence of the pattern is apt to produce. The meaningless stripes and spots and other tormentings of the simple twill of the web, which are so common in the woven ornament of the eighteenth century and our own times, should be carefully avoided: all these things are the last resource of a jaded invention and a contempt of the simple and fresh beauty that comes of the sympathetic *suggestion* of natural forms: if the pattern be vigorously and firmly drawn with a true feeling for the beauty of line and *silhouette*, the play of light and shade on the material of the simple twill will give all the necessary variety."

Morris's attention is said to have been drawn to the industry of weaving in the first place by the mere accident of seeing a man in the street selling toy models of weaving machines, when it occurred to him to buy one and to practise upon it for himself. After some preliminary experiments more or less successful, he then endeavoured to obtain a full-sized hand-loom. What he wanted was an old one of the old style, with hand-shuttle, &c., such as formerly had been in traditional use at Spitalfields, but had become by that time practically obsolete, save, it might be, among the very oldest weavers of the place. The matter was one in which, in default of an expert possessed of the necessary qualifications among his own colleagues or employés, Morris was obliged to turn to help from outside. It so happened that he was most unfortunate in respect of the several agents whom he trusted, one after another, and employed to procure and set up a loom for him. A series of disappointments caused so much delay that it was not until towards the close of the seventies that, a Jacquard loom having been erected in Ormond Yard, Morris was enabled to organize weaving systematically as a branch of the firm's work. From that time the industry grew, and was carried on regularly without a break. At the present time the looms are situated at Merton Abbey, and have been ever since the works there came into the possession of Messrs. Morris and Co. Morris drew a number of designs for silk damasks and brocades and woven wool-tapestries, as well as a limited number for fabrics of silk and linen and of silk and wool. The latter combination, as in the case of the "Dove and Rose" material—quite apart from the beauty of the design—has a beauty of texture which is peculiarly delightful; the weightier substance of the wool drawing the slighter-bodied surface of the silk into delicate ripples upon which the light plays with charming effect. The "Bird and Vine" is a beautiful and characteristic design in woollen tapestry, while the "Peacock and Dragon," in the same material, is a large pattern for which the artist himself had a special liking. One more example may be selected, among productions of a later date, viz., the diagonal woollen tapestry named the "Trail." The unit of this pattern is as simple as can be—a conventional leaf and a single spray of flowers; yet the richest effect is obtained by the simple but ingenious device of varying the colour of the woof threads, so that the flowers appear alternating horizontally in red, white, and pink. The general colour of the web is a warm green in several tones.

At one time Morris essayed to revive the art of weaving

velvet with gold tissue, after the method of the superb and famous webs of Florence and Venice in the fifteenth century. It was an interesting experiment, and such that will in all probability prove to have been unique in England during the present century. A loom was constructed especially for the purpose, and an exquisite design by Morris was reproduced in blue, white, and orange velvet pile, with gold thread interwoven in parts, Morris assisting personally in the process of manufacture. But it was found far too costly to be practical. Only a small quantity of this most sumptuous material was ever woven, and the attempt was not repeated.

It was about the middle of the seventies when Morris, who by that time had ceased to reside at Queen Square, happened to be in want of some special shades of silk for embroidery. But being unable to get what he needed by other means, he determined to start dyeing on his own account. Accordingly, the scullery at No. 26, Queen Square, being fitted with coppers, was chosen, rough and primitive as was the accommodation, for the dyeing; while the kitchen was turned into a drying ground, under the charge of the caretaker. From these small beginnings sprang what developed subsequently into one of the most indispensable of all the operations of the firm, to wit, that of dyeing, "since upon it," to use Mr. Morris's own words, "is founded all the ornamental character of textile fabrics" It was in fact the necessity of obtaining a sufficient supply of water for this purpose that induced Mr. Morris, when in treaty for some more commodious place of manufacture than the Queen Square house afforded, to decide upon the firm's present workshops on the Wandle. Among the several alternatives possible, yet such as would have involved the having to journey further afield, Merton Abbey, being at a distance not exceeding nine miles from London, presented the most convenient spot. Thither the process of dyeing was transferred, and there it has been carried on since the summer of 1881. The place had been used formerly for dyeing, and tradition says that, in the time of a previous occupier, Lord Nelson

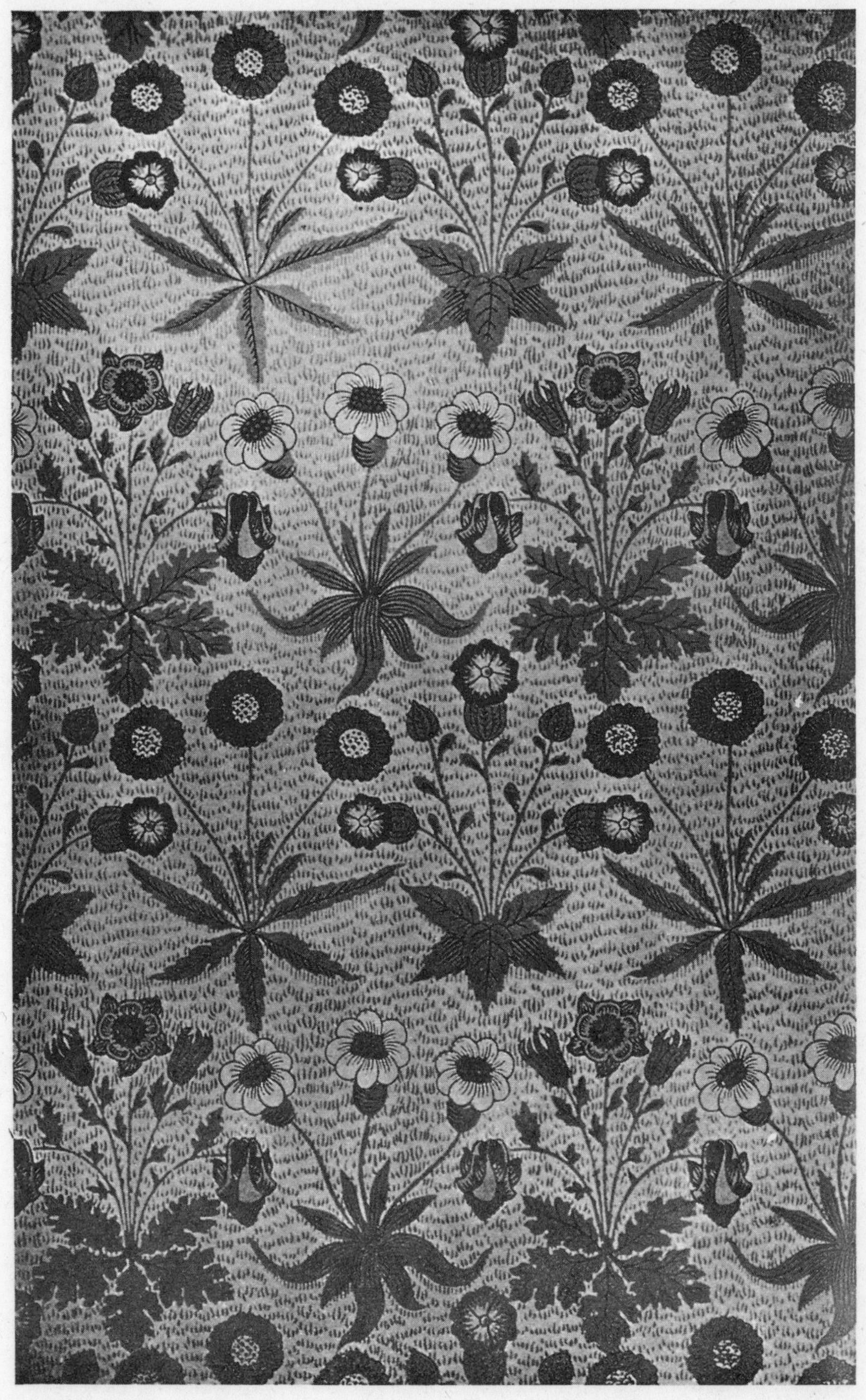

THE "DAISY" WALL-PAPER. DESIGNED BY WILLIAM MORRIS.

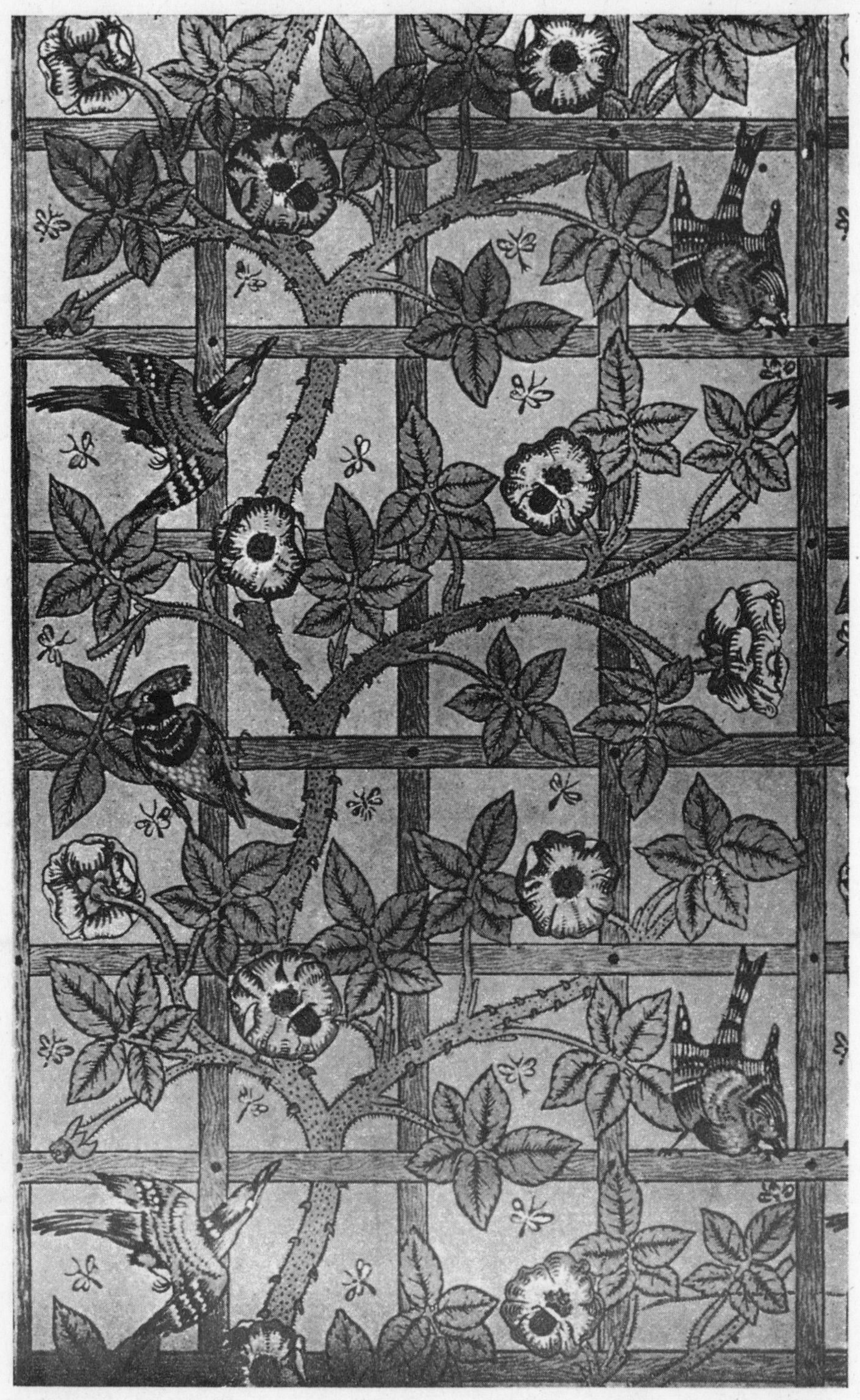

THE "TRELLIS" WALL-PAPER.

DESIGNED BY WILLIAM MORRIS.
BIRDS BY PHILIP WEBB.

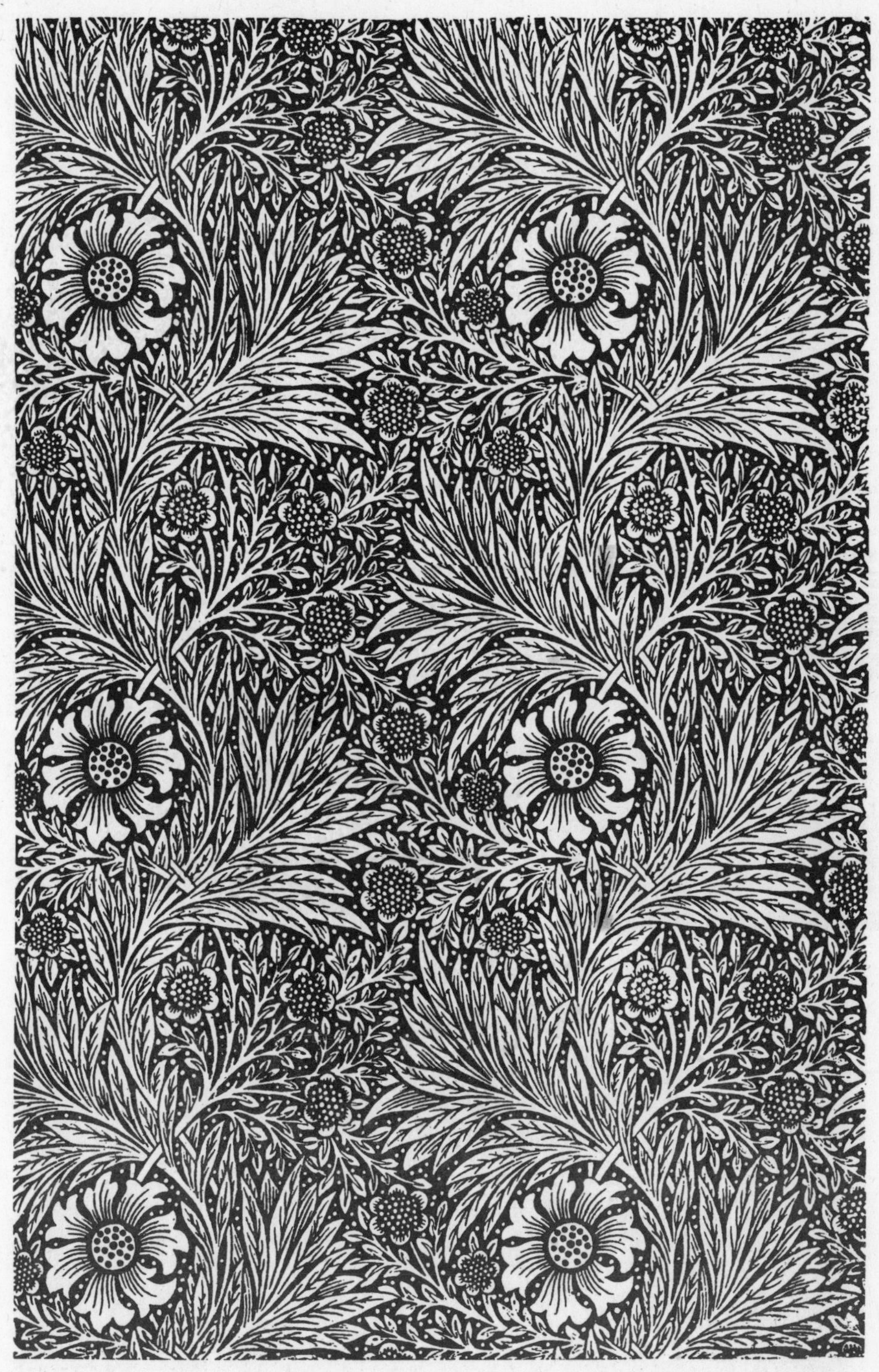

THE "MARIGOLD" WALL-PAPER. DESIGNED BY WILLIAM MORRIS.

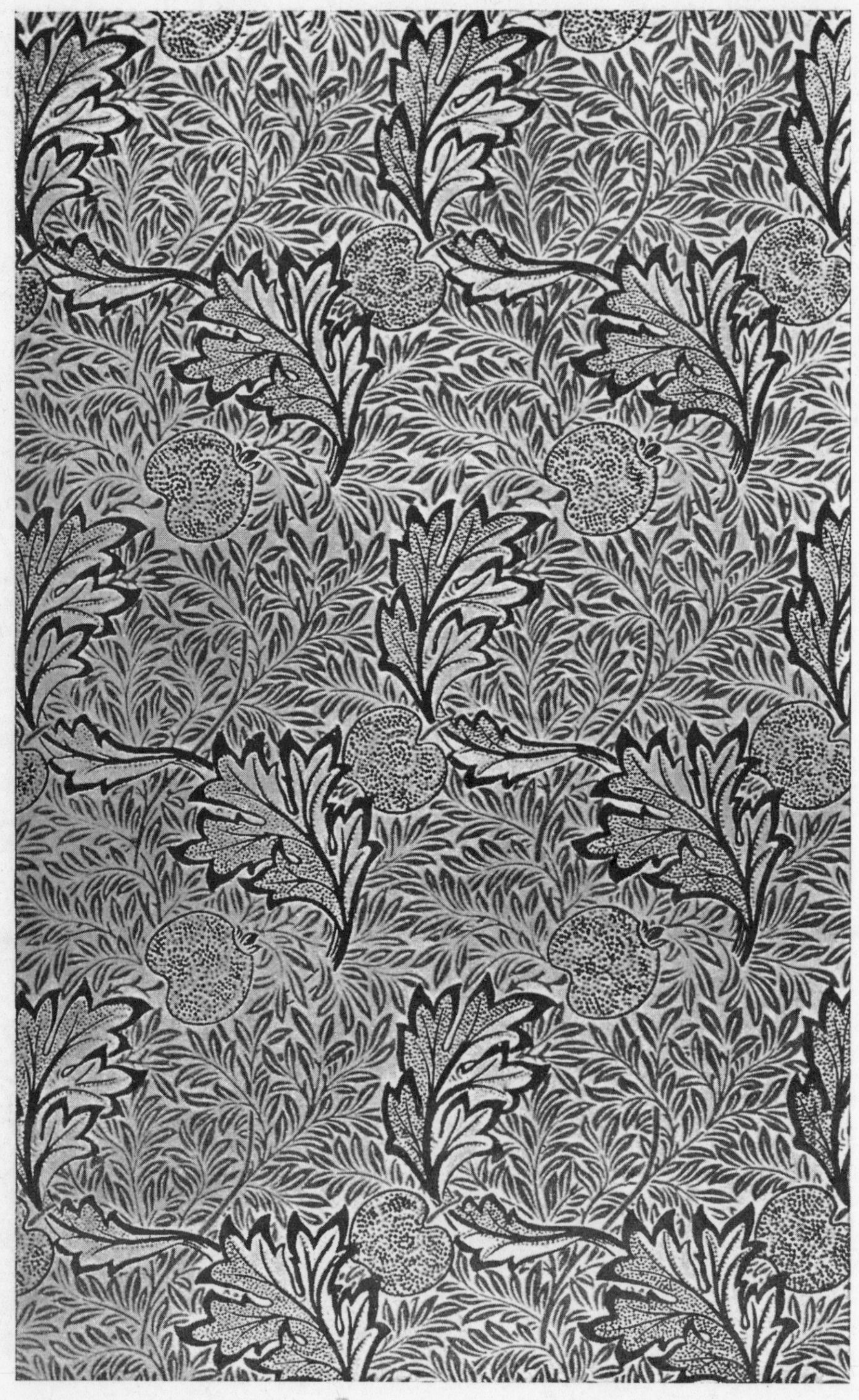

THE "APPLE" WALL-PAPER. DESIGNED BY WILLIAM MORRIS.

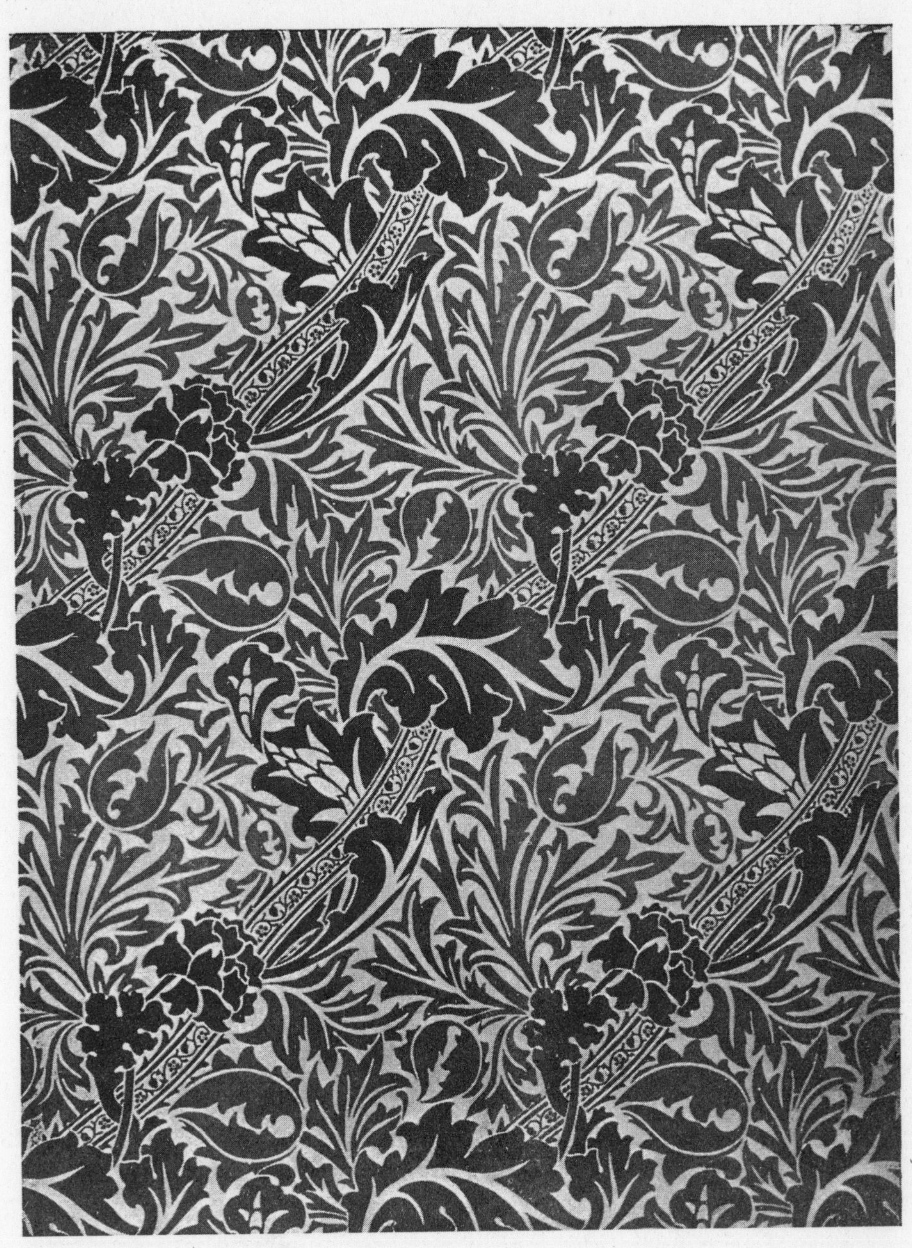

THE "BRUGES" WALL-PAPER. DESIGNED BY WILLIAM MORRIS.

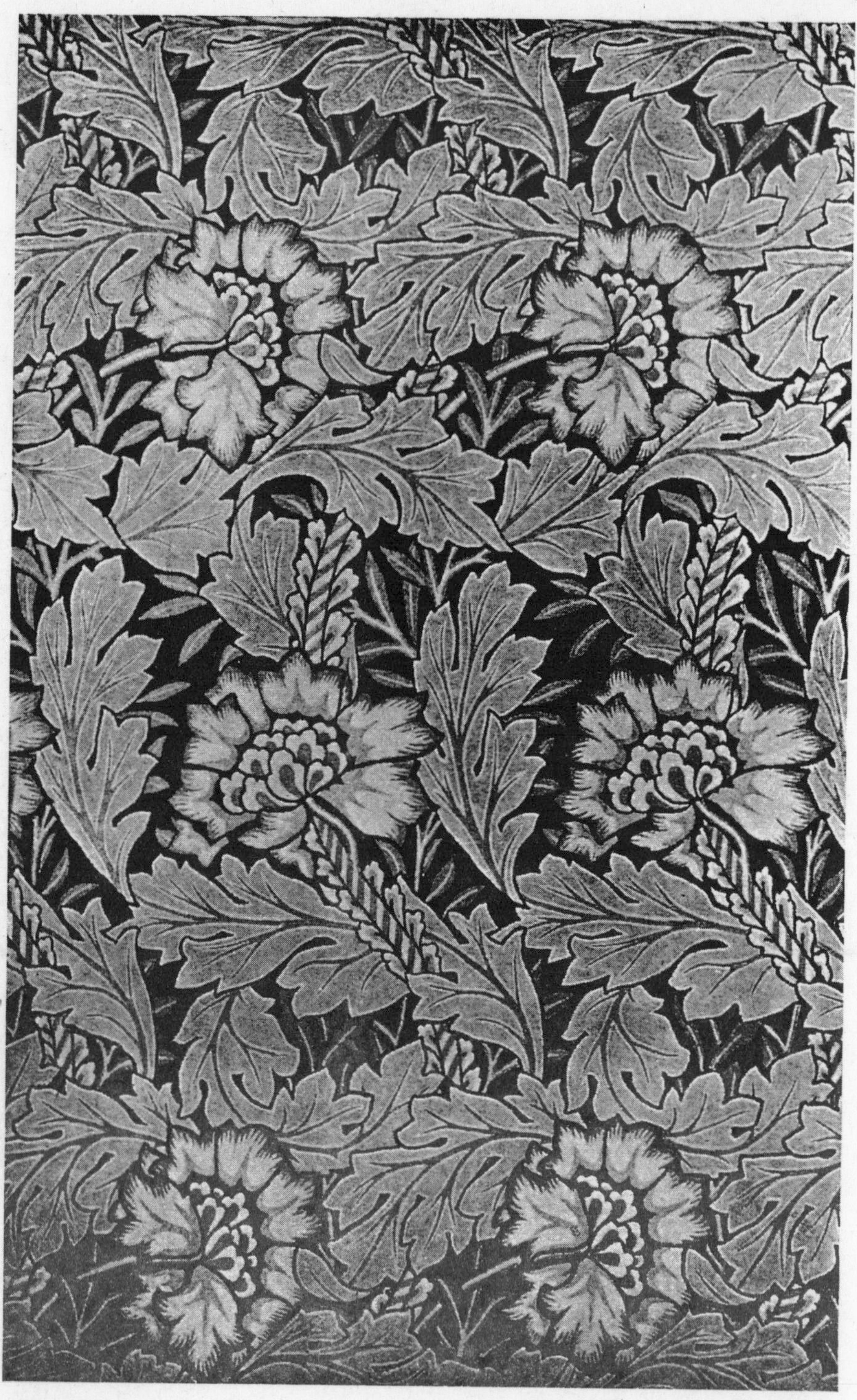

SILK AND WOOL TAPESTRY, "THE ANEMONE." DESIGNED BY WILLIAM MORRIS.

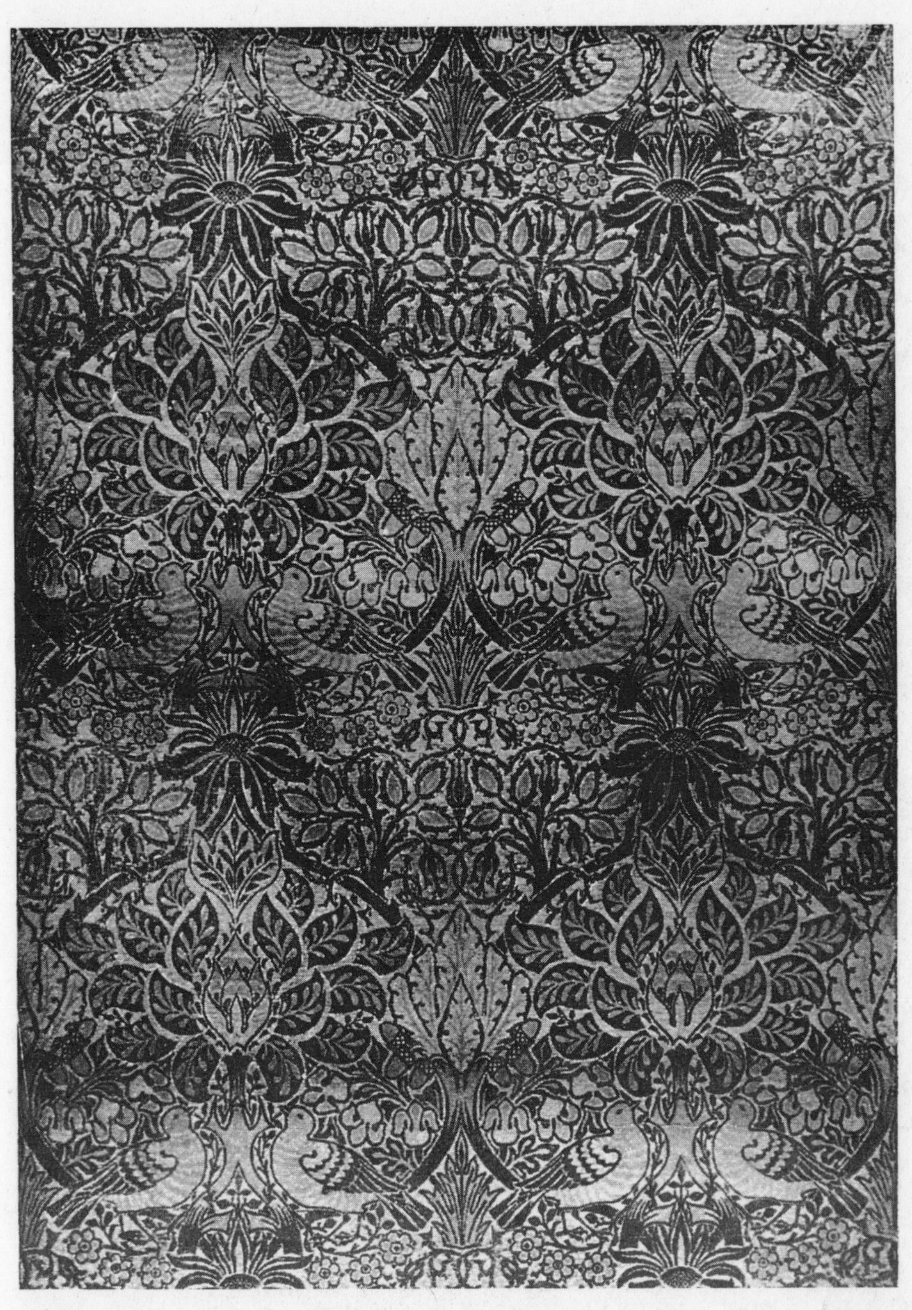

SILK AND WOOL TAPESTRY, "THE DOVE AND ROSE." DESIGNED BY WILLIAM MORRIS.

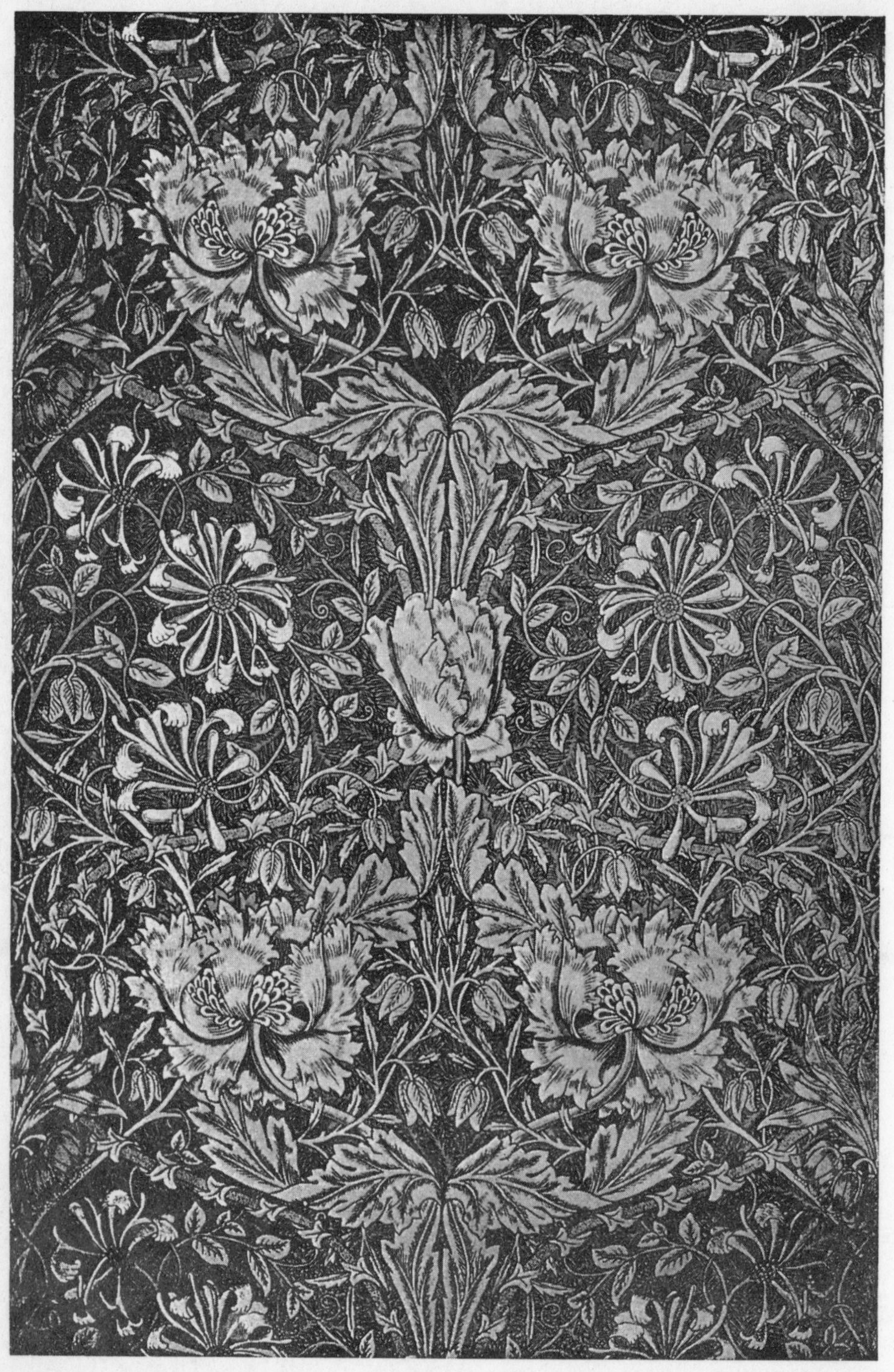

THE "HONEYSUCKLE" CHINTZ. DESIGNED BY WILLIAM MORRIS.

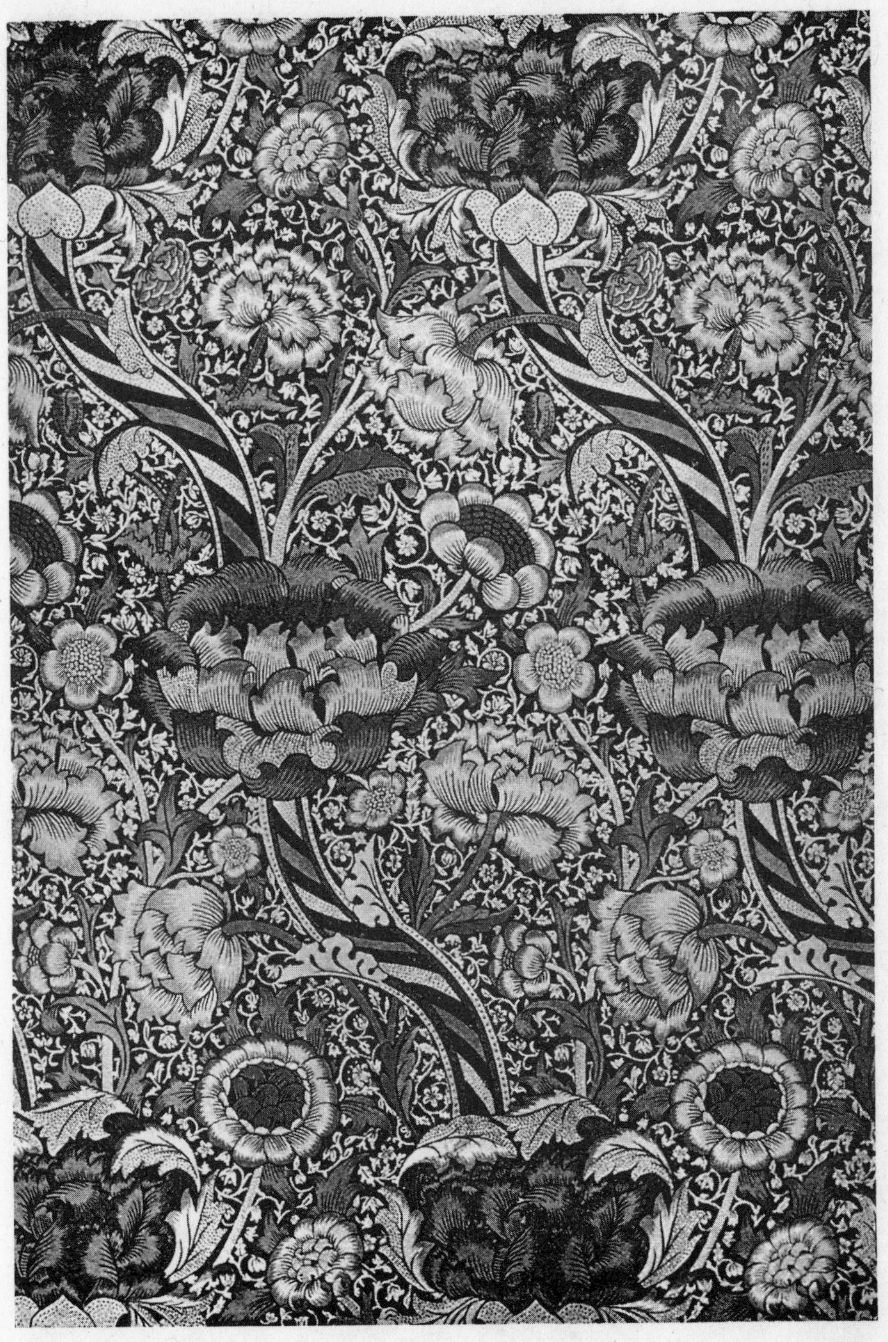

THE "WANDLE" CHINTZ. DESIGNED BY WILLIAM MORRIS.

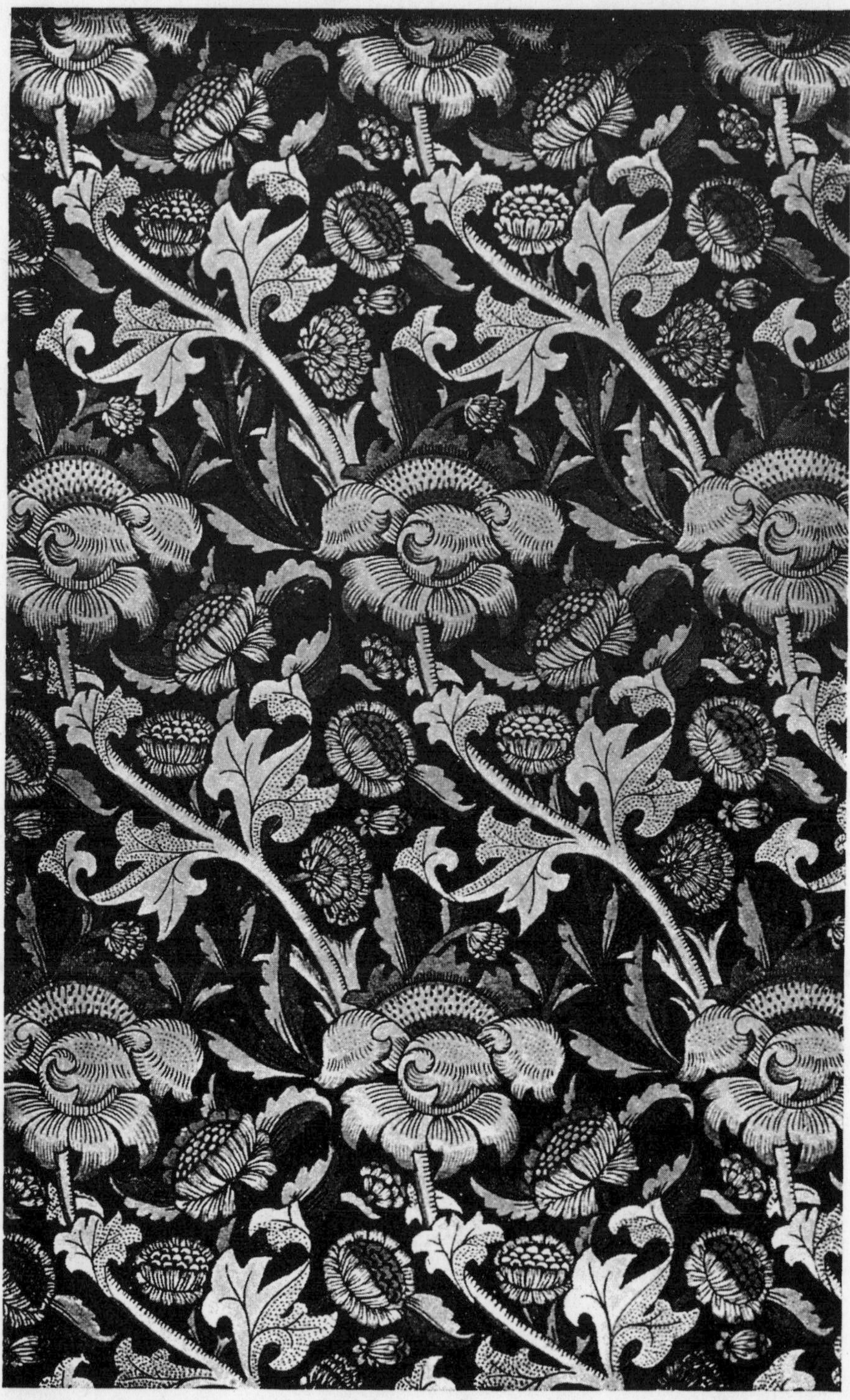

THE "WEY" CHINTZ. DESIGNED BY WILLIAM MORRIS.

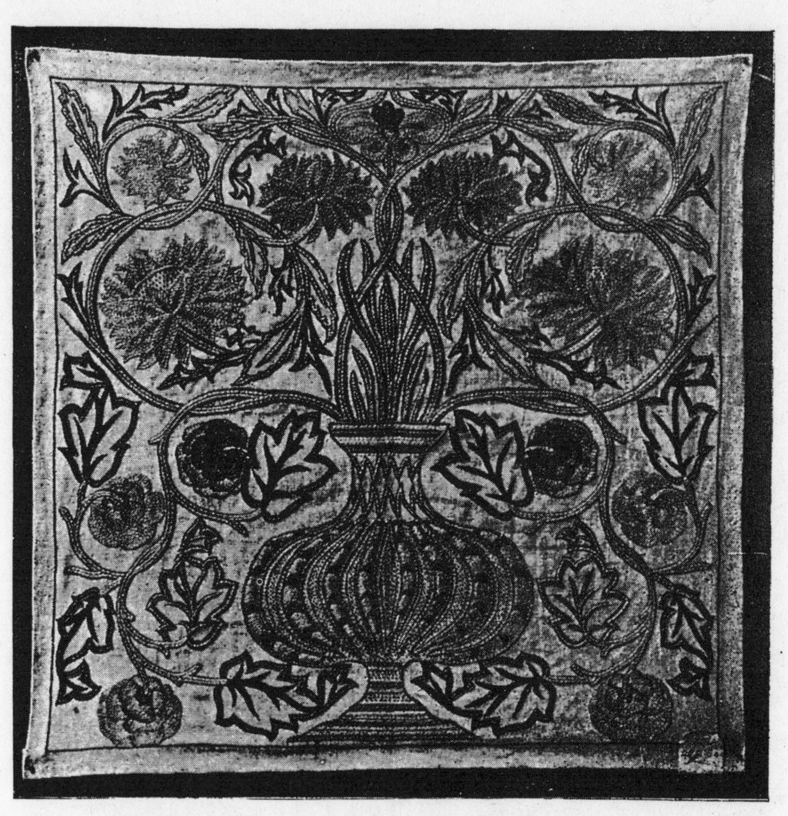

SILK EMBROIDERY,
"THE FLOWER-POT."

DESIGNED BY
WILLIAM MORRIS.

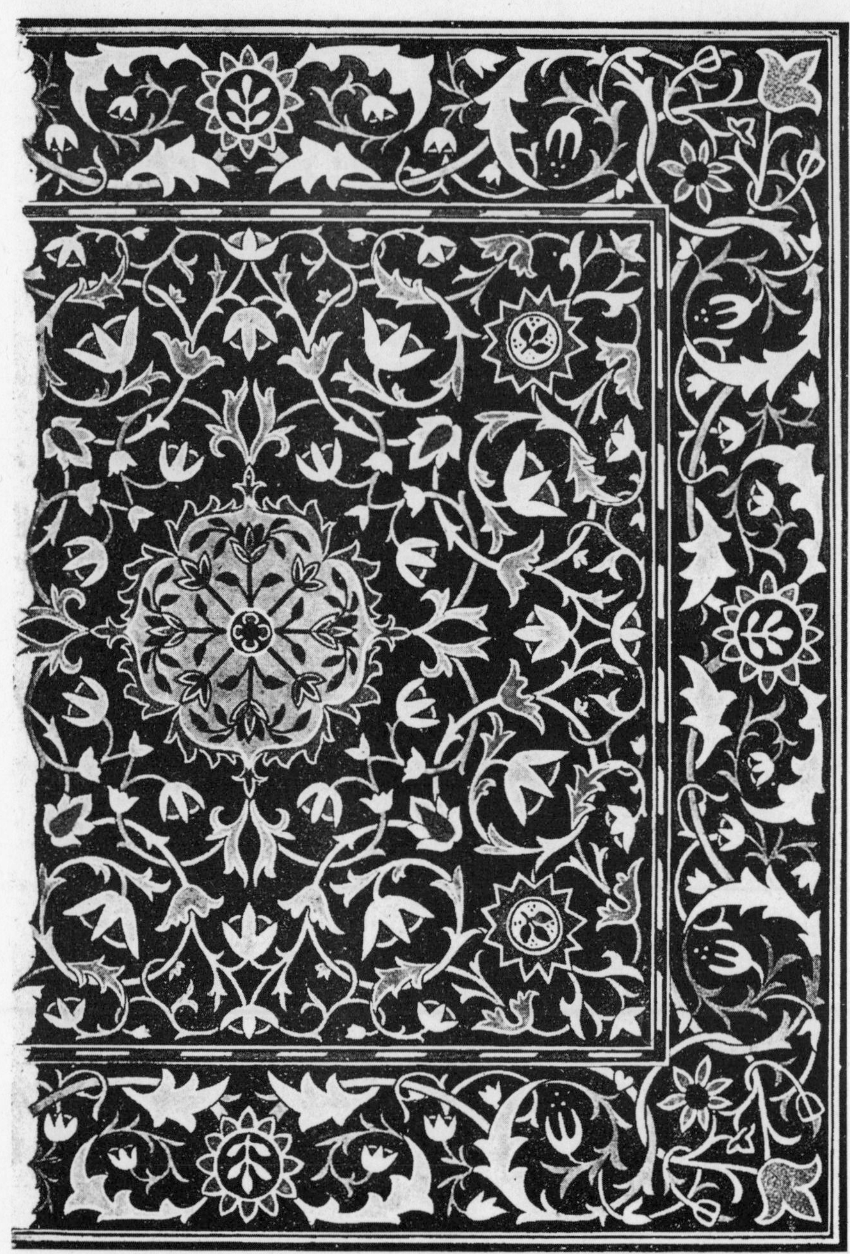

SKETCH DESIGN FOR "SMALL BARR" CARPET. BY WILLIAM MORRIS.

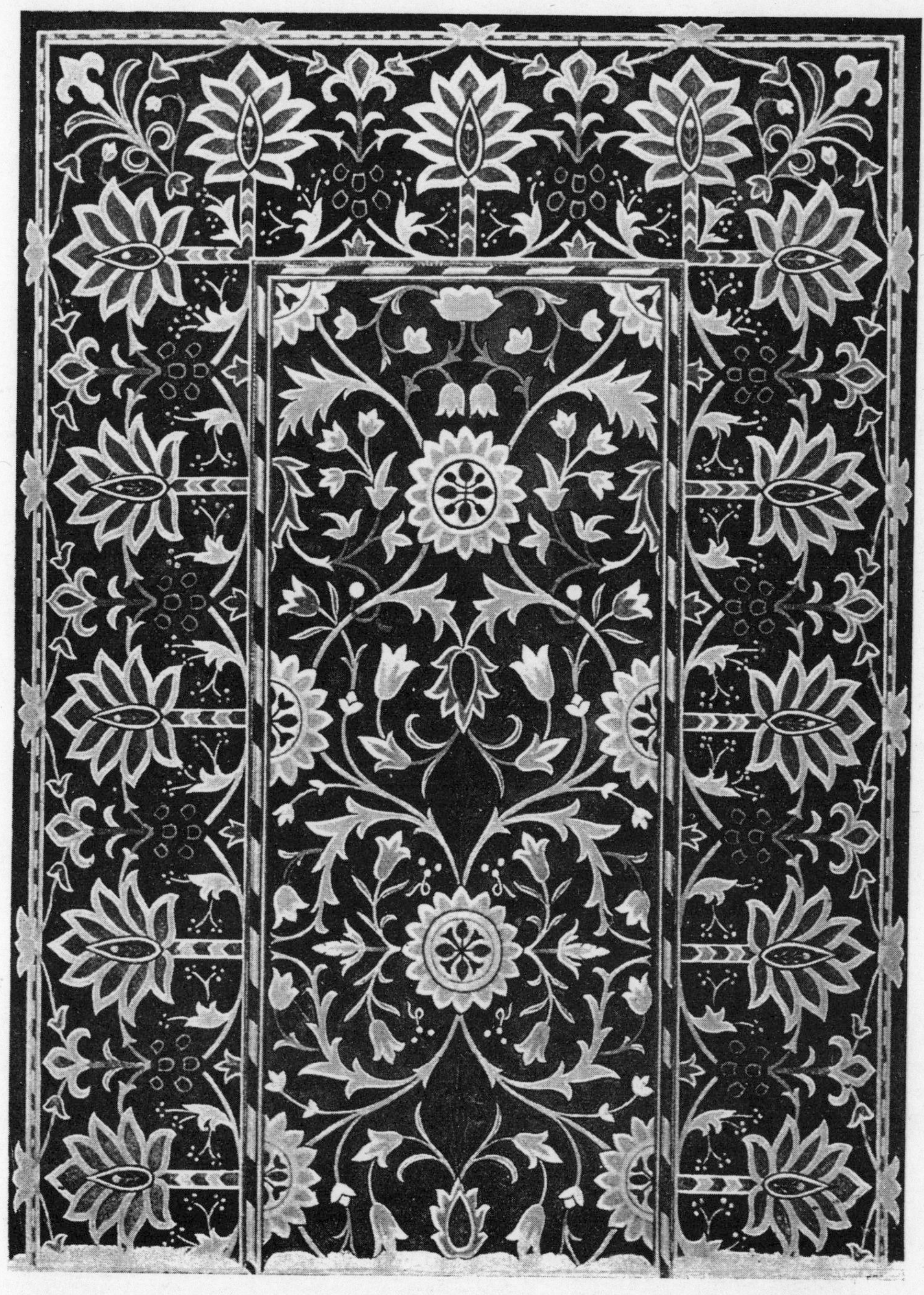

SKETCH DESIGN FOR "THE LITTLE FLOWERS" CARPET. BY WILLIAM MORRIS.

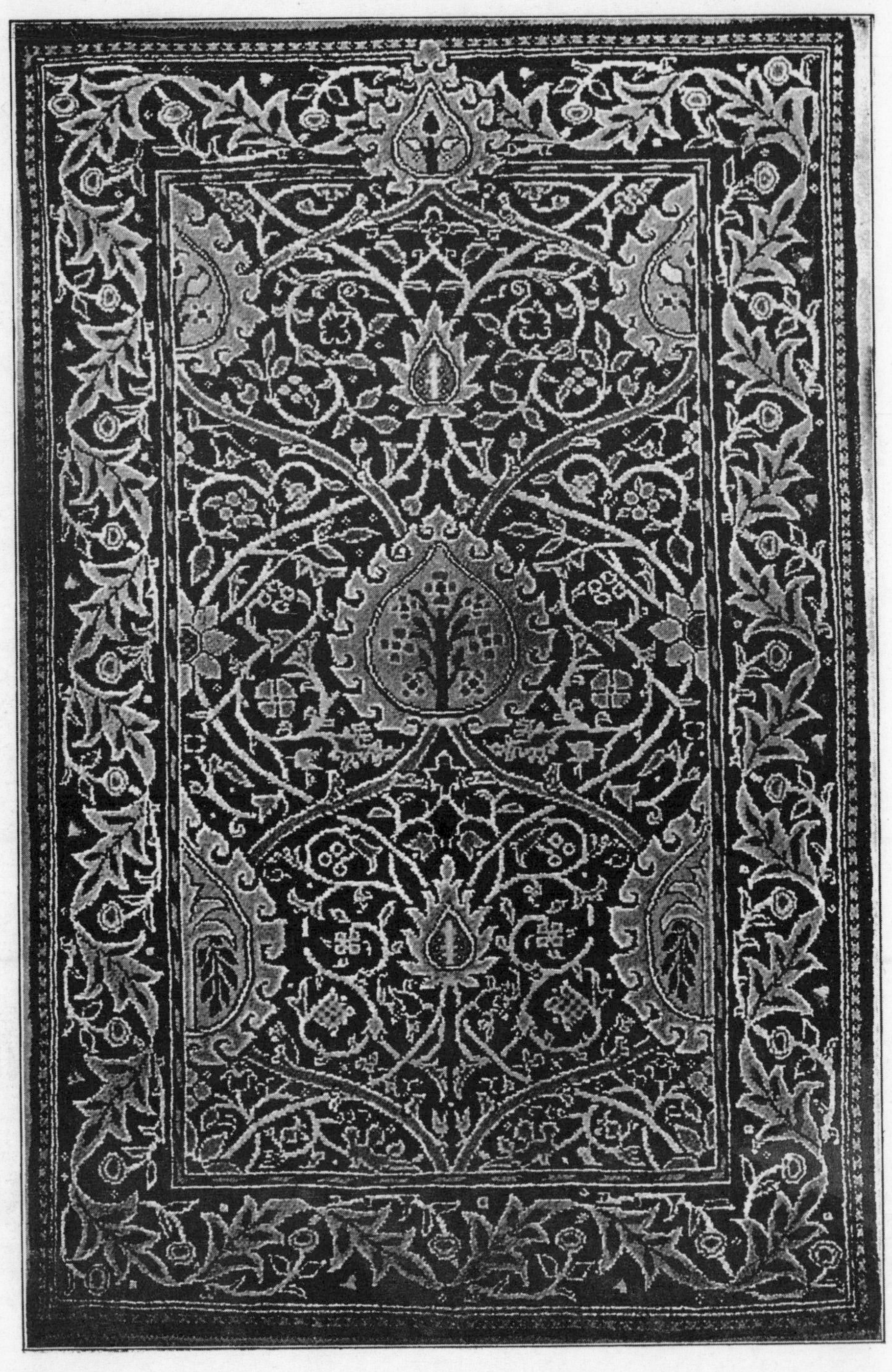

THE "BLACK TREE" CARPET. DESIGNED BY WILLIAM MORRIS.

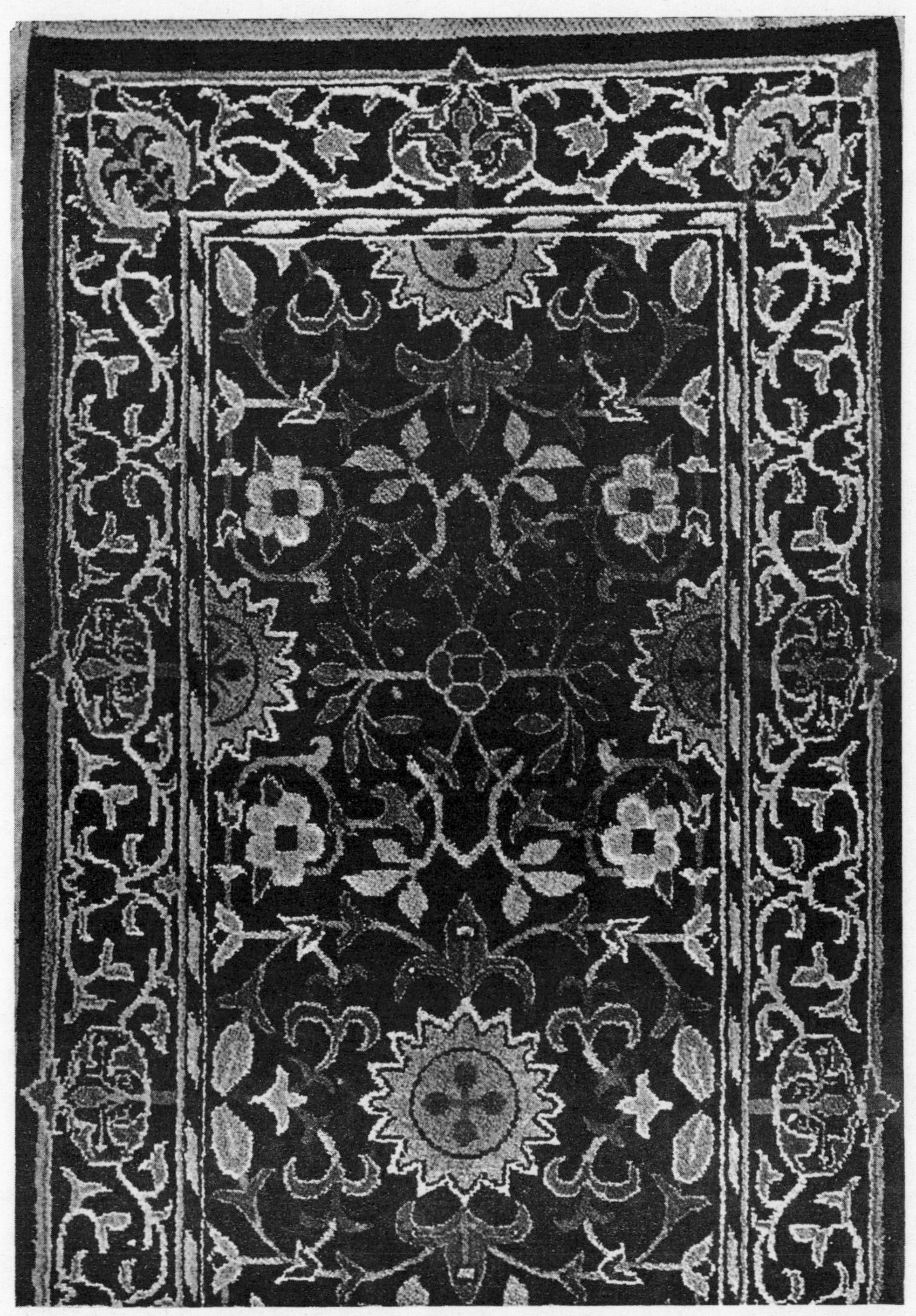

THE "LITTLE TREE" CARPET. DESIGNED BY WILLIAM MORRIS.

THE "REDCAR" CARPET. DESIGNED BY WILLIAM MORRIS.

visited the works and was shown the various processes of the craft.

Morris began by dyeing skeins of embroidery silk, and then proceeded to dye wool for tapestry and carpets, in the manufacture of which the firm use none other than their own dyed wool. Morris himself went to Leek in order to improve his acquaintance with the technicalities of the process under the guidance of Mr. Thomas Wardle, the well-known expert and eminent authority on the dyer's craft. And so, when Morris referred to the subject in his lecture at the Health Exhibition in 1884, he was entitled to remind his audience that he was "speaking as a dyer, and not a scientific person"; he spoke, that is, as one who had had practical experience of the matters whereof he treated; in contradistinction to a theorist whose knowledge must be confined within the limits of mere book-lore; or on the other hand to an experimenting chemist. Indeed, as an artist, Morris felt very strongly that the so-called improvements effected by chemical science had proved in the highest degree injurious to the craft of dyeing. In his writings on the subject he enumerates the successive additions that have been made to the repertory of dye-stuffs in historical times, with a view to showing how that the practice of primitive ages was materially identical with that of later ages, and had in fact remained unspoilt during all the intervening centuries down to quite recent days. "No change at all," says Morris, "befell the art either in the East or the North till after the discovery of America; this gave the dyers one new material in itself good and one that was doubtful or bad. The good one was the new insect dye, cochineal, which at first was used only for dyeing crimson. . . . The bad new material was log-wood, so fugitive a dye as to be quite worthless as a colour by itself (as it was at first used) and to my mind of very little use otherwise. No other *new* dye-stuff of importance was found in America, although the discoverers came across such abundance of red-dyeing wood growing there that a huge country of South America has thence taken its name of Brazil." "About the year 1656, . . . a

Dutch chemist discovered the secret of getting a scarlet from cochineal" on a tin basis, "and so produced a cheaper, brighter, and uglier scarlet, much to the satisfaction of the civilized world." "In the last years of the eighteenth century a worthless blue was invented. . . . About the same time a rather valuable yellow dye (quercitron bark) was introduced from America." Nothing else of moment occurred "up to the time of the discovery of the process of Prussian blue dyeing in about 1810, . . . which has cheapened and worsened black-dyeing in so far as it has taken the place of the indigo vat as a basis." "Now these novelties, the sum of which amounts to very little, are all that make any difference between the practice of dyeing under Rameses the Great and under Queen Victoria, till about twenty years ago." (These words were published in 1882. A few sentences from another work may best describe what befell at the time indicated. The date, to be precise, was 1858.) "Then came," says Morris, "one of the most wonderful and most useless of the inventions of modern chemistry, that of the dyes made from coal-tar, producing a series of hideous colours, crude, livid—and cheap,—which every person of taste loathes, but which nevertheless we can by no means get rid of until we are able to struggle successfully against the doom of cheap and nasty which has overtaken us." These newly-discovered methods, "from a so-called commercial point of view, have been of the greatest importance; for they have, as the phrase goes, revolutionized the art of dyeing. The dye-stuffs discovered by the indefatigable genius of scientific chemists, which everyone has heard of under the name of aniline colours, . . . are brighter and stronger in colour than the old dyes . . . and, which is of course of the last importance to the dyer, infinitely easier to use. No wonder, therefore, that they have almost altogether supplanted the older dyes, except in a few cases: surely the invention seems a splendid one! Well, it is only marred by one fact, that being an invention for the benefit of an art whose very existence depends upon its producing beauty, it is on the road, and far advanced on it, towards destroying all beauty in the art. The fact is, that every one of these colours is hideous in itself, whereas all the old dyes are in themselves beautiful colours—only extreme perversity could make an ugly colour out of them. Under these circumstances it must, I suppose, be considered a negative virtue in the new dyes, that they are as fugitive as the older ones are stable; but even on that head I will ask you to note one thing that condemns them finally, that whereas the old dyes when fading, as all colours will do more or less, simply gradually changed into paler tints of the same colour, and were not unpleasant to look on, the fading of the new dyes is a change into all kinds of abominable and livid hues. I mention this because otherwise it might be thought that a man with an artistic eye for colour might so blend the hideous but bright aniline colours as to produce at least something tolerable; indeed, this is not unfrequently attempted to-day, but with small success, partly from the reason above mentioned, partly because the hues so produced by 'messing about,' as I should call it, have none of the *quality* or character which the simpler drug gives naturally: all artists will understand what I mean by this." Elsewhere, comparing the two classes of dyes, Morris refers to pre-aniline colours as follows: "As to the artistic value of these dye-stuffs, most of which, together with the necessary mordant alumina, the world discovered in early times (I mean early *historical* times), I must tell you that they all make in their simplest forms beautiful colours; they need no muddling into artistic usefulness, when you need your colours bright (as I hope you usually do), and they can be modified and toned without dirtying, as the foul blotches of the capitalist dyer cannot be. Like all dyes, they are not eternal; the sun in lighting them and beautifying them consumes them; yet gradually and for the most part kindly. . . . These colours in fading still remain beautiful, and never, even after long wear, pass into nothingness, through that stage of livid ugliness which distinguishes the commercial dyes as nuisances, even more than their short and by no means merry life." In fine, "it is most true that the chemists of our day have made discoveries almost past belief for their wonder; they have given us a set of colours which has made a new thing of the dyer's craft; commercial enterprise has eagerly seized on the gift, and yet, unless all art is to disappear from our woven stuffs, we must turn round and utterly and simply reject it." The above passage is extracted from the lecture on "The Lesser Arts of Life." Morris refers, in very similar terms, in his essay "Of Dyeing as an Art," to aniline dyes, which are "deduced," as he says, "by a long process from the plants of the coal-measures. Of these dyes it must be enough to say that their discovery, while conferring the greatest honour on the abstract science of chemistry, and while doing great service to capitalists in their hunt for profits, has terribly injured the art of dyeing, and for the general public has nearly destroyed it as an art. Henceforward there is an absolute divorce between the *commercial process* and the *art* of dyeing. Anyone wanting to produce dyed textiles with any artistic quality in them, must entirely forego the modern and commercial methods in favour of those which are at least as old as Pliny, who speaks of them as being old in his time." After this it is scarcely necessary to add that no aniline dyes are admitted, on any pretext, into the vats of Messrs. Morris and Co.

"The art of dyeing, I am bound to say," writes Morris, who was well qualified to express an opinion on the subject, "is a difficult one, needing for its practice a good craftsman, with plenty of experience. Matching a colour by means of it is an agreeable but somewhat anxious game to play." In several places he has left on record his own personal experiences in the use of various dyes. Thus, in the lecture on "Textile Fabrics," already quoted, he says of indigo that "as long as it keeps its colour and nature, it "is insoluble and therefore unfit for dyeing; it has therefore to be turned into white indigo by means of deoxidation, which is effected . . . chiefly by fermentation; the white indigo is then soluble by alkalies; this deoxidation is called by the dyers 'setting the vat'; and this setting by means of fermentation, the oldest and best way, is a very ticklish job, and the capacity of doing so indicates the past master in dyeing," though perhaps it "seems an easy process" enough. The ancient blue dye-stuff has at any rate one advantage, which, as Morris points out, is of no little account: "I may note also that no textiles dyed blue or green, otherwise than by indigo, keep an agreeable colour by candle-light: many quite bright greens turning into sheer drab." Elsewhere Morris writes: "I myself have dyed wool red," (which was to his mind "above all a dyer's colour,") "by the selfsame process that the Mosaical dyers used. . . . If I want for my own use some of the red dye above alluded to, I must send to Argolis or Acharnania for it." And although this "red insect dye, . . . called by the classical peoples coccus, and by the Arabs Al kermes," shares "somewhat in the ill qualities of madder for silk,"—it is apt, that is, to take off the gloss, and was for that reason never used so largely for silk dyeing as were some other dyes,—Morris says, again, that he has "dyed silk in kermes and got very beautiful and powerful results by means of it. . . . Yellow dyes," he continues a little further on, "are the commonest to be met with in nature, and our fields and hedgerows bear plenty of greening-weeds, as our forefathers called them, since they used them chiefly for greening blue woollen cloth. . . . Of these I have tried poplar and osier twigs, which both gave a strong yellow, but the former not a very permanent one." These quotations must suffice. The whole subject of dyeing will be found dealt with both fully and clearly in Morris's Arts and Crafts Essay.

From self-colour dyeing was but one step to pattern printing on textile fabrics of velveteen, of cotton or linen. "The art of dyeing," says Morris, "leads me naturally to the humble but useful art of printing on cloth. . . . As to the craft among ourselves, it has, as a matter of course, suffered grievously from the degradation of dyeing, and this not only from the worsening of the tints both in beauty and durability, but from a more intricate cause. I have said that the older dyes were much more difficult to use than the modern ones. The processes for getting a many-coloured pattern on to a piece of cotton, even so short a while back as when I was a boy, were many and difficult. As a rule, this is done in fewer hours now than it was in days then. . . . The natural and healthy difficulties of the old processes, all connected as they were with the endeavour to make the colour stable, drove any designer who had anything in him to making his pattern peculiarly suitable to the whole art, and gave a character to it—that character which you so easily recognize in Indian palampores, or in the faded curtains of our grandmothers' time, which still, in spite of many a summer's sun and many and many a strenuous washing, retain at least their reds and blues. In spite of the rudeness or the extravagance of these things, we are always attracted towards them, and the chief reason is, that we feel at once that there is something about the designs natural to the craft, that they can be done only by the practice of it; a quality which, I must once more repeat, is a necessity for all the designs of the lesser arts. But in the comparatively easy way in which these cloths are printed to-day"—worst of all by means of the cylinder-machine—"there are no special difficulties to stimulate the designer to invention; he can get any design done on his cloth; the printer will make no objections, so long as the pattern is the right size for his roller, and has only the due number of colours. The result of all this is ornament on the cotton, which might just as well have been printed or drawn on paper, and in spite of any grace or cleverness in the design, it is found to look poor and tame and wiry. That you will see clearly enough when someone has had a fancy to imitate some of the generous and fertile patterns that were once specially designed for the older cloths: it all comes to nothing—it is dull, hard, unsympathetic. No; there is nothing for it but the trouble and the simplicity of the earlier craft, if you are to have any beauty in cloth-printing at all. And if not, why should we trouble to have a pattern of any sort on our cotton-cloths? I for one am dead against it, unless the pattern is really beautiful; it is so very worthless if it is not."

Again, in the Arts and Crafts Essay on "Textiles,"

Morris says: "The remarks made on the designs for mechanically woven cloths apply pretty much to these printed stuffs: only, in the first place, more play of delicate and pretty colour is possible, and more variety of colour also; and in the second, much more use can be made of hatching and dotting, which are obviously suitable to the method of block-printing. In the many-coloured printed cloths, frank red and blue are again the mainstays of the colour arrangement; these colours, softened by the paler shades of red, outlined with black and made more tender by the addition of yellow in small quantities, mostly forming part of brightish greens, make up the colouring of the old Persian prints, which carry the art as far as it can be carried."

The above conditions which he lays down as requisites for the craft, Morris has indeed fulfilled abundantly in the number of beautiful chintzes, cretonnes, and printed velveteens of which he has been the author. He made designs for these materials long before he was personally in a position to effect the production of them. The firm's earliest blocks for the purpose of pattern-printing on textiles were cut by Mr. Clarkson, then of Coventry Street, who also cut a roller, to their order, for stamped velvet, when the firm had been in existence about ten years. By him also, at the beginning, was undertaken the printing of chintzes, &c., for the firm. Later on this department of their work was carried out on behalf of Messrs. Morris and Co. by Mr. Wardle of Leek. But eventually when Morris acquired possession of the works at Merton he was able to carry on all these processes on his own premises. Of Morris cretonnes and chintzes the "Bird and Anemone," in a single print, and one in many colours, the "Strawberry Thief," a favourite pattern of the artist's own, may well compare as illustrating the variant treatment of ornament in which bird forms are introduced. The first is a simple repeat, while the second is constructed on the basis of a doubled pattern. The "Honeysuckle" is an exquisite combination of somewhat naturalistic with thoroughly conventional forms; a task that is by no means easy of achievement. The "Wandle" design is composed entirely of conventional forms. With its large peony-like rosettes breaking, at regular intervals, the course of the pronounced diagonal band which forms the chief feature; its intervening spaces filled with a profusion of flowers relieved against a background of deep blue, which again is varied by a sort of delicate underprinting in white, this is one of the richest designs imaginable. It is a marvel that a fabric, so poor by comparison, should admit of a decorative effect so splendid as this.

It is about ten or twelve years since pattern-printing on white velveteen was first attempted by Morris and Co., a branch in which their productions have hitherto proved to be unrivalled—the designs, of course, being Morris's and such, perhaps, as no hand but his could produce. Of these the "Acanthus," though early in point of date, has hardly been surpassed for simple dignity by later designs; while the "Florence" and the "Cherwell" are both admirable and well adapted, as patterns, for the particular material. There is one, however, than which it is impossible to conceive anything more splendid of its kind. It is known as the "Severn," and is printed on white velveteen; yellowish brown dots, closely powdered upon the surface, forming a background against which the main features of the design, large conventional flowers and acanthus foliage, outlined in brown, stand out white and clear. Together with these, light green leaves and rose-red tulips make up the most delicate harmony of colours. The same design is printed on a cotton cloth, but the difference of texture is such that the two fabrics cannot well be compared with one another.

To the art of embroidery, as has been pointed out in a previous chapter, Mr. Morris gave his attention right early. "Of the design for" this branch of work he writes, "it must be said that one of its aims should be the exhibition of beautiful material. Furthermore it is not worth doing unless it is either very copious and rich, or very delicate—or both. For such an art nothing patchy or scrappy, or half-starved, should be done: there is no excuse for doing anything which is not strikingly beautiful. . . . It may be well here to warn those occupied in embroidery against the feeble imitations of Japanese art which are so disastrously common amongst us. The Japanese are admirable naturalists, wonderfully skilful draughtsmen, deft beyond all others in mere execution of whatever they take in hand; and also great masters of style within certain narrow limitations. But with all this a Japanese design is absolutely worthless unless it is executed with Japanese skill. In truth, with all their brilliant qualities as handicraftsmen, which have so dazzled us, the Japanese have no architectural, and therefore no decorative, instinct. Their works of art are isolated and blankly individualistic, and in consequence, unless where they rise, as they sometimes do, to the dignity of a suggestion for a picture (always devoid of human interest), they remain mere wonderful toys, things quite outside the pale of the evolution of art, which, I repeat, cannot be carried on without the architectural sense that connects it with the history of mankind." It may be permitted to interpolate here some further remarks of Morris's, bearing as they do upon the same subject. "It is true," so he says in the lecture on "The Lesser Arts of Life," "that these non-architectural races (let the Chinese stand as a type of them) have no general mastery over the arts, and seem to play with them rather than to try to put their souls into them. Clumsy-handed as the European or Aryan workman is (of a good period, I mean) as compared with his Turanian fellow, there is a seriousness and depth of feeling which, when brought to bear upon the matter of our daily life, is in fact the soul of Architecture, whatever the body may be; so that I shall still say that among ourselves, the men of modern Europe, the existence of the other arts is bound up with that of Architecture." And again, speaking of certain properties of Chinese work, Morris says, "They were indeed valuable qualities in the hands of a Chinaman, deft as he was of execution, fertile of design, fanciful though not imaginative; in short, a born maker of pretty toys; but such daintinesses were of little avail to a good workman of our race,—. . . he had other work to do . . . than the making of toys." The last features to be looked for, then, in Morris ornament for embroidery, or indeed any other craft, are those which characterize either Chinese or Japanese designs. Thus for instance the employment of gold thread is almost unknown in Morris's embroideries. Whereas the capabilities of needlework done while held in the hand, as distinct from that executed while stretched in a frame, have been developed to a high degree of perfection. In particular very beautiful effects have been obtained by means of darning stitch in twist silks upon special hand-woven cotton and linen cloths, the entire surface of the material being covered with solid embroidery. As to the colours used it is needless to say that they display to utmost advantage the rich and harmonious combinations which distinguish the style of Morris. It should be noted beside that the accidental irregularities of the dyeing process, which rarely produces absolute uniformity of tint throughout, imparts to the Morris embroidery-silks additional charm and variety of effect.

William Morris allowed the use of some of his designs to the Royal School of Art Needlework in Exhibition Road, Kensington, with whose aims and objects, from the time of its foundation in 1872, he was naturally in sympathy. A bed-hanging from his design was worked in the school for the Honourable Mrs. Percy Wyndham. In the "Handbook of Embroidery," by L. Higgin, edited by Lady Marian Alford, and published by authority of the School of Art Needlework in 1880, were reproduced three Morris designs, viz., two diapers for embroidered wall-hangings (one of them, with honeysuckle and other flowers, being printed in colours), and thirdly a border, an adaptation of the same motif as the "Marigold" pattern in wall-paper. These instances however are exceptions. The majority of Morris's embroidery designs remain the property of the firm and are executed through the department of which his daughter, Miss May Morris (Mrs. Sparling), has for some years past been in charge. This lady is not only an excellent worker and teacher of embroidery, but also herself of unusual talents as a designer. The amount of embroidery undertaken by the firm for ecclesiastical purposes is insignificant: the greater portion consisting of domestic work in the shape of curtains, table-cloths, squares for cushions, and some smaller articles. Although a catalogue of names is powerless to convey any idea of the description or beauty of Morris needlework, the "Tulip and Rose," "Olive and Rose," "Rose Wreath," "Vine and Pink" and "Flower-pot" pattern by Mr. Morris for embroidered cushion-covers; as also his splendid curtain executed in coloured silks upon a background of yellowish green linen—all of them shown at one or other of the Arts and Crafts Exhibitions in London—may be mentioned as especially fine and characteristic examples of his designs for embroidery.

The record-roll of the domestic arts taken up by William Morris's firm would not have been complete without that of carpet-making. The earliest of Morris's designs for this craft was for Kidderminster carpet. It was a very simple one, called the "Grass" pattern, and was followed by the "Lily," a small pattern again, comprised of lilies and fritillaries, arranged upon the scale principle, with a narrow border of chevrons when it was intended to serve as a stair-carpet. There being no means of executing these carpets upon the premises, they had to be woven elsewhere for Messrs. Morris and Co. It happened that the designs were not registered, and one of them, the "Lily," was appropriated by an unscrupulous manufacturer, who produced it on his own account, after having made some minute alteration in it by leaving out part of the ply. The manufacturer, when confronted with Mr. Morris, owned that he could not rebut the charge; and there the matter ended, to obtain redress being out of the question. Wilton and Axminster and, latterly, Brussels carpets have in turn been designed by Morris and executed on behalf of the firm. It goes without saying that these are all of the best quality—indeed Morris would not have been satisfied with anything less—as regards material; and as for design they are not a whit below Morris's high standard in other wares. They are both pleasant to look at and in every way suited to their purpose. But it was not any such kinds of carpets as these that Morris had in mind when writing or speaking of the art of carpet-weaving. By the latter he meant, to use his own words, "the real thing, such as the East has furnished us with from time immemorial, and not the makeshift imitation woven by means of the Jacquard loom, or otherwise mechanically." This is what, elsewhere, he says on the same subject: "Carpet-weaving is somewhat of the nature of tapestry: it also is wholly unmechanical. . . . Carpets form a mosaic of small squares of worsted, or hair, or silk threads, tied into a coarse canvas, which is made as the work progresses. Owing to the comparative coarseness of the work, the designs should always be very elementary in form, and *suggestive* merely of forms of leafage, flowers, beasts, and birds, &c. The soft gradations of tint to which tapestry lends itself are unfit for carpet-weaving; beauty and variety of colour must be attained by harmonious juxtaposition of tints, bounded by judiciously chosen outlines; and the pattern should lie absolutely flat upon the ground. On the whole, in designing carpets the method of *contrast* is the best one to employ, and blue and red, quite frankly used, with white or very light outlines on a dark ground, and black or some very dark colour on a light ground, are the main colours on which the designer should depend. In making the above remarks I have been thinking only of the genuine or hand-made carpets. The mechanically-made carpets of to-day must be looked upon as makeshifts for cheapness' sake. . . . The velvet carpets need the same kind of design as to colour and quality as the real carpets; only, as the colours are necessarily limited in number, and the pattern must repeat at certain distances, the design should be simpler and smaller than in a real carpet. A Kidderminster carpet calls for a small design in which the different planes, or plies, as they are called, are well interlocked." In another place, speaking of old Persian carpets, Morris describes one class of them as having been "designed on scientific principles which any good designer can apply to works of our own day without burdening his conscience with the charge of plagiarism." And as for the other class of ancient carpets, with Persian floral designs, he says, "These, beautiful as they are in colour, are as far as possible from lacking form in design; they are fertile of imagination and rich in drawing; and though imitation of them would carry with it its usual disastrous consequences, they show us the way to set about designing such like things, and that a carpet can be made which by no means depends for its success on the mere instinct of colour." Again, "To us pattern designers," says Morris, "Persia has become a holy land, for there in the process of time our art was perfected, and thence above all places it spread to cover for a while the world, east and west." He would commend "the designers of time past . . . and the usefulness of the lives of these men . . . whose names are long forgotten, but whose works we still wonder at. In their own way they meant to tell us how the flowers grew in the gardens of Damascus, or how the hunt was up on the plains of Kirman, or how the tulips shone among the grass in the Mid-Persian valley, and how their souls delighted in it all, and what joy they had in life; nor did they fail to make their meaning clear to some of us." So much for the past. But the future of Eastern art had only gloomy prospects for William Morris. He could not sufficiently deplore the action of the Government in "manufacturing cheap Indian carpets in the Indian gaols. . . . In this case the Government . . . has determined that it will make its wares cheap, whether it make them nasty or not. Cheap and nasty they are, I assure you; but, though they are the worst of their kind, they would not be made thus, if everything did not tend the same way. And it is the same everywhere and with all Indian manufactures. . . . In short, their art is dead, and the commerce of modern civilization has slain it. What is going on in India is also going on, more or less, all over the East; but I have spoken of India chiefly because I cannot help thinking that we ourselves are responsible for what is happening there." "Withal," wrote Morris in another place, "one thing seems certain, that if we don't set to work making our own carpets it will not be long before we shall find the East fail us: for that last gift, the gift of the sense of harmonious colour, is speedily dying out in the East before the conquests of European rifles and money-bags."

Stirred, then, by some such apprehensions as are expressed by him in the foregoing passages, and at the same time conscious, no doubt, of his own personal fitness, before all others, for the task, William Morris formed the fixed determination to rescue, by his own effort, the perishing art of carpet-weaving. He began accordingly to make a systematic study of an antique Persian carpet, examining and analysing its every detail, until at length he had mastered the method of construction to the extent of being able to start weaving in the same manner with his own hands. Thus, from his own designs and with his own dyed wool, a certain quantity of pile-carpet squares were produced, under the immediate direction of his helping hand, in a loom set up in the back attic at Queen Square. But ere long the industry outgrew these narrow bounds, and was transferred to the coach-house adjoining Morris's house at Hammersmith, where looms were set up and a certain number of women were employed in the weaving. Thence it was that these splendid pile fabrics of Morris and Co.'s came by the name of "Hammersmith" carpets, by which they are now always known. In some instances the device of a hammer, in allusion to the place of manufacture, was woven into the borders of the carpets. In this connection it may be mentioned by the way that no other formal trademark was adopted by the firm; unless indeed one excepts the device of two doves, flying together somewhat in the attitude of the swallows on willow pattern china,—a badge which was designed by Madox Brown and was in use by the original company in the early period of their career. From Hammersmith the carpet-weaving was moved to Merton Abbey, where it is now carried on, and constitutes not the least flourishing industry of the firm.

In the matter of carpets, no less than in that of every other craft taken in hand by Morris, his own words provide the best commentary that could be found; since his own productions do not fail to satisfy the most stringent canons which he formulated for the right conduct of the art. And his carpet-making furnishes a very excellent case in point. Here was a craft with definite limitations such as might on no account be ignored nor over-stepped; a craft moreover which had already on its native soil been carried to what anyone might have assumed to be the goal of its highest attainable perfection. Its former glories had long since passed away, and yet Morris undertook to resuscitate it, nor was daunted by the magnitude of the task. To embark on the enterprise of manufacturing carpets for modern folk living in modern dwellings did not seem to afford much scope for the employment of the artistic faculty; yet by applying in present day carpet-making those principles that diligent research had discovered to him were they which governed the practice of the art at its zenith, Morris proved it to be capable of yet further development, and more beautiful, than it had undergone for centuries. Those who visited the Arts and Crafts Exhibition of 1893 will recall the magnificent pile carpet exhibited by Messrs. Morris and Co., which was the principal object in the West Gallery there. It was designed by Morris and manufactured specially for Mr. Sanderson at Buller's Wood—whence its name. This carpet does not come under the head of those more common and rudimentary patterns referred to in the lecture of Morris above quoted. On the contrary, it belongs to the more elaborate and complex order. It is not copied, of course, from oriental work, but evolved rather out of the English artist's brilliant powers of invention. At the same time it is such that no Persian handicraftsman in the palmiest days of the carpet-weaving art need have been ashamed of, if but he had been entitled to claim it as his own.

Allied to carpet-craft is "the noblest of the weaving arts," to wit, that of tapestry, known under the specific name of Arras. The conditions of carpet and tapestry weaving are alike, and such that entail a very similar mode of execution, similar material and similar apparatus. The latter is simplicity itself. In fact, neither industry is one which demands "the help of anything that can fairly be called a machine: little more is needed than a frame which will support heavy beams on which we may strain our warp: our work is purely hand-work—we may do what we will according to the fineness of our warp." Tapestry making "requires but a very small amount of technical, though often much artistic, skill." The purpose of the craft is the production of "what may fairly be called woven pictures; webs whose elaboration and want of repetition of pattern would scarcely allow of any reasonable effect being produced by mere mechanical weaving." In the Arts and Crafts Essay on "Textiles" is Morris's description of the art as it should be: "It may be looked upon," he says, "as a mosaic of pieces of colour made up of dyed threads, and is capable of producing wall ornament of any degree of elaboration within the proper limits of duly considered decorative work. As in all wall-decoration, the first thing to be considered in the designing of Tapestry is the force, purity and elegance of the *silhouette* of the objects represented, and nothing vague or indeterminate is admissible. But special excellences can be expected from it. Depth of tone, richness of colour, and exquisite gradations of tints are easily to be obtained in tapestry; and it also demands that crispness and abundance of beautiful detail which was the especial characteristic of fully developed Mediæval Art."

The method of weaving which William Morris proposed to revive was the traditional one, the same which survives to this day at the Gobelins factory, viz., that of the vertical loom, or *haute lisse* as it is called to distinguish it from the *basse lisse*, or horizontal loom, where the weaver looks down upon the face of the web as he works; whereas in the case of the high warp loom the weaver is seated at the back and can only see the front of the web by looking through the warp threads at its reflection in a mirror. This system of weaving is demonstrated in the model of a *haute lisse* tapestry loom which Mr. Morris gave to the South Kensington Museum in 1893 (Catalogue number

156). At the time when it occurred to him to start hand-weaving according to the ancient plan, it was a thing extinct in this country. In fact the last work of the kind in England was the industry which had been carried on at Mortlake and which was stopped by the Protector Cromwell. Thus there was no working model at hand to which Morris could refer for practical illustration of the method of weaving. It is true that the other system had been inaugurated by the opening of the Royal Tapestry Works at Windsor, as Morris showed in his lecture on "The Lesser Arts of Life," wherein he remarked: "I am sorry to have to say that an attempt to set the art going, which has been made, doubtless with the best intentions, under royal patronage at Windsor, within the last few years, has most unluckily gone on the lines of the work at the Gobelins, and if it does not change its system utterly, is doomed to artistic failure, whatever its commercial success may be." The prediction was fulfilled only too surely. The Windsor tapestry factory did not manage to attract the custom of the public by means of the landscapes and other realistic representations which it produced, and a few years ago the establishment was definitely closed, the plant sold, and the staff of workers disbanded. Nor was there much to be learnt elsewhere. For, as to the craft in France at the present day, its "poor remains" lie "in that mud of degradation" into which they were dragged by "the establishment of that hatching nest of stupidity, the Gobelins," which changed tapestry weaving, from having been "a fine art" and a noble, into a mere "upholsterer's toy." "If you are curious on the subject of its technique you may see that going on as in its earlier, or let us say real, life at the Gobelins at Paris; but it is a melancholy sight: the workmen are as handy at it as only Frenchmen can be at such work, and their skill is traditional too, I have heard; for they are the sons, grandsons, and great-grandsons of tapestry weavers. Well, their ingenuity is put to the greatest pains for the least results: it would be a mild word to say that what they make is worthless; it is more than that; it has a corrupting and deadening influence upon all the Lesser Arts of France, since it is always put forward as the very standard and crown of all that those arts can do at the best: a more idiotic waste of human labour and skill it is impossible to conceive. There is another branch of the same stupidity, differing slightly in technique, at Beauvais; and the little town of Aubusson in mid-France has a decaying commercial industry of the like rubbish." Thus Morris felt constrained to refer to the art of tapestry as something that "must be spoken of in the past tense." And moreover he deemed it necessary to apologize to his audience for addressing them at any length on so ineffectual a subject as an art which had "practically perished." At the same time, "There is nothing whatever," he urged "to prevent us from reviving it if we please, since the technique of it is easy to the last degree." These words appeared in 1882. Already by that date Morris had achieved somewhat in the direction of the revival he advocated. In default of any existing instance available where the actual weaving process might be observed, Morris had had to pick up the details of the craft, as best he might, from an old French official handbook, published prior to the Revolution. He caused a handloom to be set up in his bedroom at Kelmscott House, Hammersmith, and, so as not to let this new undertaking of his interfere with his ordinary occupations, he used to rise betimes and practise weaving in the early hours of the morning. By following out the instructions he gathered from his printed guide, Morris gradually overcame the difficulties of the craft and became a proficient weaver himself. With his own hand he wove a beautiful piece of tapestry, designed by himself with birds and foliage, for a private gift. In one or two respects he even improved upon the instructions given in the French book. For example, the plan therein recommended for marking on the warp threads the design to be woven was to use charcoal. But experience showed Morris that this method was inadequate, because the charcoal, in the process of working, quickly got rubbed off, before the outline of the pattern had stood long enough to be carried into execution.

Accordingly, with the aid of Mr. Campfield, he devised a more permanent means of fixing the outline, by holding a brush, dipped in Indian ink, to the warp thread at the point required, and then twirling the thread round between the finger and thumb so as to mark it thoroughly and thus avoid the risk of obliteration. In his earliest experiments in weaving, conducted, on behalf of the firm, as far back as the year 1878, Mr. Morris had the assistance of Mr. H. Dearle, to whom he imparted what he himself had learned of the art. Their first efforts were confined to floral designs, with the occasional introduction of birds into the composition. The first time that figure-weaving was attempted was at Merton in 1881, the subject being the "Goose Girl," from a cartoon by Mr. Walter Crane. Thenceforward, with one exception, the figures were always designed by Sir Edward Burne-Jones. Among the earlier tapestries of the firm of Morris and Co. were two of the type known by the technical name of "Verdura;" both shown at the Exhibition of Arts and Crafts in 1888. One of them, an upright panel, designed by W. Morris, is an admirable instance of the adaptability of his bold, sweeping leaf-scrolls to this kind of work. It is called "The Woodpecker," after the main incident depicted in it, and is ornamented above and below with ribbon scrolls bearing verses from the pen of Mr. Morris—verses included in the collection of "Poems by the Way." The other is a horizontal panel, woven for Mr. Alexander Ionides. It is named "The Forest." The foliage and flowers were designed by Mr. Morris and Mr. Dearle respectively, but the animals introduced into the composition—a lion and a fox—were from cartoons by Mr. Philip Webb. These however, being in the latter's wonted zoological style, do not seem quite in keeping with their severely conventional surroundings. Designs in which the contrary elements of realism and decoration are combined in so marked a way as this seldom produce satisfactory results. More commonly a loss of organic unity is the result. In the particular case in point one cannot help deploring the fact, and feeling that a far more harmonious effect would have been obtained had the whole of this tapestry been designed by William Morris alone, or at any rate by none other than those who, by training, have acquired his ornamental manner. However, Morris himself thought otherwise. In the two tapestry panels entitled "Flora" and "Pomona," each with an allegorical figure designed by Burne-Jones, very similar "verdura" backgrounds occur; rabbits and birds being introduced in the "Flora" panel with excellent effect amid the flowers and wreathing acanthus foliage. Either panel has scrolls with two quatrains, written by Morris and published in "Poems by the Way" in 1891.

Messrs. Morris and Co.'s first large figure-subject tapestry, and perhaps also their best known work of this kind, was "The Star of Bethlehem" panel, designed by Burne-Jones for Exeter College Chapel at Oxford, and completed in April, 1890. It was but fitting that the two friends should have the opportunity to unite together thus in the beautifying of their old college. Unfortunately this splendid piece of tapestry, the joint product of Morris and Burne-Jones, is ill-shown in the position in which it is fixed, against the south wall of the edifice: and yet it is a veritable treasure and deserves to be made more of than it is, since—alas, that it should have to be said!—it is the only artistic object in the chapel that enshrines it. The new building is indeed such that could not possibly commend itself to Mr. Morris, who always regretted the disappearance of the plain old building that stood in its place in his undergraduate days. How much beauty of decorative detail in "The Star of Bethlehem" tapestry was due to Morris and Co. may be perceived by comparison of their woven panel with Burne-Jones's drawing as brought to its final state in 1891. The discrepancies in the two versions represent the amount that the artist in his cartoon left blank for Morris and Co. to fill in before they executed it in arras; these very parts being supplied eventually by Burne-Jones with ornaments of an entirely different design. The lilies, irises, tulips, borage, heartsease, and other flowers in the foreground of the tapestry were indicated but slightly and sketchily in the original, and all of them

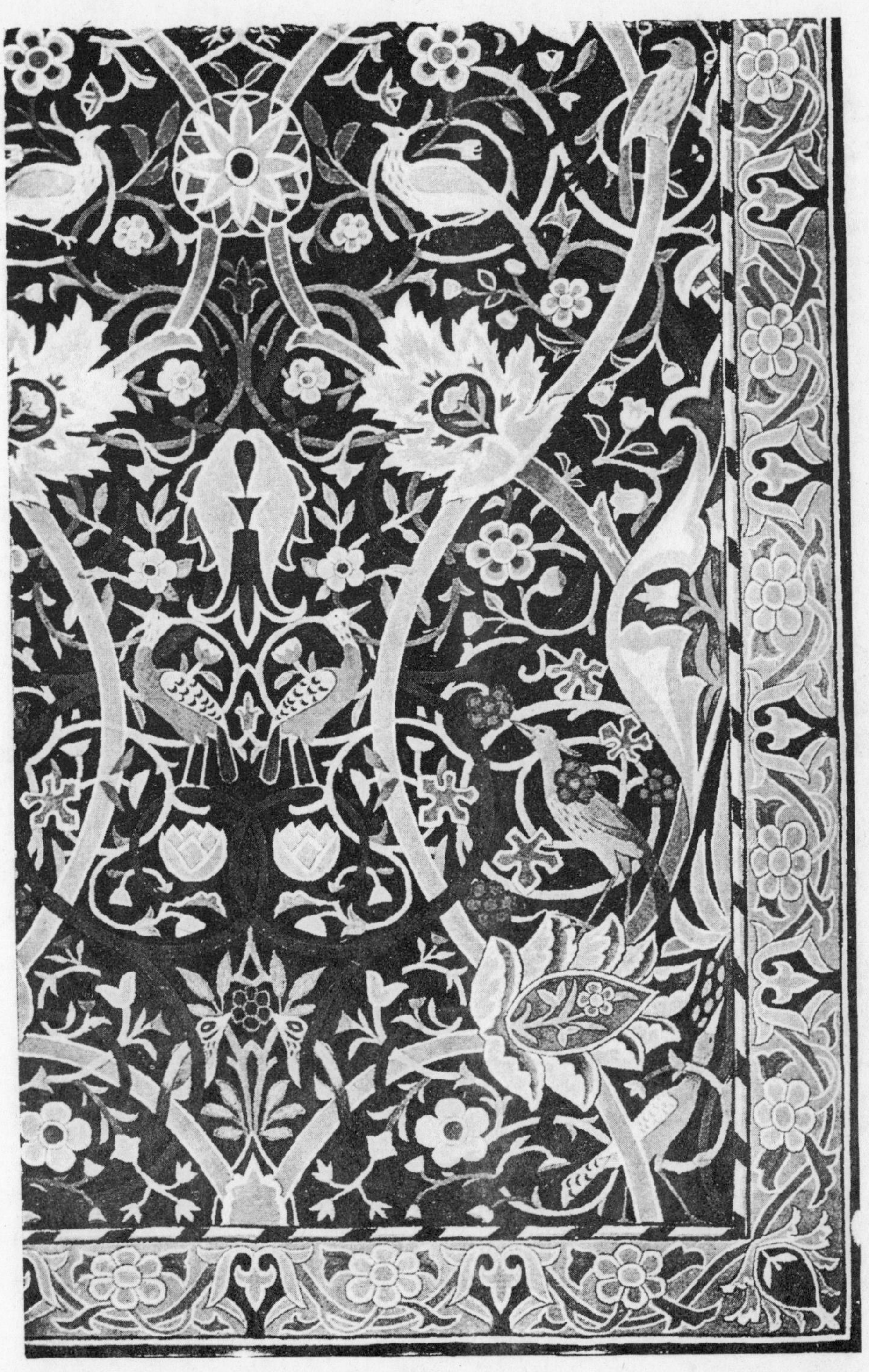

SKETCH DESIGN FOR "BULLER'S WOOD" CARPET. BY WILLIAM MORRIS.

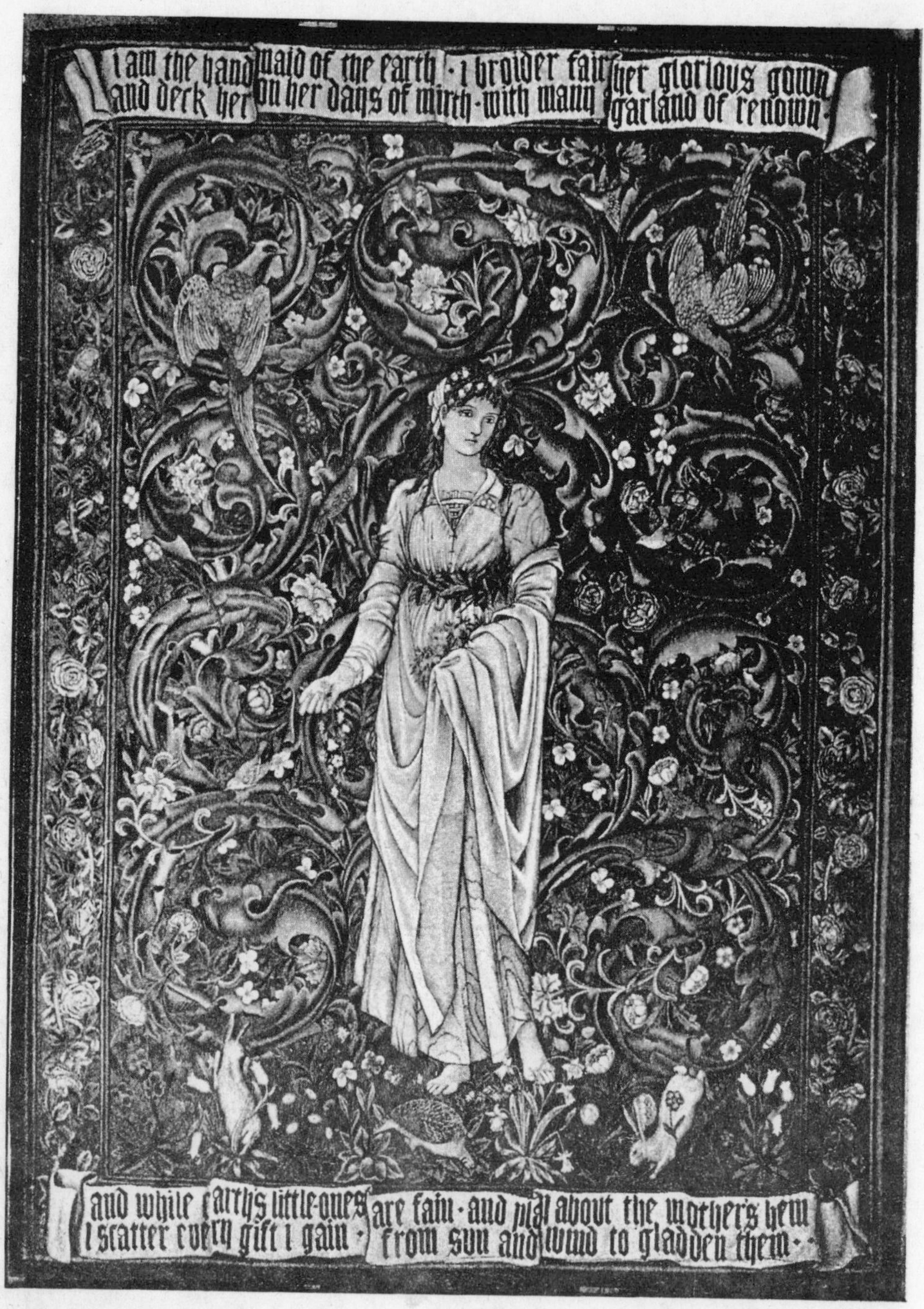

ARRAS TAPESTRY, "FLORA."

DESIGNED BY WILLIAM MORRIS.
THE FIGURE IS BY SIR EDWARD BURNE-JONES, BART.

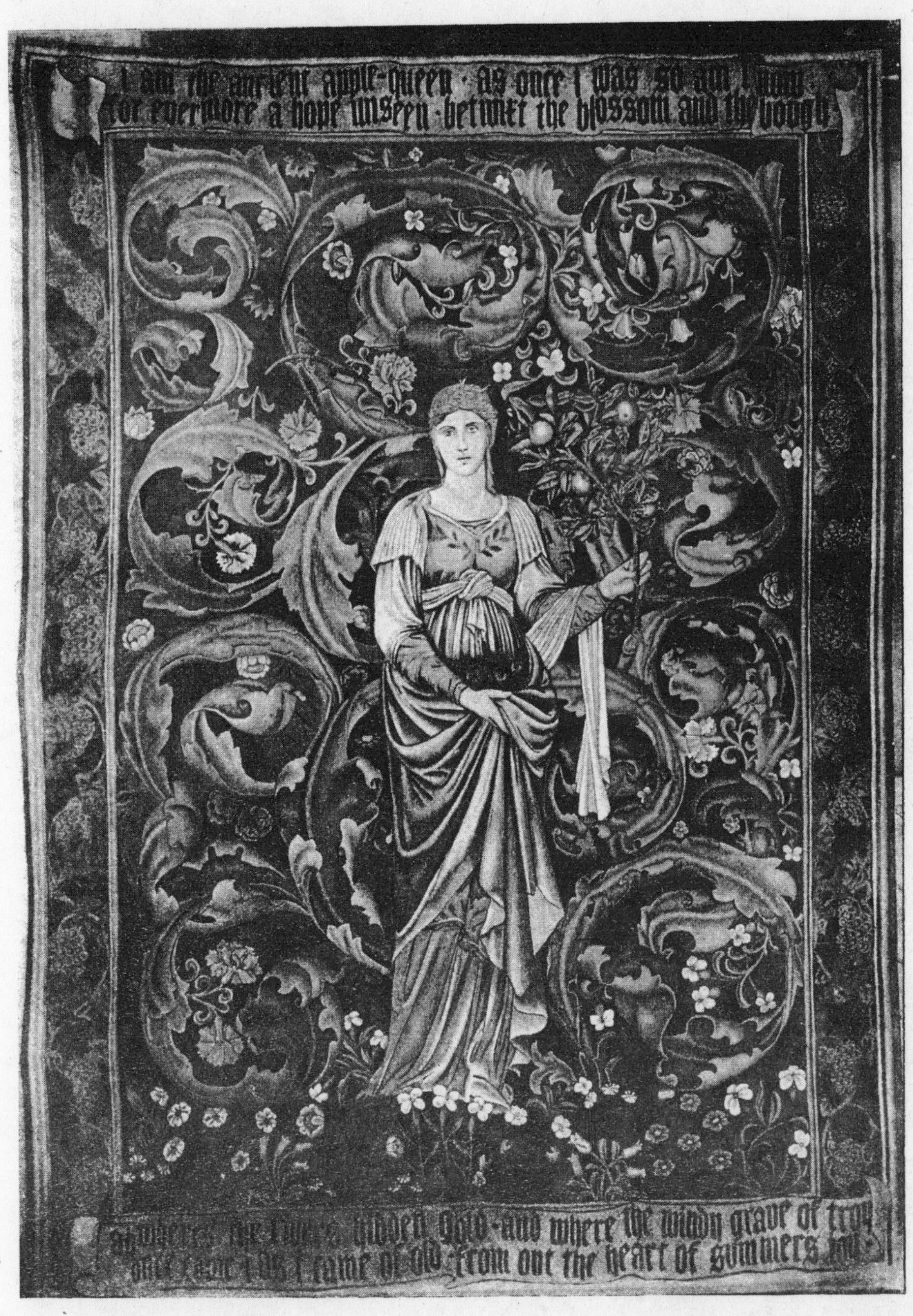

ARRAS TAPESTRY, "POMONA."

DESIGNED BY WILLIAM MORRIS.
THE FIGURE IS BY SIR EDWARD BURNE-JONES, BART.

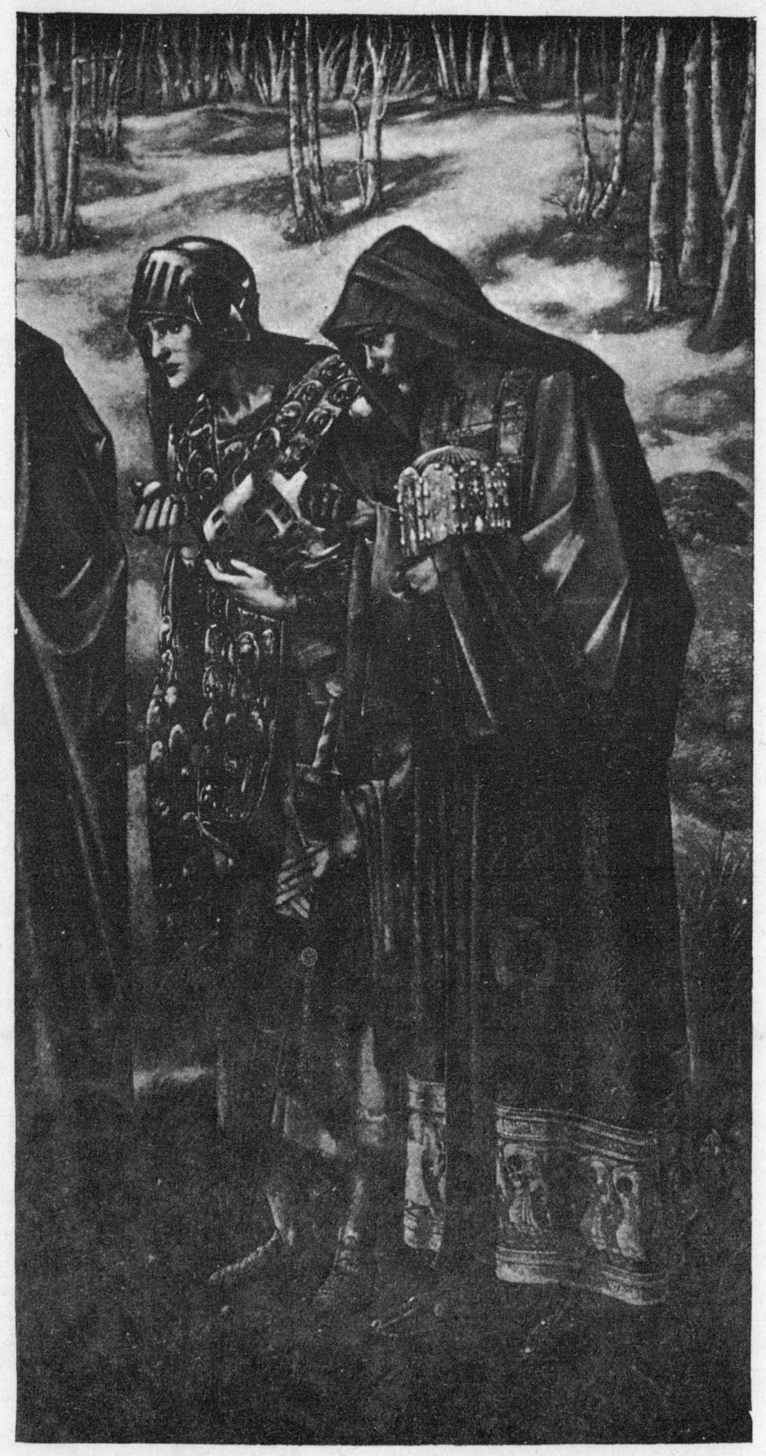

DETAIL OF WATER-COLOUR PAINTING.

"THE STAR OF BETHLEHEM." BY SIR E. BURNE-JONES, BART.

BY PERMISSION OF THE CORPORATION OF BIRMINGHAM.

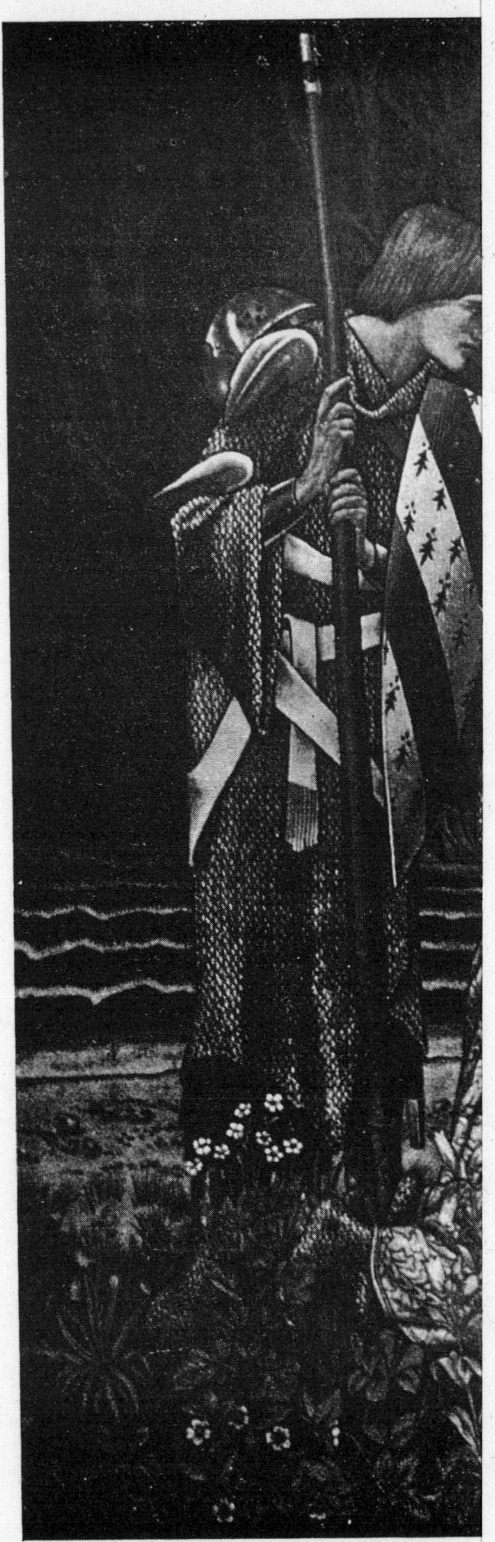

DETAIL OF ARRAS TAPESTRY
AT STANMORE HALL.

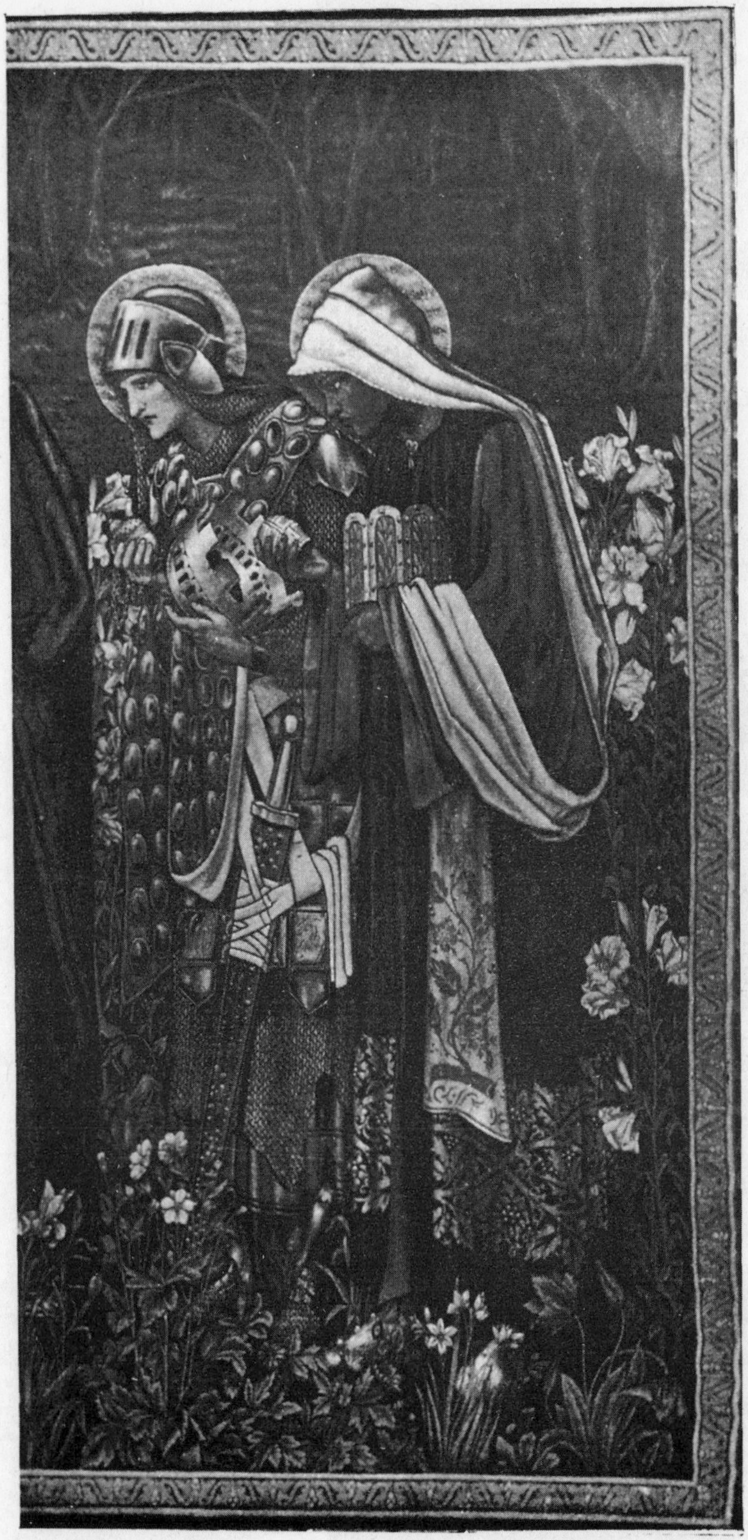

DETAIL OF ARRAS TAPESTRY, EXETER COLLEGE, OXFORD. "THE STAR OF BETHLEHEM." DESIGNED BY SIR E. BURNE-JONES, BART.

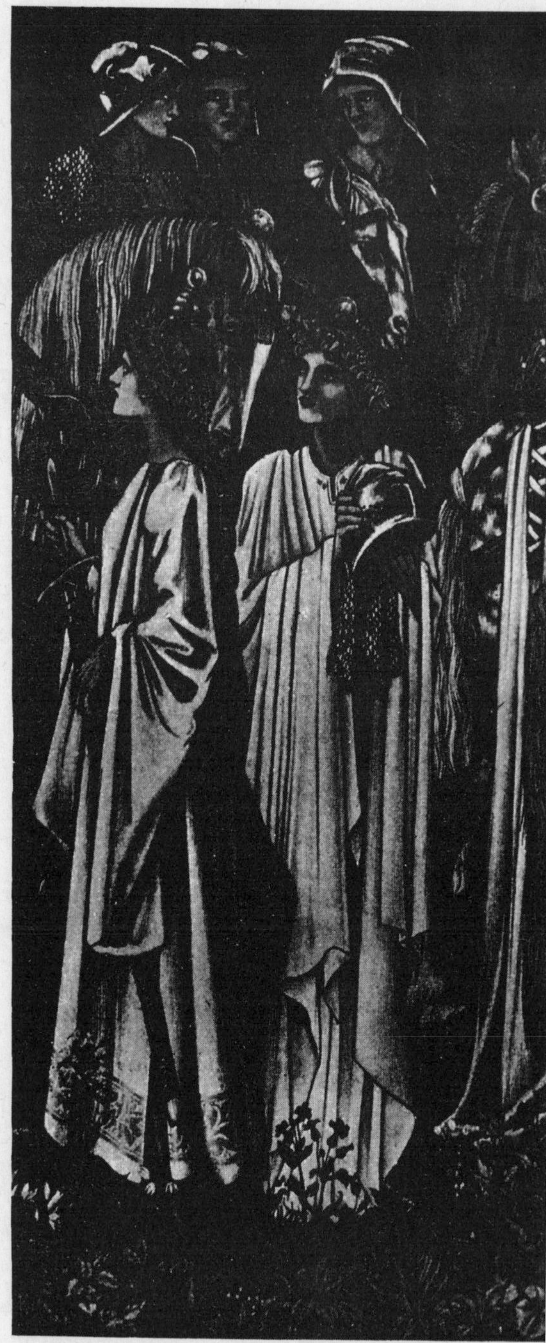

DETAIL OF ARRAS TAPESTRY
AT STANMORE HALL.

FROM "
HOLY GI

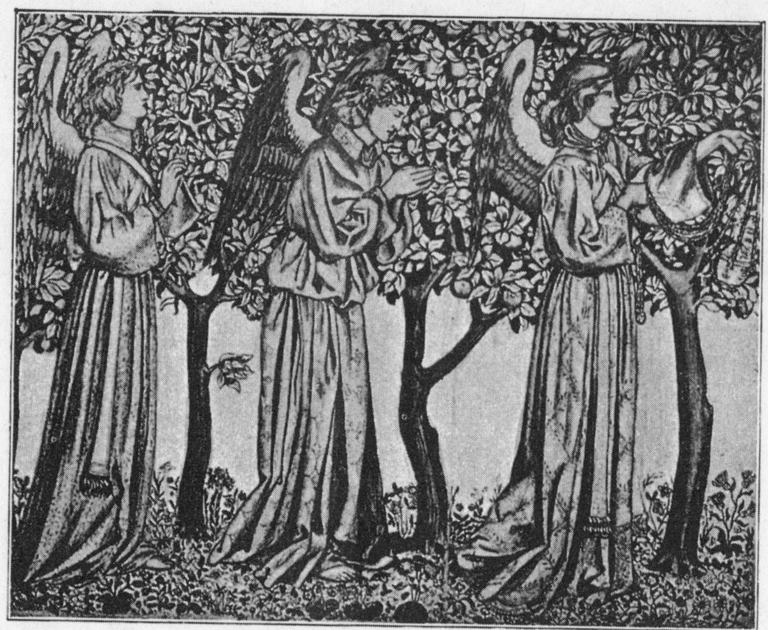

ANGELS IN ADORATION.

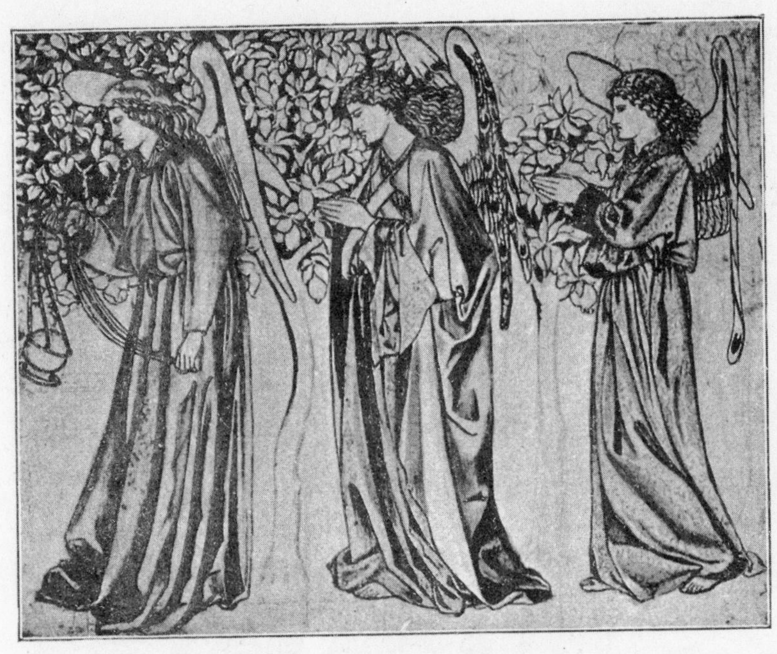

FROM CARTOONS BY WILLIAM MORRIS
IN THE POSSESSION OF MR. C. FAIRFAX MURRAY.

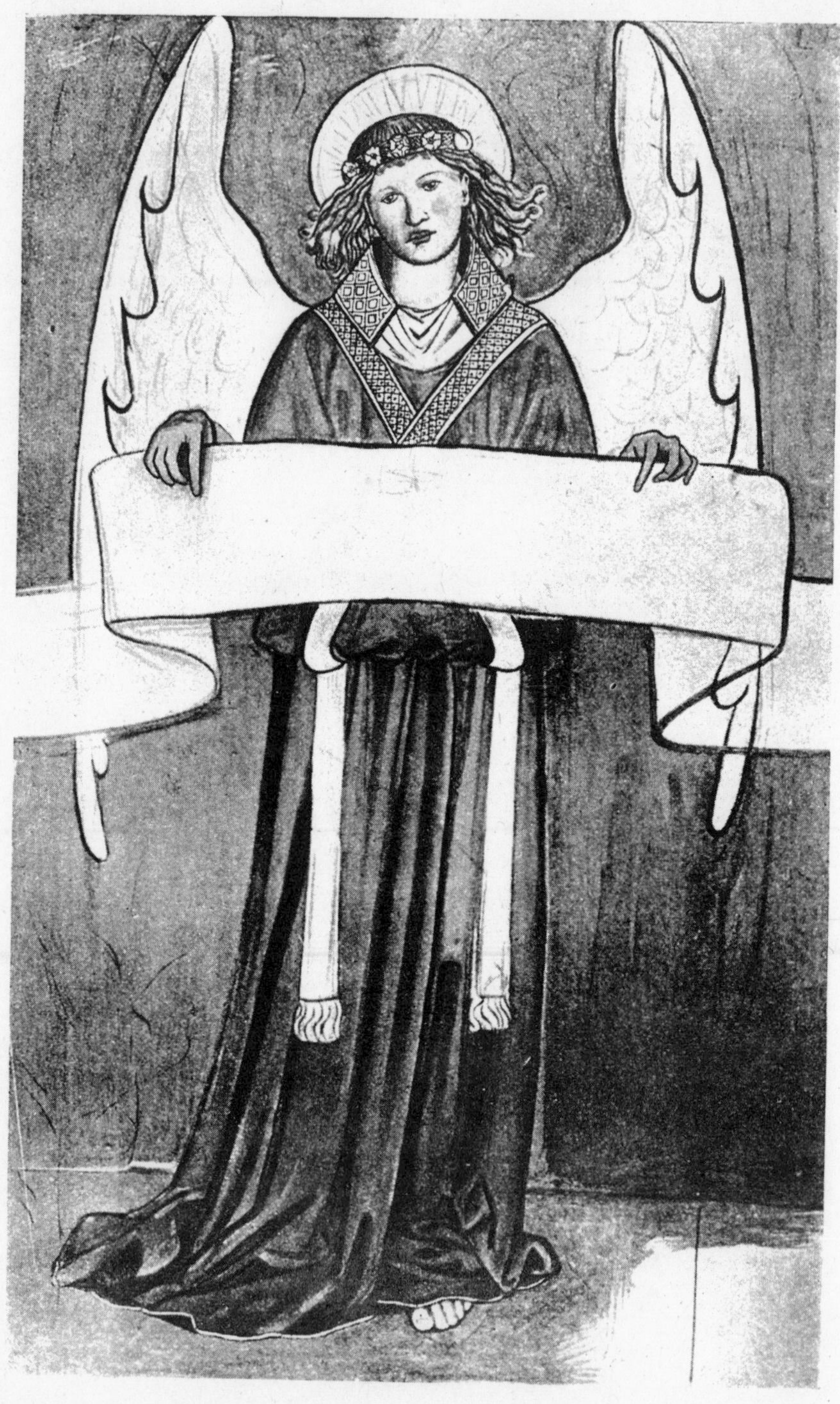

ANGEL WITH SCROLL.

CARTOON BY WILLIAM MORRIS. IN THE POSSESSION OF MR. C. FAIRFAX MURRAY.

had to be drawn afresh in definite shape by Morris and Co., as were also the patterns on the draperies, the jewellery, &c. The firm was called upon twice subsequently to produce replicas of "The Star of Bethlehem," one of them being a commission from Mr. Wilfrid Scawen Blunt.

In one single instance, and that a notable one for the very reason that he did so, Mr. Morris provided a set of four figures from drawings by his own hand, to be reproduced in arras tapestry, which was shown at the Arts and Crafts Exhibition of 1893. These, by the way, were the same figures which he had designed in the first instance for the roof of Jesus College Chapel, Cambridge. Only, whereas the angels in the original decoration hold in their hands a scroll inscribed with the words of an ancient hymn, in place thereof in the latter case the figures display some verses from the pen of William Morris, beginning, "Midst bitten mead and acre shorn," &c., and published under the title-heading of "The Orchard" in "Poems by the Way." This specimen (apart from the figures, which, contrary to his wont, as has been shown, Morris designed himself) may serve as a typical example of how, among the several persons participating in the execution of any given piece of tapestry at Merton Abbey works, each one's share was apportioned. The fruit trees in the background were designed by Mr. Morris; the flowers in the foreground by Mr. Dearle; and the diapers and minor details of the ornament by those whose hands were engaged in the actual weaving.

The Morris window in Salisbury Cathedral, designed by Burne-Jones and representing groups of ministering and praising angels, has been mentioned already. The identical figures have since been adapted, in subdued blues and reds, with a dull but rich-coloured background of foliage and flowers, with borders, &c., and worked out in two panels of arras tapestry by Messrs. Morris and Co.; and that with results so fine that the disquieting question perforce suggests itself whether these cartoons are not more appropriate to the latter medium. In that event it follows—does it not?—that they are scarcely in the best manner of design for stained glass too. Had the lead-glazing and the consequent subdivision of surface been, as they ought, an integral part of the original conception, it must have been a literal impossibility to convert the cartoons, by the omission of their lead lines or by any other means, into proper designs for tapestry treatment, short of altering their whole form and character. It is not too much to affirm that no design submitted for stained glass without the lead lines being marked would be accepted from any student in the National Art competition, of which Mr. Morris himself was a judge. But, to remove any possible doubt on the point, take an instance of stained glass as it is seen at its perfection of maturity in the fifteenth century, say in the ante-chapel of New College, Oxford, or of All Souls'; at Thornhill Church, Yorkshire, or at Fairford: imagine a window from any one of these places re-drawn upon paper and then executed in arras in in the loom. The thing is preposterous! The very character and conditions which go to make the excellence of a design for one branch of art work, almost necessarily disqualify the same design from being carried out in any different material; the measure of its fitness for the one being in inverse ratio to its fitness for the other. And if this rule be such as holds good generally, even in respect of arts which are nearly akin to one another; how much more forcibly does it apply in the case of two so diverse as glass painting and tapestry weaving! The principle, after all, is one which Morris himself has laid down and emphasized again and again in his own writings and public utterances. However, since tapestry is of the nature of woven picture-work, paintings certainly lend themselves, of all branches of art, to more legitimate adaptations than any other for this medium. Thus the figures painted at Jesus College, when, years afterwards, they were modified and introduced into a tapestry hanging, did not seem to have suffered in the process, nor to be in any way out of keeping with the composition. On the other hand, there can be little disputing that "The Star of Bethlehem," designed as it was *ab initio* for tapestry, is far more satisfactory in that form even than when worked up from the cartoon into the large water-colour picture commissioned by the directors of the Municipal Art Gallery at Birmingham. Another and a later work of the class of adaptations in tapestry, to wit, a copy of Sandro Botticelli's "Primavera," cannot claim to be particularly happy in effect. It was exhibited at the Arts and Crafts Exhibition in 1896. For the choice of subject it may not indeed be fair to hold Mr. Morris responsible, since the tapestry was woven specially to the order of Mr. Blunt. Of this panel Mrs. Mabel Cox, in "The Artist," remarks: "The colouring is especially good, the faded tones of the old colours being reproduced without any loss of the rich glow. To do this is to encounter no small difficulty, considering the material under command." But the same writer, while pronouncing that the subject "is certainly a good design for tapestry," is obliged to admit that "it is by no means certain . . . that lovers of Botticelli's masterpiece will be pleased to see it in its new form."

Of Morris and Co.'s tapestry the most important work altogether, and one that may justly be described as monumental, is that executed from Sir Edward Burne-Jones's designs for the dining-room at Stanmore Hall. The scheme of this decoration is to illustrate the Arthurian romance, more particularly that part of it which deals with the quest of the San-Graal. The main division consists of a series of figure-subject panels. Their height is uniformly eight feet, but they vary in width according to the dimensions of the several spaces they have to fill round the room. Of these panels it will suffice to describe one, which, though neither the largest nor the most conspicuous, is yet, in point of beauty, second to none in the set. The subject is "The Failure of Sir Lancelot." It contains but two figures. In the foreground Sir Lancelot is represented lying asleep, his back leaning against the stone side of a water-cistern, his feet pointing to the door, shut against him and guarded by an angel-warder of the Temple of the Holy Grail. The angel's wings, blue as the depths of a sapphire, harmonize with the paler blue of his sleeves;

while his white and yellow brocaded robe contrasts with the rich crimson surcoat of the mailed knight, whose limbs are encased partly in plate, partly in chain, armour. The execution of the latter must have needed almost as much technical skill as do human features. In this case the difficulty was greatly enhanced by the fact that the whole composition is in a subdued tone of colour, with beams of strong light streaming through the chinks of the door and glinting, where they fall, upon armour and blades of grass. A masterly reserve together with the utmost delicacy of treatment were required to save a scene treated in such a manner as this from degenerating into melodrama. But the feat has been accomplished nevertheless. Other panels depict "The arrival of Sir Galahad to take his place in the Siege Perilous," "The Knights departing on the Quest," "The Failure of Sir Gawaine," "The Vision of the Holy Grail," and, what is really a part of the last subject, a ship riding at anchor at a short distance from the shore which, strewn with shells and overgrown with tufts of coarse grass, occupies the foreground.

The panels which form the upper and principal division of the Stanmore Hall tapestries are woven separately from the lower part, which runs beneath in the form of a detached band nearly five feet deep. Along the top of this dado is a scroll, with a legend giving a brief explanation of the particular subject which is represented immediately above. Below the scroll is represented a deer-haunted thicket, upon the branches of which are hung the escutcheons of the Knights of the Round Table, all with their proper heraldic charges. The different pieces of tapestry which compose this magnificent set were placed *in situ* severally, as they were finished; the entire work from first to last occupying between three and four years to complete.

In the various specimens of tapestry woven by Messrs. Morris and Co. the same texture is not to be found in every case. Thus, for bold effects a thicker wool was used, which required fewer stitches in a given space, and entailed therefore less work proportionately than the finer specimens. At one time the firm endeavoured to obtain in the coarser tapestries a better finish in the faces, and so on, by introducing in those parts a greater number of warp threads and using a finer wool, but, the result not proving satisfactory, the experiment was not renewed. In some cases, where a richer effect is desired than could be obtained from wool alone, the high lights and other details are worked in with silk. For the Stanmore series, notwithstanding their large scale, a moderately fine web was decided upon, of a uniform texture, *i.e.*, the warp threads sixteen to the inch throughout. Questioned with regard to the latter work by a representative of "The Daily Chronicle," Mr. Morris explained that one of the larger panels, the same that was exhibited at the Arts and Crafts Exhibition in 1893, had taken two years to weave. It was the handiwork of three persons, as many that is as could sit comfortably side by side across the warp. "The people who made it—and this is by far the most interesting thing about it—are boys, at least they are grown up by this time—entirely trained in our own shop. It is really freehand work, remember, not slavishly copying a pattern, like the '*basse lisse*' method; and they came to us with no knowledge of drawing whatever, and have learnt every single thing they know under our training. And most beautifully they have done it! I don't think you could want a better example than this of the value of apprenticeship. Our superintendent, Mr. Dearle, has of course been closely watching the work all the time, and perhaps he has put in a few bits, like the hands and the faces, with his own hands; but with this exception every bit has been done by these boys."

In the case of the tapestry designed by Sir Edward Burne-Jones, it was not that artist's usual custom to supply full-size working cartoons. His original drawings for the Stanmore series are not above fifteen inches high. He prepared these compositions from studies of figures and groups drawn with his wonted care; but, for the rest, there was little else beyond slight colour-tinting to serve as guide in the execution of the work. Such being the condition in which the designs came into Messrs. Morris and Co.'s hands, it was necessary for each of these drawings to be enlarged by photography, in squares varying in size and number according to the full dimensions required. These enlarged sections were then fitted together, and the whole, now of the proper size, submitted, together with a small coloured sketch showing the scheme of colouring proposed by the firm, to the designer for his approval or revision. On these enlargements Burne-Jones confined himself, for the most part, to working up the heads and hands; preferring to leave the ornamental accessories, the patterns of brocades on the draperies, the flowers, &c., to Messrs. Morris and Co., on whose behalf they were generally undertaken by Mr. Dearle, who has been associated with Mr. Morris in the work for many years past. Over and above Mr. Dearle's share in the matter, considerable latitude in the choice and arrangement of tints in shading, &c., was, and is, invariably allowed to the executants themselves, who are, in fact, both by nature and training, artists and no mere animated machines. All three of the tapestry looms at Merton are constructed on the high warp system, that being the method of hand-weaving which Mr. Morris approved, and the only one, therefore, which he cared to revive.

One of the vicissitudes of the firm was a fire which occurred in October, 1877, caused, as it was believed, through the igniting of a beam in the chimney of the hinder part of the house at Queen Square, the result being that the back premises were gutted and much valuable property belonging to the firm destroyed, to say nothing of the dislocation of business or of the disorder and inconvenience unavoidable during the rebuilding. The loss included the stock of linoleum then ready for use and lying stored up in that part of the building which was burnt. No branch of decoration, however humble and commonplace, came amiss to William Morris. He designed and caused to be carried out two patterns for linoleum, that useful form of floor-covering which is commonly not to be obtained except of such fashion that a great many persons are deterred from using it. For is it not next to impossible for anyone of taste to put up with the vicious counterfeits of parquetry, encaustic tiles, mosaic, Chinese matting, Brussels carpet, Berlin wool-work, and such like, which comprise the more part of commercial patterns in oil-cloths, linoleums, &c.? Morris was clearly of that opinion when he undertook to design for this material.

Messrs. Morris and Co.'s furniture was not of William Morris's own design, flat ornament being essentially his *métier*. Long before the business of Morris, Marshall, Faulkner and Co. was started, Madox Brown had been designing furniture, and in that capacity had had the mortification of being refused a place in the exhibitions of the old Hogarth Club, because, forsooth, his designs were not, in the eyes of the committee, to be regarded as "fine art proper." When, however, the firm, largely owing to his instrumentality, had come into existence, both Madox Brown and Rossetti, too, supplied a certain number of designs for furniture. A larger quantity were provided by Mr. Webb; and, still more recently, Mr. George Jack, a pupil of Mr. Webb's, designed furniture for the firm. Morris used to regret the decay of the art of carving at the present day, and the consequent difficulty of obtaining suitable carving for the ornamentation of furniture, &c. However, that of Mr. Jack supplies some admirable examples, while other furniture of the firm is decorated with inlay or painted ornament of good design in a style to harmonize with Morris fabrics. In the early days the cabinet-making and carpentry were carried on in the workshop belonging to the firm in Ormond Yard. Quite lately they purchased the business of Messrs. Holland and Son, in whose former premises all the cabinet-work, &c., on the part of Messrs. Morris and Co. is now executed.

The firm since their foundation have undertaken in whole or in part the furnishing and decorating of a large number of private houses; as, for instance, the Old Swan House at Chelsea and Stanmore Hall, Stanmore, the country residence of Mr. W. K. D'Arcy. The interior of the latter, a very characteristic house, is thus described in "The Studio" of September, 1893: "The interest lies in the applied decoration added to a building seventy years old, which had been remodelled some time since by Mr. Brightwen Binyon. But it is only with the final re-decoration that we are concerned here. In this Messrs. William Morris and Co. have had a free hand, not merely in such matters as usually fall within the scope of decorators, but in the hangings, furniture, and carpets. Hence the work shows a curious instance of one very individual artist fettered by existing features not in themselves remarkable, in a building not ideally adapted to his particular style; but, on the other hand, with control of many matters that do not usually come within the limits of either architect or decorator—particularly the carpets, which, designed specially for the places they occupy, form an extremely important feature in Mr. Morris's scheme of colour. The dining-room, however, was built anew, and in it one feels the larger scope at the artist's disposal has resulted in more complete beauty. Its chimney-piece of solid white marble is . . . of the fashion Mr. Morris employed many years ago in his own house at Bexley Heath." A description has been given above of the series of tapestries designed to represent scenes from the legend of King Arthur, and manufactured by Morris and Co. for the dining-room at Stanmore. "The tables and chairs, the buffet . . . and the dining hatch, deserve special notice, while the carpet is perhaps the most noteworthy item in a splendid room, since it is one of Mr. Morris's most successful designs and large enough to extort admiration on that ground alone. The ceiling, in delicately moulded plaster, also commands attention, and yet keeps its right place. The painted ceilings, both in the entrance hall and staircase, deserve study, not because they are 'hand-painted,' but because of their beautiful forms and dainty colours. The delicate tones, like those of embroidery on old white silk, are in shades of pinks, purples, tender greens, and spring yellows, on a pale creamy ground, the whole bright yet light and with an aërial effect. . . . This lightness of the ceilings and carpets, with the untouched oak of much of the panelling and furniture, gives an air of gaiety . . . most unusual in work of this school. On the walls of the vestibule a delicate pattern in . . . silk and linen, and in the drawing-room a rich warm silk tapestry, unite in preserving the same harmony of sumptuous decoration kept within proper proportion. One has but to compare Stanmore Hall with houses of equally elaborate adornment to feel that in this respect it has no rival. The large ornament and bold forms Mr. Morris delights in, prove their power to blend into a perfect whole, elaborate but in no way overwhelming. The modelled ceiling in the vestibule, and several others in the house, are left in pure low-toned white, so that their rich decoration keeps its place. The staircase, with its solid balustrade of oak inlaid with dark walnut, is an important feature in the central hall."

The firm have appeared before the public in yet another way, to wit, in the capacity of stage decorators, to whom two plays by Mr. Henry Arthur Jones owed their settings more or less. The first was "The Crusaders," which had a run of three months from the beginning of November, 1891, at the Avenue Theatre; the other, "The Case of Rebellious Susan," of which the first performance, under the management of Mr. Charles Wyndham, took place at the Criterion Theatre early in the year 1895, acts 1 and 3 being arranged by Messrs. Morris and Co.

The firm have been represented from time to time at exhibitions of industrial art in the provinces as well as in the metropolis. The several Arts and Crafts Exhibitions that have been held in London and in Manchester, for instance, were supplied with plentiful selections of Messrs. Morris and Co.'s products in the various branches of design and handicraft in which they are engaged. In such ways as this, so far from being close-handed or jealous of exposing his designs too openly, Mr. Morris was well known for his liberality. Quite careless of his own interests in the matter of copyrights, &c., he used freely to send specimens of his wall-papers and textiles to different local schools of art all over the country, until unhappily it was found that unfair advantage of his

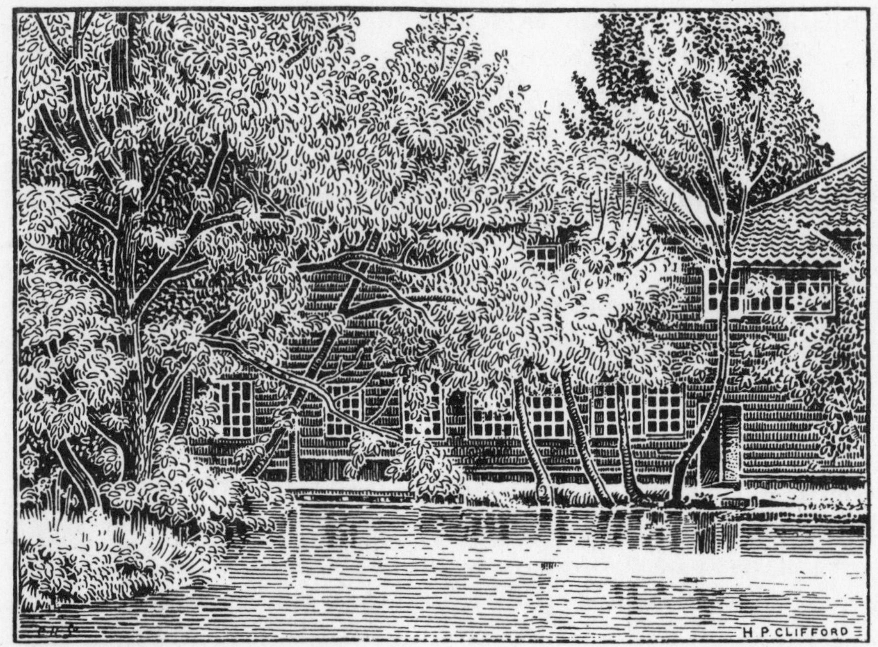

MESSRS. MORRIS & CO.'S WORKS. MERTON ABBEY.

generosity was so often taken that of late years the supplies had to be stopped.

In 1877 Messrs. Morris and Co. took their present premises at 449, Oxford Street, comprising shop-front, show-rooms, offices, &c., but the business still continued to be carried on in part at the old place in Queen Square until the end of 1881, when everything that remained was definitely transferred thence to the Oxford Street house. Meanwhile the firm had acquired the property at Merton, Surrey, and set up their works on the former site of the abbey there, in June, 1881. Morris kept the place in much the same condition in which he found it, with the exception of some slight renovations to the weaving-shed. Since it is often interesting to learn how others see us—how such things strike a foreigner, a short extract on the subject of Morris and Co.'s works from "Passé le Detroit," by M. Gabriel Mourey, may not be amiss here. The French critic gives his impressions thus: "The art workshops of Merton Abbey stand in an immense field amid tall trees and charming scenery. Workshops did I say? It is an ugly word that conjures up visions of grimy smoke, creaking machinery, and bodily toil. No, there is nothing of all that. It is a sort of large farmhouse built on one floor, surrounded by foliage and greenery, close by the bank of a small stream, the Wandle, which winds in and out with happy, joyous murmurs. Such is the workshop of Merton Abbey. Nothing is manufactured there except by hand. No machine-power is used, either steam or electric, but implements of the simplest construction, the most primitive in kind, the old tools, the old handicrafts of four or five centuries ago. The predominant feature is that the artisan is allowed almost perfect liberty of talent and imagination in the development of his work. This is especially the case in the tapestry and glass-work studios, where the most exquisite marvels of art are turned out. The workman takes part in the work, becomes artist, and imparts his own personality to the thing created, of which a rough plan has first been drawn up by the master. The hand-press is used . . . or the velvet and cretonne work is done directly with the hand. Thus is avoided that monotonous stiffness peculiar to the work of modern machinery, and further, it encourages the workman to take a more personal interest in his labour."

On the same subject Mr. Alan S. Cole writes in "The Art Journal" in 1893: "I may be mistaken, but I believe that in this country Mr. Morris stands alone in the variety of intricate hand-woven silks, &c., which he produces. Many are, no doubt, resuscitations of ingenious twelfth-century methods. But for an occasional distant whistle and rumble of trains, a twelfth-century Sicilian weaver might, without sense of anomaly, take his seat in the weaving-shed at Merton, and find himself almost as much at home with the handicrafts pursued there as he was seven hundred years ago with those which engaged him in the palace at Palermo. . . . In Mr. Morris's factory, apparently in contradiction of a modern spirit of specializing and separately pursuing branches of textile manufacture and treatment, are to be found in operation the three technically distinct forms of weaving—namely, tapestry, carpet, and ordinary shuttle weaving. . . . Besides these, there are rooms for dyeing wools and threads used in the looms and frames, a long upper story where cotton and other printing by hand-blocks is done, and store-rooms and offices. Adjoining the irregular group of workshops, and commanding a view of the garden, with its trees, and stream, is a last century house, in which is Mr. Morris's studio, and from which he has easy access to his workrooms. An extra ounce of indigo to strengthen the dye, an additional five minutes' immersion of threads in the vat, a weft of colour to be swept through the warp in a moment of inspiration, a dappling of bright points to lighten some over-sombre hue in the grounding of a carpet, are some of the details in technical and artistic administration constantly receiving the attention of the director of the establishment, who thus secures a standard of artistic production at which the systematized operations of a steam-driven factory have not arrived."

Again, a writer in "The Spectator" of November 24th, 1883, in an article "On the Wandle," describing the Abbey works at Merton, says that to anyone "passing through the gates from the high road, the mill and Wandle present themselves much mixed up together. The river as we saw it was shimmering in the sunlight of a bright November afternoon; little eddies of the stream carried light and glimmer into dark corners, round the many angles of the scattered building. Near its edge the stream is shedded over, to protect some bright-brown wooden pegs, turning on a wheel, through the mysteries of which bright blue stuff is dripping and splashing. . . . Here is none of the ordinary neat pomposity of 'business premises.' . . . We turn through doors into a large, low room, where the hand-made carpets are being worked. It is not crowded. In the middle sits a woman finishing off some completed rugs; in a corner is a large pile of worsted of a magnificent red, heaped becomingly into a deep-coloured straw basket. The room is full of sunlight and colour. The upright frames face you at right angles, with a long row of windows looking close upon the bright-shining river. . . . The strong, level afternoon light shines round the figures of the young girls seated in rows on low benches along the frames, and brightens to gold some of the fair heads. Above and behind them rows of bobbins of many-coloured worsteds, stuck on pegs, shower down threads of beautiful colours, which are caught by the deft fingers, passed through strong threads (fixed uprightly in the frames, to serve as a foundation), tied in a knot, slipped down in their place, snipped even with the rest of the carpet, all in a second of time, by the little maidens. Twenty-five rows does each do in a day,—that means about two inches of carpet. One of the rugs being made is of silk, instead of worsted, very exquisite in quality of surface. . . . It is a delightful workroom. . . . Out again by the Wandle, and across a bridge . . . you pass through a garden; the paths and grass are covered with golden leaves, and the fallen chestnuts roll under your feet, a faded sunflower hangs its head pathetically over the stream. . . . You pass an open door and see men working over vats . . . where the dyeing is done; . . . but we turn into another room, where the hand-looms are working busily, the shuttles flying to and fro between the webs with a speed like lightning. . . . There are many looms, and beautiful-coloured threads are being woven into beautiful materials on every side. Men work the looms; the only women we saw employed at the mill were those working the hand-made carpets. We go on to the rooms where the printing and the stained glass is done. Both are reached by outside wooden staircases. In the glass room we see cartoons by Burne-Jones and by Morris himself in process of being copied. There are many other rooms, for stores, in the old mill. In no part of it does there seem any crowding, either of things or people; the work seems all going on cheerfully and steadily, without hurry." The writer continues: "In the work we have been seeing what a strength there is of individuality, and what an entire absence of commonplace self-importance; what a natural way of doing things, and what a sense of distinction in all that is done! . . . The genius of inventiveness and the love of beauty are the ruling principles, not the making of money. The machinery used in the manufacture is accommodated, made subservient and elastic, to a standard of excellence which has no place at all in the ordinary manufacturer's horizon, but is quite outside and beyond it. If a piece of ordinary machinery can only in part carry out the conception, however easy and inexpensive the use of it would be, it is not used, but something else invented or adapted which shall carry out what is wanted as perfectly as it is possible to carry it out. If a dye is beautiful in colour, but does not give a fast colour, no time is spared in inventing a combination which will make it fast. The ordinary manufacturer, even were he to perceive the beauty of the colour, would see no advantage in overcoming difficulties and incurring expense in order to use it. He would ignore it as practically useless. He could not spare the time or money to try experiments." At Merton, on the other hand, "No time, trouble or money is spared in making the work as perfectly true to the conception as human means can make it. . . . The results are evolved out of individual choice, the means alone adjusting themselves as different requirements present themselves to the mind of the inventor, but the choice is peremptory. . . . Here, at last, we can see some practical outcome of the principles of which Mr. Ruskin is the prominent preacher. Here are examples of what the human machinery can do at its best, heart, head and hand all in their right places relatively to one another. . . . No wonder that the character of this work done on the Wandle has a high distinction in it." . . . It "is uncommon because it is so natural, so indicative of the pure, ungreedy side of human nature, so real as an outcome of individual choice. We may like it or dislike it, but very certain it is that the inventor himself liked it." It is what it is because of its independence of the "belief in any artificial standard of beauty" or correctness ordained by "momentous academies or individuals." It is the honest outcome of "genuine preference," and has unsophisticated nature "at the root of its creation."

It is gratifying to be assured that, if the closing of the Kelmscott Press became, to adopt the cant phrase of the newspapers, "an artistic necessity" on Mr. Morris's death, no such fate threatens or need threaten the business of art decoration. Mr. Morris took measures some years before he died to establish the firm on a secure and independent footing, so that its work might be carried on without break or hindrance in the event of his decease. Moreover, he entrusted it into the hands of his two partners and friends, Messrs. F. and R. Smith, brothers, who have worked with him for close on twenty-five years past, and who, as they enjoyed his confidence during his lifetime, so, now that he is removed, are fully sensible of the responsibility of carrying on his work as he would have wished it to be. And not only have Mr. Dearle, the resident manager at Merton Abbey, and other artists learnt, under Morris's training, to assimilate his style and methods so closely as to be able to produce designs scarcely distinguishable from their master's; but also a considerable number of Morris's original sketches and cartoons that have never yet been carried out, remain in the hands of the firm for future use, as occasion may require. It is understood that Sir Edward Burne-Jones will still supply the firm with designs for their stained glass; a recent order of this kind, and one in fact which has been accepted since Mr. Morris's death, being the west window of St. Philip's, Birmingham.

It is not right to omit to mention here that the firm of Messrs. Morris, Marshall, Faulkner and Co. early took up the art of wood-engraving, although, for the sake of convenience, the treatment of this subject is reserved for another chapter.

It remains but to add a brief account of the constituent elements of Morris's ornamental design and of the leading features which characterize it. And first as to his employment of the primal form, the human figure. Morris's capabilities in this regard, though not known so generally as they deserve to be, were decidedly of a high order, as may be gathered from the beautiful decorations he made for the roof of Jesus College Chapel, and from the not less beautiful cartoons in the possession of Mr. Fairfax Murray. In these figures may be discerned a refined type of features of a character all his own, akin to and yet quite distinct from the type of either Rossetti or Burne-Jones. One cartoon, in colours, represents an angel holding a scroll; the other, in monochrome, six angels in adoration. It is twofold and was designed for wall-painting. One half of it was lent by the owner to the Arts and Crafts Exhibition in 1893. At the same exhibition was shown a small figure-panel of singular charm, drawn for embroidery and carried out in that medium by the designer's daughter, Mrs. Sparling. Next, as regards animal shapes, Morris would seem to have restricted himself principally to dragons, rabbits, and various kinds of birds, such as the peacock, the dove, the thrush, the woodpecker, and the partridge. But it was chiefliest in the adaptation of floral and vegetable forms that he excelled. In this sphere one of Morris's most characteristic types was that "glittering leafage" which, for want of a more accurate name, it is convenient to designate as the Acanthus. "No form of ornament," says Morris, "has gone so far or lasted so long as this; it has been infinitely varied, used by almost all following styles" (*i.e.*, after the Greek) "in one shape or another, and performed many another office besides its original one." So trite and stereotyped indeed had this familiar variety of foliage become that it might have been supposed that its last word, as it were, had long since been said in ornament; its powers of further growth exhausted. On the contrary, however, to such magnificent developments was it brought by Morris's creative genius,—its grand coils of foliage turning and counter-turning this way and that, its serrated edges bent over and back again,—that it seems to have been redeemed and made fertile anew with a splendid vitality, before which open out possibilities wellnigh limitless.

Nor did the associations of his Oxford days fail to impress themselves upon Morris's art. Thus he made frequent use of the fritillary—or snake's-head, as it is popularly called—whose chequered, purplish head is one

of the characteristic sights in the grass-fields by the riverside, particularly at Iffley, where it may be seen nodding in profusion in the late spring. Another favourite form of his was the long and slender spike of the wild tulip, which, as Morris must have been aware, although it is not proved that he ever saw it flowering there in his time, grew in the meadow bordering on the Cherwell, to the south of the Botanical Gardens at Oxford. Or was this rather one of those flowers which he borrowed from Persian ornament? Morris indeed loved best the familiar forms of our English flowers, and most "the queen of them all—the flower of flowers," the rose. This flower is one which "has been grown double," says he, "from I don't know when. The double rose was a gain to the world, a new beauty was given us by it, and nothing taken away, since the wild rose grows in every hedge. Yet even then one might be excused for thinking that the wild rose was scarce improved on, for nothing can be more beautiful in general growth or in detail than a wayside bush of it, nor can any scent be as sweet and pure as its scent. Nevertheless the garden rose had a new beauty of abundant form, while its leaves had not lost the wonderfully delicate texture of the wild one. The full colour it had gained, from the blush rose to the damask, was pure and true amidst all its added force, and though its scent had certainly lost some of the sweetness of the eglantine, it was fresh still, as well as so abundantly rich." On the whole, however, Morris's counsel—which he followed himself—was: "Be very shy of double flowers; choose the old columbine where the clustering doves are unmistakable and distinct, not the double one, where they run into mere tatters. Choose . . . the old china-aster with the yellow centre, that goes so well with the purple-brown stems and curiously coloured florets, instead of the lumps that look like cut paper, of which we are now so proud. Don't be swindled out of that wonder of beauty, a single snowdrop; there is no gain and plenty of loss in the double one. More loss still in the double sunflower, which is a coarse-coloured and dull plant, whereas the single one, though a

late comer to our gardens, is by no means to be despised, since it will grow anywhere, and is both interesting and beautiful, with its sharply chiselled yellow florets relieved by the quaintly patterned sad-coloured centre clogged with honey and beset with bees and butterflies." Though this advice of Morris's for avoiding "over-artificiality in flowers" is given, as a matter of fact, with a view to the selecting of plants for a garden, it nevertheless applies to the choice of flowers in ornament as well. "Many plants," there are, in his opinion, "which are curiosities only, which Nature meant to be grotesque, not beautiful, and which are generally the growth of hot countries, where things sprout over quick and rank. Take note that the strangest of these come from the jungle and the tropical waste, from places where man is not at home but is an intruder, an enemy. . . . But there are some flowers (inventions of men, *i.e.*, florists) which are bad colour altogether, and not to be used at all. Scarlet geraniums, for instance, or the yellow calceolaria, which are indeed not uncommonly grown together profusely, in order, I suppose, to show that even flowers can be thoroughly ugly." Such forms then one need not look to find in Morris's designs. But the flowers one does recognize therein, besides those already enumerated, are the peony and poppy, the honeysuckle, carnation and iris, larkspur and anemone, the daisy and the marigold. These were the mainsprings of Morris's inspiration. And it is this he intended to convey when he said that ornament should have a meaning, should express something, viz., that it ought to give the impression of having been founded upon some object in actual existence, instead of being, like most of the "ornament" of the Louis XIV., XV., and XVI. periods, a mere shapeless and senseless elaboration of nothing at all. At the same time Morris's decorative work is as far as possible from being didactic. He never used it as the vehicle for the expression of a lesson or theory; never set himself to preach or to expound through the medium of ornament, as some do. His is the very type of æsthetic design. "He was too true an artist to

follow art into its byways of moral significance and thereby cripple its broader arms." This was Hall Caine's account of Rossetti; but the words might apply with even greater truth to William Morris. No bogey of the pulpit or of the platform lurks within the folds of his velvets; no homily is to be discovered in the colours of his chintzes; no allegory latent in the lines of his wall-papers. Their charm is just what it appears to the eye to be: there is nothing else concealed beneath their surface. One may enjoy the beauty of them, and one may revel in it to one's heart's content with the confident assurance that the designer is not the man to take a mean advantage of one's being absorbed in admiration for the purpose of cozening one, as a reluctant child is cozened, into swallowing a stealthy pill enfolded in a delicious wrapping of sweet-stuff. Artless as a child himself, Morris was in absolute sympathy with, and shared, the child's view of the case. And since few things are more distasteful to anybody than to be edified *malgré lui*, Morris does not attempt to do so surreptitiously. But when, on the other hand, he has a message to deliver, as for instance in his Socialistic writings, he states the matter plainly and straightforwardly, in terms, at times, outspoken even to bluntness. There is no fine writing then, nor any precious periods nor phrases to dazzle and captivate the senses.

With Morris, then, art and literature were kept quite distinct; their functions never confounded by him. He was too whole-hearted in his devotion to both to impair the integrity of either by making it subservient to the other or dependent upon that other for support. Indeed in his case neither had need to be supplemented by the other; nor to derive any powers of fascination from without, but held to its own perfection in either sphere untrammelled. Quotations from prose and poetry may have to be tacked on to the Academy picture so as to pander to the taste of a public incapable of feeling any appreciable joy in beauty for its own sake; of enthusiasm for anything but what embodies a sentiment or has a story belonging to it. But it was otherwise with Morris's work. Take, for example, the verses he wove into his tapestries. The lettering of the words, the folds of the ribands on which they were inscribed, both alike being carefully considered and integral parts of the design, are pure ornament—no less than that and no more. The only Morris pattern that can be said to have even a remote connection with literature is the "Brother Rabbits" cretonne; and that merely by way of a reminiscence of the amusement afforded by the foibles of "Brer Rabbit" in Joel Chandler Harris's "Uncle Remus." The design does not attempt of course to illustrate the book. For practical convenience, to avoid confusion in the ordinary course of business, it was indispensable for Morris's numerous designs to be distinguished each by a different name. But as often as not the title was purely arbitrary and had little or no connection with the particular pattern in point. Thus a list of names was taken from the tributaries of the Thames, but these names, it is needless to say, made no pretence to be suggestive of the subject-matter of the designs by which they were borne respectively.

The correlation of the arts is a subject upon which, of late years, a great deal has been said and written. The principle is one which is supposed to dominate the æsthetic school above all others; yet one hears little enough of its perilous tendencies, or of how conspicuously and how successfully Morris escaped them; or how again and again he insisted that it was wrong for anything to be expressed in the terms of one art which would have been expressed better in the terms of another. The process leads invariably to a nondescript product, that, by whichsoever standard it be measured, fails to come up to the proper requirements. One has heard much talk of "painter-poets," "musician-painters," and recently even of "poet-upholsterers"—titles for which there is about as much warrant as for that of "Cardinal-Archbishop." One has heard tell also of "painted poems," "painted allegories," "sculptured poems," and, even worse hybrids, of different "colour-symphonies," "nocturnes," "variations," "harmonies," "scherzos," and more nonsense and to spare of the like sort. Morris could not away with any of these eccentric methods of "making enemies"—which, being interpreted, is, of course, advertising oneself; nor indeed would his straightforward principles have allowed him to stoop to such artifices, to prostitute his art in such wise. In a word, his designs owe their attractiveness to no adventitious charm of association or issue outside themselves, but stand supreme, resting their claim to homage on nothing else but their own inherent merits, their æsthetic qualities of form and colour combined with their appropriateness for the purpose for which they are intended to be used. And so Morris called himself only "an ornamentalist, a maker of would-be pretty things"!

As in the realm of poetry William Morris made good his claim to be the representative of Chaucer and of Spenser; so, in the genealogy of art, none has so indisputable a title as he to be the lineal descendant of the Gothic artists. There is not the slightest taint of the Renaissance or of Japanese influence in his work—in which respect, indeed, his position is remarkable and almost unique among the designers of modern times. Withal there may be traced in him a certain strain of Persian and of Byzantine origin. In the blending of these several elements, now one, now another being present in greater proportion than the rest, might give a certain complexion to any given design; but above all else the strong individuality of William Morris himself always prevailed, making all his decoration of one perfectly sustained and consistent style; and such that no one having the most superficial acquaintance with ornamental design could mistake Morris's for anybody else's work. However, it was not vouchsafed him to be spared the usual fate which a master of style must suffer at the hands of those less gifted than himself. "His power is proved,"—to quote once more from a writer in "The Spectator," whose views on this very point happen to be in direct antagonism to those of Mr. Robert Buchanan,—"by his many imitators. Nearly all the better kind of designs in the shops are, as far as they are good, cribs from Morris, just altered sufficiently 'to prevent unpleasant-

T

ness.' His willow-pattern paper is taken very boldly, stamped upon a carpet, and a trellis of little squares added by the accommodator. Even Paris taste, that mixture of fantastic extravagance, persistence in mediocrity, and industrious finish of detail, took up the style of Morris colours some years ago, and flavoured it with the usual touch of French morbid cynicism by calling the colours '*teints dégradés*.'" What an inversion of the order of things! And how quickly must the memory of the beautiful old colours (the only colours known and used until the lurid discoveries of Perkins blinded men's eyes with the glare and vulgarity of coal-tar) have faded from the mental vision of French folk, how utterly become obliterated, if the same colours when presented once more to them, not a quarter of a century afterwards, could strike them only as being some novel form of corruption! It is quite a mistake to imagine that Morris either had himself introduced or approved of the introduction of the dull and gloomy colours in the popular estimate associated with the art movement. In one of the addresses included in "Hopes and Fears for Art" Morris, though not denying that crudeness of colouring is a possible danger, warned his audience in most emphatic terms against "getting . . . colour dingy and muddy, a worse fault than the other because less likely to be curable. All right-minded craftsmen who work in colour," he continues, "will strive to make their work as bright as possible, as full of colour as the nature of the work will allow it to be." And again he says: "Do not fall into the trap of a dingy, bilious-looking yellow-green, a colour to which I have a special and personal hatred, because (if you will excuse my mentioning personal matters) I have been supposed to have somewhat brought it into vogue. I assure you I am not really responsible for it."

"I am an artist," wrote Morris, "or workman, with a strong inclination to exercise what capacities I may have, and a determination to do nothing shabby if I can help it." Now one of the worst forms of shabbiness in Morris's eyes, was plagiarism, which he abhorred for artistic no less than for ethical reasons. "Everyone ought to do his own work," was the maxim by which he was guided himself and would have others guided, because he knew, only too well, the paralysing and destructive effects exercised on the faculty of invention by indolent and disingenuous copyism. This, then, is what he says on the duty of exerting one's own originality in decorative design: "Your convention must be your own, and not borrowed from other times and peoples; or at the least you must make it your own by thoroughly understanding both the nature and the art you are dealing with. If you do not heed this, I do not know but what you may not as well turn to and draw laborious portraits of natural forms of flower and bird and beast, and stick them on your walls anyhow. It is true you will not get ornament so, but you may learn something for your trouble; whereas, using an obviously true principle as a stalking-horse for laziness of purpose and lack of invention will but injure art all round, and blind people to the truth of that very principle."

In his evidence before the Royal Commission on Technical Education in 1882, after stating that the business he carried on comprised weaving, dyeing, cotton printing, carpet weaving, glass painting and cabinet making, Morris said: "I make mostly my own designs; I do not employ designers because, amongst other reasons, it is so very difficult to get a due amount of originality out of them; the designs which one gets are too hackneyed, and there is the same sort of idea harped upon for ever and ever. Mine is quite a peculiar trade." And, in reply to the question: "Your forte is originality?" he answered in the affirmative. "It is necessary for our business merely as a commercial affair. I need not say it is desirable in everything in which one applies design to the industrial arts." The vast amount of original design produced by Morris is almost incredible. If "great genius means," as Mr. Marion Crawford says it does, "great and constant creative power before all things;" if "it means wealth of resource and invention; . . . quantity as well as quality," then William Morris was surely a genius of greatness preeminent. It would be difficult for anyone who had not been admitted, as it were, behind the scenes at Messrs. Morris and Co.'s, nor been shown the mass of sketch-designs and cartoons prepared by William Morris's own hand for execution in various mediums; or for anyone who had not been in the habit of calling at his house and finding him, as was his wont, at work or, if resting for a few minutes, with the ink or the colour scarcely dried upon the paper before him; it would be difficult for such an one to comprehend the prodigious industry of the man. It was simply astounding. Indeed he is not exaggerating when he says, in one of his lectures, that having once tried to think what would happen to him if he were forbidden his ordinary daily work, he knew that he should die of despair and weariness, unless he could straightway take to something else which he could make his daily work; and that the reason clearly was because he loved the work itself; nay, even mechanical work was pleasant to him, provided that it were not too mechanical. Thus he who, while insisting on the universal duty of work, yet would have had labour press unduly on no man, was unsparing of himself. The precepts Morris enjoined on others were in his own case no empty formulas. If any man ever practised to the letter what he preached, it was William Morris, who set an example of untiring activity and application that might well put other people to shame. Never was a more busy, a more conscientious worker than he. Thoroughness was one of his most prominent qualities. Nothing was allowed by him to be done hurriedly or carelessly; nothing left in an unfinished state that could be finished; nothing passed as satisfactory until it had been brought as near as human hands could avail to bring it, to that ideal standard he had conceived of it in his own mind. Formerly he used even to set out with his own hands and square up his designs for tapestry and carpet weaving. But, careful as he was in the preparation of his patterns beforehand, once they were executed, the originals in his eyes were of no further use. In short, he regarded them as so many tools, as means merely to an end, which end attained in the concrete form of the manufactured article, the *raison d'être* of the design had ceased for him. He used readily to part with, in exchange for books or anything else which he happened for the moment to want, original and unique drawings of his own which one would have supposed of almost priceless worth.

It may be permitted to borrow once more from M. Mourey on the subject of Morris's share in the revival of the industrial arts of this country. Morris, says the French writer, "is especially keen on the art of the Middle Ages, the complex and fertile depths of which he has penetrated with wonderful acuteness, even to restoring it in all its beauty. And it is through those unknown workers who have by their labours and the fruits of their imagination profusely adorned not only cathedral stones but the most trifling objects, that William Morris has been able to bring about this Restoration of Decorative Art of which he himself is the originator and master. He is indeed an earnest worker who has sounded the older methods and early formulas, and has attempted and realized all with wonderful breadth and originality. . . . Now this imagination, this power to create, this rare gift of transforming one's subject into seductive harmony of form, happy combination of lines, enchanting rhythms of colour, or developing it by unexpected deductions, enriching it with one's fancy until it blossoms forth in beauty, melancholy, or merely fresh and simple tones—what other worker in decorative art possesses to such a degree as he? But apart from his innate gift, the tools employed are well known: earnest, attentive and sincere study of nature; thorough and well-grounded knowledge of past epochs instead of that servile imitation with which we content ourselves; and above all —what so often proves a true stumbling-block in decorative art—scrupulous heed that the caprices of invention, colour and form shall be in perfect accord with the requirements of the material."

"And his influence? To give a fair answer to this question one must have lived an English life. It has indeed been deep, restorative, transforming the outward and decorative side of life, adorning the home with the pleasures of art—and we all know how full of significance that word *home* is. We meet with the fertile results of his mind on all sides. . . . It is a real style he has created, a style which owes its origin to that perfect, clear and expressive style of the Middle Ages, which alone is capable of providing the nineteenth century with material and ideas suitable to it, which passes by Japanese and Persian art to develop in the original, fruitful imagination and temperament of the northern."

A writer in "The Edinburgh Review," speaking of Morris's wide-spread influence in art decoration, says: "Even in the ordinary work exposed for sale in furniture shops the effect of the change is manifest; tradesmen . . . have been compelled to do their best to follow the change in public demand. And this improvement in household taste is the direct work of Morris more than of anyone else. He set the example of designing furniture in accordance with the requirements and expression of structure (in which respect furniture properly follows much the same principles as architecture); of considering harmony of colour in the carpets, papering, and other decorations of a room; of treating designs based on natural foliage on true decorative principles, conventionalizing the forms employed, and teaching the public the importance of beauty of line and of preserving the balance and spacing of decorative detail. . . . Morris's perceptions in this class of work were not based on any mere dilettante preferences. They were the result of a close and unremitting study of the subject. It is said by those who knew him well that no man had such a thorough and exhaustive knowledge of the technical processes of old work, so far as we now have the means of knowing them. Design in all the decorative arts is, or should be, based upon or largely influenced by technique; it was the perception of this, and the knowledge of the technical requirements and possibilities in connection with each class of material, which led him to the right path in the treatment of design."

Mr. Herbert Horne, in "The Saturday Review," rightly

said of Morris that "in his genius for fine craftsmanship he was alone; a unique figure of our time." He then points out the beneficial influence of a cultured age like the fifteenth century, and how such an influence "is nowhere shown to more evident advantage than in the production of those goods and fabrics which are intended for the uses of daily life, but into which the element of beauty enters in some degree or another; the craft of cabinet making, for example," or "the weaving of figured textiles;" and he contrasts that desirable state of things with the present. "In an age like our own, when the sphere of the practical utilities of life is wholly divorced from the sphere of art, this element of beauty is apt to be mistaken, or lost sight of, by those who practise these crafts, and an indifference to produce beautifully is soon followed by an indifference to produce well. It is here precisely that the conditions of good craftsmanship assert themselves; reminding us that the craftsman is neither wholly concerned with mere utility on the one hand, nor with mere beauty on the other; but that his productions must be fitted to the uses for which they are intended; that they must be well made; and that they must be made with a due sense of beauty. For us, the tradition of such craftsmanship has long been broken; and, to recover it, the craftsman is forced to revert to methods which have been lost or forgotten, to the productions of some other age than our own. In this attempt Morris went beyond anyone of his time. The success, for example, with which he revived the older and simpler methods of the dyer's art, and the use of vegetable dyes, has contributed not a little to the beauty of his tapestries, his silks, and his other textile and printed fabrics. His painted glass, his decorative paintings and furniture . . . all show the fine instinct with which he returned to sound principles of good craftsmanship, employing only the simplest and best of materials." "He has done much," says another writer, "to rehabilitate the pride in workmanship that was at one time a characteristic of English workmen, but which of late years, under the influence of commercialism," and other causes, "we are said to have lost."

Enough has now been said to show that William Morris was no mere dabbler but a specialist in the arts; how that he grappled with the technical difficulties—aye, and the commercial difficulties, too—of one handicraft after another; how that, once having taken up any particular branch of industry, he never let it go until he had made himself an expert in all the intricacies of it; and how, while handling it as any practical man of business might do, over and above all that, he dignified it through the riches of his own transcendent imagination, bringing it into accord with his own refined sense of beauty. It is thus impossible to over-estimate the influence of William Morris in the improvement of household taste. When he "began his crusade against ugliness and bad work, the art of house decoration," says a writer in "The Standard," "was at its lowest ebb," and "there was little produced which was not positively repulsive both in execution and design." But, thanks to Morris, the remedy for so deplorable a state of things is with us. In the establishment of the decorative firm which bears his name he provided the public with both an illustration of his teaching and also a practical means of putting it into effect in their own surroundings. How great a multitude of houses he has thus directly or indirectly beautified none can tell—it is indeed incalculable. "Plain painting," says Mr. Walter Crane, has "displaced graining and marbling; frankly but freely conventionalized patterns" have "routed the imitative and nosegay kinds. Leaded and stained glass" have "filled the places which were wont to be filled with the blank despair of the ground kind. The white marble mantelpiece" has "turned pale before rich hangings and deep-toned wall-papers, and" has been "dismantled and sent to the churchyard. These" are "some of the most marked effects of the adoption of the new, or a return to older and sounder ideas in domestic decoration." In short, as Mr. Harry Quilter says, the artistic reform achieved by William Morris is such that "has changed the look of half the houses in London, and substituted art for ugliness all over the kingdom."

CHAPTER SIX: MORE POETRY.

THAT Morris's poetry subsequent to "The Defence of Guenevere," dealt no more with any incident from the Arthurian cycle is a point to be noted. Of that book itself the concluding and larger portion is devoted to such subjects as are recorded in the pages of mediæval chroniclers, of whom Froissart stands for representative, instead of that remoter age of myth and legend to which King Arthur belongs. That Morris ever wavered in his allegiance to Malory is too much to assert. However, if he was yet in any sort of doubt as to his choice of subjects after "The Defence of Guenevere," he made up his mind, on the appearance of the first instalment of Tennyson's "Idylls" in the following year, to occupy other ground thenceforward. But that "The Defence of Guenevere" would be followed next in order of publication by "The Life and Death of Jason," readers of the former work might possibly not have foreseen. Between Morris's lays of chivalry and his epic of classical theme there was indeed no very obvious connection. From Guenevere to Medea; from the "Quest of the Holy Grail" to the "Quest of the Golden Fleece," the way back might well be regarded as long and over long. But Morris, like every mediæval student and lover of romance, could not fail, sooner or later, to find himself in spirit with Caxton, with Memling, and with the actors in Scott's "Quentin Durward" and "Anne of Geierstein," amid the magnificence of the Court of Burgundy, where Gothic arts and Gothic manners were brought to fullest development. Thence with the ducal founder of the illustrious order of knighthood, second to one only, that of the Garter to wit, in all Christendom, he would be transported by a perfectly historical train of thought, across the gulf of intervening centuries to antique Colchis and the mythic Argonauts. One may take it, in short, that Morris's rendering of the theme is just such as would have presented itself to the mind of the Duke of Burgundy and his contemporaries. The Flemish tapestries of the period furnish the best possible commentary upon this kind of conception of classic story; and it would be in entire accord if Morris's

"Life and Death of Jason" could be illustrated by a similar series of arras panels to those which (formerly belonging to Lausanne Cathedral, and now in the Museum at Berne) represent the histories of Julius Cæsar and of Trajan, or the piece of arras from the Chevalier Bayard's Château near Grenoble, now at South Kensington, representing "A Scene from the Siege of Troy."

"The Life and Death of Jason," in seventeen books, appeared in 1867. It is of epic proportions, being, in fact, "one of the longest narrative poems in the language." The body of the work is composed in rhymed heroic measure, the monotony of which is relieved by the occasional introduction of lyrical songs in octosyllabic metre. It is to be noted here, as Mr. Saintsbury remarks, that "Mr. Morris did to the heroic couplet what Milton and Wordsworth did to blank verse. He broke it up, changed its centres of gravity, subjected it to endless varieties of *enjambement*, or overlapping. It was his main care to end a paragraph, to begin a speech, in the middle of a couplet or line," "after the fashion set by Keats," as another writer points out. This plan of not winding up, but carrying the flow of the verse on and on, from one paragraph over to the next, is peculiarly suited to the structure of poetry of mediæval type such as this. It soothes the senses like the untiring, melodious drone of plain-chant, which herein seems (unlike the secular "church-music" of modern composers) to partake of the never-ceasing song of celestial choirs.

The differences between the "Jason" and the "Guenevere" are in some respects more pronounced than the differences between the latter and "The Earthly Paradise," parts of which coincide in point of time more nearly with "The Defence of Guenevere" than the "Life and Death of Jason" does. By comparison with Morris's "Guenevere," as portrayed both in "The Defence" and in "King Arthur's Tomb," his Medea is almost a piece of marble statuary. Even where her vengeance culminates in the destruction of her rival and in the murder of her own children with her own hands, Medea does not attain to that tragic intensity displayed, for instance, in "The Haystack in the Floods." The unmitigated savagery of the latter, when the Lady Jehane is torn from the arms of her lover and his head beaten to pieces at her very feet as she is in the act of straining forward for one last kiss of his lips; the depths of dogged despair with which she resigns herself to the awful ordeal of fire or water sooner than yield herself to the man she loathes, have no parallel in "The Life and Death of Jason." The stream of Morris's verse no longer seethes with passion, nor forces its turbid way about boulders obstructing its passage, but flows evenly now through smooth channels, iris-fringed, amid flowery meads interspersed with quiet homesteads. Withal the air is not charged with the fiery heat of noonday, but there is diffused over everything, so to speak, a softer, tenderer light, resembling more the subdued glow of afternoon. The very din of battle has a far-away sound that scarcely tends to disturb the prevailing serene sense of repose. This calm, however, is not that which betokens loss of vital energy or power, but rather peace and victory achieved through striving, and at the end of strife.

Notwithstanding that the plot of the story, in its episodes as well as in its main outline, differs but little from the genuine classical one, the setting of the various tableaux is as far removed as possible from any scenes depicted on Greek vases as it is also from the ancient sculptured imagery of frieze or pediment. The whole environment of "The Life and Death of Jason," as told by William Morris, is taken, of all bygone epochs in the world's history, from some one more nearly Gothic than any other. The flavour and glamour of old-world romance clings to the associations conjured up, times and again, by the occurrence of such mediæval words as "aumbrye" and "sere-cloth," "dais" and "vane," "pleasance," "close," "undercroft" and "cloister," while the characters that figure in the shifting panorama of the tale pass by with rhythmic tread as in some stately pageant, surrounded by an atmosphere now sweet with the fragrance of swinging censers, now resonant with the lilt of carols and the silvery peal of bells. To have chosen a subject purely classical and to have given it thus a treatment altogether romantic was a project venturesome even to temerity, but Morris succeeded to the extent that, instead of seeming to do violence against fact and archæology, he made it assume the air of being quite plausible and consistent. If Mr. Lang is correct in supposing that "it was natural in Morris to 'envisage' the Greek heroic age in this way," it is equally certain that "it would not be natural in most other writers." In this new and enchanting fashion of telling a story in verse it was impossible to fail to recognize the rare faculty of a master-poet. "It was all more or less exquisite," says Mr. Saintsbury; "it was all more or less novel." With its honeyed cadence it exercises a spell and fascination like that of some strange, languorous vision.

A special witchery is, of course, intended in the beautiful chant wherewith the nymph beguiles Hylas to his undoing. This song, beginning,

> "I know a little garden close,
> Set thick with lily and red rose,"

is one which Morris himself prized highly; for, lest it should lie buried in the larger work, he resuscitated it purposely under the title of "A Garden by the Sea" in "Poems by the Way." Again, there is Medea's incantation song, by means of which she bewitches into harmlessness the monster that guards the Golden Fleece. Of all the songs in the book the longest, falling, as it does, not far short of 300 lines, is that in antiphonal verses in which the Sirens try to wile Jason's crew, and Orpheus responds with counsels of prudence. The other lyrics in "Jason" are Orpheus's song in Book IV., "O bitter sea, tumultuous sea," &c.; another, in which he encourages the crew of the Argosy, in Book IX.; one, where he sings a marvellous retrospective ode in praise of Saturn's days, in Book X.; and an Epicurean song addressed to Death, in Book XII. Lastly, there is the song of the Hesperides in Book XIV.

Musical language and graphic, while it is at the same time vividly concise—a feature noticed already in "The

Defence of Guenevere"—is no less a marked characteristic of "The Life and Death of Jason;" as, for example:

> "Dusk grows the world, and day is weary-faced;"

or where Medea warns Jason of the terrible consequences awaiting herself in the event of the failure of their enterprise, as follows:

> "But what thing will be left to me but fire?
> The fire of fierce despair within my heart.
> * * * *
> * * And in no long space
> Real fire of pine-wood in some rocky place
> Wreathing about my body greedily,
> A dreadful beacon o'er the leaden sea."

In this:

> "Already did a bright fire glare
> And made the hot air glassy with its heat;"

or in this picture of

> "The slim-leaved, thorny pomegranate,
> That flung its unstrung rubies on the grass;"

or where, a few lines lower down, the description of the Garden of the Hesperides is continued:

> "Nor was there lacking many a living thing
> Changed of its nature; for the roebuck there
> Walked fearless with the tiger; and the bear
> Rolled sleepily upon the fruit-strewn grass
> Letting the conies o'er his rough hide pass,
> With blinking eyes, that meant no treachery.
> Careless the partridge passed the red fox by;
> Untouched the serpent left the thrushes brown,
> And as a picture was the lion's frown."

Or in this, which contains a striking alliteration:

> "And therewithal must I dread many a hand
> And writhe beneath the whistle of the whip;"

or, once again:

> "Darksome night is well-nigh done,
> And earth is waiting silent for the sun."

The poem derives a peculiar charm from the gracefully balanced phrasing of antithesis, of which a few instances only must suffice:

> " And shall we find the worst, who sought the best ? "

or again :

> " And so began short love and long decay,
> Sorrow that bides, and joy that fleets away ; "

or this, where Medea bids Jason

> " Either die a man or live a king ; "

or this :

> " Haste, for the night
> Is young no more, and danger comes with light ; "

or again :

> " Therefore she knows
> Why this thing perishes, and that thing grows ; "

or the conclusion of the following passage :

> " O thou fearful one,
> Who knowest all my life, who in the breath
> Wherein thou prayest help still threatenest death."

Of longer passages it is impossible to forbear to quote from the description of the starting of the Argonauts on their quest :

> " 'Twixt the thronging people solemnly
> The heroes went afoot. * * *
> * * * * *
> And as they went the roses rained on them
> From windows glorious with the well-wrought hem
> Of many a purple cloth ; and all their spears
> Were twined with blossoms that the fair earth bears ;
> And round their ladies' token-gifts were set
> About their helmets, flowery wreaths, still wet
> With beaded dew of the scarce vanished night.
> * * * * *
> Nor could the heroes leave their fathers' home
> Unwept of damsels, who henceforth must hold
> The empty air unto their bosoms cold,

And make their sweet complainings to the night
That heedeth not soft eyes and bosoms white.

* * * * *

But on they went, and as the way they trod
His swelling heart nigh made each man a god;
While clashed their armour to the minstrelsy
That went before them to the doubtful sea.

* * * * *

Faster they strode and faster, till a cry
Again burst from them, and right eagerly
Into swift running did they break at last,
Till all the wind-swept quay being overpast,
They pressed across the gangway, and filled up
The hollow ship as wine a golden cup."

Fine as is the above, it cannot come up to another passage, the account of the sowing of the dragon's teeth and the brood that sprang from them. The episode is one which might easily have been merely grotesque, whereas, with his masterly treatment, Morris succeeds in making it appear as though it were being really enacted before the mind's eye:

"Then Jason took the sack, and with it went
About that field new turned, and broadcast sent
The white teeth scattering, but or ere he came
Back to the altar and the flickering flame,
He heard from 'neath the earth a muttered sound
That grew and grew, till all that piece of ground
Swelled into little hillocks, like as where
A stricken field was foughten, but that there
Quiet the heroes' bones lie underneath
The quivering grasses and the dusky heath;
But now these heaps which labouring earth upthrew
About Mars' acre ever greater grew,
And still increased the noise, till none could hear
His fellow speak; and Jason only stood
As stands the stout oak in the poplar wood
When winds are blowing. Then he saw the mounds
Bursten asunder, and the muttered sounds
Changed into loud strange shouts and warlike clang,
As with freed feet at last the earth-born sprang
On to the trembling earth, and day and light
Shone on bright arms clean ready for the fight."

The account of the slaying is concluded as follows:

"So satiate of the fight
Quickly the earth-born were, and their delight
With what it fed on perished, and one hour
Ripened the deadly fruit of that fell flower."

"The Life and Death of Jason," it has been observed, showed that the poet "had left the shadows of ballad minstrelsy and entered the pleasant sunlight of Chaucer." It "was a surprise, and was welcomed as the sustained performance of a true poet"—sustained, indeed, through upwards of ten thousand lines. No wonder, then, that it "took by storm that portion of the public which has scholarship as well as taste." The work evoked a prompt and generous tribute from Morris's brother-poet Swinburne, who, in "The Fortnightly Review" of July, 1867, after a brief reference to "The Defence of Guenevere," went on to say: "The shortcomings of this first book are nowhere traceable in the second now lying before us. A nine years' space does not lie between them in vain; enough has been learned and unlearned, rejected and attained. . . . This 'Jason' is a large and coherent poem, completed as conceived; the style throughout on a level with the invention. In direct narrative power, in clear forthright manner of procedure, not seemingly troubled to select, to pick and sift and winnow, yet never superfluous or verbose, never straggling or jarring; in these high qualities it resembles the work of Chaucer. . . . In all the noble roll of our poets there has been since Chaucer no second teller of tales, no second rhapsode comparable to the first, till the advent of this one. . . . No higher school has brought forth rarer poets than this. . . . Here is a poem sown of itself, sprung from no alien seed, cut after no alien model; fresh as wind, bright as light, full of the spring and the sun. It shares, of course, the conditions of its kind; it has no time for the subtleties, and hardly time for the ardours of tragic poetry. Passion in romance is of its nature subordinate to action. . . . Only by rare and brief jets does the poet let out the fire of a potent passion which not many others can kindle and direct. For the most part the river of romance flows on at full, but keeping well to its channel, unvexed by rains and undisturbed by whirlpools. . . . The descriptive and decorative beauties of this romance of 'Jason' are excellent above all in this, that, numberless though they be, they are always just and fit.

Not a tone of colour, not a note of form, is misplaced or dispensable. The pictures are clear and chaste, sweet and lucid as early Italian work. There are crowds and processions, battle-pieces and merry-makings, worthy of Benozzo or Carpaccio. Single figures or groups of lovers in flowery watery land, worthy of Sandro or Philippo. The sea-pieces are like the younger Lippi's. . . . They do not taste salt or sound wide; but they have all the beauty of the beach. . . . But the root of the romance lies, of course, in the character of Medea; and here, where it was needfullest to do well, the poet has done best. At her first entrance the poem takes new life and rises out of the atmosphere of mere adventure and incident. . . . Her incantations and her flight with Jason have no less of fanciful and tender power. The fifteenth book, where she beguiles Pelias to death at the hands of his daughters, is a sample of flawless verse and noble imagination unsurpassed by any here. For dramatic invention and vivid realism of the impossible, which turns to fair and sensible truth the wildest dreams of legend, there has been no poet for centuries comparable. But the very flower and crest of this noble poem is the final tragedy at Corinth. Queen, sorceress, saviour, she has shrunk or risen to mere woman; and not in vain before entering the tragic lists has the poet called on that great poet's memory who has dealt with the terrible and pitiful passion of women like none but Shakespeare since. . . . Rarely but in the ballad and romance periods has such poetry been written, so broad and sad and simple, so full of deep and direct fire, certain of its aim, without finish, without fault. . . . The workman . . . has here approved himself a master, acceptable into the guild of great poets, on a footing of his own to be shared or disputed by no other."

Mr. Pater draws particular attention to certain aspects of the "Jason" already mentioned, viz., its "mediævalisms, delicate inconsistencies, which, coming in a poem of Greek subject, bring into this white dawn thoughts of the delirious night just over, and make one's sense of relief deeper. The opening of the fourth book of 'Jason' describes the embarkation of the Argonauts. As in a dream the scene shifts, and we go down from Iolchos to the sea through a pageant of the Middle Age in some French or Italian town. The gilded vanes on the spires, the bells ringing in the towers, the trellis of roses at the window of the close planted with apple trees, the grotesque undercroft with its close-set pillars, change by a single touch the air of these Greek cities, and we are in Glastonbury, by the tomb of Arthur. The nymph, in furred raiment, who seduces Hylas, is conceived frankly in the spirit of Teutonic romance; her song is of a garden inclosed, such as that with which the old church glass-stainer surrounds the mystic bride of the Song of Songs. Medea herself has a hundred touches of the mediæval sorceress."

"The advent of a new poet," says Mr. Hewlett, "characterized by an unconsciousness like that of the ancient rhapsodists, and avowedly the disciple of the first English poet who most nearly resembled them, yet able to adapt his themes and his language to the demands of modern taste, was sure . . . of a hearty welcome if only on the score of novelty. On the appearance of Mr. Morris's 'Jason' he was hailed in almost every quarter as a poet who fulfilled these conditions; and the poem has deservedly taken rank among the purest of modern classics." The same writer reckons among the "salient beauties" of this poem "vivid clearness of description, choice simplicity of diction, ordered tunefulness of measure."

"In this almost entirely open-air poem," says Mr. Buxton Forman, "we follow Jason and his companions about over the world with a full, fresh, delicious sense of space and health and beauty; and we never have to think of these men as mean or low by reason of their creed or actions: they are simply big-souled adventurers, not to be daunted in their search for what the world yields of great and desirable. Mr. Morris is never more at home than when he is out of doors. He seems to revel in nature; and, full as his head must be of old lore, it is difficult to imagine when and where he has found time to acquire it, except by fits and starts in open-air ramblings, for not an elemental trait escapes him when he gets into his landscape vein. Far too fresh are his leafy, woody, airy, sunny scenes to be conceivably the result of a second-hand study; they bear the impress of nature directly on them. . . . The poet who wrote the description of a storm in the first book of 'Jason' . . . must have studied out in the broad air, and deep in the woods, and down on the river beds, . . . open-eyed, open-eared, drinking in the beauties of prospect and sound fresh from the springs of nature. . . . All is fragrant, fresh, and instinct with originality. . . . Nearly half the materials are used in building the story up to the point whereat, through Medea's helpful love, Jason obtains the fleece; and with the other half the downward slope to his early death is symmetrically constructed. The conception of Medea is daring and powerful: the austere sorceress of the popular idea is here subdued to an exquisitely tender maiden with much strength of character; and the latent fierceness of her nature is shown in cunning touches throughout the early parts of her story. . . . We get a taste of Medea's potential fierceness when, on board Argo with the fleece, she urges the adventurers to hasten the work of running down the ship of her brother Absyrtus. This luckless prince falls by Jason's spear; and herein is one of Mr. Morris's excellent modifications: had Medea reddened her hand with a brother's blood at this point, as in the orthodox version, we must have lost interest in her; but as the tale stands we are able to regard her as a fair specimen of crafty antique womanhood, undeprived of the grace of sweet maidenliness. *Gratuitous* ferocity is no part of this conception of Medea, even when we pass from the 'Life' to the 'Death' of Jason. . . . The whole of the last book, depicting his fall from allegiance to Medea, and his fading life after her vengeance and departure, is magnificent. His mere death immediately after his treachery would scarcely have been affecting; but Mr. Morris restores him to his healthy love of great emprise and to something of his old love for Medea, and thus renders his premature death highly pathetic. Lying in the dark shadow of his beached Argo, looking across the sea, he broods on his inactivity since the loss of Glauce; and bringing together the ruins of the past he begins to build them into the future, and to hope that Medea, hearing of new exploits, may come and seek him on his lonely throne. In this fine frame of mind he lapses into sleep—his last sleep; for as he lies the fated beam falls from Argo and crushes him with his new aspirations."

In the first edition of "The Life and Death of Jason" in 1867, the fly-leaf at the end of the volume announced as in preparation by the same author a work entitled "The Earthly Paradise," containing the following tales in verse:

Prologue—The Wanderers; or, the search for Eternal Youth.
The Story of Theseus.
The Son of Crœsus.
The Story of Cupid and Psyche.
The King's Treasure House.
The Story of Orpheus and Eurydice.
The Story of Pygmalion.
Atalanta's Race.
The Doom of King Acrisius.
The Story of Rhodope.
The Dolphins and the Lovers.
The Fortunes of Gyges.
The Story of Bellerophon.
The Watching of the Falcon.
The Lady of the Land.
The Hill of Venus.
The Seven Sleepers.
The Man who never Laughed again.
The Palace East of the Sun.
The Queen of the North.
The Story of Dorothea.
The Writing on the Image.
The Proud King.
The Ring given to Venus.
The Man Born to be King.
Epilogue.

In the next year, as appears from a letter from Ford

Madox Brown to Mr. Rae, dated April, 1868, Morris, while on a visit to Rossetti, finished the last of the stories for his forthcoming volume of "The Earthly Paradise," the first part of which appeared in June. It contained, beside the Prologue, which now no longer bore its subtitle, ten of the stories heralded in the original list and two fresh items, viz., "The Love of Alcestis" and "Ogier the Dane." The title of the penultimate story was changed to "Pygmalion and the Image." The table of contents for the second part, as advertised in the volume issued in 1868, was as follows:

The Story of Theseus.
The Hill of Venus.
The Story of Orpheus and Eurydice.
The Story of Dorothea.
The Fortunes of Gyges.
The Palace East of the Sun.
The Dolphins and the Lovers.
The Man who never Laughed again.
The Story of Rhodope.
Amys and Amillion.
The Story of Bellerophon.
The Ring given to Venus.
The Epilogue to the Earthly Paradise.

What further important modifications this scheme underwent may best be made clear by perusal of the list of contents of the book as it stands complete. It will then be seen that, assumed the identity of "The Palace East of the Sun" with the poem which actually appeared bearing the title "The Land East of the Sun and West of the Moon," only half the number of those tales that had been projected for the last part of "The Earthly Paradise" found a place in it finally. "The Story of Bellerophon," however, was expanded and divided into two separate poems, so that room was left for five new subjects instead of six. The first part of the work, originally one, was subsequently halved to form the first two volumes. The work, as it progressed, had grown so much in bulk that it was found impracticable to compress the whole of the second part into one. Volumes III. and IV., therefore, were issued separately, with a short interval between, the last volume appearing in 1870. The contents of the four parts of "The Earthly Paradise," as published, are as follows:

Vols. I. and II. (Spring and Summer).
The Wanderers.
Atalanta's Race.
The Man Born to be King.
The Doom of King Acrisius.
The Proud King.
Cupid and Psyche.
The Writing on the Image.
The Love of Alcestis.
The Lady of the Land.
The Son of Crœsus.
The Watching of the Falcon.
Pygmalion and the Image.
Ogier the Dane.

Vol. III. (Autumn).
The Death of Paris.
The Land East of the Sun and West of the Moon.
Acontius and Cydippe.
The Man who never Laughed again.
The Story of Rhodope.
The Lovers of Gudrun.

Vol. IV. (Winter).
The Golden Apples.
The Fostering of Aslaug.
Bellerophon at Argos.
The Ring given to Venus.
Bellerophon in Lycia.
The Hill of Venus.

"The Earthly Paradise," which has been fitly described as "a vast collection of the world's old tales retold," and as "a stately treasure-house of the noblest poetry," is, as it has been well said again, "a library in itself." It is not the size of the work alone—although that, since it fills four goodly volumes, is considerable—which makes it the poet's greatest work, and that upon which his fame must chiefly rest. It is the essential qualities of the book itself which constitute it his masterpiece.

Now, first of all, it is necessary to allude to a matter which, though one might have thought there was no possible room for misunderstanding on the subject, has nevertheless proved a pitfall whereat one writer after another has stumbled. The point is this. The opening words of the "Apology" prefixed to "The Earthly Paradise" run:

> "Of Heaven or Hell I have no power to sing."

Now the context ought to make it abundantly obvious that it is no question whether Morris had or had not the gift of delivering a dissertation on eschatology. But, lest possibly the word "Paradise" in the title of the work might mislead; lest it might be supposed to be his purpose as the friend and associate of Rossetti, to tread with the latter in the footsteps of the author of the "Divina Commedia," the poet wants to make the nature of his work clear at the outset. And so, in introducing himself to his readers, he disclaims any attempt to follow Dante, at the same time that he avows in effect his discipleship to Chaucer. That is all: a very simple affair. And yet what a deal of solemn nonsense has been written on this text; how it contained Morris's avowal of his materialism, and what not! "Of things mystical and spiritual he frankly says he knows nothing," writes one; another, "he had no melodramatic imagination." But all this sort of thing is utterly beside the mark.

Next, as to the Prologue, the drift of it may be stated in the words of Dr. Francis Hueffer: "Guided probably by a vague tradition of pre-Columbian discovery of America by the Vikings, the prologue relates how during a terrible pestilence certain mariners leave their northern home in search of the land where old age and death are not, and where life is surrounded by unbroken pleasure. Sailing west they come to a fair country. They gaze on southern sunshine and virgin forest and fertile champaign, but death meets them at every step, and happiness is farthest from their grasp when the people worship them as gods and sacrifice at their shrine. Escaping from this golden thraldom they regain their ship, and after many dangers and privations are driven by the wind to an island inhabited by descendants of the ancient Greeks, who have preserved their old worship and their old freedom. Here the weary wanderers of the main are hospitably received and here they resolve to dwell in peace, forgetful of their vain search for the earthly paradise. At the beginning and the middle of every month the elders of the people and their guests meet together to while away the time with song and friendly converse. The islanders relate the traditions of their Grecian home, the mariners relate the sagas of the North, and Laurence, a Swabian priest who had joined the Norsemen in their quest, contributes the legends of Tannhäuser and of the ring given to Venus by the Roman youth. Here, then, there is full scope for the quaint beauty of romantic classicism, and for the weird glamour of the northern myth."

"Much more dramatic, I venture to think," writes Mr. Andrew Lang, "than any passage in 'Jason' is that where the dreamy seekers of Dreamland, Breton and Northman, encounter the stout King Edward III., whose kingdom is of this world. Action and fantasy are met, and the wanderers explain the nature of their quest. . . . This encounter is a passage of high invention. . . . The tale of the wanderers was Mr. Morris's own; all the rest are of the dateless heritage of our race, fairy tales coming to us, now 'softly breathed through the flutes of the Grecians,' now told by Sagamen of Iceland. The whole performance is astonishingly equable."

Although the local colour, details, and many incidents of the various tales which constitute "The Earthly Paradise" are due to the poet's creation, in no instance do the plots of the tales which he has chosen pretend to be original. It may, therefore, be useful to record the several sources from which these stories "oft-besung" are derived; and first of "The Man Born to be King." Herr Julius Riegel, in his critical and analytical work, "Die Quellen von William Morris' Dichtung," declares that the original of this story is without doubt the legendary history of the Emperor Henry III. A somewhat similar tradition attaches to the Emperor Conrad II. Another version of the same is found in the "Gesta Romanorum," where, however, the hero is an emperor named Dolfinus; and yet again it is related of the Emperor Constantius I., surnamed Chlorus. "The Proud King" is another story from the "Gesta Romanorum." Morris gives him the name Jovinian. The story finds a close parallel in the legend of Count Robert of Sicily, as told by Longfellow. "The Writing on the Image," a tale from the "Gesta Romanorum," is also recounted by William of Malmesbury. "The Lady of the Land" is founded on the fourth chapter of "The Voiage and Travaile" of Sir John Maundevile, under the heading "Of Ypocras Daughter, transformed from a woman to a dragoun:" the "Lady of the Land" being the daughter of the famous physician Hippocrates, and the land the Isle of Cos. "The Watching of the Falcon" is taken from the thirteenth chapter of Maundevile, from the section headed "Of the Wisshinges, for Wacchinge of the Sperhauk." "Ogier the Dane," the last story in the first part of the work, may be traced to two old French poems, entitled "Chevalerie Ogier le Danois" and "Enfances Ogier le Danois;" but neither of these versions is followed so closely in Morris's poem as is the account in Tressan's "Corps d'Extraits de Romans de Chevalerie," published at Paris in 1782. The tale, which bears the long title, "The Land East of the Sun and West of the Moon" is remarkable as being the first story of Scandinavian origin in "The Earthly Paradise." It is the story of Gregory the Star-gazer, of the time of the Norwegian King Magnus, and has much in common with the Saga of Theodoric of Verona. The hero of the tale, who is on no account to be confounded with the Knight of the Swan or Lohengrin, may further be identified with the Wayland Smith of popular folk-lore. "The Man who never Laughed again" is obviously taken from an Oriental source, and indeed is nearly identical with the Arabian story, translated by Jonathan Scott, of "The King, his Son, Concubine, and Seven Viziers." It embodies the root idea, which is worked out in the old romance of "Melusine," and in De la Motte Fouqué's "Undine," viz., of a mystery on the wife's part, into which, on pain of disaster and the wreck of the happiness of them both, the husband is forbidden to inquire. "The Lovers of Gudrun" is purely Icelandic, and is to be found in the "Laxdæla Saga." "The Fostering of Aslaug" is from the Saga of Rágnar Lódbrók, and is a sort of sequel to the "Völsunga Saga." "The Ring given to Venus," from the "Gesta Regum Anglorum" of William of Malmesbury, the same *motif* employed by M. Prosper Mérimée in "Venus d'Ille," is, in its main incident, to be contrasted with the legend of St. Edmund Rich, placing a ring upon the finger of the Madonna's image in St. Mary's Church at Oxford. "The Hill of Venus" is, of course, the well-known German romance of "Tannhäuser." The remainder of the tales are taken from classical literature, "The Son of Crœsus" being related by Herodotus.

Three varieties of metre are in turn employed in "The Earthly Paradise," viz., rhymed five-foot couplets, rhymed four-foot couplets, and thirdly, *settima rima*, or the seven-line stanza of Chaucer, used in "Troilus and Criseide." In the story of "The Man who never Laughed again" occurs an exquisite song in heroic rhymed triplets, a song whose "love-laden words" are borne to the ears of the listener

> "On tender music, mother of sweet tears."

And again there is a song in praise of Venus, beginning,

> "Before our lady came on earth
> Little there was of joy or mirth,"

in "The Hill of Venus." From the story entitled "The Golden Apples" may be extracted a stanza of superbly descriptive music:

"Amid regrets for last night, when the moon,
Risen on the soft dusk, shone on maidens' feet,
Brushing the gold-heart lilies to the tune
Of pipes complaining, o'er the grass down-beat
That mixed with dewy flowers its odours sweet,
The shipmen laboured, till the sail unfurled
Swung round the prow to meet another world."

And this also:

"So on they went; the many birds sang sweet
Through all that blossomed thicket from above,
And unknown flowers bent down before their feet;
The very air, cleft by the grey-winged dove,
Throbbed with sweet scent, and smote their souls with love."

Here, from another poem, is a graphic figure to express a ship's passage through the waters:

"The broad bows pierced the land of fishes through."

Here is a powerful metaphor of the twilight that precedes the dawn:

"Ere yet the sun
Had slain the stars outright;"

and here, from "The Ring given to Venus," is a picture of wasting land and encroaching sea:

"the doubtful place
"Where the sea sucked the pasture's blood,"

portrayed more graphically by Morris in ten words than by Swinburne in so many lines, *e.g.*, in the magnificent poem, "By the North Sea," in "Studies in Song:"

"Like ashes the low cliffs crumble,
    The banks drop down into dust,
The heights of the hills are made humble,
    As a reed's is the strength of their trust:
As a city's that armies environ,
    The strength of their stay is of sand:
But the grasp of the sea is as iron,
    Laid hard on the land.

A land that is thirstier than ruin;
    A sea that is hungrier than death."

"The Land East of the Sun and West of the Moon" deserves a better description than an "idle dream." It is a tale which, as Mr. Hewlett says, "is eminently characteristic of the Norse imagination, and if not founded upon one of its native products, attests how thoroughly Mr. Morris had become imbued with its genius. The incidents of the narrative, especially the hero's first vision of his Fairy-love, as she dances and sings at dawn on the meadow with her sisters, holding in her hand the doffed swan-skin, which is her earthly disguise, are exquisite in their simplicity and grace." Mr. Buxton Forman is of opinion that there is no one poem in the whole collection "comparable with 'The Land East of the Sun and West of the Moon' in point of exquisite sustained imagination and what"—the term being used to denote his qualities as the typical singer of the English tongue, "the man whose utterances are most completely and musically dissevered from prose,"—"may be called the *Shelleyan* singing faculty." It is in this tale that there occurs the beautiful and well-known Christmas carol beginning:

"Outlanders, whence come ye last?"

with the alternate refrain:

"The snow in the street and the wind on the door;"

and

"Minstrels and maids stand forth on the floor."

In the same tale is also a very exquisite passage:

"Red roses fair
To wreathe my love that wanders here,
Gold-hearted lilies for her hand!
And yet withal that she may stand
On something other folk think sweet,
March violets for her rosy feet;
The black-heart amorous poppy, fain
Death from her passing knee to gain,
Bows to the gilliflower there:
The fiery tulip stands to stare
Upon her perfect loveliness,
That 'gainst the corn-cockle will press
Its fainting leaves: further afield
The untended vine black fruit doth yield,
That bore long torment of the heat,
At last in bliss her lips to meet;
The wind-flowers wotting of the thing
Must gather round there in the spring,
And live and die and live again,

That they might feel the joyous pain
At last, of lying crushed and rent
Beneath her feet, while well content
Above their soft leaves she doth sing.
What marvel, love, that everything
That far apart the troubled year,
Midst toil and doubt, gives otherwhere,
Must gather in this land round thee,
Living and dying, still to see
A wonder God shall not make twice."

"'The Man Born to be King' is" continues Mr. Hewlett, "a scarcely less admirable example of pure narrative. In the homeliness of the detail the essential life-likeness of the description consists. . . . In both these poems skilful management of the eight-syllable couplet lends an added charm to the diction. We may take, as a typical specimen, a passage from the latter, which combines these features in a single picture." The scene that follows is one which seems like a reminiscence of the poet's in Mesopotamia, on the banks of the Cherwell, or on the Thames at Iffley.

"So long he rode he drew anigh
A mill upon the river's brim,
That seemed a goodly place to him,
For o'er the oily smooth mill-head
There hung the apples growing red,
And many an ancient apple tree
Within the orchard could he see,
While the smooth mill walls, white and black,
Shook to the great wheels' measured clack,
And grumble of the gear within;
While o'er the roof that dulled that din
The doves sat crooning half the day,
And round the half-cut stack of hay
The sparrows fluttered twittering."

Two short but typical passages may be extracted from "Bellerophon in Argos" and "Bellerophon in Lycia" respectively:

"Thus have I sat, and cursed the God who made
The day so long, the night so long delayed;"

and

"Life seemed gone,
And she had fought the Gods, and they had won."

Of all the classical stories in "The Earthly Paradise" these two which have Bellerophon for hero exhibit the poet's gifts to the utmost advantage. The intensely real horror of the description of the Monster slain by Bellerophon makes one's flesh creep to read it, although the passage is too long for quotation. Again, how sure and how powerful is the delineation, whether it be of Sthenobœa's phlegmatic nature when it is awaked to inexperienced and unsuspected excess of "glorious thirst" at the first sight of the man who is fair

"Beyond the beauty of the sons of men,"

or of Philonoë and her gentler but not less deep-seated passion for the same object. So, on the eve of the fulfilment of her love, she reflects with a wistful regret on the happiness of anticipation which has sustained her hitherto, and which, in the very fulfilment, must pass away never to be recalled again:

"Alas! alas!
To-morrow must I say that all this was
And is not—this sweet longing?—what say men—
It cometh once and cometh not again,
This first love for another? Holds the earth
Within its circle aught that is of worth
When it is dead?—and this is part of it,
This measureless sweet longing that doth flit,
Never to come again, when all is won.
And is our first desire so soon foredone,
Like to the rose-bud, that through day and night
In early summer strives to meet the light
And in some noon-tide of the June, bursts sheath,
And ere the eve is past away in death?
Belike love dies then like the rest of life?
—Or falls asleep until it mix with strife
And fear and grief?—and then we call it pain,
And curse it for its labour lost in vain."

In such lines as these the poet does not shrink from dealing with one of the most excruciating tragedies that a human being can be called upon to endure and yet live—the workings of the inexorable law of change. This, which is a dominant idea in Ibsen's "Little Eyolf," might have been noticed as making its first appearance in Morris in

"The Life and Death of Jason," where the latter writes his cruel letter informing Medea that he no longer loves, and must therefore abandon her:

> "I hear thee talk of old days thou didst know—
> Are they not gone?—wilt thou not let them go,
> Nor to their shadows still cling desperately,
> Longing for things that never more can be?"

Another and a later instance is to be found in "The Doom of King Acrisius" in the touching lines beginning "Love while ye may."

"Many are of opinion," says Mr. Watts-Dunton, "that 'The Lovers of Gudrun' is his finest poem; he worked at it from four o'clock in the morning till four in the afternoon, and when he arose from the table he had produced 750 lines!" Rossetti, for one, thought very highly of this poem, as appears from a letter, written in December, 1869, to Mr. Frederic Shields, in which he remarks: "Have you seen Morris's new volume of the 'Paradise?' It contains glorious things, especially 'The Lovers of Gudrun.'" Mr. Robert Steele, writing years later in "The Academy," states explicitly that this was Rossetti's favourite poem, and, moreover, that it "is, in the opinion of some well qualified to judge, one of the finest and strongest poems of this century." Of the same poem Mr. Buxton Forman wrote: "Saga literature yielded Mr. Morris his material and the manner of laying out, and introduced a fresh element of freshness into his book; but no Saga afforded him the tender refinement with which Gudrun, Ingibiorg, and Refna are drawn, the largeness with which the fierce and fond elements of Gudrun's character are brought out, or the subtlety wherewith Bodli, the Agonistes of the piece, is depicted in his severe nobility, dashed with a single red streak of perfidy—in his complex combination of strong purpose and weak yielding to temptation. Bodli is the profoundest conception Mr. Morris has given us; he is a man of an exceedingly fine nature, of intense warmth in his affections, and, when led to indulge his passion for Gudrun at the expense of his friend, he bids good-bye for ever to happiness, and knows he has done so—his very nobility of nature crushing his heart with remorse at the one perfidy into which he has fallen. He honestly believes that he loves Gudrun better than Kiartan does; and even in that belief he can get no solace from a marriage brought about by a betrayal of his friend, though that friend looked very like a man who meant to betray his love. The utter unsatisfaction of Bodli after he has put hope away from Gudrun's heart is finely drawn: he cannot rest away from her, and he is miserable with her. Marriage, however, appears to have been a matter of course in those days; and Gudrun's obvious line of conduct, on conviction that the noblest youth of Iceland was not, as supposed, at her disposal, was to take the man at her feet, recognised as the next noblest, and get what happiness she might from a union based on a one-sided love. But not a suspicion of joy to either man or woman arises from the partnership contracted under these sombre conditions. . . . And so matters go hideously on, until Kiartan's coming back and marrying Refna drive Gudrun frantic with sorrow at having missed the man who has really loved her, and whom she most loves; rage with the husband through whose agency the miscarriage of her happiness has chanced, and jealousy of the woman who has apparently inherited the affection once for her alone. Under Mr. Morris's treatment it is of course through no coarse and brutal enmity between his Dioscuri that the catastrophe comes about. . . . The soul which the poet has put in Bodli is far superior to the wreaking of animal hatred on his betrayed friend; and Kiartan, though a much simpler study in psychology, is no less noble than Bodli, so no more capable of low hate. . . . Kiartan, a man fitted eminently for a large, simple life of success, might never have shown greatness or smallness but for Bodli's perfidy; and when these two fine fellows are thrown into collision on the swirl of the current of Gudrun's fierce love, that would fain consume the thing loved for very hell of jealousy, each desires only to fall by the other's sword—Bodli advancing his blade to meet the parry and retort of Kiartan, and Kiartan throwing down his arms unexpectedly to take in his breast the sword of

Bodli. . . . The culminating refinement of the poet upon saga barbarism comes in the magnificent pathos of Bodli's speech over his dead rival." In short this is a masterpiece "in the extreme sense of the word:" and in the whole of "The Earthly Paradise" there is not "any one poem that approaches 'The Lovers of Gudrun' in point of breadth, depth and grandeur." But, after all, as Matthew Arnold said, the best tribute is that "which consists not in covering the poet with eloquent eulogy of our own, but in letting him, at his best and greatest, speak for himself. Surely the critic who does most for his author is the critic who gains readers for his author himself, not for any lucubrations on his author; gains more readers for him, and enables those readers to read him with more admiration." And again he says, "the characters of a high quality of poetry are what is expressed *there*. They are far better recognised by being felt in the verse of the master, than by being perused in the prose of the critic." One prefers, therefore, not to mar the splendours of this poem by inadequate scraps of quotations, and although it were presumptuous to suppose that anyone previously disinclined to a study of William Morris would be led thereto by a recommendation in these pages, at the same time if it should chance that there be anybody who, though at present unacquainted with the great master's poems, is willing to make trial of one, let him select "The Lovers of Gudrun," of all Morris's writings that surely which is most deserving of the description "the best tale pity ever wrought." To have introduced that sublime poem to the notice of even one only to whom it was previously unknown, and to have prevailed upon that one to share the certain joy of knowing it, were an object indeed worth the winning.

Thus much for particular stories in "The Earthly Paradise." It is now necessary to notice certain characteristics of the work in general.

Morris is peculiarly fortunate and suggestive in his choice of epithets, as, for instance, when he speaks of the "dusty" grain in a manger. Others recur so frequently as to have become noted as mannerisms of the poet, *e.g.*, "wan" water, "dusky" swifts, and "pink-foot" doves, just as "blameless," "godlike," "pious," and the rest, are of the stock phrases of Homer and Virgil; while others again are strikingly unconventional, as when Morris describes a woman's countenance as being "pale as privet." The scenery and architecture, and in fact the general *entourage* of the Middle Ages which distinguish the "Jason," are not less conspicuous features of "The Earthly Paradise," and that not only in the romance tales, in which, of course, one would expect to find it so, but also in the classical tales as well. Thus one reads of Greek warriors wearing hauberks and bearing pennons; one meets with chapmen, or, again, a woman carrying a maund; the folk dwell in bowers and sleep upon tester-beds; they stroll in pleasances, enter precincts, and pass through posterns. In a word the associations of the days of chivalry impart an indescribable charm to "The Earthly Paradise." But its mediævalisms are not merely superficial. How thoroughly had Morris assimilated the attitude of mind of the period, its feelings and mode of expression, may be gathered from two examples. The first occurs in the tale of "The Man Born to be King," in which a religious recounts how, being on his way to housel one who lay at the point of death, although the district was but scantily populated, he yet caused the bell to be rung before him, for just such a motive as would have actuated St. Francis of Assisi or the Paduan St. Antony.

> "I took between mine hands the Lord,
> And bade the boy bear forth the bell,
> For though few folk were there to tell
> Who passed that way, natheless I trow
> The beasts were glad that news to know."

The other instance, from its utter unconsciousness, bespeaks perhaps even more than the foregoing the poet's mediæval habit of thought. In the twenty-third stanza of "Atalanta's Race" Morris applies the epithet "shapeless" to a bear's cubs. The expression is incidental, without further elaboration of the idea, and might easily escape observation. And yet what a jewel of ancient lore does it enshrine! The notion is older than the time of Pliny, and there is of course nothing in it that is unfamiliar to the student of mediæval bestiaries. It may not, then, be irrelevant to the subject to quote from Mr. Robert Steele's selections from the encyclopædia of Bartholomew Anglicus, to which Morris himself wrote a preface in 1893. "The bear bringeth forth a piece of flesh imperfect and evil shapen, and the mother licketh the lump, and shapeth the members with licking. . . . For the whelp is a piece of flesh little more than a mouse, having neither eyes nor ears, and having claws some-deal bourgeoning, and so this lump she licketh, and shapeth a whelp with licking." It is in such allusions as these that the unmodern tone of mind of the writer is revealed.

Morris was especially happy in his understanding and delineation of that fantastic borderland of half-dead, half-formed reliefs—that twilight phase of religion, when, on the one side, whole-hearted heathenism, as a system, had dwindled and already become discredited, and that residuum which yet survived of it, and had not lost hold on men's minds, was but the worst and lowest part of it, to wit, its superstition and its occultism; and when, on the other side, Christianity, acknowledged and accepted in its externals, had nevertheless not sunk deep enough into the conscience of the race to have effected any essential transformation of life and conduct. The passages which chiefly illustrate Morris's powerful appreciation of this dual condition of things occur in "The Hill of Venus" and in "The Ring given to Venus," which latter "contains, in the procession of the dead gods from the sea to land, perhaps the very finest thing," says Mr. Saintsbury, "that Mr. Morris has ever done." Here the two conflicting elements are blended in the person of Palumbus, who is both a Christian priest and at the same time an adept in the black arts; and find their commentary in the bitter cry of Satan, wrung from him in the anguish of his perplexity:

"Shall this endure for ever, Lord?
Hast thou no care to keep thy word?
And must such double men abide?
Not mine, not mine, nor on thy side?
For as thou cursest them I curse:—
Make their souls better, Lord, or worse."

The same thing appears once more in "The Lovers of Gudrun." The middle of this story coincides with the introduction of Christianity into Iceland, "where, though welcomed by the young, it has obtained the bare assent of the elder generation." One of the closing scenes of the tale shows Kiartan's surviving brothers and kindred gathered together round the board. The memory of the murdered man has been pledged in silence; whereupon his mother starts up, and, with a ruthless ferocity ill-becoming her venerable years, as it is inconsistent with her newly-adopted creed, strives to incite the family to avenge the blood of the slain. One glance from the widow was responded to by

"Grey Thorgerd's smile
Scornful and fierce, who therewithal rose up
And laid her hand upon a silver cup,
And drew from out her cloak a jewelled sword,
And cast it ringing on the oaken board,
And o'er the hall's noise high her clear voice shrilled:
'If the old gods by Christ and mass are killed
Or driven away, yet am I left behind,
Daughter of Egil, and with such a mind
As Egil had; wherefore if Asa Thor
Has never lived, and there are men no more
Within the land, yet by this king's gift here,
And by this cup Thor owned once, do I swear
That the false foster-brother shall be slain
Before three summers have come round again,
If but my hand must bring him to his end.'"

Instances might be multiplied, but the above must suffice.

One delightful characteristic of the stories contained in "The Earthly Paradise"—a characteristic which is shared also by the "Jason," and by the later work, the "Sigurd"—is that the poet tells them, as stories of the sort should alone be told, with a childlike directness of statement that seems to disarm all doubt or question as to the reality of the various occurrences related. The supernatural element abounds, but there is no approach to an apology for it. The course of the narrative runs on evenly and smoothly without any appreciable transition from the most matter of fact and ordinary incident to the most marvellous and extraordinary, just as though the narrator himself believed implicitly in the objective truth of everything he relates; nay, further, as though he were not conscious of making any unusual demand on the credulity of his readers. The god in the car appears and vanishes in the most natural and facile manner conceivable, without any hitch, so to speak, or creaking of the wheels of the mechanism by means of which he was introduced upon the scene.

Another point to notice is Morris's excessively delicate handling of all subjects which involve sexual relationship, subjects which, as given in the blunt language of the originals, or of the classical dictionary, scarcely seem, of their very nature, to admit of refining. Take, for instance, the well-known story of Danae's being imprisoned by her father in a tower of brass to insure her never conceiving; and of how the craft of Acrisius was outwitted by the lust of Jupiter, who, visiting the maiden in a shower of gold, became by her the father of Perseus, the predestined destroyer of his royal grandsire. It is impossible to read Morris's account of this incident in "The Doom of King Acrisius," and not to be struck with admiration at the way in which, without slurring over, he yet succeeds in transfusing the whole matter with a chaste exaltation which banishes every trace of coarseness; or, it may be added, without being convinced of the flagrant injustice of connecting the poet's name with any faintest suspicion of "fleshliness." To anyone so minded what an opportunity offered in "The Hill of Venus" to elaborate the merely sensuous, at the expense of the ethical, side of the picture! Here, again, Morris does not take refuge in vague generalities. Yet every detail of the story goes to point the surelier to the moral that no amount of indulgence of passion can ever avail to satisfy the cravings of the human heart. The description of the knight Walter's disillusionment is terrible in its convincing force. For a long while, indeed, his life in the Venusberg seemed to leave nothing to be desired. But this flawless enjoyment was bound sooner or later to come to an end. The time came when he began to be assailed by misgivings of he knew not what.

> "Then what had happed? was the sun darker now?
> Had the flowers shrunk, the warm breeze grown a-chill?"

The very vision vouchsafed him of the passionate lovers of past time—the vision that was meant to reassure him, by contrasting his present lot with theirs who had perished, that he alone enjoyed the supreme favour of the goddess, compelled him on the contrary to ask himself what guarantee he had that his life of pleasure should last if theirs had not endured. When he appealed to Venus herself with the question—

> "Am I the only one
> Whose eyes thy glorious kisses have made dim?
> And what then with the others hast thou done?
> Where is the sweetness of their sick love gone?"

the passionate cry remained unanswered. Although the goddess might stifle further questions of his lips with kisses, she could not stifle the heart-searching questions within him; until at last he could endure the torturing doubts no longer, and turned his back and fled from the Venusberg with its allurements, whose emptiness he had probed and proven, crying thus in his desperate need:

> "Ah, at last
> I know that no real love from me I cast;
> Nought but a dream; and that God knoweth too."

Such, then, being the high tone of Morris's poetical work, a more unfounded charge than that which on the opposite score was ultimately brought against him it would be impossible to imagine, or as Mr. Hewlett puts it, "Mr. Morris's subtle delineation in 'The Hill of Venus' of the successive phases of carnal slavery and emancipation—the spiritual chaos that precedes the sudden lapse, the gradual disenchantment, in spite of every effort to defer 'the dreadful dawn,' the long-drawn weariness of satiety, and the self-loathing sense of degradation that attends the awakening recoil—opposes as powerful a protest as any in modern poetry against the teaching of the school with which his name has been undeservedly associated."

Between the appearance of "The Defence of Guenevere" and the first instalment of "The Earthly Paradise" a space, as has been mentioned above, of ten years intervened. During that time it has been represented by several critics, while they admit his great advance in technical skill, that Mr. Morris underwent a change in mental attitude that can only be described as for the worse!

These writers contrast the vigorous, nay almost rugged, manliness of the earlier collection of poems with the brooding despondency, the abject repugnance at the prospect of death which they detect in the subsequent work. They complain that the ghastly intrusion of this sentiment, like the unwelcome presence of a skeleton at a feast, by forcing itself repeatedly upon the attention of the reader—and that too with increasing importunity, so they affirm, as the poem proceeds—in effect goes a long way to mar the beauty of the entire work. As an instance of this lamentable blemish they have singled out, among others, the song from the story of "Ogier the Dane," with its burden

> "Kiss me love! for who knoweth
> What thing cometh after death?"

But the whole theory of Morris's deterioration of tone in this regard, based and built as it is on the assumption that the writing of the several poems was but little antecedent to the dates of their respective publication, is an erroneous one. The facts do not admit it, and it must fall to the ground. For, as has been shown already, not only was the particular lyric in question all but contemporary with "The Defence of Guenevere," but further, the inception of "The Earthly Paradise" itself, and the mapping out also of the poem generally, took place years before the work was committed to the public. There simply was not time, therefore, for a radical change of conviction in William Morris, such as is alleged, to have come about. The alteration, if any, was one not of mind, but of mood. The truth is, that, with his poet's large heart and faculty of intense sympathy, Morris was capable of ranging by rapid turns from the realization of one to another of the most varied and opposite situations and phases of emotion. He was not the man, however, to allow himself to be overmastered for a length of time by any one mood, least of all by a morbid or enervating one. If he alludes frequently to the subject of death, it is as a mediæval writer might have done, for whom familiarity has robbed it of its worst terrors. It is not, indeed, to be denied that towards the latter part of the Middle Age period there were some over whom the coming Renaissance of paganism cast its grim shadows before. These were, for the most part, of exalted rank, like Charles VII. of France, for instance, and his son Louis XI., men whose craven precautions to ward off the inevitable—precautions which in the case of victorious Charles actually proved fatal to himself—became a byword of elaborate futility. But on the other hand the rank and file of Christendom, being unbeguiled by the snares of princely place and sham classical culture, from the beginning of the Gospel era down to the close of the Middle Ages, were haunted by no unwholesome nor inordinate dread of death, but faced it calmly and with fortitude. Robust, and knowing not the hypersensitiveness of these latter days, they had no occasion to resort to our vain periphrases such as "If anything should happen to me," or the like, but spoke of their end freely and quailed not. And this their spirit is little different from that which animated the author of "The Earthly Paradise," a true mediæval poet, though one born, he is constrained to own, out of his due time. No more than they did William Morris shrink from the mention of dissolution. It is only the critics of an introspective and degenerate age who have interpreted his references to death as betraying on his part a habit of cowardly terror, that had no existence apart from their imagination. In the "Envoi" of "The Earthly Paradise" the poet does say "death have we hated;" but it is merely as a child might hate, with an innocent and perfectly natural hatred, engendered not through brooding on the dismal thought of death, but because, though he knows not what it is nor what it means, of this at least he is conscious, that it is something utterly at variance with the vigorous young life that warms and pulses through every fibre of his being. Granted that the note of "*carpe diem*" is sounded at intervals, that the desire of evading death is expressed not rarely with wistful longing and regret in the pages of "The Earthly Paradise" nevertheless it will not be found to be dominant. To have omitted such utterances altogether would have been an abandoning, if not an actual breaking, of the thread which serves to bind together the several parts of the work. As it is, it amounts merely to this, that the *motif* of the plot is sustained effectively throughout. For surely the very object of the Wanderers is to seek—is it not?—upon earth some favoured spot where, as within Eden's self, they may win means of refuge from the cares of ordinary mortals, from sickness, old age, and death; and it is no reproach therefore if this idea is not lost sight of by the poet. It occurs no more than is necessary to insure unity of purpose and cohesion to what would otherwise be a scrap-book of miscellaneous and disconnected tales. It might have been supposed, on the contrary, that no one could fail to be touched by the pathos of the situation, that as the days and months glide by, the melancholy conviction presses itself upon the Wanderers that, in spite of all efforts made, all hardships endured, so far from their having reached or having any prospect of reaching, the goal of their hopes, the end from which there is no escape is but drawing surely nearer and nearer. It is not more just to pronounce this as a detriment in "The Earthly Paradise" than to say that the sense of strain and stress on the part of the fair story-teller, compelled to keep up the Khalifa's interest without abate to avoid her impending execution, spoils the "Thousand and One

Nights," or that of parrying pestilence the "Decameron."

Mr. Pater observes in the interval between the publication of "The Defence of Guenevere" on the one hand, and "The Life and Death of Jason" and "The Earthly Paradise" on the other, a "change of manners . . . wrought, . . . entire, almost a revolt"—one of the characteristics, according to his view, "of æsthetic poetry. Here there is no delirium or illusion, no experience of mere soul while the body and the bodily senses sleep, or wake with convulsed intensity at the prompting of imaginative love, but rather the great primary passions under broad daylight. . . . This simplification interests us, not merely for the sake of an individual poet—full of charm as he is—but chiefly because it explains through him a transition which, under many forms, is one law of the life of the human spirit. . . . Complex and subtle interests which the mind spins for itself may occupy art and poetry or our own spirits for a time; but sooner or later they come back with a sharp rebound to the simple elementary passions—anger, desire, regret, pity, and fear. . . . This reaction from dreamlight to daylight gives, as always happens, a strange power in dealing with morning and the things of the morning. Not less is this Hellenist of the Middle Age master of dreams, of sleep and the desire of sleep—sleep in which no one walks, restorer of childhood to men—dreams, not like Galahad's or Guenevere's, but full of happy, childish wonder as in the earlier world. It is a world in which the centaur and the ram with the fleece of gold are conceivable. The song sung always claims to be sung for the first time. There are hints at a language common to birds and beasts and men. Everywhere there is an impression of surprise, as of people first waking from the golden age, at fire, snow, wine, the touch of water as one swims, the salt taste of the sea. And this simplicity at first hand is a strange contrast to the sought-out simplicity of Wordsworth. Desire here is towards the body of nature for its own sake, not because a soul is divined through it. And yet it is one of the charming anachronisms of a poet who, while he handles an ancient subject, never becomes an antiquarian, but animates his subject by keeping it always close to himself, that betweenwhiles we have a sense of English scenery as from an eye well practised under Wordsworth's influence, as from 'the casement half opened on summer nights' with the song of the brown bird among the willows, the

> 'Noise of bells, such as in moonlit lanes
> Rings from the grey team on the market night.'

Nowhere but in England is there such a 'paradise of birds,' the fern-owl, the water-hen, the thrush in a hundred sweet variations, the ger-falcon, the kestrel, the starling, the pea-fowl; birds heard from the field by the townsman down in the streets at dawn; doves everywhere, pink-footed, grey-winged, flitting about the temple, troubled by the temple incense, trapped in the snow. The sea-touches are not less sharp and firm, surest of effect in places where river and sea, salt and fresh waves, conflict."

"For us the most attractive form of classical story is the monk's conception of it, when he escapes from the sombre atmosphere of his cloister to natural light. The fruits of this mood, which, divining more than it understands, infuses into the scenery and figures of Christian history some subtle reminiscence of older gods, or into the story of Cupid and Psyche that passionate stress of spirit which the world owes to Christianity, constitute a peculiar vein of interest in the art of the fifteenth century." Continuing, Mr. Pater shows (in a passage already quoted) how these remarks apply in particular to the "Jason." Still, the mediævalisms and delicate inconsistencies of the latter poem also abound in the succeeding work; and "It is precisely this effect, this grace of Hellenism relieved against the sorrow of the Middle Age, which forms the chief motive of 'The Earthly Paradise;' with an exquisite dexterity the two threads of sentiment are here interwoven and contrasted. A band of adventurers sets out from Norway, most northerly of northern lands, when the plague is raging—the bell continually ringing as they carry the Sacrament to the sick. . . . It is below the very coast of France, through the fleet of Edward the Third, amongst the gaily-painted mediæval sails, that we pass to a reserved fragment of Greece, which by some divine good fortune lingers in the western sea into the Middle Age. There the stories of 'The Earthly Paradise' are told, Greek story and romantic alternating; and for the crew of the 'Rose Garland,' coming across the sins of the earlier world with the sign of the cross, and drinking Rhine-wine in Greece, the two worlds of sentiment are confronted. One characteristic of the pagan spirit the æsthetic poetry has, which is on its surface—the continual suggestion, pensive or passionate, of the shortness of life. This is contrasted with the bloom of the world, and gives new seduction to it—the sense of death and the desire of beauty, the desire of beauty quickened by the sense of death."

The first part only of "The Earthly Paradise" had appeared when Mr. John Morley, in the "Fortnightly Review," of which he was editor, expressed the grateful and refreshing sense of relief produced by this one with its absence of subjective sentiment, after the work of other contemporary poets. "Mr. Morris's central quality is a vigorous and healthy objectivity," he wrote, and "people who talk conventional cant about word-painting . . . should turn to a page of 'Jason' or 'The Earthly Paradise' and watch how the most delicious pictures are produced by the simplest and directest means."

"Mr. Morris's descriptions, condensed, simple, absolutely free from all that is strained and all that is artificial, enter the reader's mind with the direct and vivid force of impressions coming straight from the painter's canvas. There is no English poet of this time, nor perhaps of any other, who has so possessed this excellent gift of looking freshly and simply on external nature in all her many colours, and of reproducing what he sees with such effective precision and truthfulness. . . . Another of Mr. Morris's most characteristic and most delightful qualities, nearly always found in men of the healthy objective temperament, is the low-toned, crooning kindliness to all the earth which one hears through all his pleasant singing; and akin to this a certain sweet sadness as of the old time."

Ford Madox Brown wrote that "The Earthly Paradise" was full of admirable things, most of which he had heard read from the poet's own lips; while Mr. Saintsbury says that Morris, with the school to which he belonged, had "rediscovered the way to one of the Paradises of Art, . . . a true and genuine Paradise, and, to my taste, one delicious and refreshing to an extent not exceeding any other." And again the same writer says of Morris's verse, "And still, charming as are many of the detached pieces to be culled from him, the atmosphere and the tenor of the whole seem to me to be more poetical than any of the parts. All over it is that 'making the common as though it were not common,' which is the best if not the only existing definition of this indefinable quality."

Miss Amy Sharp justly remarks of the tales in "The Earthly Paradise" that "no one . . . can have the smallest difficulty in following their clear, smooth, beguiling narrative. . . . They consistently avoid all stress of heart-searching topics, and the charm of their execution is exactly what analysis kills instead of demonstrating." With reference to the language of the work Mr. Arthur Symons says that the words are always "happily chosen, . . . they have the grace of being quite the best that could happen, not that fineness which is of long search, rarity and dear buying. Certainly this was deliberate on his part; and deliberate was his use of the simplest words, which sometimes became a little cloying, and of the simplest rhythms, in which he uses few licenses, and almost never attempts an individual effect in any single line. . . . His rhymes are faint, gliding into one another stealthily; dying away, often, upon such vaguely accentuated words as 'patiently,' 'listlessly.' He aims at the effect of improvisation, and his verse becomes a sort of pathetic sing-song, like a croon, hardly ever rising or sinking in tone. With its languid, lulling monotony, its 'listless chime,' it has (especially in those heroic couplets which were finer in his hands than any other measure) the sound of a low plashing of sea-ripples on a quiet shore, a vague and monotonous and continuous and restful going on."

"'The Earthly Paradise'" says Mr. Hewlett, "is a work of which our generation may well be proud. Whatever else may be thought of its drift it is dignified by seriousness of purpose; amid copious variety it preserves a unity of structure, and bears throughout the honourable stamp of artistic craftsmanship." "If it is sometimes voluble"—to borrow from Mr. George Saintsbury once more—"it is never prosaic; the setting-pieces, intercalated prefaces, and epilogues for the several months are, as they should be, of the very best; the proem is noble, and the general contents are sublime." One more quotation, to conclude, from Mr. Buxton Forman in "Our Living Poets:" "Putting aside the question of relative merits in the various tales, it is not too much to say that the whole 'Earthly Paradise' is such a work as cannot be found in modern literature regarded as a repertory of Aryan myth, tradition and legend. Founded almost exclusively on tales current at different epochs among nations of the great Indo-European family, this work is a more complete and homogeneous collection of the myths and traditions of that family than any one hand has yet got together and fused, by stress of individuality in the rendering, into a luxuriant and beautiful form. And when to this work is added 'The Life and Death of Jason' with its many complete episodes, Mr. Morris's unflagging energy in working at these legends, that are and always must be so dear to every Englishman, becomes a matter for no small astonishment. . . . Whatever he dreams, or whatever dream of other men he makes his own for the nonce, is rendered vivid by so much reality, so much healthiness of landscape and sky, so much truth of human interest, psychology so sterling as far as it goes, that with the easy musical flow of his rhythm and his perfectly individual simplicity of song-language, these works must be an heirloom of price for later generations as long as English poetry is read."

CHAPTER SEVEN: KELMSCOTT MANOR.

FOR five years from the time he left the Red House at Upton, in Kent, William Morris was without a home in the country. His friend, Rossetti, being desirous "of establishing some country quarters for work, where," so he wrote, "I can leave my belongings, and return to them as opportunity offers;" and such an arrangement as that proposed being agreeable to Morris as well, they began to look out for a suitable place to take together. They had been searching already some little time, "when this one," writes Rossetti from Kelmscott Manor, "was discovered in a house-agent's catalogue—the last place one would have expected to furnish such an out-of-the-world commodity" Out-of-the-world indeed! for in those days there was no railway station nearer than at Faringdon, a drive of seven miles. However, in 1873, a station on the Oxford and Fairford line was opened at Lechlade, a distance of between three and four miles from Kelmscott. Before the end of May, 1871, Morris had decided with Rossetti to rent Kelmscott Manor, and in less than two months' time their joint occupation was begun. Morris held the house from that time to the day of his death, a space of five-and-twenty years. He used to stay there longest in the autumn months, but at other times whenever he was overworn with too much work, or otherwise in need of a change, he had only to go down there and find the rest and refreshment that he needed. How devoted he was to the place he signalized in more ways than one. Undoubtedly he had it in his mind when he said to his audience in one of his lectures: "There may be some here who have the good luck to dwell in those noble buildings which our forefathers built, out of their very souls, one may say; such good luck I call about the greatest that can befall a man in these days."

In "News from Nowhere" Morris describes a journey up the river to Kelmscott—not his "first visit by many a time. I know these reaches well; indeed, I may say that I know every yard of the Thames from Hammersmith to

Cricklade." The teller of the tale, fancying himself in the neighbourhood of Hampton Court, says, "And as we slipped between the lovely summer greenery, I almost felt my youth come back to me, and as if I were on one of those water excursions which I used to enjoy so much in days when I was too happy to think that there could be much amiss anywhere." The visit in the romance is represented as taking place at just the year's season at which Morris first took up his abode at Kelmscott, and it may well be that he is recording here his exact impressions at the time. He dwells with tender sympathy on the description of the various river-side scenes he loved, from the "beginning of the country Thames" with its "bough-hung banks," until his arrival at the very threshold of his home—"the mowing-field; whence came waves of fragrance from the flowering clover amidst of the ripe grass. In a few minutes we had passed through a deep eddying pool into the sharp stream that ran from the ford, and beached our craft on a tiny strand of limestone gravel, and stepped ashore . . . our journey done. . . . The river came down through a wide meadow on my left, which was grey now with the ripened seeding grasses; the gleaming water was lost presently by a turn of the bank, but over the meadow I could see the mingled gables of a building where I knew the locks must be. . . . I turned a little to my right, and through the hawthorn sprays and long shoots of the wild roses could see the flat country spreading out far away under the sun of the calm evening. . . . Before me the elm boughs still hid most of what houses there might be in this river-side dwelling of men; but to the right of the cart-road a few grey buildings of the simplest kind showed here and there." It may be remarked at this point, by way of explanation, that the soil in the neighbourhood being light, the trees that flourish thereabouts are chiefly elm-trees. "Almost without my will my feet moved on along the road they knew. The raised way led us into a little field bounded by a backwater of the river on one side; on the right hand we could see a cluster of small houses and barns, new and old, and before us a grey stone barn and a wall partly overgrown with ivy, over which a few grey gables showed. The village road ended in the shallow of the aforesaid backwater. We crossed the road, and again, almost without my will, my hand raised the latch of a door in the wall, and we stood presently on a

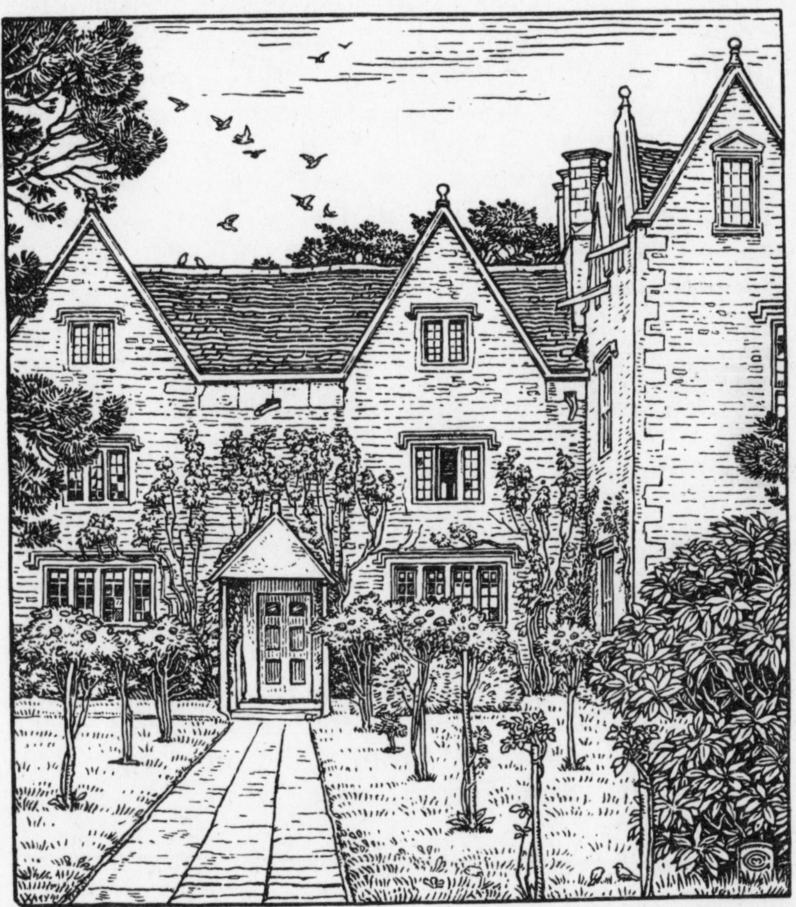

KELMSCOTT MANOR. ENTRANCE FRONT.

stone path which led up to the old house. . . . The garden between the wall and the house was redolent of the June flowers, and the roses were rolling over one another with that delicious superabundance of small well-tended gardens which at first sight takes away all thought from the beholder save that of beauty. The blackbirds were singing their loudest, the doves were cooing on the roof-ridge, the rooks in the high elm-trees beyond were garrulous among the young leaves, and the swifts wheeled whirring about the gables. And the house itself was a fit guardian for all the beauty of this heart of summer. . . . 'This many-gabled old house, built by the simple country-folk of the long-past times, regardless of all the turmoil that was going on in cities and courts, is lovely still.'" His companion in the story then led him "close up to the house, and laid her shapely, sun-browned hand and arm on the lichened wall as if to embrace it, and cried out, 'O me! O me! How I love the earth, and the seasons, and weather, and all things that deal with it, and all that grows out of it—as this has done!' . . . We stood there a while by the corner of the big gable of the house. . . . We drew back a little, and looked up at the house: the door and the windows were open to the fragrant sun-cured air. . . . We went in. . . . We wandered from room to room,—from the rose-covered porch to the strange and quaint garrets amongst the great timbers of the roof, where of old time the tillers and herdsmen of the manor slept. Everywhere there was but little furniture, and that only the most necessary, and of the simplest forms. The extravagant love of ornament which I had noted . . . elsewhere seemed here to have given place to the feeling that the house itself and its associations was the ornament of the country life amidst which it had been left stranded from old times, and that to re-ornament it would but take away its use as a piece of natural beauty.

"We sat down at last in a room . . . which was still hung with old tapestry, originally of no artistic value, but now faded into pleasant grey tones which harmonized thoroughly well with the quiet of the place, and which would have been ill-supplanted by brighter and more striking decoration. I . . . became . . . scarce conscious of anything, but that I was there in that old room, the doves crooning from the roofs of the barn and dovecot beyond the window opposite to me." He then noted the contrast between his living companion and "the grey

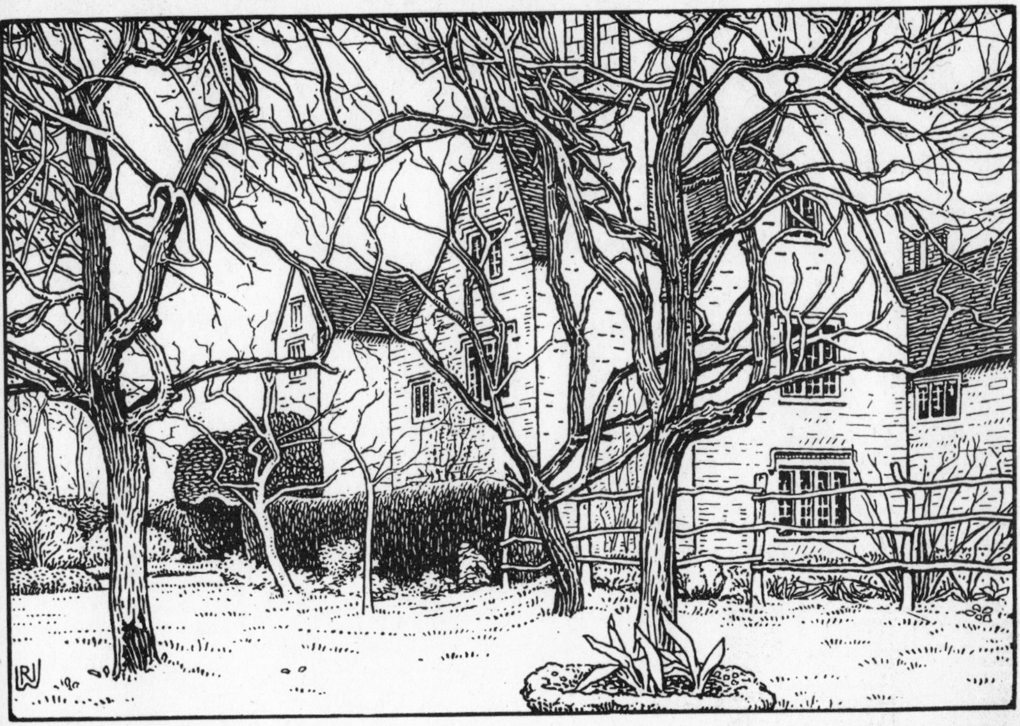

KELMSCOTT MANOR. FROM THE GARTH.

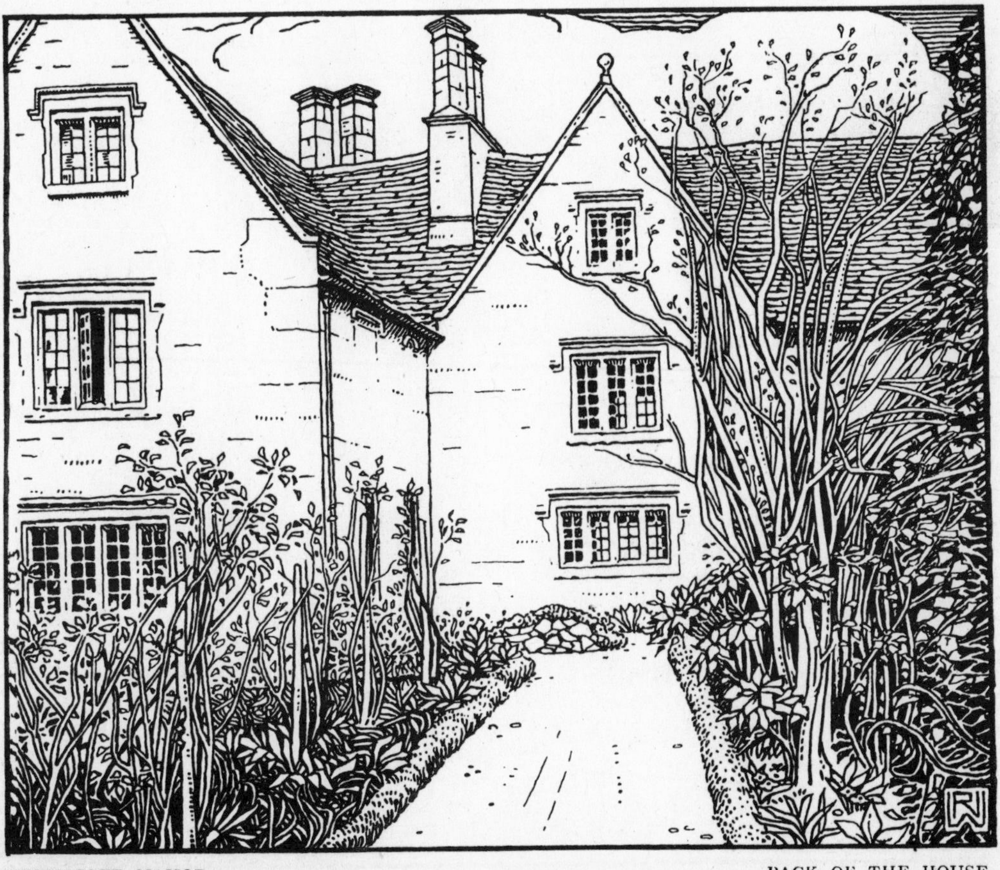

KELMSCOTT MANOR. BACK OF THE HOUSE.

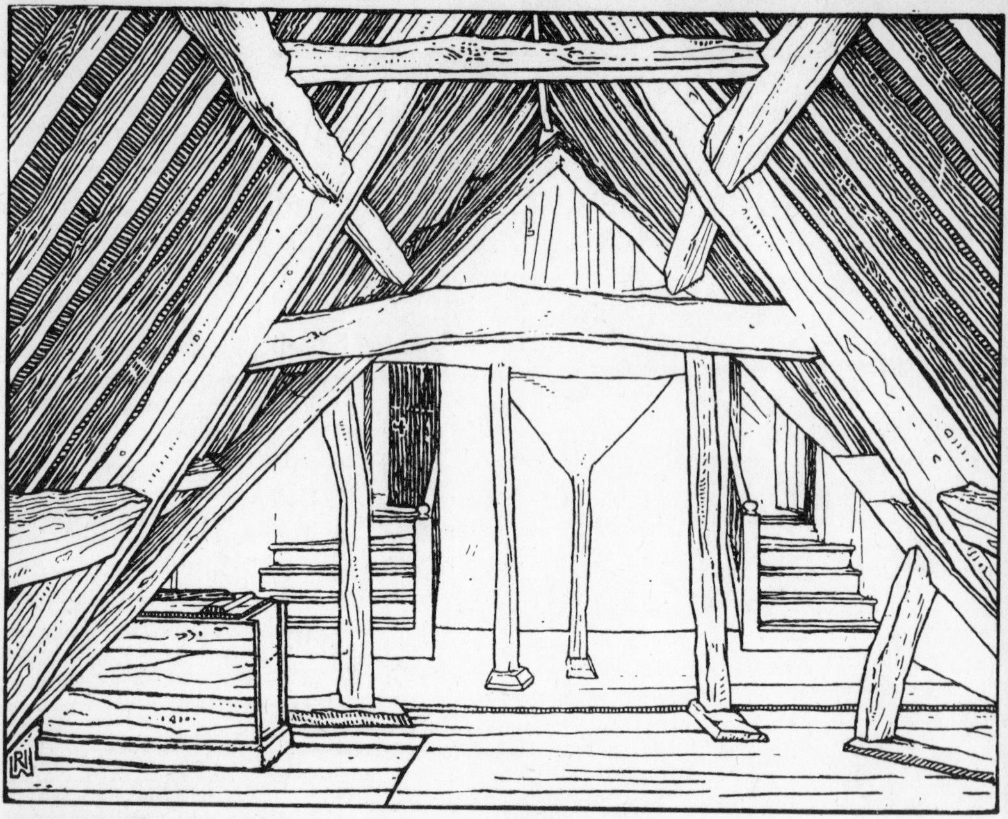

KELMSCOTT MANOR. THE GARRET.

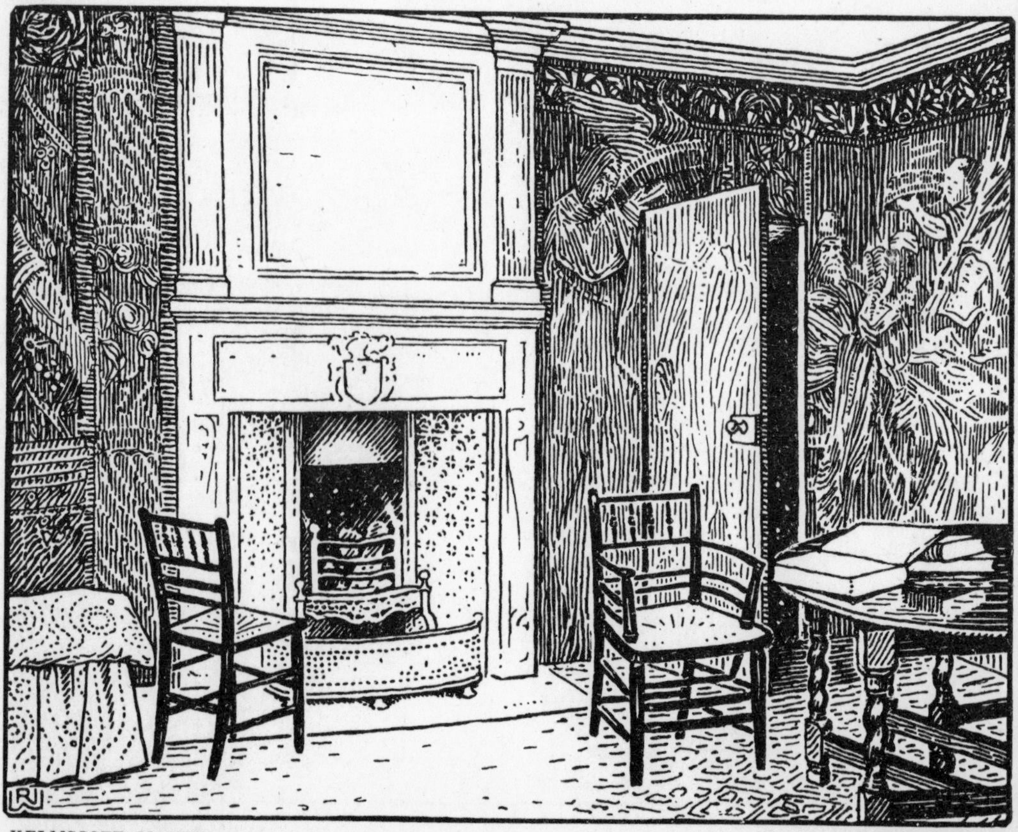

KELMSCOTT MANOR. THE TAPESTRY ROOM.

faded tapestry with its futile design, which was now only bearable because it had grown so faint and feeble." Presently he goes "downstairs and out of the house into the garden by a little side door which opened out of a curious lobby." He is still in the "lovely garden," "when a little gate in the fence, which led into a small elm-shaded field, was opened" and a friend "came up the garden path, who exclaimed, 'I thought you . . . would like to see the old house. . . . Isn't it a jewel of a house after its kind?'" Such is the picture he drew of Kelmscott, and one not so much idealized but that to recognize the original of it is easy enough.

Again in an article, dated at "Kelmscott, October 25," and published in "The Quest" (Birmingham), of November, 1895, William Morris, under the title "Gossip about an old House on the Upper Thames," furnishes another account of his country home. "The village of Kelmscott," he begins, "lies close to" the river, "some five miles (by water) from the present end of the navigation at Inglesham." After a short survey of the neighbourhood, he then proceeds to describe the "mass of grey walls and pearly-grey roofs which makes the House, called by courtesy the Manor House, though it seems to have no manorial rights attached to it. . . . It lies at the very end of the village on a road which, brought up shortly by a backwater of the Thames, becomes a mere cart track leading into the meadows along the river. . . . Entering the door in . . . the high impointed stone wall, . . . you go up a flagged path through the front garden to the porch which is a modern but harmless addition in wood. The house from this side is a lowish three-storied one with mullioned windows (in the third these are in the gables), and at right angles to this another block whose bigger lower windows and pedimented gable lights indicate a later date. The house is built of well-laid rubble-stone of the district, the wall" in part plastered over with thin plaster. "The roofs are covered with the beautiful stone slates of the district, the most lovely covering which a roof can have, especially when, as here and in all the traditional old houses of the country-side, they are 'sized down'; the smaller ones to the top and the bigger towards the eaves, which gives one the same sort of pleasure in their orderly beauty as a fish's scales or a bird's feathers. Turning round the house by

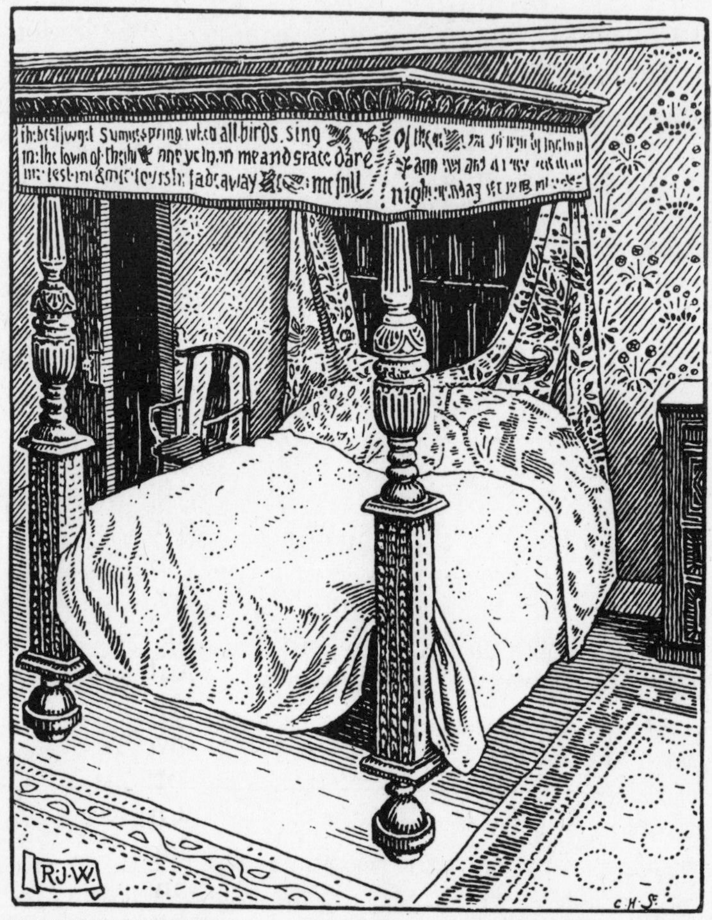

KELMSCOTT MANOR. 17TH CENTURY CARVED BEDSTEAD, WITH NEEDLEWORK HANGINGS DESIGNED AND WORKED BY MAY MORRIS.

the bigger block, one sees where the gable of the older and simpler part of the house once came out, and notes with pleasure the simple expression of the difference of levels in the first floor and the third floor, as by the diversity of windows and roofs: the back of the house shows nothing but the work of the earlier builders, and is in plan of the shape of an E with the tongue cut out. . . . Standing a little aloof from the north-east angle of the building, one can get the best idea of a fact which it is essential to note, and which is found in all these old houses hereabouts, to wit, all the walls 'batter,' *i.e.*, lean a little back. . . . We must suppose that it is an example of traditional design from which the builders could not escape. To my mind it is a beauty, taking from the building a rigidity which would otherwise mar it; giving it (I can think of no other word) a flexibility which is never found in our modern imitations of the houses of this age." After a few words on the adjoining farm buildings, the dovecot, and garden, Morris continues: "Going under an arched opening in the yew hedge which makes a little garth about a low door in the middle of the north wall, one comes into a curious passage or lobby" which "leads into what was once the great parlour. . . . I have many a memory of hot summer mornings passed in its coolness amidst the green reflections of the garden. Turning back and following a little passage leading from the lobby aforesaid to the earlier part of the house" one comes, at the end of the passage, upon "a delightful little room quite low ceilinged, in the place where the house is 'thin in the wind,' so that there is a window east and a window west. . . . This room is really the heart of the Kelmscott house, having been the parlour of the old house. . . . Outside this little parlour is the entrance passage from the flagged path aforesaid, made by two stout studded partitions, the carpentry of which is very agreeable to anyone who does not want cabinet work to supplant carpentry." He then describes the upstairs part, of which the feature is the tapestry room "over the big panelled parlour. The walls of it are hung with tapestry of about 1600, representing the story of Samson: they were never great works of art, and now, when all the bright colours are faded out, and nothing is left but the indigo blues, the greys and the warm yellowy browns, they look better, I think, than they were meant to look . . . and, in spite of the designer, they give an air of romance to the room which nothing else would quite do. Another charm this room has, that through its south window you not only catch a glimpse of the Thames clover meadows, and the pretty little elm-crowned hill over in Berkshire; . . . you can see not only the barn . . . with its beautiful sharp gable, the grey stone sheds and the dove-cot, but also the flank of the earlier house and its little gables and grey-scaled roofs, and this is a beautiful outlook indeed." Morris does not even omit to speak of "the attics, *i.e.*, the open roof under the slates, a very sturdy beam roof of elm often unsquared; it is most curiously divided under most of the smaller gables into little chambers where, no doubt, people, perhaps the hired field labourers, slept in old time: the bigger space is open, and is a fine place for children to play in, and has charming views east, west and north: but much of it is too curious for description. . . . The older part of the house *looks* about 1573, and the later (in this country-side) *looks* 1630 to 1640. . . . Here then," the writer concludes, "are a few words about a house that I love; with a reasonable love I think: for though my words may give you no idea of any special charm about it, yet I assure you that the charm is there; so much has the old house grown up out of the soil and the lives of those that lived in it; needing no grand office-architect, . . . but some thin thread of tradition, a half-anxious sense of the delight of meadow and acre and wood and river; a certain amount (not too much let us hope) of common-sense, a liking for making materials serve one's turn, and perhaps, at bottom, some little grain of sentiment—this I think was what went to the making of the old house. Might we not manage to find some sympathy for all that from henceforward!"

It was on a "memorable day," shortly after Morris and Rossetti had entered upon their joint occupancy of Kelmscott Manor, that Mr. Theodore Watts, being there at the time on a visit to Rossetti, first met Morris "and was blessed," so he writes in "The Athenæum," "with a friendship that lasted without interruption for nearly a quarter of a century." In the same paper Mr. Watts-

Dunton mentions another occasion on which himself was staying, together with the late Dr. Middleton, as guests of Morris's at Kelmscott. "The beautiful old house and the quaint, romantic chamber that served for studio, became," says Mrs. Esther Wood, "the resort of poets and artists, critics and connoisseurs, disciples and aspirants, in companies small indeed, but brilliant and memorable as any that gathered round the young Pre-Raphaelites in Newman Street, or the maturer masters of art and song that assembled in Cheyne Walk, Chelsea. Mr. William Morris and his family were there frequently."

In a letter addressed to his mother from Kelmscott, a few days after his arrival there in 1871, Rossetti writes: "This house and its surroundings are the loveliest 'haunt of ancient peace' that can well be imagined—the house purely Elizabethan in character, though it may probably not be so old as that. . . . It has a quantity of farm buildings of the thatched squatted order, which look settled down into a purring state of comfort. . . . My studio here is a delightful room, all hung round with old tapestry. . . . It gives in grim sequence the history of Samson. . . . I hope you will see this lovely old place some time when it is got quite into order, and I am sure it will fill you with admiration. The garden is a perfect paradise, and the whole is built on the very banks of the Thames, along which there are beautiful walks for miles." Rossetti found the quiet of this peaceful spot particularly restful and soothing to him. He used constantly to be going there for periods of longer or shorter duration at intervals during three years. Indeed he resided there almost entirely between 1872 and 1874. He wrote much poetry and painted a certain number of pictures there. Ford Madox Brown painted a great part of his picture "Cromwell on his Farm" in the open air at Kelmscott in 1872. In the winter of that year Rossetti moved his studio to the large drawing-room on the ground floor, on account of the cold in the tapestry-room. For he had returned with Mr. George Hake to Kelmscott Manor from Scotland, whither he had gone for some while in the autumn of 1872 for the benefit of his health. Dr. Thomas Gordon Hake visited Rossetti at Kelmscott and described the scenery of the place in his poem "Reminiscence." Rossetti left Kelmscott altogether in July, 1874; after whose withdrawal, for a period of about ten years, Mr. F. S. Ellis had a share in the place with Morris and had the right, as part occupier, to go there when it was convenient to himself to do so.

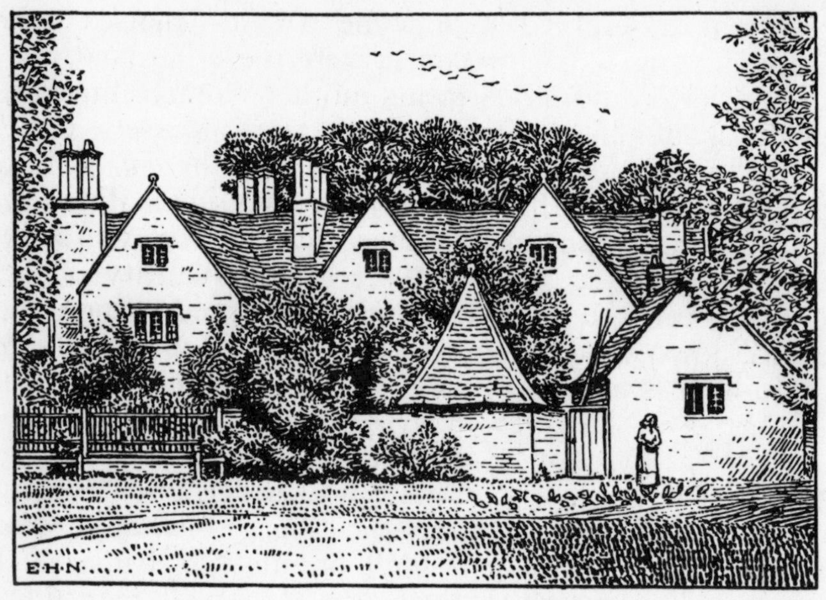

KELMSCOTT MANOR. FROM THE MEADOW AT THE BACK.

CHAPTER EIGHT: ICELANDIC LITERATURE AND TRAVEL.

ERE the second half of "The Earthly Paradise" had taken definite shape, Mr. Morris underwent a new experience, which not only left its mark, as it has been shown, upon the book he had in hand at the time, but was destined to affect materially the whole subsequent course of his literary career. "Considered in the light of a poet and story-teller," says Mr. Buxton Forman, William Morris "may be said to have started on his career as an Anglo-Norman mediævalist, drawing, however, considerable inspiration from the Greek and Latin classics, and gradually, with a widening area of knowledge and reading, taking in at first hand influences from the sturdy literature of the Northmen who peopled Iceland."

And this is how it all happened. In the year 1868 Mr. Morris became acquainted with the Icelandic scholar, Mr. Eiríkr Magnússon. At that time the vast field of Icelandic literature was practically an unknown territory to William Morris, who, however, immediately plunged into the subject with his characteristic enthusiasm. In order to attain the utmost possible proficiency in the language, Morris entered upon the systematic study of Icelandic under the guidance of Mr. Magnússon. The first book they read together was the "Story of the Dwellers at Eyr." Master and pupil continued in close collaboration together until the withdrawal of the former in 1871, on his appointment to his present post at the University Library at Cambridge. The first-fruits of the joint labours of the two friends was the translation of "The Saga of Gunnlaug the Worm-tongue and Rafn the Skald," which appeared in the "Fortnightly Review" of January, 1869 (a "beautiful little Saga," as Mr. Forman calls it," and "a piece pervaded by an exquisite sentiment, with a far larger element of intellectual life than the 'Story of Grettir' has"); and a separate volume entitled "The Story of Grettir the Strong," published also in 1869, translated from the "Grettis Saga," "one of the most remarkable prose works of ancient Icelandic literature." "Opposite the title-page of his 'Grettis

Saga,'" writes Mr. Forman, "Mr. Morris has inscribed a beautiful and noble-spirited sonnet—the two quatrains expository of a sad-faced and tender paganism, and the terminal sestett embodying somewhat of the poet's inevitable modern refinement of idea on the same subject." The sonnet ends thus:

> "Nay, with the dead I deal not; this man lives,
> And that which carried him through good and ill,
> Stern against fate while his voice echoed still
> From rock to rock, now he lies silent, strives
> With wasting time, and through its long lapse gives
> Another friend to me, life's void to fill."

"But there is no need of such evidence as this," comments Mr. Forman, "to prove the whole-hearted friendliness with which the fortunes of Grettir have been followed closely by the poet, and put into his own tongue. An almost exuberant sympathy with the hero of the saga appears and reappears in every chapter of the volume in some deftly-turned simplicity or vigorous piece of narration of vigorous proceedings. Many readers might perhaps find the story of Grettir dry. . . . The only love-passages that lend an interest to the book for such readers are in the foreign matter introduced into the saga in a late stage of its development, . . . passages, some of which are identical with passages in the romance of 'Tristram.'"

There followed, in May, 1870, "Völsunga Saga. The Story of the Volsungs and Niblungs with certain Songs from the Elder Edda." Like the foregoing, this translation was the work of Messrs. Morris and Magnússon, whose aim was, as they said, to make their "rendering close and accurate, and, if it might be so, at the same time, not over prosaic." In the preface they declare that "it is to the lover of poetry and nature, rather than to the student, that we appeal to enjoy and wonder at this great work, now for the first time, strange to say, translated into English." In the process of explaining the nature of the contents of the book, the translators say, "We have inserted entire into the text as Chapter XXXI. the first lay of Gudrun, the most lyrical, the most complete, and the most beautiful of all the Eddaic poems; a poem that any age or language might count among its most precious possessions. . . . In conclusion, we must again say how strange it seems to us that this Volsung tale, which is, in fact, an unversified poem, should never before have been translated into English. For this is the Great Story of the North, which should be to all our race what the Tale of Troy was to the Greeks." The prologue, in verse, by William Morris, consists of six seven-line stanzas, of which the concluding and most beautiful one runs as follows:

> "So draw ye round and hearken, English Folk
> Unto the best tale pity ever wrought!
> Of how from dark to dark bright Sigurd broke,
> Of Brynhild's glorious soul with love distraught,
> Of Gudrun's weary wandering unto naught,
> Of utter love defeated utterly,
> Of Grief too strong to give Love time to die!"

Here, says Mr. Forman, the reader "will find sentiment enough and romance enough—flashes of a weird magnificence that all the ice-hills of the Land of Ice have not been able to overreach with their long dusk shadows, and that all the 'cold grey sea' that rings the island of Thule has not washed free of its colour and heat. The marvels of this marvellous story are strongly upborne by the only firm pillars art has ever had—those, namely, whose bases are fixed in the utterly real, and whose capitals reach the topmost heights of the imaginative and ideal. The science of human souls shown in the general conception of the book, and the particular conception of each character, is perfect and deep and piercing—albeit those characters do not depart from the simplicity of primitive people. . . . Sigurd Fafnir's-bane . . . is not the rough character that Grettir is: he is not behind him in readiness to kill enemies, and so on, but there is a certain courtliness about him without the dishonesty of the court, and a comeliness without the effeminacy of the polished produce of later times. Grettir is a brute, but a noble brute; Sigurd is noble, but not a brute by a long way; and yet . . . the one fierce, headstrong savage of the 'Grettis Saga' seems to me a greater conception, artistically, than Sigurd or any other man of 'Völsunga.' As a work, however, this latter must carry the palm from its more grisly rival, for the variety's sake of its incidents and characters, and for the strength's sake of the finer feelings treated in it and ignored in the other. The one figure of the warrior-woman, Brynhild, so mere a woman for all her king-slayings and war-deeds, is priceless; and the working out of the final crash—full of passion and death and disaster —is a thing not often surpassed in any literature. . . . The Eddaic songs, translated and appended to the 'Völsunga' volume are very fine. Mr. Morris has doubtless done well to render these early poems in short irregular unrhymed stanzas, if stanzas they are to be called; and he has, without loss of ease and simplicity, given a good sprinkling of the alliterations which the Icelandic poets used for the adornment of their verse. His renderings of periphrastic expressions, too, have a peculiar excellence; and though this be the case, the finest of all the poems is peculiarly free from such expressions, probably by reason of the great earnestness of that poem's depicted sorrow, and the intense reality and simplicity of the whole scene." In short, to apply to this work in particular what has been said of his translations of the poems and tales of the Norsemen in general, it may fairly be claimed for William Morris that, by his successful renderings into our language he has "popularized in England some of the most beautiful poetry of a race with which we are closely connected by ties of ancestry and by the possession of a kindred tongue."

"The Story of Frithiof the Bold," in fifteen chapters, a translation by W. Morris alone, from the Icelandic, appeared between the months of March and August, 1871, in Volume I. of "The Dark Blue." The purpose of this serial was, as it announced, to "combine the salient points of existing monthly periodicals;" and accordingly "it was determined that an appeal should be made to the members of the University of Oxford, by means of circulars, begging them to contribute to and assist this new magazine" —hence its name. It may be mentioned here that Morris's contributions to different magazines and periodicals were numerous. Thus at this period, for instance, he contributed to "The Fortnightly Review" in August, 1868, "The God of the Poor: a Poem;" in October, 1868, "The Two Sides of the River: a Poem;" in April, 1869, "On the Edge of the Wilderness," a five-foot line poem in the form of a dialogue between Puellæ and Amans; and in February, 1871, "The Dark Wood," all of which were afterwards included in "Poems by the Way," the last-named poem appearing in that work with a new title, "Error and Loss." There were published also in "Good Words," April, 1869, a poem entitled "Hapless Love;" and in "The Academy," February 1st, 1871, four stanzas, entitled "The Seasons," reprinted in "Poems by the Way" with a variant in place of the original version of the last stanza on "Winter."

To continue the subject of translations from the Icelandic: in 1875 Messrs. Magnússon and Morris issued a volume entitled "Three Northern Love Stories, and other Tales." The contents, of which the first two items, as has been mentioned, had already appeared, are as follows:

The Story of Gunnlaug the Worm-tongue and Raven the Skald.
The Story of Frithiof the Bold.
The Story of Viglund the Fair.
The Tale of Hogni and Hedinn.
The Tale of Roi the Fool.
The Tale of Thorstein Staff-smitten.

The work was augmented with Notes and an Index.

Lastly, the two friends, Morris and Magnússon, cooperated in the preparation of the Saga Library for Mr. Bernard Quaritch. The first volume of this series, done into English out of the Icelandic, appeared in 1891, and contains:

The Story of Howard the Halt.
The Story of the Banded Men.
The Story of Hen Thorir.

The second volume appeared in 1892, and contains "The Story of the Ere Dwellers" (Eyrbyggja Saga) with "The

Is it enough for our rest,
the sight of this desolate strand,
And the mountain-waste voiceless as death
but for winds that may sleep not nor tire?
Why do we long to wend forth
through the length and breadth of a land,
Dreadful with grinding of ice,
and record of scarce hidden fire,
But that there 'mid the grey grassy dales
sore scarred by the ruining streams,
Lives the tale of the Northland of old,
and the undying glory of dreams?

* * * *

No wheat and no wine grows above it,
no orchard for blossom and shade;
The few ships that sail by its blackness
but deem it the mouth of a grave."

The remainder of the poem is not descriptive of the scenery.

In the preface to the second volume of the Saga Library, anent "The Story of the Heath-slayings," occurs a passage where Morris describes an object which he went to see, of peculiar interest: "A remarkable popular tradition . . . lives still in the country of Hunawaler, to the effect that, after the battle of the Heath, Bardi built up the work to this day called Burg-Work, and there defended himself against the Burgfirthers, being twice attacked by them in force. . . . Whatever may be the real origin of the popular tradition, the incontestable fact remains, that once upon a time the peak-shaped fell, . . . towering to the height of some 800 feet above the level of the sea, between the two steads of Mickle-Burg . . . and Little-Burg . . . in Willow-dale, was transformed by the labour of man into a military fortress. We ourselves had an opportunity of visiting the work in our trip to Iceland in 1871, and to inspect the by no means inconsiderable fortifications thrown, in the shape of walls made of large flat slabs, across all clefts in the natural basaltic rock which offered access to the top, standing over four feet thick, and in some places as many as ten feet high."

While Morris was away in Iceland Rossetti wrote to Bell Scott, to give him what news there was to give of their common friend: "We did not expect to hear again from Morris till his return, as the steamer which took him brought the first letter we got, on its passage back, and no other steamer could come thence till the one by which he will return—I believe about the 9th or 10th. However, a few days ago a letter did come (entrusted to some Danish merchantman sailing thence) and gave a very pleasant account, though not an elaborate one. He is enjoying himself thoroughly, finds the people so hospitable (where there are any) that his party has no lack of bearable provisions, and their rides consist of a cavalcade of no less than twenty-eight horses. Tent-sleeping they do not suffer from at all, even in cold weather, as the cold is thoroughly excluded. He has seen all kinds of localities connected with the sagas. He took sketching materials, but does not say if he has used them." On September 15th, after Morris's return, Rossetti writes to Bell Scott again, saying that Morris "has kept a diary in Iceland, but not for publication." Two years later Mr. Morris went to Iceland again. On this occasion he was not accompanied by Mr. Magnússon; and the stay he made in the island was of shorter duration than the first. It was whilst on this second visit of his that Morris passed through the great central desert of Iceland with its sand, "that founders the horses," strewn with huge boulders. The fields of lava, like beds of rough clinkers, seemed to him almost trackless. The lava, as he was interested to observe, by the way, owes its name in Icelandic to the traditional story of two unhappy bareserks, who, after bathing in a volcanic spring, were speared as they stepped out, and, slipping on a raw ox-hide, placed there for that purpose, fell back into the midst of the boiling water and thus were done to death by treachery. The violent winds that sweep over the country incessantly are another characteristic of the place. Morris noted, moreover, that there is not much vegetation in the island, but that parts of it are very beautiful, particularly where the wild swans gather. The inhabitants he found slow of speech with strangers, but great talkers once their tongues were loosed. They would sometimes refuse at first to provide Morris and his party with accommodation, unless they had what they considered something better to offer than fish and potatoes. The tent, however, was not called much into requisition, for in the end the travellers generally were sheltered with a roof over their heads. Their means of conveyance were ponies, and often a whole company would join them and ride with them from their last halting-stage to the next, to explain to them the points of interest on the way and introduce them to other people. Not a place in the island but there was localized some event or other which was to be read of in the sagas. To find the whole population fully acquainted with the traditions of their race, and able to show the exact spot where this or that scene had been enacted, was a unique experience for Morris, and one that he prized highly. The sagas date mainly from his favourite period, the thirteenth century. But whilst he held these to be of special value, he did not overlook the importance of the later ones; nor the fact that the people went on casting their national history in this form as late as the middle of the seventeenth century, when the celebrated raiding of the country by Algerian (or, as they called them, "Turkish") freebooters occurred, the last event to be recorded in saga shape.

How deeply Morris was impressed with this astounding country, as he used to call Iceland, may be judged, for instance, from the way he wrote of it in a notice of the Royal Academy Exhibition in 1884, in which, referring to the subject of a certain picture by Mr. Peter Graham, he described it as such that "cannot but move anyone who has visited the northern latitudes; there is a sense about it of romance and interest in life amidst poverty and a narrow limit of action, and maybe of thought, which is characteristic of a poor but historic country-side, and reminds me of many a morning's awakening in a country which one may call the northern limit of history, as it is certainly one of its richest treasure houses, Iceland to wit." And again, criticising a picture of Mr. Brett's, he says, "I am not ashamed, for instance, to remind him of what a mine lies untouched in Iceland; I could tell him of places there as wild and strange as the background of a fairy story, every rood of which has a dramatic tale hanging by it; and scenes moreover not unpaintable for a man like him, who mingles so much patience and determination with his skill." Again, in concert with Mr. Magnússon, Morris writes in the Introduction to the Saga Library: "Although Iceland is a barren northern island, of strangely wild, though to the eye that sees, beautiful scenery, the inhabitants of it neither are nor were savages cut off from the spirit and energy of the great progressive races. . . . Still more, while over the greater part of Europe at least, all knowledge of their *historical* past has faded from the memory of the people, and the last vestiges of their prehistorical memories are rapidly disappearing, in Iceland every homestead, one may almost say every field, has its well-remembered history, while the earlier folk-lore is embedded in that history, and no peasant, however poor his surroundings may be, is ignorant of the traditions of his country, or dull to them; so that a journey in Iceland to the traveller read in its ancient literature is a continual illustration, freely and eagerly offered, of the books which contain the intimate history of its ancient folk. . . . The fact that the Icelandic historians and tale-tellers were cut off from the influence of the older literature of Europe, was, we think, a piece of good luck to them rather than a misfortune. For the result was that, when the oral traditions and histories came to be written down and had to receive literary form, the writers had to create that form for themselves, and thereby escaped the meshes of the classical Latin pedantry which so grievously encumbers the mediæval literature of the rest of Europe, even in early times—a pedantry which would be unendurable if it were not that the mediæval writers misconceived it and made something else of it than was originally intended; since they saw it through the medium of feudal Christianity, and in this guise handed it down to us."

Morris's interest, however, was not confined to that merely of a student of Norse language, legend and history. His travels also enabled him to add to his experience as a handicraftsman. For instance, he observed, as he stated in his lecture at the Health Exhibition in 1884, that the fashion of "the looms in use in Iceland and the Faroes within the last sixty years for weaving ordinary cloth, plain or chequered," was in all essentials identical with the Greek looms of 400 B.C. Again, in offering a conjectural explanation of certain textile fabrics named in edicts of St. Louis and long a subject of debate among scholars, Morris's own impression was, he said, that these materials "were like the rudely flowered stuff traditionally made by the Italian peasants to-day, in the Abruzzi, for instance. . . . This impression is chiefly founded on the fact that exactly the same make of cloth is woven in Iceland for coverlets, saddle-cloths, and the like, the inference being that it was formerly in use very widely throughout Europe."

An episode, on its own merits scarce worthy of passing mention, must yet be related, on account of the great stir it occasioned in the literary world at the time; and also on account of the protracted paper warfare of which it was the opening skirmish. Inconsistently regardless of the fact that, to use his own words, "sooner or later all literature finds its own level, whatever criticism may say or do in the matter," a certain writer thought fit to expose "The Fleshly School of Poetry" in "The Contemporary Review" of October, 1871. The article in question was signed with the *nom de guerre* of Thomas Maitland. Professedly a review of Rossetti's volume of poems, at that date some eighteen months old, it was in effect a vehement attack upon Rossetti, and upon Swinburne and William Morris as well; the latter however being dealt with the most sparingly of the three. The strategic device employed by the author of the article to conceal his identity speedily led to his being discovered. For not only had Mr. Robert Buchanan, writing in the guise of a separate individual, assigned himself a prominent rank among the poets of the day—allotting them for the cast of "Hamlet," he placed his own name fourth in order, for the character of Cornelius, before Rossetti, Swinburne and Morris, on whom he bestowed respectively the parts of Osric, Rosencrantz, and Guildenstern—but he even went so far in advertising his own compositions as to specify those which Rossetti, so he alleged, had plagiarized. Now this, in view of the fact that the accusation he was bringing against Rossetti was, in the first place, one of immorality, and that not merely in the poet's treatment of his themes, but also in the actual subject matter, amounted to a deliberate attempt to throw dust in the eyes of the public, and deserved all that Rossetti and Swinburne could urge, by way of indignant retort, against "the stealthy school of criticism." Mr. Morris for his part did not deign to reply. And Mr. Buchanan, though professing—strangely enough, for he was undeniably the aggressor—to consider himself aggrieved in the matter, has long since withdrawn the worst of his charges. Therefore, whether or not he may have had any justification for pointing a moral in the case of Rossetti or Swinburne, is no concern here. But what shadow of pretext had he for including William Morris's name unless it was to help to adorn a much-varnished tale? In a sort of disclaimer which appeared in "The Academy" in the July following Rossetti's death Mr. Buchanan wrote: "Mr. Morris may be passed by without a word; he needs no apology of mine." Retracted or not retracted, however, the charge of fleshliness in any event should never have been brought against the poetry of William Morris. His prime offence indeed appears to have been that, with a friend's generosity, he had praised the volume of Rossetti's poems which happened to have met with Mr. Buchanan's disapproval. "The book," thus wrote Mr. Morris in "The Academy" of May 14th, 1870, "is satisfactory from end to end," and "I think these lyrics, with all their other merits, the most complete of their time; nor do I know what lyrics of any time are to be called *great* if we are to deny the title to these." Morris wrote no less enthusiastically on the appearance, some years afterwards, of Rossetti's sonnets, which he described as being "unexampled in the English language since Shakespeare's for depth of thought, and skill and felicity of execution."

As to the notices of Mr. Morris's "holiday-makings"

out. It will be a very fine work." (The writer then goes on to refer to the article in "The Contemporary Review," already noticed.) The year 1872 was not over when there appeared, antedated 1873, the poem of which the full title is "Love is Enough, or the Freeing of Pharamond. A Morality." In this work, as Mr. Gosse observes, Morris "essayed a stately analysis of certain transcendental phases of emotion." There is a deeper strain of reflection in "Love is Enough" than any part of "The Earthly Paradise" can show. An abstract of the former poem may be gathered from Mr. Hewlett's article in "The Contemporary Review," already quoted: "Pharamond, the hero, is . . . represented to us as having been in former years a pattern-king, undaunted in adversity, unspoilt by prosperity,—a gallant soldier in the field, a wise judge on the throne. But we only see him as the slave of phantasy, haunted by dreams of an ideal love which benumb his energies and destroy his peace. Faint with the sickness of hope deferred, he deserts his people . . . and attended by one faithful follower, wanders over land and sea, enduring grievous perils, until he realizes in a lowly maiden the fair enchantress of his visions. He returns home to find his throne occupied and his people's affections estranged." But he does not wait long to bandy words with the usurper, nor to reproach his subjects for their disloyalty. "He abdicates without a pang, and cheerfully retires to love and obscurity. . . . Azalais his love . . . appears but once, to fall instantly in love with the sleeping stranger, and accept without scruple or inquiry the recognition with which he greets her on waking." The henchman Oliver's "unquestioning devotion to his master is truthfully . . . pourtrayed." "An abstract personage such as Love is apt to talk too metaphysically to be readily intelligible to a concrete audience." Between each scene he "appears before the curtain in an emblematic disguise;" his "ministers are supposed to chaunt the lyrical interludes that follow. . . . The universality of love's dominion is gracefully typified by exhibiting its influence over three couples of unequal rank, a newly-wedded Emperor and Empress, in whose honour the morality is played, the actor and actress who fill the leading parts, and a rustic pair selected from the throng of spectators. The simple, tender converse of the latter is full of charm." Mr. Buxton Forman is of opinion that this "dramatic and lyric morality derives the more marked features of its poetic method from the Icelandic; and it is to the second period that both this and several renderings of Icelandic sagas belong, though some of them remained in manuscript till a recent date. The period is that in which Morris shows a prevailing feeling of Northern hardiness, has abandoned the three Chaucerian stock metres, and developed a metric system with anapæstic movement surpassing in every vital particular all that has been done in anapæstic measures since Tennyson showed the way in 'Maud.'" In somewhat similar strain writes Mr. Robert Steele, who says that "'Love is Enough' . . . marks still further advance in the handling of a difficult metre and in its use of the 'tale within a tale' method. Moreover it is distinguished by its lovely lyrics, too often passed over in silence." These songs, composed in long stanzas with double rhymes, are indeed the most delightful feature of the book. Two stanzas, one out of the second, and the concluding one from the fourth interlude, may be given as typical of the style and melodious metre of the rest:

"And what do ye say then?—that Spring long departed
Has brought forth no child to the softness and showers;
—That we slept and we dreamed through the Summer of flowers;
We dreamed of the Winter, and waking dead-hearted
Found Winter upon us and waste of dull hours."

And

"Is he gone? was he with us?—ho ye who seek saving,
Go no further; come hither; for have we not found it?
Here is the House of Fulfilment of Craving;
Here is the Cup with the roses around it;
The World's Wound well healed, and the balm that hath bound it:
Cry out! for he heedeth, fair Love that led home."

It was about the time of the dissolution of the original partnership of Morris, Marshall, Faulkner, and Co., in 1874, that William Morris changed his town residence

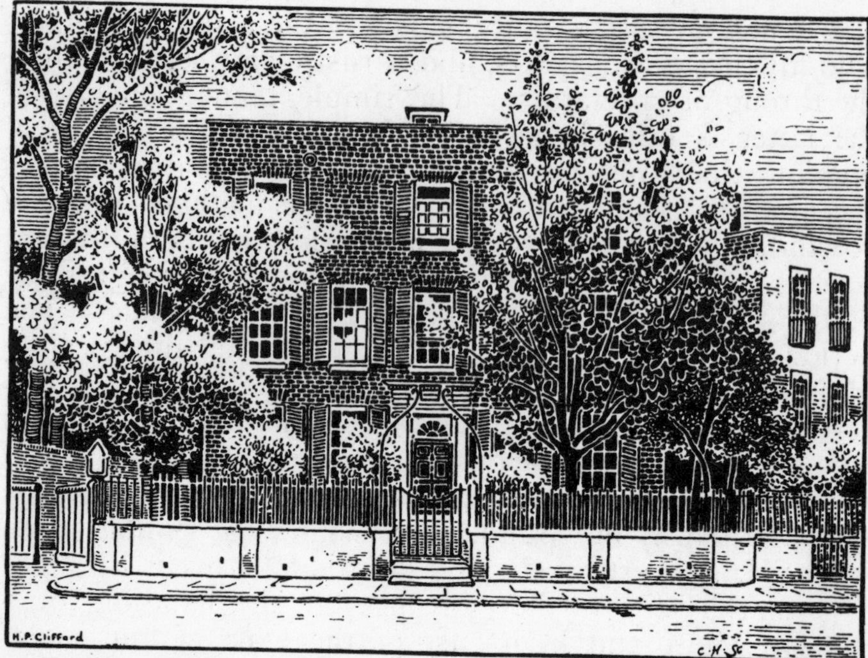

KELMSCOTT HOUSE. UPPER MALL, HAMMERSMITH.

from Queen Square, Bloomsbury, to Horrington House, Chiswick, which he held until he moved, only a few years later, to No. 26 on the Upper Mall, Hammersmith. This house, which faces the river, he named, after his country home on the Upper Thames, Kelmscott House. It is said to have been occupied formerly by Dr. George Macdonald, and, earlier still, by Francis Ronalds, the electrician, who came to live there in 1816. By him were conducted some of the very first experiments in telegraphy, in the garden at the back of the house and in the sheds adjoining—the same buildings which Morris made use of for his carpet weaving, and turned subsequently into Socialist club and lecture-rooms.

But to resume the subject of poetry. Morris's next departure after "Love is Enough" was again of quite a different order. "The Aeneids of Virgil. Done into English Verse" appeared in 1875 (dated 1876). Mr. Nettleship has remarked of this translation that "the number of lines in each book in the original is accurately reproduced, that the periods were ended as Virgil ended them, and that Virgil's unfinished lines are never finished by his translator." In short it is a very close rendering. Mr. Watts-Dunton says that while giving "us an almost word-for-word translation" Morris "yet throws over the poem a glamour of romance which brings Virgil into the sympathy of the modern reader." Another writer has said of this work of Morris's that "modulated to the metre of Chapman's Homer and written largely in the Elizabethan language, it is a . . . piece of ingenious and often exquisite word-workmanship, which testifies . . . to an amazing literary dexterity;" while, according to Mr. Steele, it "was an attempt on Mr. Morris's part to express his own view of the poem. The substance of the Aeneid is a collection of folk-lore tales; and in telling them to a modern audience he wished to remove them from the 'classical' atmosphere, and to replace it by the simpler, earlier one. In this aim he has succeeded." In connection with the Virgil it is convenient, in this place, to mention "The Odyssey of Homer. Done into English Verse" by W. Morris, although this work was, in point of time, dissevered from the former altogether, and did not in fact appear until the year 1887. It is written in anapæstic couplets.

"Some competent critics are dissatisfied," writes Mr. Watts-Dunton, with Morris's translation of the Odyssey; "yet in a certain sense it is a triumph. The two specially Homeric qualities—those, indeed, which set Homer apart from all other poets—are eagerness and dignity. Never again can they be fully combined, for never again will poetry be written in the Greek hexameters and by a Homer. . . . Morris gave us a translation of the entire Odyssey, which, though it missed the Homeric dignity, secured the eagerness as completely as Chapman's free-and-easy paraphrase, and in a rendering as literal as Buckley's prose crib, which lay frankly by Morris's side as he wrote." A writer in "The Westminster Gazette" has described how he called upon Morris one day and happened to find the poet in the act of working at his version of the Odyssey, with the help of Bohn's translation. His visitor expressed astonishment, and ventured to suggest that, if Morris did indeed consider it necessary to use a translation at all, that by Messrs. Butcher and Lang would be far more suitable. Morris replied that in the first place he was not confident enough to dispense with a translation altogether; but that at the same time he had chosen purposely the most prosaic and had avoided the one named, not wishing to let any of the phrases in it, fine as they were, run in his head and get reproduced in his own rendering. Of the two works "The Standard" says: "Previous renderings of the great books of antiquity have either endeavoured to produce the local colour of the original with as great accuracy as possible, or to transfer the thoughts of the ancient poet to modern readers by employing the diction of the generation for whom the version is intended. Mr. Morris adopted a third course. . . ." He strove "to show us the Aeneids and the Odyssey as seen through Scandinavian spectacles. That is . . . he gave us the poem as if it had reached him through the Eddas of the Viking age." A more sympathetic writer, Mr. Lang, remarks: "The reader of Mr. Morris's poetical translations has in his hands versions of almost literal closeness, and (what is extremely rare) versions of poetry by a poet."

In 1876 Mr. Morris caused to be printed for private circulation only, not for sale, three poems, viz., "The Two Sides of the River," "Hapless Love," and "The First Foray of Aristomenes." The last was a fragment, in heroic measure, of a poem never carried out, called "The Story of Aristomenes." "The Two Sides of the River" had been published, as stated, eight years, and "Hapless Love" seven years, previously. The whole work did not exceed the size of a pamphlet of some two and twenty pages.

In 1877, the following year, was published the work which Morris himself, it is said, preferred to all his other efforts in epic form, and that one of which he was proudest, viz., "The Story of Sigurd the Volsung, and the Fall of the Niblungs." This poem may almost be called a colossal work. It consists of four books, which again are subdivided into nine, ten, fifteen and seven sections respectively. The names and arguments of the several books are as follows:

Book I. Sigmund. In this book is told of the earlier days of the Volsungs, and of Sigmund the father of Sigurd, and of his deeds, and of how he died while Sigurd was yet unborn in his mother's womb.

Book II. Regin. Now this is the first book of the Life and Death of Sigurd the Volsung, and therein is told of the birth of him, and of his dealings with Regin the master of masters, and of his deeds in the waste places of the Earth.

Book III. Brynhild. In this book is told of the deeds of Sigurd, and of his sojourn with the Niblungs, and in the end of how he died.

Book IV. Gudrun. Herein is told of the days of the Niblungs after they slew Sigurd, and of their woeful need and fall in the House of King Atli.

This long poem is written throughout in anapæstic rhyming couplets. In "The Story of Sigurd" the flame which had burnt lowest in the "Jason," and flickered but fitfully in "The Earthly Paradise" (flaring up on such rare occasions, for example, as when Sthenobœa plays Potiphar's wife to Bellerophon's Joseph, or when again Gudrun, having lost the only man she loved, was driven frantic at the marring of her own life and Kiartan's by their two unsatisfactory marriages), broke forth afresh, rekindled into fervour,—not indeed with the same fierce, consuming fire of Guenevere's passion, but with a steady, radiant glow, communicated, as it were, from the furnace of Hindfell. Mr. Richard Le Gallienne describes "Sigurd the Volsung" as a "splendidly forceful" poem; "a masterly version of the famous myth, and, indeed, largely derived from the 'Völsunga Saga.' To the vigour and dramatic power of the book quotation can do little justice, as its most striking effects are cumulative, as in the splendid battle descriptions, and in such a scene as the haunting death of King Gunnar. Of the strong movement of the verse, the opening lines will give some idea, though even here quotation is like bringing one wave to convey the idea of an ocean." Nevertheless it is not possible to forbear to give these grand and sonorous lines:

"There was a dwelling of Kings ere the world was waxen old;
Dukes were the door-wards there, and the roofs were thatched with gold;
Earls were the wrights that wrought it, and silver nailed its doors;
Earls' wives were the weaving-women, queens' daughters strewed its floors,
And the masters of its song-craft were the mightiest men that cast
The sails of the storm of battle adown the bickering blast.
There dwelt men merry-hearted, and in hope exceeding great
Met the good days and the evil as they went the way of fate:
There the Gods were unforgotten, yea whiles they walked with men,
Though e'en in that world's beginning rose a murmur now and again
Of the midward time and the fading and the last of the latter days,
And the entering in of the terror, and the death of the People's Praise."

Of Sigurd's magnificent speech, on his mother's disclosing to him the precious treasure stored up, "a hope of much fulfilment," to wit, "the shards of Sigmund's sword," one must be content to quote but the concluding verses:

"'They have shone in the dusk and the night-time, they shall shine in the dawn and the day;
They have gathered the storm together, they shall chase the clouds away;
They have sheared red gold asunder, they shall gleam o'er the garnered gold;
They have ended many a story, they shall fashion a tale to be told:
They have lived in the wrack of the people; they shall live in the glory of folk;
They have stricken the Gods in battle, for the Gods shall they strike the stroke.'"

Once more, here are the words of Brynhild's invocation when first she meets with Sigurd, the opening line of which recalls another in the same poem where Morris pictures daybreak as the moment of the "sun's uprising, when folks see colours again":

"'All hail, O Day and thy Sons, and thy kin of the coloured things!
Hail, following Night, and thy Daughter that leadeth thy wavering wings!
Look down with unangry eyes on us two to-day alive,
And give us the hearts victorious, and the gain for which we strive!
All hail! ye Lords of God-home, and ye Queens of the House of Gold!
Hail, thou dear Earth that bearest, and thou Wealth of field and fold!
Give us, your noble children, the glory of wisdom and speech,
And the hearts and the hands of healing, and the mouths and the hands that teach!'"

The death-song of the noble King Gunnar, fallen into the pitiless power of Atli, and thrust, harp in hand, into the pit of adders and serpents, is not less majestic but too long unfortunately for quotation.

Mr. Andrew Lang has observed that "Mr. Morris took the form of the story which is most archaic, and bears most birth-marks of its savage origin—the version of the 'Völsunga,' not the German shape of the 'Nibelungenlied.' He showed extraordinary skill, especially in making human and intelligible the story of Regin, Otter, Fafnir, and the Dwarf Andvari's Hoard." It is interesting to note the different points of view in the several treatments of the myth—a comparison which is worked out somewhat fully by Dr. Francis Hueffer, as follows: "Of the two modern versions of the tale which are most thoroughly inspired by the ancient myth, one, that of Wagner in his tetralogy 'Der Ring des Nibelungen,' is dramatic in form, the other, Morris's 'The Story of Sigurd the Volsung,' bears all the characteristics of the epic. To this difference of artistic aim, the difference of shape which the tale takes in the hands of the two poets may be traced. In one point, however, they agree. Both Wagner and Morris go back to the old Icelandic sources in preference to the mediæval German version of the tale embodied in the 'Nibelungenlied.' From this the German poet borrows little more than the localization of his drama on the banks of the river Rhine, the English poet scarcely anything but his metre—the *langzeile* or long line with six high-toned and any number of unaccentuated syllables. The ordinary modern reader taking up the 'Völsunga Saga' or either of the Eddas without preparation would probably see in them little more than a confused accumulation of impossible adventures and deeds of prowess, with an admixture of incest, fratricide, and other horrors. But on looking closer one discovers a certain plan in this entanglement. . . ." To "the modern poet who is courageous enough to grapple with such a subject, two ways are open. . . . Either he may wholly abandon the sequence of the old tale and group its *disjecta membra* round a leading idea as a centre, or else he may adhere to the order and essence of the legend as originally told, only emphasizing such points as are essential to the significance of the story, and omitting or throwing into comparative shade those incidents which by their nature betray themselves to be arbitrary additions of later date. Wagner has chosen the former way, Morris the latter. This fact, and the divergent requirements of the drama and the epic, sufficiently account for their difference of treatment. . . . With an astounding grasp of detail, and with a continuity of thought rarely equalled, Wagner has re-moulded the confused and complex argument of the old tale, omitting what seemed unnecessary, and placing in juxtaposition incidents organically connected but separated by the obtuseness of later saga-men. Morris, as has been said before, proceeds on a different principle. His first object is to tell a tale, and to tell it as nearly as possible in the spirit and according to the letter of the old Sagas. In this he has succeeded in a manner at once indicative of his high poetic gifts and of a deep sympathy with the spirit of the Northern myth, which breathes in every line and in every turn of his phraseology."

"It is the influence of the Northern sagas," says Mr. Arthur Symons, "which took possession of Morris as they took possession of Wagner, both having passed through a period of complete absorption in the knightly and romantic Middle Ages; and both, at the last, going back to the primitive antiquity of legend, and of Northern legend. With Morris we feel that certain energies, latent in the man from the first, and, indeed, compressed within certain limits by the exercise of a most energetic will, have at last been allowed free play. The simple, artificial English of the earlier books gives place to a new, and in a sense not less artificial style, returning upon earlier English models, and forging for itself monosyllabic words which are themselves energies. In 'The Story of Sigurd,' which remains his masterpiece of sustained power, he goes sheer through civilization, and finds an ampler beauty shadowed under the dusk of the gods. He gets a larger style, a style more rooted in the earth, more vivid with the impulse of nature; and the beauty of his writing is now a grave beauty, from which all mere prettiness is clean consumed away. And now, at last, he touches the heart; for he sings of the passions of men, of the fierceness of love and hate, of the music of swords in the day of battle. And still, more than ever, he is the poet of beauty; for he has realized that in beauty there is something more elemental than smiling lips, or the soft dropping of tears."

A wider significance in "The Story of Sigurd" has been perceived by some writers, like Mr. A. L. Lilley, for example, who discourses thus in "The Commonwealth:" "Morris found the definite inspiration of his song in Teutonic legend, in the gigantic primeval world of Scandinavian myth. To it we owe his greatest work, the 'Sigurd,' and that cycle of half-prose, half-verse romances which his death left incomplete. Nothing can better illustrate the essential unlikeness of Morris to his age than a comparison of the way in which he treated this legendary material with that in which it has been treated by Wagner and Ibsen. On the one hand is the wild incalculableness of life, its destructive rage and wrath bursting forth inevitably and unaccountably from its centres of sanest and deepest feeling. On the other is life well in hand, a great ordered body of feeling and purpose, moving, with struggle and effort, indeed, but with certainty too, and self-control, to its appointed end, and that an end of assured justice and good. . . . For Morris 'Sigurd' is . . . the protagonist of right, of a true social order. Whatever shadows may rest upon his soul, the battles have to be fought and won, the struggle against external wrong must go on continually, 'for the hope of the days to be.' Morris found in the Teutonic ideal of tribe-fellowship, of the subordination of the individual life to the age-long life of the House, or of the Kindred, all the elements of a reasonable joy and purpose and satisfaction for the individual life itself. Within the limits of a true social order he believed with his whole soul that there lay the elements of all that is essentially individual—of art, of morals, of religion."

The above view of the matter may or may not be justified; for how is it possible to be quite certain as to what unconscious influences may have been at work in the poet's mind at the time of his writing "The Story of Sigurd?" But that, even had they been present, Morris would willingly have allowed them—one cannot say to obtrude themselves, for that is out of the question, but even so much as to modify his treatment of the theme in any way, is not probable. If indeed he did so it was quite an exceptional case. And why, it may be argued, should he have chosen so indirect a means of saying what he could have said, nay, often did say, when occasion was, in direct and forthright fashion? It seems, then, far more in keeping with his taste and general custom to suppose that his purpose was simply to tell a pleasant tale in the pleasantest manner possible. Be that as it may, however, there is no doubt as to the extraordinary genius of the man who could write a poem so scholarly and so beautiful as this. "Think of the forces at work," writes Mr. Watts-Dunton, "in producing a poem like 'Sigurd.' Think of the mingling of the drudgery of the dryasdust with the movements of an imaginative vision unsurpassed in our time; think, I say, of the collaborating of the 'Völsunga Saga' with the 'Nibelungenlied,' the choosing of this point from the saga-man, and of that point from the later poem of the Germans, and then fusing the whole by imaginative heat into the greatest epic of the nineteenth century. Was there not work enough here for a considerable portion of a poet's life?" In fine, "The Story of Sigurd the Volsung" is such that, for those high qualities, as Mr. Forman observes, "which derive from knowledge of life, feeling for national myth, epic action and tragic intensity combined, . . . stands among the foremost poems not only of this century but of our literature."

CHAPTER NINE: THE PARTING OF THE WAYS.

THOSE persons who had been in the habit of complaining that they found the subjects of William Morris's pen—his "Guenevere," "Jason," "Earthly Paradise," "Love is Enough," and "Sigurd," his translations of the Æneid and Norse Sagas, of merely literary and archæological interest; too much belonging to an unreal land of dreams and legend; or, if not mythological, at any rate too far away in scene and circumstance to apply to their needs and be of practical help in the present, were destined before long to receive a surprise, it may be said a shock, in some of his later poems, and in most of his later prose writings. "A serious generation," so we were told, "found something wanting in 'the idle singer of an empty day;' they wanted more body in their poetry—more 'criticism of life'—a more courageous endeavour to stand up to the problems of the age and make the best of them, instead of fleeing for refuge into fairyland." They experienced from reading "The Earthly Paradise" the drowsy sensations of "lotus eating." They felt themselves aggrieved at "the constant effort to detach poetry from modern life and connect it with a past age of romance." They reproached the poet that he shrank from grappling with the questions of the day; yet it may be doubted whether, when Mr. Morris did come forward to express his views on a matter of public concern, his critics were satisfied. Anyhow, he vindicated himself once and for all from the charge of indifference to contemporary affairs. It was in the autumn of the year 1876. Through the length and breadth of Europe an outburst of indignation had followed the notorious Bulgarian atrocities; and more particularly in this country the demand for redress had rung forth clamant, peremptory. It seemed as though the misgovernment of the Turk really was going to be put a stop to once and for all. Time glided by, however, and nothing was done; when at the end of a few weeks a reaction set in and dominant opinion seemed unaccountably to have veered round, so that there was actually a likelihood of England, under the Tory ministry, being driven to take up arms on the side of Turkey. Then it was that Mr. Morris addressed a letter, dated October 24th, to "The Daily News," under the heading "England and the Turks." Had we gone to the help of the victims of the Turks, Mr. Morris would have rejoiced, he said, "in such a war, and thought it wholly good. . . . I should have thought I had lived for something at last: to have seen all England just and in earnest, . . . and our country honoured throughout all the world." But, on the contrary, as things were, after three weeks he found England, to his sorrow, "mocked throughout all the world." The many resolutions that had but recently been passed calling for the punishment of the Turkish "thieves and murderers" had proved mere empty words; while the rumour in the air to the effect that England was going to war on behalf of the Turks filled Mr. Morris with consternation, and impelled him to protest in the most formal and forcible way he could. "I who am writing this," he said, "am one of a large class of men—quiet men, who usually go about their own business, heeding public matters less than they ought, and afraid to speak in such a huge concourse as the English nation, however much they may feel, but who are now stung into bitterness by thinking how helpless they are in a public matter that touches them so closely." Such a war as threatened was a monstrous shame, a disaster, a curse. Of so "cynically unjust" a proceeding Morris was convinced that "nothing could come . . . but shame in defeat, shame in victory." "I appeal," he said, "to the working men, and pray them to look to it that if this shame falls upon them they will certainly remember it and be burdened by it when their day clears for them, and they attain all, and more than all, they now are striving for." And in conclusion, "I beg with humility to be allowed to inscribe myself, in the company of Mr. Gladstone and Mr. Freeman, and all men that I esteem, as an hysterical sentimentalist,"—for such, after all, was the worst taunt with which their opponents knew how to reproach them. The whole letter is astonishingly modern and apposite to present circumstances. In fact, with the alteration of certain names of persons and places, it reads as if it had been written but yesterday.

Mr. Morris again had occasion to come before the public under somewhat similar circumstances at the beginning of 1878. At that time, it will be remembered, there seemed imminent prospect of England being dragged into the Russo-Turkish struggle, in active support of the Ottoman cause. The sentiment of this country was divided on the subject, and party feeling was strong on either side. Various meetings were held in different parts to discuss the situation. In London, on January 16th, two meetings were held to advocate the preservation of neutrality by the nation in respect of Eastern affairs. The first meeting took place in the afternoon at Willis's Rooms. It was organized by the committee to promote the free navigation of the Straits of the Dardanelles and the Bosphorus, the Hon. and Rev. W. H. Fremantle in the chair. William Morris was present, and delivered a speech in which he pronounced the Turks to be, in his opinion, irreformable (prophetic words which have received the saddest confirmation in the recent massacres of Armenians in Constantinople and in the East—events fresh in everybody's memory), denounced the "war at any price" party, and concluded by insisting that "the country ought to offer the most earnest resistance to schemes that were a disgrace to the names of peace, goodwill, and justice."

In the evening of the same day another meeting with the same objects was convened at Exeter Hall by the Eastern Question Association and the Workmen's Neutrality Committee, Morris being present on this occasion also. In the early part of the proceedings was read from the platform a song, in five stanzas of eight lines each, commencing "Wake, London lads," written by William Morris in support of the intention of the meeting. A copy of these verses, printed on a broadside for distribution, had been placed in the hands of every person entering the hall, so that, when they were sung by the choir to the tune of "The Hardy Norseman's Home of Yore," a large number of the audience took part in the singing. Mr. Mundella, M.P., was in the chair, and at the close Mr. Morris seconded the vote of thanks to him for presiding. The platform tickets for this Neutrality Demonstration bore a vignette designed by Burne-Jones, entitled "Blind War." As they would have of course to be given up by all who availed themselves of them, specimens of the ticket must now be exceedingly rare. Mr. Fairfax Murray, however, has a copy both of the platform ticket and of the broadside, bound up in a volume of pamphlets collected by the late William Bell Scott, bearing on the Eastern Question.

From this time forward, except the translation of the Odyssey in 1887, already mentioned, Morris published no volume of poetry until the appearance of "Poems by the Way," in 1891; neither, until the same year (1891), which witnessed also the first issue of the Saga Library, had he published any more translations from the Icelandic since the appearance of "Three Northern Love Stories" in 1875. The contrast is very striking between the prolific output of poetry in his earlier years, *i.e.*, from 1858 to 1877, during which time six important works (including "The Earthly Paradise," itself equivalent to four) appeared, and the later period, from 1878 to his death in 1896, during which he published but two poetical works, or three, if the verse translation of "L'Ordene de Chevalerie," comprised, under the title of "The Ordination of Knighthood," together with "The Order of Chivalry," in one volume, in 1893, be counted.

It would seem almost as though there were few middle courses open for a poet to choose between the two extreme alternatives of his art on the one hand, and the world of living humankind on the other. Of the class who are absolutely unconcerned with anything beyond their own art, Keats may be taken as an example, in whose poetry hardly a single allusion to contemporary affairs is to be found; Keats whose imagination was lulled into a sort of charmed sleep, out of which all his life through he never waked to any of the sterner realities of daily existence. There is the poet, on the contrary, who, at starting, is keenly alive to the problems of his day; ay, he whose gift of foresight is so much more penetrating than that of the vast mass of his contemporaries that it enables him to anticipate far ahead of them all—so far, indeed, that he becomes himself unpractical. Such a man was Byron, who, born aristocrat though he was, did not hesitate to utter sentiments that were counter to all the hereditary prejudices of his class, and could not fail to estrange and isolate him. "The king-times," he wrote, "are fast finishing; there will be blood shed like water and tears like must, but the peoples will conquer in the end. I shall not live to see it, but I foresee it." A political career being impossible for him under these circumstances, he threw himself, as Matthew Arnold points out, upon poetry as his organ, and from his advanced position turned deliberately, in all a pessimist's despair of the present, to excess and luxury, for distraction. Morris avoided either of these courses, as also he was wise enough to avoid another error of an opposite kind, viz., the poet's who, striving to be the prophet of his age, and to proclaim his message through the medium of his poetry, misses the point at which he has aimed, and, becoming overwhelmed in a maze of tortuous emotions, only succeeds in providing intellectual conundrums for learned Browning societies to wrangle over. With Morris it was altogether different. Arriving at last, through a process the reverse of Byron's, that is, through poetry and the arts, face to face with the tremendous study of modern life, he yet kept his poetry as far as possible disengaged from the entangling mesh of social and political problems, and at the time when these came uppermost in his mind he practically abandoned poetry. Hence the disproportionate quantity produced in his later years. Hence also the fact that such poems as he did produce were all of them shorter pieces; his perfect sense of the fitness of things showing him the incompatibility of heroic poetry with any modern theme. For a nineteenth century epic is assuredly a contradiction in terms. "An epic poem on a historical subject," as the "Edinburgh Review" rightly says, "is a form of composition which the experience of poets and the progress of criticism seem to have condemned. It is difficult to imagine an epic written now upon the Peninsular or the Crimean War. As civilization advances the poet is driven to deal with purely imaginative stories, or with legends of a remote past. Information becomes more accessible, and men become more sensitive to inaccuracies in matters of fact. How could a poet re-cast the Crimean War so as to give it anything of the poetic shape of the Wars of Thebes or Troy? He would meet with insuperable obstacles both in style and subject. How could he prevent his language from becoming at times irredeemably prosaic? . . . The true material for an epic would seem to be, not recent fact, but the remote memories of a people's past, glorified and shaped by the imagination of successive generations, or the artistic efforts of successive minstrels." The age of skald and bard, mouthpieces and inspirers of the people, is now passed away. Much as one may regret it, one has to face the fact that at the present day the oracle of the masses finds its chosen mode of utterance in the prose of the newspaper; and that poetry—good poetry—is not the language that suits them. The only kind that does appeal to them is the doggerel recited on the stage of the music-hall. But to such depths of laurelled degradation it was of course inconceivable that Morris could ever have suffered himself to sink.

But unmodern in theme and mould as was William Morris's poetical work, it is not to be denied that, at an early date in his career, he betrayed symptoms of unrest and dissatisfaction with our existing condition of things. Thus an examination of "The Earthly Paradise" will disclose tokens of a conflict, as it were, going on in the poet's mind between his art and his politics, either striving for the mastery. Mr. Oscar Triggs, indeed, professes to trace a logical and continuous development of ideas in Morris from the beginning, and to show that both his later and earlier writings harmonize and interpenetrate. "The poet's Socialism," writes the American critic, "grew out of his love of art, which inflamed him with a desire to bring all men within its domain, while the 'Earthly Paradise' reveals a man who chose to live before he wrote. He invites us to

> 'Forget six counties overhung with smoke,
> Forget the snorting steam and piston stroke,
> Forget the spreading of the hideous town ;
> Think rather of the pack-horse on the down,
> And dream of London, small, and white, and clean,
> The clear Thames bordered by its gardens green ;'

and shows us Chaucer's London that he may recover for us the conditions of life which made possible the peculiar spring-tide quality of Chaucer's poems. And before he wrote he repeated for himself the principles of living, only from which pure art can spring. The latter work announces the prophecy implied in the former." "Just consider," said Morris in an address to the Society for the Protection of Ancient Buildings, "the immeasurable difference between the surroundings of the workmen of the present day and the workmen of the fourteenth century. Consider London of the fourteenth century—a smallish town, beautiful from one end to the other; streets of low whitewashed houses, with a big Gothic church standing in the middle of it; a town surrounded by walls, with a forest of church towers and spires, besides the cathedral and the abbeys and priories; every one of the houses in it, nay, every shed, bearing in it a certain amount of absolute, definite, distinct, conscientious art. Think of the difference between that and the London of to-day, whose houses either have no attempt at ornament or architecture about them, or, where they have ornament, make us regret that there is such a thing; and at least where art exists, it is paid for by the foot, and only comes in as part of the conditions of contract which rules all society among us; whereas in the old town the ornament grew spontaneously out of the method of work. The modern conditions of labour were not known in the old time. Yet even this difference between the towns in the fourteenth and nineteenth centuries does not express the difference which exists between the workmen of the two ages. It is far greater than that. Just consider what England was in the fourteenth century. The population, rather doubtful, but I suppose you may take it at about four millions. Think then of the amount of beautiful and dignified buildings which those four millions built; of whom there were, of course, the regular proportion of women, children, and idlers. As we go from parish to parish in England we see in each a church which is, or at all events has been, beautiful, and in every town we see important and sometimes huge and most elaborate buildings, the very sight of which fills us with a kind of awe at the patience and skill which produced them. But further, we have to consider not only those churches and houses which we see, but also those which have been destroyed, and all those other beautiful abbey buildings, *e.g.*, of which only a few relics have been left, and of which Cobbett truly says that at the time of the Reformation England must have looked like a country which had been subject to a cruel invasion. Those buildings also, though they contained little upholstery contained much art: pictures, metal work, carvings, tapestry, and the like, altogether forming a prodigious mass of art, produced by a scanty population. Try to imagine that. Why, if we were asked, supposing we had the capacity, to reproduce the whole of those buildings with their contents, we should have to reply, 'The country is not rich enough—every capitalist in the country would be ruined before it could be done.' Is not that strange? Surely there must be some reason for that." And so the more Morris pondered on these things, the more wide and accurate his knowledge of history and of the literature and art of the Middle Ages became, the more thoroughly was he persuaded that "the art of that time was the outcome of the life of that time," and the more was he struck by the terrible contrast presented by the life of the workmen of the past and the life of the workmen of to-day, and the more profound grew his sense of dissatisfaction with the present conditions of society. But to go back again some twenty years, it is in "The Life and Death of Jason," perhaps the last place where one would look to find it,—

so remote is the classic legend both in scene and subject from the life of our own day—that the first note of discontent is sounded. Apostrophizing therein his master Chaucer, Morris refers to ourselves as being "meshed within this smoky net of unrejoicing labour." On the other hand, in the Prologue to "The Earthly Paradise," published a year later, he seems to repudiate, as being but a "dreamer of dreams," the care and responsibility of taking part in measures of reform. "Why should I strive," he asks, "to set the crooked straight?" and in protest asseverates that he is only "the idle singer of an empty day." For the issue was undecided; was perhaps even undefined as yet. But the mere fact of the poet reasoning on the matter at all shows that the idea of setting the crooked straight *had* already presented itself to him, in some form or other, as a possible duty to be undertaken, and that the rival claims had ere now begun to contend within him. "His mood changed from 'The Earthly Paradise,'" writes Mr. Walter Crane, "though even there, in the opening verses, the very fact that he seemed conscious of the turmoil and trouble of the world outside would indicate what afterwards happened—that he would finally be compelled to listen to it, to form an opinion, and take his part in the great industrial battle. That he did not hesitate on which side, or with whom, to cast his lot, is not to be wondered at when one considers the thoroughness of his nature."

Abundant indications of revolutionary tendency are to be found in the body of the poem. Thus, in "Bellerophon in Argos," there occurs the stirring injunction:

> "Yea, and bethink thee, mayst thou not be born
> To raise the crushed and succour the forlorn,
> And in the place of sorrow to set mirth,
> Gaining a great name through the wondering earth?"

If the high purpose here set forth may not be pronounced as necessarily Socialistic, at any rate the author's views with regard to the injustice of privileged class government are definite and unmistakable. Take, for instance, another passage from the last-quoted poem:

"Do thou bide at home,
And let the king hear what may even come
To a king's ears; meddle thou not, nor make
With any such; still shall the brass pot break
The earthen pot—a lord is thanked for what
A poor man often has in prison sat."

In another passage he says:

"Some smiled doubtfully
For thinking how few men escape the yoke
From this or that man's hand, and how most folk
Must needs be kings and slaves the while they live,
And take from this man, and to that man give
Things hard enow:"

in another:

"Like the wise ants, a kingless, happy folk
We long have been, not galled by any yoke."

And in another:

"Ever must the rich man hate the poor."

At the end of the tale of "The Proud King" the writer bursts forth:

"But ye, O kings, think all that ye have got
To be but gawds cast out upon some heap,
And stolen while the Master was asleep."

And once again he gives vent to his indignation as follows:

"Many-peopled earth!
In foolish anger and in foolish mirth,
In causeless wars that never had an aim,
In worshipping the kings that bring thee shame,
In spreading lies that hide wrath in their breast,
In breaking up the short-lived days of rest,—
In all thy folk care nought for, how they cling
Each unto each, fostering the foolish thing,
Nought worth, grown out of nought, that lightly lies
'Twixt throat and lips, and yet works miseries!"

And here he expresses his yearning desire for the realization of his ideal:

"Ah! good and ill,
When will your strife the fated measure fill?
When will the tangled veil be drawn away
To show us all that unimagined day?"

A section of Morris's admirers would have preferred to

have him engaged incessantly and exclusively in active propaganda of Socialism. If the truth must be told, his having written poetry at all is an awkward fact, and one of which they are rather ashamed. In the eyes of these people every moment Morris gave to art and letters was so much wasted time that needs apology, that can be justified only on the plea that it was the recreation he allowed himself as a relief from the arduous strain of political agitation. But this is a poor compliment to pay their hero. It is practically an assertion that in the vast amount of poetry and prose romance he produced he was not in earnest! Was ever trifling so elaborate and so sustained known before? No; it will not do. Morris's poetry was neither the plaything to which he resorted for pastime, nor the narcotic by which he induced oblivion. As long as he was able to do so with a free conscience he devoted himself to poetry heart and soul. But there was that spirit latent within him which was bound to assert itself sooner or later; that spirit which, when he at first became conscious of it, maybe he would fain have repressed, but such that nevertheless was destined to become the ascendant and in effect the controlling force of his life. The first intimations of its presence occur in the "Jason," as has been shown above; it makes itself felt more manifestly and more persistently in the "Earthly Paradise." To all seeming dormant (or is it stifled by effort?) in "Love is Enough" and in "Sigurd," it breaks forth imperious thereafter, never again to be subordinated, but to become ever more and more paramount as the poet's years increased.

The die had long since been cast, long since the choice of paths made irrevocably, when, in 1891, Morris published his "Poems by the Way." The collection ranged over a long period—included, in fact, all the best of the shorter poems that Morris had written since "The Defence of Guenevere." Of these a considerable number had already been published in magazines and papers, viz., beside those named already, the poem called "Of the Three Seekers," in "To-Day," January, 1884; "Meeting in Winter," in

Macmillan's "English Illustrated Magazine," March, 1884; "The Hall and the Wood," in the same of February, 1890; and "The Day of Days," in "Time," November, 1890. The last should be included among the Socialist poems, like "The Message of the March Wind," "Mother and Son," "The Voice of Toil," "The Day is Coming," and "All for the Cause," which had previously made their appearance in political journals or pamphlets. There were also certain verses for pictures by Burne-Jones, *e.g.*, the four stanzas for "The Briar Rose" series of paintings, exhibited at Messrs. Thomas Agnew and Sons' in 1890; and others for tapestry, *e.g.*, "The Woodpecker," "Pomona," "Flora," and "The Orchard." But not the least notable feature in "Poems by the Way" was a series of ballads translated from the Icelandic and the Danish, and a certain further number of original ballads inspired by them. In the poem "Mother and Son," according to "The Academy," "the piece that is perhaps the strongest Mr. Morris has written, . . . there are strokes with a fearless ring that reminds one strongly of Rossetti's 'Jenny;' and the whole volume, indeed, not only betokens a splendid vitality of gift . . . but recalls at every turn that its author is one of a famous fraternity . . . who have been animated, despite all their differences, by a certain common spirit, and endowed with a similar cunning in the craft of song." "In none of his previous works," says another writer, "does Mr. Morris show an eye and a hand so sure as here;" and "in all that is noble in temper and beautiful in art this volume could hardly be surpassed, even by the poet of 'Sigurd.' . . . Howsoever rapturously the poet may delight in the rich and wonderful world in which he finds himself, the moment he stays to reflect, the moment he stays to ask himself what it all means, there comes upon him that high seriousness, that 'sad earnestness,' which is the foundation of the great poetry of Hellas. . . . Although in Mr. Morris's case the high poetic temper does not wane, but, on the contrary, waxes with years, its expression is mellower now." The work, representing, as it does, manifold phases of thought and emotion, certainly could not be charged with aloofness from human interests, the characteristic which, as it has been shown, many had deplored in Morris's earlier poems. The song, once languorous, it was remarked, now "vibrates oftener;" the former "faint voices . . . have begun to speak in more human tones." A writer in "The Academy" recognizes in "Poems by the Way," "a passion for equal justice, a sympathy with outcast classes, and a vision of coming redress," as imparting to this work a strength and substance which could not be claimed for Morris's work in the days of "The Earthly Paradise." Again, "another influence . . . that of the old Norse life and literature . . . just like that of Socialism, is certainly one that has given additional vigour and glory to the poet's verse."

CHAPTER TEN: LECTURES, ARTICLES, AND OPINIONS.

FROM the year 1878 to the last year of his life Morris became more and more prominent as a lecturer and writer on all sorts of subjects connected with the arts; and that not merely in respect of their technical processes, in which he was an adept, but in the social and economical bearings of the question. With him, indeed, were not to be dissociated the two aspects, the political gaining ever greater importance in his eyes, and becoming even more predominant in his writings and public utterances as time advanced. The amount of brain-work entailed in the preparation of so many lectures, articles, &c., as are enumerated below—and the following cannot pretend to be an exhaustive list of Morris's labours in this field—is enormous, and such that cannot easily be estimated.

In 1878 Morris delivered an address before the Trades' Guild of Learning, entitled "The Decorative Arts, their Relation to Modern Life and Progress." In the same year the lecture was issued in pamphlet form with its original title, but when it came out again in 1882 in the volume "Hopes and Fears for Art: Five Lectures delivered in Birmingham, London, and Nottingham, 1878-1881," its title was changed to "The Lesser Arts." The above-named volume comprised "The Art of the People," delivered before the Birmingham Society of Arts and School of Design in the Town Hall at Birmingham on February 19th, 1879, and "The Beauty of Life," a lecture delivered exactly a year later, to the very day, before the same Society by Mr. Morris in his new capacity of President. (This lecture was first published in Birmingham in 1880 under its original title of "Pleasure *versus* Labour and Sorrow.") The two concluding items in "Hopes and Fears for Art" are "Making the Best of it," a paper read before the Trades' Guild of Learning and the Birmingham Society of Artists; and "The Prospects of Architecture in Civilization," delivered at the London Institution. Two more lectures by Morris, entitled respectively "The History of Pattern Designing," and

"The Lesser Arts of Life," were published in 1882. The volume in which these last-named lectures appeared has a preface by Morris's friend, Professor Middleton, in conjunction with whom he wrote for the ninth edition of the "Encyclopædia Britannica" (Edinburgh, 1884), an article on the subject of "Mural Decoration."

Prior to this, on November 14th, 1883, at a meeting organized by the Russell Club at Oxford, Morris delivered a lecture on "Art under Plutocracy" in the hall of University College. Professor Ruskin, with whom, long as they had been acquainted, Morris never came much into personal contact, was present on the high-table daïs to support the lecturer on this occasion, and in a short speech referred to Morris as "a great conceiver, a great workman, at once a poet and an artist." He urged the necessity of union, and called upon the young men to help in giving the best direction to the "great forces which, like an evil aurora, were lighting the world, and thus to bring about the peace which passeth understanding." In concluding the lecture, in which he had denounced the modern industrial and economical system, Morris said, "It is my business here to-night and everywhere to foster your discontent," and, as a practical step, advised his audience to marry, as it would be called, "beneath" them in order to break down the existing social barriers between class and class. Fancy that in a College Hall! It was not to be expected that the Reverend Master, with the responsibilities of office upon him, could sit and listen quietly to such counsels being given to undergraduates in his very presence; accordingly Mr. Franck Bright rose up, and in the most emphatic manner protested that the College Hall had not been lent for any such purpose. The lecture was published in the February and March numbers of the magazine "To-Day," 1884. On January 23rd, 1884, Morris delivered, before the Secular Society of Leicester, a lecture on "Art and Socialism," afterwards published at Leek. In the above-named magazine, "To-Day," in July, 1884, appeared a notice of "The Exhibition of the Royal Academy" of the current year "by a rare visitor"—for so

Morris described himself. In this article the writer states that the aims of a painter should be briefly:

1st. Expression of Imagination;
2nd. Decorative Beauty;
3rd. Realization of Nature;
4th. Skill of Execution.

"Success," he says, "in any of the three first of these aims, *together with the last*, will give a picture existence as a work of art." Morris further observes that the way the Chantrey Bequest is administered is "the sort of thing which gets the Academy the bad name it has got, and makes it perhaps the most contemptible public body in England—which is saying much." In the Lecture Room of the International Health Exhibition Mr. Morris delivered, on July 11th, 1884, a lecture on "Textile Fabrics," afterwards published for the Executive Council of the Exhibition, and the Council of the Society of Arts. In 1887 Morris published a pamphlet "The Aims of Art," a lecture incorporated with six others more or less political and economical, in "Signs of Change" (1888). To "The Fortnightly Review" of May, 1888, he contributed an article on "The Revival of Architecture," and to the same periodical in November an article on "The Revival of Handicraft," in which he discussed the probabilities of hand-workmanship recovering the place usurped from it by machinery as a means of production. On November 1st in the same year, at the New Gallery, he lectured on "Tapestry and Carpet Weaving," one of a series of lectures organized by the Arts and Crafts Exhibition Society.

Morris wrote for "The Nineteenth Century" of March, 1889, a paper on "Westminster Abbey and its Monuments," in which he said, "we may call" the Abbey Church "the most beautiful of all English buildings, and unsurpassed in beauty by any building in the world;" and again, "Placed in the centre of the shabbiest, ugliest, and most ridiculous capital in the world, with London squalor on the one hand, and London eclectic fatuity and sham on the other, it upholds for us the standard of art or the pleasure of life, contrasted with dirt and its degradation, beyond all other buildings." In another place he says, on the same subject, "We live in the middle of this world of brick and mortar, and there is little else left us amidst it, except the ghost of the great church at Westminster, ruined as its exterior is by the stupidity of the restoring architect, and insulted as its glorious interior is by the pompous undertaker's lies, by the vainglory and ignorance of the last two centuries and a half—little besides that and the matchless Hall near it;" and again elsewhere he describes Henry VII.'s chapel as a "most romantic work of the late Middle Ages," rendered, however, as to its exterior, little more than "an office study" by Wyatt's disastrous rebuilding. The article in "The Nineteenth Century" was occasioned by Mr. Shaw-Lefevre's scheme for erecting a memorial chapel for further interments and monuments, for which the available room in the Abbey Church is rapidly becoming exhausted. Criticizing the existing monuments, Morris divided them into two categories, viz., those which do, and those which do not "harmonize" with the architecture of the church. Disfiguring as the official undertakers' monuments are, they have at least fulfilled a good end, not contemplated by those who erected them, to wit, they have saved the walls they cover from the hand of the "restorer." But as to the memorials of more recent times, "the busts produced by modern sculpture are not quite congruous with the architecture of people who knew how to carve." Mr. Morris insists then, as of absolute necessity, that "no more monuments of any kind should be placed in the Abbey Church, on any pretext whatever." In the matter of the proposed mortuary annexe, as Morris observes elsewhere, "the welfare of the noblest building ever raised by Englishmen ought to be the first thing considered." His passionate admiration for the ancient abbey increased as years went by. Thus, in the year previous to his death, writing to "The Times" to protest against the "restoration" of the royal tombs, Morris said that it would amount to nothing short of a "national disaster,"

drawing of the office. The draughtsmanship of the architects of ancient buildings was not particularly splendid nor complete. For most of the beautiful buildings throughout the country nothing, in fact, beyond the roughest draught was prepared. "They . . . grew up simply, without any intermediary between the mind and the hands of the people who actually built them." And the chief reason was that the builders of those days "were traditionally acquainted with the best means of using the material, which, happily for them, they were forced to use—the materials that were all round about them in the fields and woods amidst which they passed their lives."

On January 26th, 1892, Morris read before the Society of Arts a paper, afterwards published, with illustrations, in the Journal of the Society, on "The Woodcuts of Gothic Books." In recognition of this service he received, at the end of the session 1891-92, the Society's silver medal.

On February 15th, 1892, Morris wrote for the Kelmscott edition of Ruskin's "The Nature of Gothic" a special preface. Herein he says that, to his mind, this chapter of "The Stones of Venice" "is one of the most important things written by the author, and in future days will be considered as one of the very few necessary and inevitable utterances of the century. . . . For the lesson that Ruskin here teaches us is that art is the expression of man's pleasure in labour; that it is possible for man to rejoice in his work, for, strange as it may seem to us today, there have been times when he did rejoice in it; and lastly, that unless man's work once again become a pleasure to him, the token of which change will be that beauty is once again a natural and necessary accompaniment of productive labour, all but the worthless must toil in pain, and therefore live in pain. So that the result of the thousands of years of man's effort on earth must be general unhappiness and universal degradation. . . . If this be true, as I for one most firmly believe, it follows that the hallowing of labour by art is the one aim for us at the present day. . . . But for this aim of at last gaining happiness through our daily and necessary labour, the time is short enough, the need . . . urgent. . . . And we may well admire and love the man who here called the attention of English-speaking people to this momentous subject, and that with such directness and clearness of insight that his words could not be disregarded." Ruskin was not indeed the first man who "put forward the possibility and the urgent necessity that men should take pleasure in Labour. . . . But in their times neither Owen nor Fourier could possibly have found the key to the problem with which Ruskin was provided," to wit, "the element of sensuous pleasure, which is the essence of all true art. Nevertheless, it must be said that Fourier and Ruskin were touched by the same instinct, and it is instructive and hopeful to note how they arrived at the same point by such very different roads." To Morris the most characteristic side of Ruskin's writings is the ethical and political part of them—elements which, from the time of his writing "The Nature of Gothic," have "never been absent from his criticisms of art; and, in my opinion," says Morris, "it is just this part of his work fairly begun in the" chapter above-named "and brought to its culmination in that great book, 'Unto this Last,' which has had the most enduring and beneficent effect on his contemporaries, and will have, through them, on succeeding generations." In a word, "John Ruskin has done serious and solid work towards the new birth of society, without which genuine art, the expression of man's pleasure in his handiwork, must inevitably cease altogether, and with it the hopes of the happiness of mankind."

"The address to the President and Council of the Royal Institute of British Architects," says "The Saturday Review," "to protest against the proposal to make the practice of architecture a closed profession, bears amongst other names that of William Morris. It is printed at the end of the Preface, p. xxxiv, to a collection of essays on the subject, entitled 'Architecture, a Profession or an Art,' published by Mr. Murray in 1892."

In 1893 was published "Medieval Lore: an Epitome

of the Science, Geography, Animal and Plant Folk-Lore and Myth of the Middle Age: being Classified Gleanings from the Encyclopedia of Bartholomew Anglicus on the Properties of Things," edited by Robert Steele, with a preface by William Morris. The latter is particularly interesting, as it sets forth the position with regard to mediæval studies. "It is not long since the Middle Ages . . . were supposed to be an unaccountable phenomenon accidentally thrust in betwixt the two periods of civilization, the classical and the modern, and forming a period without growth or meaning, a period which began about the time of the decay of the Roman Empire, and ended suddenly, and more or less unaccountably, at the time of the Reformation. The society of this period was supposed to be lawless and chaotic; its ethics a mere conscious hypocrisy; its art gloomy and barbarous fanaticism only; its literature the formless jargon of savages; and as to its science, that side of human intelligence was supposed to be an invention of the time when the Middle Ages had been dead two hundred years. The light which the researches of modern historians, archæologists, bibliographers and others have let in on our view of the Middle Ages has dispersed the cloud of ignorance on this subject. . . . For many years there had been a growing reaction against the dull 'gray' narrowness of the last century. . . . At last the study of facts by men who were neither artistic nor sentimental came to the help of that first glimmer of instinct, and gradually something like a true insight into the life of the Middle Ages was gained. . . . The men of those times are no longer puzzles to us; we can understand their aspirations, and sympathize with their lives, while at the same time we have no wish (not to say hope) to put back the clock, and start from the position which they held. For, indeed, it is characteristic of the times in which we live, that whereas in the beginning of the romantic reaction, its supporters were, for the most part, mere *laudatores temporis acti*, at the present time those who take pleasure in studying the life of the Middle Ages are more commonly to be found in the ranks of those who are pledged to the forward movement of modern life." In another place Morris speaks to the same effect: "I will be bold to say that many of the best men among us look back much to the past, not with idle regret, but with humility, hope, and courage; not in striving to bring the dead to life again, but to enrich the present and the future." But to return to the preface to "Medieval Lore." "The reader before he can enjoy . . . what was once a famous knowledge-book of the Middle Ages," says Morris, "must cast away the exploded theory of the invincible and wilful ignorance of the days when it was written; the people of that time were eagerly desirous for knowledge, and their teachers were mostly single-hearted and intelligent men, of a diligence and laboriousness almost past belief. This 'Properties of Things' of Bartholomew the Englishman is but one of the huge encyclopedias written in the early Middle Ages for the instruction of those who wished to learn, and the reputation of it and its fellows shows how much the science of the day was appreciated by the public at large, how many there were who wished to learn. . . . It is a hopeful sign of the times when students of science find themselves drawn towards the historical aspect of the world of men, and show that their minds have been enlarged and not narrowed by their special studies, a defect which was too apt to mar the qualities of the seekers into natural facts in what must now, I would hope, be called the just-passed epoch of intelligence, dominated by Whig politics, and the self-sufficiency of empirical science." Elsewhere Morris speaks of "the great period of genuine creation" which was "once called the Dark Ages by those who had forgotten the past, and whose ideal of the future was a comfortable prison." Morris held that if those ages are dark it is only because our own blindness makes them so to us, and to speak of them as dark, therefore, is but a confession of ignorance on our own side. "The part which they played in the course of history was not only necessary to the development of the life of the world, but was so special and characteristic that it will leave its mark on future ages in spite of the ignorant contemplation of them, from which we are slowly emerging."

Once more on this subject Morris says: "The past art of what has grown to be civilized Europe from the time of the decline of the ancient classical peoples, was the outcome of instinct working on an unbroken chain of tradition: it was . . . human and fruitful ever: many a man it solaced, many a slave in body it freed in soul; boundless pleasure it gave to those who wrought it and those who used it: long and long it lived . . . while it kept but little record of its best and noblest; for least of all things could it abide to make for itself kings and tyrants: every man's hand and soul it used, the lowest as the highest, and in its bosom at least were all free men: it did its work, not creating an art more perfect than itself, but . . . freedom of thought and speech, and the longing for light and knowledge, and the coming days that should slay it: and so at last it died in the hour of its highest hope, almost before the greatest men that came of it had passed away from the world. It is dead now; no longing will bring it back to us; no echo of it is left among the peoples whom it once made happy."

On June 19th, 1893, Morris read a paper on "The Ideal Book" before the Bibliographical Society in Hanover Square, a paper afterwards published among the Society's Transactions of the year. In July, 1893, Morris wrote a preface to the collection of "Arts and Crafts Essays," published in one volume in 1893. Herein he sets forth "the way in which it seems to me we ought to face the present position of" the "revival in decorative art. . . . And in the . . . first place, the very fact that there is a 'revival' shows that the arts aforesaid have been sick unto death. . . . The position which we have to face then is this: the lack of beauty in modern life (of decoration in the best sense of the word), which in the earlier part of the century was unnoticed, is now recognized by a part of the public as an evil to be remedied if possible; but by far the larger part of civilized mankind does not feel the lack in the least, so that no general sense of beauty is extant which would *force* us into the creation of a feeling for art which in its turn would *force* us into taking up the dropped links of tradition, and once more producing genuine organic art. Such art as we have is not the work of the mass of crafts-men unconscious of any definite style, but producing beauty instinctively. . . . Our art is the work of a small minority, composed of educated persons, fully conscious of their aim of producing beauty, and distinguished from the great body of workmen by the possession of that aim." Elsewhere Morris observed: "The workman of to-day is not an artist as his forefather was, . . . it is the hope of my life that this may one day be changed, that popular art may grow again in our midst; that we may have an architectural style, the growth of its own times, but connected with all history." Again he says, "the line of traditions is broken." It takes a thousand years in a straight line to produce a traditional style, and "we have nothing like a stream of inspiration to carry us on. The age is ugly—to find anything beautiful we must 'look before and after.' . . . No, if a man nowadays wants to do anything beautiful he must just choose the epoch which suits him and identify himself with that—he must be a thirteenth century man, for instance." And yet again he says: "Whatever there is of" the art of our own day "that is worth considering is eclectic," for "the present century has no school of art but such as each man of talent or genius makes for himself to serve his craving for the expression of his thought while he is alive, and to perish with his death." In many other places Morris insisted on the impossibility of any art flourishing which was the exclusive possession of the so-called cultivated classes only. "The truth is . . . the laboured education of a few will not raise even those few above the reach of the evils that beset the great mass of the population: the brutality, of which such a huge stock has been accumulated lower down, will often show, without much peeling, through the selfish refinement of those who have let it accumulate." Again: "The reflex of the grinding trouble of those who toil to live that they may live to toil weighs upon them also, and forbids them to look upon art as a matter of importance: they know it but as a toy, not as a serious help to life. . . . They think that as labour is now organized art can go indefinitely as *it* is now organized, practised by a few, adding a little interest, a little refinement to the lives of those who have come to look upon intellectual interest and spiritual refinement as their birthright. No, no, it can never be." "We cannot have art by striving after its superficial manifestation." But to return to the Preface of the "Arts and Crafts Essays;" Morris goes on to say he does not "ignore the fact that there is a school of artists belonging to this decade who set forth that beauty is not an essential part of art; which they consider rather as an instrument for the statement of fact, or an exhibition of the artist's intellectual observation and skill of hand. . . . The modern 'Impressionists' loudly proclaim their enmity to beauty, and are no more unconscious of their aim than the artists of the revival are of their longing to link themselves to the traditional art of the past. Here we have then, on the one hand, a school which is pushing rather than drifting into the domain of the empirical science of to-day, and another which can only work through its observation of an art which was once organic, but which died centuries ago, leaving us what by this time has become but the wreckage of its brilliant and eager life, while at the same time the great mass of civilization lives on content to forgo art almost altogether. . . . Now it seems to me that this impulse in men of certain minds and moods towards certain forms of art, this genuine eclecticism, is all that we can expect under modern civilization; that we can expect no *general* impulse towards the fine arts till civilization has been transformed into some other condition of life, the details of which we cannot foresee. Let us then make the best of it, and admit that those who practise art must nowadays be conscious of that practice. . . . But having made the admission let us accept the consequences of it, and understand that it is our business as artists, since we desire to produce works of art, to supply the lack of tradition by diligently cultivating in ourselves the sense of beauty, . . . skill of hand, and niceness of observation, without which only a *makeshift* of art can be got." Morris's contributions to the book consist of essays on "Textiles," "Printing," and "Of Dyeing as an Art." These three papers had already appeared in the several catalogues of the exhibitions of the Society; two of them in the same form in which they were republished, while the third, the essay on "Printing," was a paper which, in its original form, had been issued in the name of Emery Walker alone. It was afterwards recast entirely, and in its new state, with important additions, it now appeared in the names of William Morris and Emery Walker together.

In August, 1893, was completed the Kelmscott Press reprint of the "Utopia," with a "Foreword" written specially for this edition by William Morris. The work, he says, is one which embodies "the curious fancies of a great writer and thinker of the period of the Renaissance." In another place Morris calls him "the representative of the nobler hopes of his day." But to resume: "The change of ideas concerning the best state of a 'publique weale,' which, I will venture to say, is the great event of the end of this century, has thrown a fresh light upon the book; so that now to some it seems . . . (in its essence) a prediction of a state of society which will be." He then goes on to point out the value of the work as a historic link in the study of sociology, connecting, as it does, the surviving communist tradition of the Middle Ages with "the hopeful and practical progressive movement of to-day. . . . The action of the period of transition from mediæval to commercial society with all its brutalities, was before his" (More's) "eyes; and though he was not alone in his time in condemning the injustice and cruelty of the revolution which destroyed the peasant life in England, and turned it into a grazing farm for the moneyed gentry; creating withal at one stroke the propertyless wage-earner and the masterless vagrant (*hodie* 'pauper'), yet he saw deeper into its root-causes than any other man of his own day. . . . The spirit of the Renaissance, itself the intellectual side of the very movement which he strove against, was strong in him; . . .

supplanted in him the chivalry feeling of the age just passing away. To him war is no longer a delight of the well born, but rather an ugly necessity. . . . Hunting and hawking are no longer the choice pleasures of knight and lady, but are jeered at by him as foolish and unreasonable pieces of butchery: his pleasures are in the main the reasonable ones of learning and music. . . . In More . . . are met together the man instinctively sympathetic with the communistic side of mediæval society; the protester against the ugly brutality of the earliest period of commercialism; the enthusiast of the Renaissance, ever looking toward his idealized ancient society as the type and example of all really intelligent life; the man tinged with the asceticism at once of the classical philosopher and of the monk. . . . These qualities and excellences meet to produce a steady expression of the longing for a society of equality of condition; a society in which the individual man can scarcely conceive of his existence apart from the commonwealth of which he forms a portion. This . . . is the essence of his book. . . . Though doubtless it was the pressure of circumstances in his own days that made More what he was, yet that pressure forced him to give us . . . a picture (his own, indeed, not ours) of the real New Birth, which many men before him had desired; and which now indeed we may well hope is drawing near to realization, though after such a long series of events which at the time of their happening seemed to nullify his hopes completely."

On November 2nd, 1893, Morris lectured at the New Gallery "On the Printing of Books;" and to the January number of Messrs. Cassell and Co.'s "Magazine of Art" in 1894, contributed a paper entitled "Some Notes on the Illuminated Books of the Middle Ages," in which he remarked that illumination is "an art which may be called peculiar to the Middle Ages, and which commonly shows mediæval craftsmanship at its best." He then sketches the progress of the art from its earliest days down to its disappearance in 1530.

At the South London Art Gallery on January 14th,

1894, Mr. Morris delivered an address on "Early England," in which he gave a graphic and interesting sketch of the fortunes of this island and its occupiers in the earliest historic times. Hammersmith, his home, was situated, he remarked, in the Hundred of Ossulton, a name which survived, although the site of that place, which might have dated from the successors of the Romans in Britain, could not be determined at the present day. Morris spoke in high terms of Ethelwulf's son, King Alfred the Great (to whom he refers elsewhere as "the only decent official that England ever had"). "No other man of genius," he said, "sat on the throne of England save Cromwell, who was mourned more during life by his friends than at death, and after all Alfred was the one man of genius who ever held that position in this country." Nothing could be more romantic than the history of Harold the Hapless, and he (Morris) could only regret that no native pen had preserved for us such a narrative of that fatal battle of Senlac as would have proceeded from an Icelandic source.

In September, 1894, Morris wrote an introductory note to an edition of Dr. J. M. Neale's carol of "Good King Wenceslas," pictured by Mr. A. J. Gaskin, of the Birmingham School. In this note Morris observes that Dr. Neale was a representative of a certain aspect of the party movement to which he belonged, an aspect "which, unless I am mistaken, has almost died out as a special characteristic of Ritualism—the historical side, to wit. This has happened, I think, because of the growth amongst thinking people generally of a sense of the importance of mediæval history, and of the increasing knowledge that the ecclesiastical part of it cannot be dissociated from its civil and popular parts. Mediæval history, in all its detail, with all its enthusiasms, legends and superstitions, is now cultivated by many who have no ecclesiastical bias, as a portion of the great progress of the life of man on the earth, the discovery of which as an unbroken chain belongs almost entirely to our own days."

In the first volume of "Bibliographica" (1895), appeared a paper by W. Morris "On the Æsthetic Qualities of the

Woodcut Books of Ulm and Augsburg in the Fifteenth Century." Morris here declares that his own choice among books of the school rests with the work of an Ulm printer, John Zainer, viz., "Boccaccio De Claris Mulieribus" (1473), and that "partly because it is a very old friend of mine, and perhaps the first book that gave me a clear insight into the essential qualities of the mediæval design of that period." The qualities, or rather the merits, in question are two, and comprise what is essential in all picture books, viz., firstly, decorative beauty; and, secondly, the telling a story. The decorative quality is produced in these books unconsciously, that is to say, it is the accidental product of the skilful workman, whose skill is largely the result of tradition, so that it "has become a habit of the hand to him to work in a decorative manner. . . . The subject-matter of the book also makes it one of the most interesting, giving it opportunity for setting forth the mediæval reverence for the classical period, without any of the loss of romance on the one hand, and epical sincerity and directness on the other, which the flood-tide of Renaissance rhetoric presently inflicted on the world. . . . The great initial S I claim to be one of the very best printers' ornaments ever made."

On December 14th, 1895, in the Bolt Court School, Fleet Street, Morris delivered a lecture, organized by the London County Council, on the subject of "Early Illustration." He commenced the lecture with an attractive sketch of the evolution of the art. Organic work in the way of illustration had, he said, two qualities, viz., the ornamental and the epical; that is, the quality of telling a story with the interest of incident. This latter quality, however, after a short life of about fifty years only from its beginning, was displaced by the rhetorical, which did not tell a story but took hold of all sorts of minor incidents that had nothing to do with it. The art of illustrating books with woodcuts was apparently of German origin, the best work of early days having been carried out in that country. The lecturer concluded by exhibiting a series of lantern slides representing various woodcuts of the fifteenth and early sixteenth centuries, beginning with the work of Germany, and passing thence to that of France, Italy, and Spain.

The recognition that William Morris received in official quarters was scant compared with that which his eminence and vast influence in the world of art and letters might have warranted. The distinction he valued most was being elected, in 1882, an Honorary Fellow of his old college, Exeter, at Oxford, where he had already taken his M.A. degree in 1875.

In 1876, and thenceforward every subsequent year to 1895—that is for twenty years in succession, until his health broke down and he could no longer serve—Morris was appointed one of the examiners of the works submitted for the National Competition of Schools of Science and Art and Art Classes at South Kensington. That the department "set great store upon his experience and judgment" was testified by the chairman in introducing him before his lecture at the Health Exhibition in 1884.

In 1882 a Royal Commission was being held to inquire into the subject of technical instruction, and Mr. Morris having been called upon to give evidence was examined on March 17th, at South Kensington, Mr. Bernhard Samuels in the chair. The minutes of the proceedings were published in a Government Blue Book. Morris's evidence, embodying as it does the results of his practical experience on the questions at issue, is so valuable that extracts from it may well be given here. The inquiry at an early stage being directed to the comparative degrees of originality of the French and of the people of this country, Morris said that he believed certainly that the latter possess this quality, and that although a great deal is talked about the superiority of the French in design, he did not think the point was one of essential difference in character between the two peoples as such. "It is," said he, "to a great extent a question of training. The French are above all things masters of style in the arts of design. For my own part I doubt if they have so much innate love of beauty as a great part of our population has. In matters of style the French are supreme; they can take two or three ugly things and combine them into a congruous whole which looks plausible at least." Asked to define the mastery of style which he had said he considered to be a national characteristic of the French, Morris replied that what he meant might be described as the ingenious faculty of working up one thing to fit in with another into a result which strikes the eye at once. At the same time, he said, "I think that in appreciation of beauty, in love for beautiful lines and colours, the French cannot be said to be superior to the English, certainly not in matters of colour. . . . So long as a thing is in a definite style it seems to satisfy the ordinary French mind, even though it is obviously ugly. . . . The department of manufacture into which design enters, that I know most of, from my own business, is textiles. . . . We English copy largely from the French in some things. I was in Manchester some time ago and a calico printer there showed me his designs, and on my asking where he got them, he told me most of them came from Paris; from what he said I judge that it is a common practice in Manchester to buy parcels of drawings from Paris, and shuffle and piece them into a variety of patterns." Continuing he said: "I think it is a thing to be rather deprecated that there should be a class of mere artists like some of these Paris designers, who furnish designs, as it were, ready made, to what you may call the technical designers, the technical designers having next to nothing to do with the drawing. . . . The designer learns about as much as is necessary for his work from the weaver in a perfunctory and dull sort of manner. . . . I think it would be better, when it could be managed, that the man who actually goes through the technical work of counting the threads and settling how the thing is to be woven through and through, should do the greater part of the drawing." Asked what practical remedy he would propose Morris replied: "What I want to see really is, and that is the bottom of the whole thing, an education all round of the workman, from the lowest to the highest, in technical matters as in others." When asked whether he considered that elementary literary instruction has much influence upon the ultimate success of a workman as a workman, Morris replied: "Yes: I should say it has undoubtedly. I often have great difficulty in dealing with the workmen I employ in London because of their general ignorance." "Would you consider that, in addition to literary instruction, instruction in drawing should be given in elementary schools, to those who are to become artizans in after life?" "I think, undoubtedly, everybody ought to be taught to draw just as much as everybody ought to be taught to read and write." In another place Morris says: "As to the kind of drawing that should be taught to men engaged in ornamental work there is only *one best* way of teaching drawing, and that is teaching the scholar to draw the human figure: both because the lines of a man's body are much more subtle than anything else, and because you can more surely be found out and set right if you go wrong. I do think that such teaching as this, given to all people who care for it, would help the revival of the arts very much: the habit of discriminating between right and wrong, the sense of pleasure in drawing a good line, would really, I think, be education in the due sense of the word for all such people as had the germs of invention in them." Or, as he expressed it before the Commission: "My own view is that drawing should be taught more or less from drawing the human figure, because it gives you a standard of correctness that nothing else can do. I should not say, however, that it was absolutely essential. There are some people who have no great turn for drawing from the figure, who would, nevertheless, make clever draughtsmen in drawing from plant-form." Touching further details of the training recommended by him, Morris said: "There are two chief things that would have to be thought of in providing facilities for study for the art of design. However original a man may be, he cannot afford to disregard the works of art that have been produced in times past when design was flourishing; he is bound to study old examples, but he is also bound to supplement that by a careful study of nature, because, if he does not, he will certainly fall into a sort of cut-and-dried conventional method of designing, which is the bane of most of these French designs that we are talking about; and the only way for a person to keep clear of that, especially one in the ordinary rank and file of designers, is to study nature along with the old examples. It takes a man of considerable originality to deal with the old examples, and to get what is good out of them, without making a design which lays itself open to the charge of plagiarism. No doubt the only help out of that is for a man to be always drawing from nature, getting the habit of knowing what beautiful forms and lines are; that I think is a positive necessity." Elsewhere, on this subject, he refers to his own experiences: "Part of the common and necessary advice given to art students was to study antiquity; and no doubt many of you," said Morris in his address delivered in 1879 before the Birmingham Society of Arts and School of Design, "like me, have done so; have wandered, for instance, through the galleries of the admirable museum of South Kensington, and, like me, have been filled with wonder and gratitude at the beauty which has been born from the brain of man." Nevertheless, Morris was quite conscious of the fact that the existence of museums and art collections is *per se* no panacea for present evils. Men are not made artists by the mere act of frequenting these institutions. It is only to those who are already "beginning to get their eyesight" that such exhibitions are of service, "but it is clear that they cannot get at the great mass of people who will at present stare at them in unintelligent wonder." And, again, he says, that under existing circumstances "our museums and art schools will be but amusements of the rich."

Referring to another aspect of the subject, Morris said before the Commission that what he had found in using the South Kensington Museum, "and perhaps I have used it as much as any man living," was that it had got more things than it knew what to do with; although he expressed himself quite adverse to breaking up the collection and distributing it among provincial centres. What was wanted were typical specimens of good work, not a mere multiplication of articles. The objects were required for educational purposes only, not as curiosities. The "museum in the metropolis should contain complete collections in all styles, and when an opportunity occurred for purchasing private collections, any gaps in the metropolitan collection should be filled up at the expense of the nation." But a good many things not wanted to fill up gaps in that collection might be sent to the provinces. "I know," he went on to say, "there are things stored away in chests which might be sent to provincial museums. As far as regards the famous Bock collection of textiles, which is one of the finest in the world—yet one that has many duplicates and other specimens almost duplicates—it could be done; and as far as regards the Indian collection also it could be done." As to the circulation of objects belonging to South Kensington, Morris did not think it a good plan. "In the first place, these things are extremely precious, and if destroyed can never be replaced; the risk in transit, though it may not be absolutely great, still is a risk, and should only be run when there is a strong necessity. I cannot help looking upon the thing from a collector's point of view, I am in terror of these things getting destroyed by accident." Resuming the subject, he said there was another objection to the circulation of these objects, viz.: "A museum, to be of any great use to those who are studying it as artists or as designers, must be arranged in a permanent manner, so that one can come day after day and see the same thing; so that a man who is a lecturer can take his class to the museum and give a lecture on such and such an article; or that a manufacturer, like myself, can take a designer to the museum and say, 'I want a thing done in such and such way.'" It is in the highest degree exasperating to come, looking for some object one particularly desires for any purpose, and to find its vacant place supplied by a white label: "temporarily removed to" so and so. "Therefore I think," said Morris, "it is very much better that the provinces should have their own museums; if small ones it does not matter so long as they are typical. . . . I would give all the national aid to such museums that could be given without robbing the great existing museum."

On the subject of provincial schools of art, Morris stated as the result of his experience as a judge in the National Art Competition: "Of course everyone knows that the character of the work done at the different schools depends very much upon the masters at the head of them. There is one thing which, I think, perhaps might be more impressed upon those masters than it is, and that is that one does not particularly want to train up the students as picture painters. There are some schools where this is overdone, but that is a matter of accident owing to the master having a turn in that direction." Again, Morris found that local manufactures had a certain influence in determining the class of designs produced in any particular district. As an instance of this he remarked: "I think that the designing for carpets is a great deal done in the places where the carpets are made. The reason I say that is, that I remember two years ago we gave the gold medal for a design for a carpet, and it turned out that the student came from the Salisbury School of Art; therefore he had been working at Wilton, no doubt. I know that the Kidderminster School always sends in a good many designs for carpets; in fact, they mostly come from Kidderminster."

Asked whether he could suggest anything that might be done at headquarters in the national competitions to encourage designing, Morris replied: "My view is that not quite enough attention is given to the turning out of the actual goods themselves; for example, we cannot give prizes for the things turned out. We can only give prizes for the designs. I think it would be a very good thing to give prizes for the goods themselves. Prizes ought to be given for careful and artistic execution, as well as for general excellence and appropriateness of design."

Recurring once more to the subject of practical designers in his own craft, Morris said: "All the weaving designers that I have met, that is to say the few I have had to deal with myself, had been trained in art schools, and could draw passably; but what really happened to them was that they had finally too much to do in the mechanical line to be able to attend much to drawing; that is where the difficulty appeared to be. . . . I think that there ought to be some opportunities afforded by the art schools for people to learn the practical part of designing: as to the workshop training in most trades, it is certainly not sufficient. The old system of apprenticeship, by which workmen learned their craft, is a good deal broken down now, and nothing as yet has taken its place. I should think that most of the young men learn their work in a very happy-go-lucky manner; they are practically not taught at all; they pick up a knowledge of their trade. There should be some systematic training."

In answer to the question whether one could introduce looms into the art schools, Morris replied "Yes, of course; they don't take up a vast amount of room. . . . It would be a great advantage for one who was learning designing to see weaving going on. I think it essential that a designer should learn the practical way of carrying out the work for which he designs; he ought to be able to weave himself. . . . There would be one advantage in learning it in the school, in the fact that the learner would not be so much hurried over the work as he would be in a factory. . . . I think it absolutely essential that the designer should be thoroughly acquainted with he particular machine which is ultimately to fabricate the material for which his design is prepared. . . . A man employs a designer to draw his patterns. One of two things happens; either the designer has learnt the method of execution in a totally perfunctory manner and takes no interest in it, but goes only by a certain set of rules, and is therefore cramped and made dull and stupid by going by them; or, on the other hand, as sometimes happens, the manufacturer goes to a more dignified kind of artist, who, knowing nothing of the way in which the thing has to be done, produces a kind of puzzle for the manufacturer. The manufacturer, having paid for it, takes it away and does what he can with it; he must do something with it, and so he chops the design up and adapts it to his purpose as well as he can. The design is spoilt, and when executed looks not better, but worse, than the ordinary cut-and-dried trade design; so that the manufacturer has got no good by employing the great artist." . . . "You believe that it is necessary that by some means, either in the school or in the factory, the designer should make himself acquainted with the exigencies of the machine and material in which the design is to be executed?" "Yes," replied Morris, "I speak as strongly as I can upon that. I think that this is the very foundation of all design."

Before concluding this chapter it may be well to gather some further details from Mr. Morris's published opinions on the subjects to which reference has already been made. And, firstly, with regard to the decorative or minor arts. "It seems to me," said Morris in his lecture on "The Lesser Arts of Life," "that the lesser arts, when they are rejected, are so treated for no sufficient reason, and to the injury of the community; therefore I feel no shame in standing before you as a professed pleader and advocate for them, as indeed I well may, since it is through them that I am the servant of the public, and earn my living with abundant pleasure. Then comes the question—what are to be considered the Lesser Arts of Life? . . . I want you to agree with me in thinking that these lesser arts are really a part of the greater ones. . . . The Greater Arts of Life, what are *they*? Since many people may use the word in very different senses, I will say, without pretending to give a definition, that what I mean by an art is some creation of man which appeals to his emotions and his intellect by means of his senses. . . . If we are to be excused for rejecting the arts it must be not because we are contented to be less than men, but because we long to be more than men. . . . You understand that our ground is, that not only is it possible to make the matters needful to our daily life works of art, but that there is something wrong in the civilization that does not do this: if our houses, our clothes, our household furniture and utensils are not works of art, they are either wretched makeshifts, or, what is worse, degrading shams of better things. Furthermore, if any of these things make any claim to be considered works of art, they must show obvious traces of the hand of man guided directly by his brain, without more interposition of machines than is absolutely necessary to the nature of the work done. Again, whatsoever art there is in any of these articles of daily use must be evolved in a natural and unforced manner from the material that is dealt with, so that the result will be such as could not be got from any other material: if we break this law we make a triviality, a toy, not a work of art. Lastly, love of nature in all its forms must be the ruling spirit of such works of art as we are considering; the brain that guides the hand must be healthy and hopeful, must be keenly alive to the surroundings of our own days, and must be only so much affected by the art of past times as it is natural for one who practises an art which is alive, growing, and looking towards the future."

Again: "Let me say it, that either I have erred," said Morris, "in the aim of my whole life, or that the welfare of these lesser arts involves the question of the content and self-respect of all craftsmen, whether you call them artists or artizans. . . . My hope is . . . that people will some day learn something of art, and so long for more, and will find, as I have, that there is no getting it save by the general acknowledgment of the right of every man to have fit work to do in a beautiful home. Therein lies all that is indestructible of the pleasure of life; no man need ask for more than that, no man should be granted less; and if he falls short of it, it is through waste and injustice that he is kept out of his birthright." Again: "I must ask you to believe that everyone of the things that goes to make up the surroundings among which we live must be either beautiful or ugly, either elevating or degrading to us, either a torment and burden to the maker of it to make, or a pleasure and a solace to him. . . . 'Art is man's expression of his joy in labour.' If those are not Professor Ruskin's words they embody at least his teaching on this subject. Nor has any truth more important ever been stated; for if pleasure in labour be generally possible, what a strange folly it must be for men to consent to labour without pleasure, and what a hideous injustice it must be for society to compel most men to labour without pleasure! For since all men not dishonest must labour, it becomes a question either of forcing them to lead unhappy lives or allowing them to live happily." And speaking of his own work Morris says: "The division of labour . . . has pressed specially hard on that part of the field of human culture in which I was born to labour. That field of the arts whose harvest should be the chief part of human joy, hope, and consolation, has been . . . dealt hardly with by the division of labour, . . . nay, so searching has been this tyranny, that it has not passed by my own insignificant corner of labour, but as it has thwarted me in many ways, so chiefly perhaps in this, that it has so stood in the way of my getting the help from others which my art forces me to crave, that I have been compelled to learn many crafts, and belike . . . forbidden to master any."

Mr. Morris's views on various styles of architecture ought to be noted, as they had an important bearing on his own artistic work. The refinement, the grace of form and proportion in Greek architecture did not blind him to its stringent limitations. He recognized that "timber-building was the origin of the Greek temple. The Greek pillar was a wooden post, its lintel a timber beam. . . . The form of the timber hall, with its low-pitched roof, its posts and beams, had got to be considered a holy form by the Greeks, and they did not care to carry dignified architecture further, or invent any more elaborate form of construction. . . . For the rest, in spite of all the wonders of Greek sculpture, we must needs think that the Greeks had done little to fix the future architecture of the world: there was no elasticity or power of growth about the style; right in its own country, used for the worship and aspirations which first gave it birth, it could not be used for anything else." "The bones of it," says Morris in another place, "its merely architectural part, are little changed from the Barbarian or primal building, which is a mere piling or jointing together of material, giving one no sense of growth in the building itself, and no sense of the possibility of growth in the style. The one Greek form of building with which we are really familiar, the columnar temple, though always built with blocks of stone, is clearly a deduction from the wooden god's-house or shrine, . . . nor had this god's-house changed. . . . In fact, rigid conservatism of form is an essential part of Greek architecture as we know it. From this conservatism of form there resulted a jostling between the building and its higher ornament. In early days, indeed, when some healthy barbarism yet clung to the sculpture, the discrepancy is not felt; but . . . it becomes more and more obvious, and more and more painful, till at last it becomes clear that sculpture has ceased to be a part of architecture and has become an extraneous art bound to the building by habit or superstition. The form of the ornamental building of the Greeks, then, was very limited, had no capacity in it for development, and tended to divorce from its higher or epical ornament. . . . The inferior parts of the ornament are so slavishly subordinated to the superior, that no invention or individuality is possible in them, whence comes a kind of bareness and blankness, a rejection, in short, of all romance, which . . . puts the style . . . aside as any possible foundation for the style of the future architecture of the world." On the other hand, "the art of the peoples collected under the Roman name" made so great an impression upon modern art that Morris saw "nothing for it but to say that it invented architecture—no less." For the Romans seized on the great device of "the arch, the most important invention to house-needing men that has been, or can be made. . . . They were the first to use it otherwise than as an ugly necessity, and, in so using it, they settled what the architecture of civilization must henceforward be. Nor was their architecture, stately as it was, any longer fit for nothing but a temple,—a holy railing for the shrine or symbol of the god; it was fit for one purpose as for another—church, house, aqueduct, market-place or castle; nor was it the style of one country or one climate, it would fit itself to north or south, snow-storm or sand-storm alike. Though pedants might make inflexible rules for its practice when it was dead or dying, when it was alive it did not bind itself too strictly to rule, but followed, in its constructive part at least, the law of nature; in short, it was a new art,—the great art of civilisation." "To my mind," says Morris in another place, "organic architecture, architecture which must necessarily grow, dates from the habitual use of the arch, which, taking into consideration its combined utility and beauty, must be pronounced to be the greatest invention of the human race. Until the time when man not only had invented the arch, but had gathered boldness to use it habitually, architecture was necessarily so limited that strong growth was impossible to it. . . . Once furnished with the arch, man has conquered Nature in the matter of building. . . . In . . . the ornamental side" (as distinguished, that is, from mere engineering), "Roman building used the arch and adorned it, but disguised its office, and pretended that the structure of its buildings was still that of the lintel, and that the arch bore no weight worth speaking of." In fact, in the strict Roman style "the construction and ornament did not interpenetrate," its architecture was *of itself* inorganic, and had "not got the qualities essential to making it a foundation for any possible new-birth of the arts." It was bound to come to an end, "yet in perishing it gave some token of the coming change," of the rise of the new and living architecture, which was born on the day when the Roman "builders admitted that their lintel was false, and that the arch could do without it." "Three great buildings mark its first feeble beginning, its vigorous early life, its last hiding away beneath the rubbish heaps of pedantry and hopelessness. I venture to call these buildings in their present state, the first the strangest, the second the most beautiful, the third the ugliest of the buildings raised in Europe before the nineteenth century. The first of these is the palace of Diocletian at Spalato; the second, the church of St. Sophia at Constantinople; the third, the church of St. Peter at Rome." (Now since Mr. Morris never visited Spalato himself, it is like enough that he was indebted to Professor Freeman's interesting "Historical Essays," Third Series, and "Sketches from the Subject and Neighbour Lands of Venice," for particulars of the palace of Diocletian.) It was there, in the first decade of the fourth century, that "the movement of new life was first felt," says Morris. "There is much about the building that is downright ugly, still more that is but a mass of worn-out tradition; but there first, as far as we know, is visible the attempt to throw off the swathings of ill-understood Greek art, with which Roman architecture had encumbered itself, and to make that architecture reasonable and consistent with the living principles of art." There one may "see for the first time the arch acting freely and without the sham support of the Greek beam-architecture." This building, then, marks "the first obscure beginning of Gothic or organic architecture; henceforth till the beginning of the modern epoch all is growth uninterrupted, however slow." "But at Spalato, though the art was trying to be alive, it was scarcely alive, and what life is in it is shown in its construction only, and not in its ornament. Our second building, St. Sophia," built by Justinian in 540, "has utterly thrown aside all pedantic encumbrances and is most vigorously alive. . . . It is not bound by the past, but it has garnered all that there was in it which was fit to live and produce fresh life; it is the living child and the fruitful mother of art, past and future. That, even more than the loveliness which it drew forth from its own present, is what makes it the crown of all the great buildings of the world." Mr. Morris's veneration for "this most lovely building" was boundless. Indeed, some have gone so far as to account for his having associated himself (as he did notably in 1876 and 1878), with the anti-Turkish party, because his whole nature revolted in horror at the idea of the Temple of the Holy Wisdom being in the hands of the infidel. At any rate, without wanting to rob William Morris of the credit of being prompted by motives of the purest philanthropy in championing the victims of Turkish violence, one may quite well believe that his zeal for the fabric of St. Sophia, perverted to uses for which it was never designed, intensified his antipathy to the alien and intruder become oppressor. "St. Sophia once built," continues Morris, "the earth began to blossom with beautiful buildings;" and, as he says in another place, "never, till the time of that death or cataleptic sleep of the so-called Renaissance, did" Gothic art "forget its origin, or fail altogether in fulfilling its mission of turning the ancient curse of labour into something more like a blessing. As to the way in which it did its work . . . . I have but little need to speak, since there is none of us but has seen and felt some portion of the glory which it left behind, but has shared some portion of that most kind gift it gave the world."

"The thousand years that lie between the date of St. Sophia and the date of St. Peter at Rome may well be called the building age of the world. But when those years were over, in Italy at least, the change was fully come; and, as a symbol of that change, there stood on the site of the great mass of history and art, which was once called the Basilica of St. Peter, that new church of St. Peter, which still curses the mightiest city of the world—the very type, it seems to me, of pride and tyranny, of all that crushes out the love of art in simple people, and makes art a toy of little estimation for the idle hours of the rich and cultivated. Between that time and this, art has been shut up in prison." "There are many artists at present who do not sufficiently estimate the enormity, the portentousness of this change. . . . How on earth could people's ideas of beauty change so? you may say. . . . Was it not rather that beauty, however unconsciously, was no longer an object of attainment with the men of that epoch? This used once to puzzle me in the presence of one of the so-called masterpieces of the New Birth; such a building as St. Paul's in London, for example. I have found it difficult to put myself in the frame of mind which could accept such a work as a substitute for even the latest and worst Gothic building. Such taste seemed to me like the taste of a man who should prefer his lady-love bald. But now I know that it was not a matter of choice on the part of anyone then alive who had an eye for beauty; if the change had been made on the grounds of beauty it would be wholly inexplicable; but it was not so. . . . St. Peter's in Rome, St. Paul's in London, were not built to be beautiful, or to be beautiful and convenient . . . but to be proper, respectable, and therefore to show the due amount of cultivation, and knowledge of the only peoples and times that in the minds of their ignorant builders were not ignorant barbarians. . . . Beauty and romance were outside the aspirations of their builders." In "News from Nowhere" St. Paul's is included among the few "poorish" and "silly old buildings" still allowed to stand as a foil to the beautiful new ones they built when Morris's dream should have been accomplished; while St. Martin's Church in the corner of Trafalgar Square is described, in the same work, as "ugly," and the National Gallery as "a nondescript, ugly, cupolaed building," and both have to make way for an open space planted with flowers and orchard trees. Elsewhere Morris says that all the houses built in the reign of Queen Anne, as well as those that are "distinctly Georgian, are difficult enough to decorate, especially for those who have any leaning towards romance, because they have still some style left in them which one cannot ignore; at the same time that it is impossible for anyone living out of the time in which they were built to sympathize with a style whose characteristics are mere whims, not founded on any principle." As to French fashions in decoration, the early seventeenth century is a period of transition from bad to worse, into the "corruption" of the "vile Pompadour period." "The fine arts, which had in the end of the sixteenth century descended from the expression of the people's faith and aspirations into that of the fancy, ingenuity and whim of gifted individuals, fell lower still. They lost every atom of beauty and dignity, and retained little even of the ingenuity of the earlier Renaissance, becoming mere expensive and pretentious though carefully-finished upholstery, mere adjuncts of pomp and state, the expression of the insolence of riches, and the complacency of respectability. Once again it must be said of the art, as of the general literature of the period, that no reasonable man could even bestow a passing glance at it but for the incurable corruption of society that it betokens." And again, "For us to set to work to imitate the minor vices of the Borgias, or the degraded and nightmare whims of the *blasé* and bankrupt aristocracy of Louis XV.'s time seems to me," says Morris, "merely ridiculous."

The only possible style of architecture for the future is Gothic, "which," said Morris, "after a development of long centuries, has still in it, as I think, capacities for fresh developments, since its life was cut short by an arbitrary recurrence to a style which had long lost all elements of life and growth."

Repeatedly, in different works of his, did Morris expose the disastrous consequences that ensued from the Renaissance movement. "The study of the Greek literature at first hand," he says "was aiding this new intelligence among cultivated men, and also, since they did but half understand its spirit, was warping their minds into fresh error. For the science of history and the critical observation of events had not yet been born; and to the ardent spirits of the Renaissance there had never been but two peoples worth notice—to wit, the Greeks and Romans, whom their new disciples strove to imitate in everything which was deemed of importance at the time." Again he refers to "that period of blight which was introduced by the so-called Renaissance," and says that the change came "at a time of so much and such varied hope that people call it the time of the New Birth: as far as the arts are concerned I deny it that title; rather it seems to me that the great men who lived and glorified the practice of art in those days were the fruit of the old, not the seed of the new order of things. . . . When the brightness of the so-called Renaissance faded, and it faded very suddenly, a deadly chill fell upon the arts: that New-birth mostly meant looking back to past times, wherein the men of those days thought they saw a perfection of art which to their minds was different in kind . . . from the ruder suggestive art of their fathers; this perfection they were anxious to imitate, this alone seemed to be art to them, the rest was childishness: so wonderful was their energy, their success so great, that no doubt to commonplace minds among them, though surely not to the great masters, that perfection seemed gained. . . . Art by no means stood still in those latter days of the Renaissance, but took the downward road with terrible swiftness, and tumbled down at the bottom of the hill where, as if bewitched, it lay long in great content, believing itself to be the art of Michael Angelo, while it was the art of men whom nobody remembers but those who want to sell their pictures." But "when the great masters of the Renaissance were gone, they, who stung by the desire of doing something new, turned their mighty hands to the work of destroying the last remains of living popular art, putting in its place for a while the results of their own wonderful individuality—when these great men were dead, and lesser men of the ordinary type were masquerading in their garments, then at last it was seen what the so-called new birth really was; then we could see that it was the fever of the strong man yearning to accomplish something before his death, not the simple hope of the child, who has long years of life and growth before him."

"This change," says Morris in another place, "we have somewhat boastfully, and as regards the arts quite untruthfully, called the New Birth. . . . But, strange to say, to this living body of . . . New Birth was bound the dead corpse of a past art. . . . On the side of art, with the sternest pedagogic utterance, it bade men look backward across the days of the 'fathers and famous men that begat them,' and in scorn of them, to an art that had been dead a thousand years before. . . . Henceforth the past was to be our present and the blankness of its dead wall was to shut out the future from us." The whole movement was retrogressive. It was no subject for self-congratulation, and Morris might fitly speak of "the miseries of the New Birth."

It simply "destroyed the building arts for Italy: while Germany, where Gothic architecture was necessarily firmer rooted in the soil, did not so much as feel the first shiver of the coming flood till suddenly, and without warning, it was upon her." The Germans then "received the Renaissance with singular eagerness and rapidity, and became, from the artistic point of view, a nation of rhetorical pedants," with the exception of Albert Dürer, whose matchless imagination and intellect, notwithstanding that his method was infected by the Renaissance, "made him thoroughly Gothic in spirit." In the space of about five years after the adoption of the Renaissance into Germany, the art of the Middle Ages fell dead, "and was succeeded by a singularly stupid and brutal phase of that rhetorical and academical art which, in all matters of ornament, has held Europe captive ever since."

The most hopeful sign Morris deemed to be the fact that there does exist amongst us a genuine and decided dissatisfaction with the present state of the arts. Sad as that state has been ever since the days of the Renaissance, with its "false taste" infecting nearly the whole of Europe, it will not have been altogether an unprofitable experience if it convince us of the utter impossibility of an organic and living style being derived from an eclectic one; and if only "we shall at last be driven into the one right way of concluding that, in spite of all risks and all losses, unhappy and slavish work must come to an end. In that day we shall take Gothic architecture by the hand, and know it for what it was and what it is."

CHAPTER ELEVEN: SOCIETIES.

HAD Mr. Morris been asked which one in preference to any other of his undertakings he considered his greatest and best, he would have had no hesitation in naming the Society for the Protection of Ancient Buildings, which owes to him more than anyone else both its origin and its success. Should all else he ever did be reprobated or forgotten, he could yet confidently rest his title to be held in grateful remembrance of posterity for this signal service alone; and it is hardly possible to lay too much stress on this department of Mr. Morris's work, or to overrate the importance he himself attached to it. Indeed it is not too much to say, that to be able to appreciate the motives that guided his course in this regard, is to possess the key to his method and conduct in general throughout his life. No cause was nearer to his heart than this; and this it is which everyone desiring to interpret aright William Morris's life's work must place first in any memorial of him. There is not a doubt that his attention was awakened to the urgency of the subject by his study of John Ruskin. Indeed, so entirely do the opinions of the two writers agree on these points, that in many a passage Ruskin expresses himself in terms that, removed from the context, might well be mistaken by anyone not previously acquainted with it for an utterance of Morris's, and *vice versâ*.

It was "chiefly owing to the necessity under which" he "felt himself, of obtaining as many memoranda as possible of mediæval buildings" then "in process of destruction, before that destruction should be consummated by the Restorer," that Ruskin laid aside for a time his work on "Modern Painters," so as to devote himself to the more pressing matter of architecture and its due treatment; with the result that he wrote "The Seven Lamps of Architecture." In this work, and more particularly in that section of it which is called "The Lamp of Memory," are these ideas expressed on which Morris's own views were based. There is one duty, contends Ruskin, "respecting national architecture, whose importance it is impossible to overrate," viz., "to preserve, as the most precious of inheritances," the buildings of past ages. To be reminded of this is "especially necessary in modern times. Neither by the public, nor by those who have the care of public monuments, is the true meaning of the word *restoration* understood. It means the most total destruction which a building can suffer: a destruction out of which no remnants can be gathered: a destruction accompanied with false description of the thing destroyed. (False, also, in the manner of parody,—the most loathsome manner of falsehood.) Do not let us deceive ourselves in this important matter; it is *impossible*, as impossible as to raise the dead, to restore anything that has ever been great or beautiful in architecture. That which I have . . . insisted upon as the life of the whole, that spirit which is given only by the hand and eye of the workman, can never be recalled. Another spirit may be given by another time, and it is then a new building; but the spirit of the dead workman cannot be summoned up, and commanded to direct other hands and other thoughts. And as for direct and simple copying it is palpably impossible. What copying can there be of surfaces that have been worn half an inch down? The whole finish of the work was in the half inch that is gone; if you attempt to restore that finish you do it conjecturally; if you copy what is left, granting fidelity to be possible (and what care, or watchfulness, or cost can secure it), how is the new work better than the old? There was yet in the old *some* life, some mysterious suggestion of what it had been, and of what it had lost; some sweetness in the gentle lines which rain and sun had wrought. There can be none in the brute hardness of the new carving. . . . The first step to restoration (I have seen it, and that again and again . . .) is to dash the old work to pieces: the second is usually to put up the cheapest and basest imitation which can escape detection; but in all cases, however careful, and however laboured, an imitation still, a cold model of such parts as *can* be modelled, with conjectural supplements. . . . Do not let us talk then of restoration. The thing is a Lie from beginning to end. You may make a model of a building as you may of a corpse, and your model may have the shell of the old walls within it as your cast might have the skeleton, with what advantage I neither see nor care: but the old building is destroyed, and that more totally and mercilessly than if it had sunk into a heap of dust, or melted into a mass of clay. . . . But, it is said, there may come a necessity for restoration. Granted. Look the necessity full in the face, and understand it on its own terms. It is a necessity for destruction. Accept it as such, pull the building down; throw its stones into neglected corners; . . . but do it honestly, and do not set up a Lie in their place. And look that necessity in the face before it comes, and you may prevent it. . . . Take proper care of your monuments and you will not need to restore them. A few sheets of lead put in time upon a roof, a few dead leaves and sticks swept in time out of a water-course, will save both roof and walls from ruin. Watch an old building with anxious care; guard it as best you may, and at any cost, from every influence of dilapidation. Count its stones as you would jewels of a crown; set watches about it as if at the gates of a besieged city; bind it together with iron where it loosens; stay it with timber where it declines; do not care about the unsightliness of the aid: better a crutch than a lost limb; and do this tenderly, and reverently, and continually, and many a generation will still be born and pass away beneath its shadow. Its evil day must come at last; but let it come declaredly and openly, and let no dishonouring and false substitute deprive it of the funeral offices of memory. . . . It is, again, no question of expediency or feeling whether we shall preserve the buildings of past times or not. *We have no right whatever to touch them.* They are not ours. They belong, partly to those who built them, and partly to all the generations of mankind who are to follow us. The dead have still their right in them; that which they laboured for . . . we have no right to obliterate. What we have ourselves built we are at liberty to throw down; but what other men gave their strength and wealth and life to accomplish, their right over does not pass away with their death; still less is the right to the use of what they have left vested in us only. It belongs to all their successors. It may hereafter be a subject of sorrow, or a cause of injury, to millions, that we have consulted our present convenience by casting down such buildings as we choose to dispense with. That sorrow, that loss, we have no right to inflict. . . . Whether enraged, or in deliberate folly; whether countless, or sitting in committees; the people who destroy anything causelessly are a mob; and architecture is always destroyed causelessly. A fair building is necessarily worth the ground it stands upon, . . . nor is any cause whatever valid as a ground for its destruction." Ruskin then goes on to point out how in these times, when "the very quietness of nature is gradually withdrawn from us," when the "ceaseless fever" of modern life reaches to the remotest corners of the land, and all vitality is being "concentrated in the central cities, . . . the only influence that can in any wise *there* take the place of that of the woods and fields is the power of ancient architecture;" a thing too precious to part with for any substitute for it that can be devised. Again Mr. Ruskin said: "Care and observation, more mischievous in their misdirection than indifference or scorn, have in many places given to mediæval relics the aspect and association of a kind of cabinet preservation. Nominal restoration has done tenfold worse, and has hopelessly destroyed what time, and storm, and anarchy, and impiety had spared. Better the unloosened rage of the fiend than the scrabble of self-complacent idiocy. Consider even now" (in 1851) "what incalculable treasure is still left in neglected and shattered churches and domestic buildings rapidly disappearing over the whole of Europe—treasure which, once lost, the labour of all men living cannot bring back again."

A moment's reflection on the practical outcome of "restoration," so-called, should establish the truth of Ruskin's propositions, and suffice to show that the invariable result of the process is to remove the past further off instead of reviving it. Let anyone who yet doubts recall the instances of ancient buildings he or she knows that have been "restored." Have they not lost far more than they can be said, on the most favourable estimate, to have gained thereby? Is any one of them really convincing? Is there not something wanting, something that fails to satisfy, about each and all of them? What sort of interest attaches to the modernized cathedral of Worcester, except the fact that it still happens to contain some mediæval remains? What man of taste would wittingly go a mile out of his way to see the new work of the spire of St. Michael's, Coventry, or the rebuilt towers of Taunton? Or take again three instances, one each from the north, the middle, and the south of England.

The first is the chapel on Wakefield Bridge. This exquisite monument underwent in the year 1847 a general "restoration," including the entire rebuilding of the western façade by Sir Gilbert Scott. But a hundred colliery chimneys' grime, soaking, with the exhalations of the polluted Calder, into the porous stone, soon began to wreak disaster; so that the condition of the new work speedily became worse than the old was at the close of five centuries. Sir Gilbert Scott, appalled at the consequences for which he could not avoid the largest share of responsibility, and anxious, no doubt, to save his credit, begged to be allowed to take down his handiwork and replace the portions of the original that yet existed. These, preserved by a happy circumstance from utter destruction, had been set up, tea-garden wise, in the grounds of Kettlethorpe Hall, distant a few miles from the town of Wakefield. But the local authorities had learnt a lesson. Disgusted at the past and profoundly distrustful of the future, they refused to sanction any further tampering with the fabric of the chapel. And so it remains to this day, the exterior crumbling to decay as fast as it can.

The second instance is the spire of the University church of St. Mary at Oxford. This was restored and amended by Mr. Buckler in 1853. Only forty years had passed when a fresh "restoration" was begun by the official architect of the University, Mr. T. G. Jackson, with the express object of undoing the "improvements" introduced by his predecessor, and reducing the spire to the semblance of what is known to have been its ancient form. Under these circumstances one can hardly help wondering how many years must go by before Mr. Jackson's new "restoration" shall be pronounced unsatisfactory and be re-restored.

The third and last instance is the reredos in Chichester Cathedral. This case is not precisely parallel to the others, as, instead of being the substitution of a copy for old work, it was avowedly a novel composition. At the same time it demonstrates the non-finality of modern taste in such matters, and, by consequence, the unwisdom of setting up in ancient buildings fresh architectural work in a style supposed to be in keeping with the old. Designed and carried out by Messrs. Slater and Carpenter, the reredos at Chichester was erected about a quarter of a century ago, saving the side wings, which were left incomplete at the time. Nor will they ever be completed. For the structure has already been discovered to fall short of the æsthetic standard of the present day, and accordingly its removal is only a question of time. Indeed, it is an open secret that nothing but respect for sentimental considerations has suffered it to stand so long.

These three examples are typical of thousands of others, less known, perhaps, but not less to be deplored. In each case those who promoted the work must be credited with having acted in perfect good faith and according to their lights; they employed architects of eminence in the profession in their day. Yet, as in the three instances mentioned, they are now seen to have been mistaken, and their opinion has had to be reversed by the next generation, even if the authors of the mischief might not have lived themselves to repent, as sometimes in fact they did. The contention, then, put forward by Mr. Morris, and by those who think with him, is that we cannot take for granted that what satisfies the judgment of the present year will satisfy equally the judgment of, say, fifty years hence. Who is there rash enough to assume that it will, when we know that work considered unexceptionable by the most critical, and applauded as "judicious"—this is the expression invariably used in such cases—by the most advanced, only half a century since, has been examined and condemned already? What certain guarantee have we that our own judgment may not have to be revised in the same way by those that shall come after us? Nay, so far from our taste having attained irreformable perfection, at the present rate of progress of human knowledge, men's eyes rapidly becoming open to see and appreciate many points that used formerly to escape observation, there seems every probability that the shortcomings of the present generation will be found out and exposed in a very much shorter space of time than it has taken us to discover those of our predecessors. We have long since learnt to execrate Wyatt, Cottingham, and the rest, for what they did at Salisbury, Hereford, and many other places. But, when one bears in mind some recent instances, such as St. Bartholomew's, Smithfield, St. Mary's Overie, Westminster Abbey, Rochester Cathedral and Peterborough, is it not probable that the Aston Webbs, the Blomfields, and, above all, the Pearsons of our own day, will, in the verdict of posterity, have to share the unenviable reproach of the Destroyer? In sooth, the dishonours are easy; it is not fair that they should score all on the side of poor Wyatt and the "restorers" of his stamp, when there are so many energetic competitors living at this moment. To have to confess ourselves unworthy to leave our mark, as every generation before us has left its mark, upon the buildings of our ancestors, is a self-denying ordinance the reverse of flattering to our vanity. Nevertheless, to be content to wait and learn, and meanwhile to prolong with the utmost care and diligence in our power the life of the priceless relics of the past, this modest programme is the only safe and proper course, as William Morris was never weary of maintaining.

It was in order to give practical effect to this belief that the Society for the Protection of Ancient Buildings was founded in the year 1877, Mr. Morris, as the leader of the movement, himself drawing up a formal statement of its principles. The "new interest, almost like another sense," he said, and the enthusiasm that had arisen for the study of ancient monuments of art, constituted in itself their most serious detriment. The "last fifty years of knowledge and attention have done more for their destruction than all the foregoing centuries of revolution, violence and contempt. For Architecture, long decaying, died out, as a popular art at least, just as the knowledge of mediæval art was born. So that the civilised world of the nineteenth century has no style of its own amidst its wide knowledge of the styles of other centuries. From this lack and this gain arose in men's minds the strange idea of the restoration of ancient buildings; and a strange and most fatal idea, which, by its very name, implies that it is possible to strip from a building this, that, and the other part of its history—of its life that is—and then to stay the hand at some arbitrary point, and leave it still historical, living, and even as it once was."

"In earlier times this kind of forgery was impossible, because knowledge failed the builders, or perhaps because instinct held them back." Any change that took place in the way of repairs or otherwise "was of necessity wrought in the unmistakable fashion of the time . . . and was alive with the spirit of the deeds done amidst its fashioning. The result of all this was often a building in which the many changes, though harsh and visible enough, were by their very contrast interesting and instructive, and could by no possibility mislead. But those who make the changes wrought in our day under the name of Restoration, while professing to bring back a building to the best time of its history, have no guide but each his own individual whim; . . . the very nature of their task compels them to destroy something, and to supply the gap by imagining what the earlier builders should or might have done. . . . The whole surface of the building is necessarily tampered with" in the process; "the appearance of antiquity is taken away from such old parts of the fabric as are left, . . . and, in short, a feeble and lifeless forgery is the final result of all the wasted labour. It is sad to say that in this manner most of the bigger Minsters, and a vast number of more humble buildings, both in England, and on the Continent, have been dealt with. . . . For what is left we plead" and, since it is impossible to restore the living spirit which was an inseparable part of the religion, thought and manners that produced the buildings of the past, we "call upon those who have to deal with them, to put Protection in the place of Restoration, to stave off decay by daily care, to prop a perilous wall or mend a leaky roof by such means as are obviously meant for support or covering, and show no pretence of other art, and otherwise to resist all tampering with either the fabric or ornament of the building as it stands; if it has become inconvenient for its present use, to raise another building rather than alter or enlarge the old one; in fine, to treat our ancient buildings as monuments of a byegone art, created by byegone manners that modern art cannot meddle with without destroying. Thus, and thus only, shall we escape the reproach of our learning being turned into a snare to us; thus, and thus only, can we protect our ancient buildings, and hand them down instructive and venerable to those that come after us."

Mr. Morris filled at first the post of Honorary Secretary single-handed; afterwards several other members were associated with him in that office, and he served on the committee thenceforward to the end of his life. He was, from the beginning, one of the most active members of the Society. He never spared himself, being always ready with voice and pen to forward the Society's objects. And, valuable as his time was, he devoted much of it to this cause; he used constantly to be going about the country, as representative of the Society, to inspect and report to the committee upon the condition of this or that ancient building, when the fact had come to their knowledge that it was in danger of demolition or—scarcely less deplorable—material damage in the euphonious name of restoration. Destruction, under this specious guise, is perpetrated not seldom on the quiet, and gets to be known only when the discovery is too late to be of any avail, even in these days; but it used to occur far more frequently before Mr. Morris took the matter up, and began to check the evil in person and through the agency of the organization he established. No one can estimate how much threatened damage to ancient buildings—damage which, once done, could never have been undone—Morris's prompt interference has averted. The task was by no means easy, and often enough turned out a most ungracious one to boot. The obstacles in the way of remedying things as they exist might well discourage the stoutest heart. In the first place the clergy, who are in occupation of the greatest proportion of the ancient buildings of this country, are, as a body, quite without training in architecture and its accessory arts. The blame, it is true, does not belong to them; but the fact, alas! remains, that not even a rudimentary course of architectural study constitutes part and parcel of the education at public schools, at the universities, or at theological colleges; that in the nomination of a minister to a living the question of his qualifications for dealing with the fabric of the old church of the parish does not enter into consideration of the patron, or influence his choice at all. The appointment is made for reasons totally different. And yet, once instituted, the parson has practically absolute control over the building, to alter, to enlarge, to pull down, to rebuild; in short, to do with it just as he please, without limit to the marring, unless, as good fortune sometimes ordains, money not forthcoming, he is forced on that account to refrain his hand, and to spare. In the second place, should the parson himself be willing to submit his own judgment to that of a specialist, to wit, an architect, the latter is but human after all, and the natural bias of self-interest must hardly fail to incline him to advise new work on a scale commensurate with the biggest possible fees. If there were a sufficiently forcible weight of public opinion many a scandalous job might be stopped in its initial stage; but there is no occasion to go further back than the recent case of Peterborough to prove that the public requires a deal of educating still. Till that desirable consummation shall have been attained, for the safeguarding of our national treasures there could not well be devised any plan so adequate as that which prevails more or less in France, Germany and Italy, viz., the scheduling of buildings as public monuments, together with their furniture and fittings; the records to be preserved among the official archives in some central place, and no alterations or additions of any sort or kind to structures so registered to be permitted without the most searching inquiries, the production of proof of the positive necessity of the proposed innovation, and a guarantee that no structural change beyond that specified shall be introduced. Even then it would be advisable for some responsible architect, or committee of architects, not paid *pro ratâ*, but in receipt of a fixed annual salary for protective services, to supervise the work while in progress, and to furnish for publication an authoritative report at the completion of the proceedings. The preliminaries and lengthy formalities attending such a mode of procedure, to say nothing of the advantage of the publicity it gives, if they accomplish nothing better, at any rate act as a wholesome deterrent to hastily-considered, and always baneful, measures of restoration. But it does not appear that William Morris advocated the regular adoption of this system, perhaps because he had no particular confidence in government officialism. At the same time he was strongly in favour of amending the present anomalous condition of affairs. "Sir, I think," so he wrote to the editor of "The Times," "that our ancient historical monuments are national property, and ought no longer to be left to the mercy of the many and variable ideas of ecclesiastical propriety that may at any time be prevalent among us." Another member of the Society appositely remarked, at one of their general meetings: "That a man with a shifting, transient incumbency should be permitted to destroy his parish church, the immemorial possession of his parishioners, among whom he was not born, robbing them and their descendants, and a more enlightened future, of perhaps the only valuable thing in the place; and that facilities for such purposes should not only be readily procured, but issued with approbation and encouragement, seems to me abominable, and a crying shame."

The Society had not been in existence two years before it was found that its business was too onerous for one General Committee that had been formed, and it became necessary to nominate sub-committees to conduct the various departments of its work. A special Restoration Committee was appointed, to undertake the consideration and sifting of the cases that had been submitted to the Society throughout a great portion of the preceding year. A Foreign Committee also was formed, to take notice of the state of ancient buildings abroad, and placed itself in communication with various archæological societies in different countries of Europe, as well as instituting special inquiries from time to time with reference to ancient monuments in India, Egypt, and elsewhere. The prospectus of the Society was translated into French, German, Italian and Dutch, and steps were taken to circulate it, and to enlist corresponding members in each of the four countries. In order to facilitate and systematize the operations of the Society at home local honorary correspondents in various districts were appointed, who might help to obtain speedy and accurate information of proposed damage to ancient buildings. The *modus operandi* of the Society in such cases is to address a letter to the person or persons immediately responsible, and to offer to provide an expert opinion on the points at issue. Sometimes the advice and help of the Society is accepted, with gratifying results; but sometimes, on the other hand, the offer meets with rejection, or even no response at all. In these events the Society follows up its previous communication by a more urgent remonstrance, and, should that fail, it has to resort to other means, such as drawing public attention to the matter through the local press, or, if it be of sufficiently general concern, in the London papers. Certain representative members of the Society meet from week to week to carry on affairs, and make themselves accountable for the labour of correspondence that its transactions necessarily entail.

A general meeting is held annually, at which the report of the past year is read, as well as a paper on some special subject bearing on the work of the Society. Mr. Morris delivered an interesting speech at the general meeting on June 28th, 1879. But by far the most important event of this year for the Society—and possibly, indeed, the most important in all their annals—was the controversy with regard to the "restoration" of St. Mark's at Venice.

As far back as March, 1872, a paragraph in "The Academy" drew attention to the virtual destruction that had already befallen Torcello, and warned those of the public who had taste enough to care about such things that a similar fate was threatening St. Mark's itself. But at that time there was, unfortunately, in this country no organization through which the voice of remonstrance might hope to make itself heard, or claim respect and compliance from the authorities abroad. Meanwhile the destructive "restoration" proceeded, until, both the north side and the south of the venerable Byzantine basilica having been renovated, it became only too evident that there was no time to lose if any of the parts remaining of the fabric were to be saved. It was actually a question, not only of replacing the old mosaics of the west front with modern monstrosities by Salviati—though that, in sooth, were bad enough—but of taking down and rebuilding the entire façade, the supremest glory of the architecture of St. Mark's, if indeed one may befittingly distinguish this from that where everything is supreme, everything glorious. At a meeting of the Society for the Protection of Ancient Buildings, held at Buckingham Street, Strand, in the first week of November, 1879, Mr. Morris, the Honorary Secretary, called attention to the urgent necessity for decisive measures to check the proposed total demolition of the west front of St. Mark's. It was resolved to prepare a memorial and invite the signatures of all who sympathized with the views of the Society, for presentation to the Minister of Public Works in Italy, in view of the fact that that official had called, or had declared his intention of calling, a commission to decide whether the work should be begun at once or be deferred for a year. Hence the need for prompt action, if the most beautiful feature of the basilica was to be saved. At the same time a meeting for the same objects was held at the Fitzwilliam Museum, at Cambridge, with Dr. Paget in the chair. Another meeting took place on November 13th, at the Midland Institute at Birmingham, at which Morris was present and spoke. He refers, in a lecture delivered at Birmingham in the following year, 1880, to "the enthusiastic meeting that I had the honour of addressing here last autumn on the subject of the (so-called) restoration of St. Mark's at Venice; you thought, and most justly thought, it seems to me, that the subject was of such moment to art in general, that it was a simple and obvious thing for men who were anxious in the matter to address themselves to those who had the decision of it in their hands; even though the former were called Englishmen, and the latter Italians; for you felt that the name of lovers of art would cover those differences. If you had any misgivings, you remembered that there was but one such building in the world, and that it was worth while risking a breach of etiquette if any words of ours could do anything towards saving it; well, the Italians were, some of them, very naturally, though surely unreasonably, irritated for a time, and in some of their prints they bade us look at home! That was no argument in favour of wantonly rebuilding St. Mark's façade: but certainly those of us who have not yet looked at home in this matter had better do so speedily, late, and over late though it be: for though we have no golden-pictured interiors like St. Mark's Church at home, we still have many buildings which are both works of ancient art and monuments of history: and just think what is happening to them, and note, since we profess to recognize their value, how helpless art is in the Century of Commerce!"

On November 15th, 1879, a large meeting was held at the Sheldonian Theatre in Oxford, the Dean of Christ Church in the chair, to discuss the expediency of appealing to the Italian Minister of Works on the subject of St. Mark's. Mr. G. E. Street, the architect, moved and

Burne-Jones seconded the first resolution, which was carried by acclamation. Other speakers in sympathy with the objects of the meeting were Professors Richmond and Holland, Dr. Acland, and Mr. W. Morris. The latter, in his speech, mentioned that the south side of the church was already spoilt, and finished by reminding his audience that "the buildings of a nation were essentially not only the property of that nation but also of the world. So above all were the golden walls that east and west had joined to build,—walls that were the symbol of a literature." There followed certain correspondence and notices on the subject in "The Times;" Morris, on behalf of the Society for the Protection of Ancient Buildings, addressing to that paper two letters, dated November 22nd and 28th respectively. He appealed most earnestly to the Italian people to do their utmost "to induce the authorities to forbid for the future all meddling with the matchless mosaics and inlaid works which are the crown of the glories of St. Mark's;" and observed that if only we could hear that the restoration of the pavement had been stopped, it would do more than anything else to allay our fears, "and would make many of us who at present dread that we shall never dare to see Venice again, look forward with redoubled pleasure to our next visit to the most romantic of cities." In the course of the correspondence other letters, all with the same intention, were addressed to "The Times" by Messrs. Street, Henry Wallis, Stillman, and Edward Poynter, R.A. Meanwhile the agitation in this country was not without its effects in Italy, where the news of the movement, together with the strong public opinion in England against the "restoration" of St. Mark's, caused considerable shame and annoyance to the authorities. In answer to the inquiries of the English correspondent there, the truth was elicited. In self-defence the Italians pleaded that it was the Austrians, during their occupation, who were the first to tamper with the basilica. Had the Venetians been wise they would have mistrusted the ways of the Austrian Danaoi, for all their seeming lavish zeal in defraying the cost of rebuilding; but alas, the Laokoon had not yet arisen; other counsels prevailed, and the Venetians took up the work where the usurpers had left it off, and proceeded to carry out the "restoration" of the south side of the church. It was at the point when this job was completed that the perpetrators themselves became alarmed, and the news of their debatings, and of the dissensions that ensued, reached England. "It was not known," said "The Times" leader of November 28th, "that the artistic conscience of Italy had already been roused, and that the mischief which was in full course had been stopped. The two previous completed acts of destruction were known only too well, and the conclusion was that the third, which had been taken in hand, would be completed too, after the same model and under the same guidance as the former ones." The repudiation on the part of the authorities of any intention of carrying out this fatal plan may have been genuine, but on the face of it there was only too much reason to fear the contrary. It seems probable enough that the work of destruction would have been carried through had not William Morris given utterance to the voice of indignant protest that this country sent forth almost unanimously. Seven years later the subject arose again in the newspapers, and the Society for the Protection of Ancient Buildings again came to the fore in defence of the integrity of the beautiful basilica, whose "golden twilight" Morris loved so well. This at least may be asserted, that if St. Mark's was saved, it had the narrowest escape; and everyone who visits the church and admires its peerless façade should remember how immeasurable a debt of gratitude is owing to William Morris for his timely intervention in defence of the building, and for the prominent part he took in organizing the agitation against the threatened effacement of one of the most exquisite monuments in the world. On the occasion of other instances of vandalism in Italy Morris addressed a letter to "The Times," in which he urged that his appeal for English support to stay such acts ought not to be without response, "when men reflect how important is the issue, and how incomparable a loss is being suffered by the whole civilized world, as one link after another in the history of art is cut away to feed the vanity of some modern designer, or the greed of some contractor eager for a job." It may perhaps be mentioned here that Morris knew Florence, and that he has been heard to describe it as "a modern city, with some ancient monuments remaining;" and Verona, with the church of St. Zeno, which he considered altogether a typical church, and the finest of its kind in Italy. Morris's admiration for "the stately and careful beauty of St. Sophia at Constantinople," and for "the sculptured cliffs of the great French cathedrals," has been noted already in previous chapters of this work.

With the object of helping to provide the necessary funds to meet the increasing expenditure of the Society for the Protection of Ancient Buildings, as year by year its work was "carried on with greater vigour, and extended over a wider field," certain lectures were organized and given by Professor Richmond, Messrs. Reginald Stuart Poole, E. J. Poynter, R.A., J. T. Micklethwaite, and William Morris. These lectures, of which two had been delivered by Morris, were issued together in one volume in 1882. In his lecture on "Pattern Designing," Morris remarks how men of old built "here, in the land we yet love, . . . their homes and temples," and built them "in such sweet accord with the familiar nature amidst which they dwelt, that when, by some happy chance, we come across the work they wrought, untouched by any but natural change, it fills us with a satisfying, untroubled happiness that few things else could bring us. Must our necessities destroy, must our restless ambition mar, the sources of this innocent pleasure, which rich and poor may share alike—this communion with the very hearts of departed men? Must we sweep away these touching memories of our stout forefathers . . . ? If our necessities compel us to it, I say we are an unhappy people; if our vanity lure us into it, I say we are a foolish and light-minded people, who have not the wits to take a little trouble to avoid spoiling our own goods. Our own goods? Yes, the goods of the people of England, now and in time to come; we who are now alive are but life-renters of them. Any of us who pretend to culture, know well that in destroying or injuring one of these buildings we are destroying the pleasure, the culture—in a word, the humanity—of unborn generations. It is speaking very mildly to say we have no right to do this for our temporary convenience. . . . Any such destruction is an act of brutal dishonesty. Do you think such a caution is unnecessary? How I wish that I could think so! . . . I think the poor remains of our ancient buildings in themselves, as memorials of history and works of art, are worth more than any temporary use they can be put to. . . . Our Society has had much to do in cases of what I should call the commercial destruction of buildings; . . . we have carefully examined these cases to see if we had any ground to stand on for resisting the destruction; . . . we have argued the matter threadbare on all sides; and . . . above all we have always tried to suggest some possible use that the buildings could be put to. . . . The Society has taken great pains . . . to try and get guardians of ancient buildings to *repair* their buildings. For we know well, by doleful experience, how quickly a building gets infirm if it be neglected. There are plenty of cases where a parish or a parson will spend two or three thousand pounds on ecclesiastical finery for a church, and let the rain sap the roof all the while." An old building ought the rather "to be watched by people that love it, and know it both in the present and the past, so that no beginnings of preventible decay might be allowed" to undermine its strength: and "surely," says Morris, "in days to come people will feel ashamed of us that we took so little trouble to guard the things they have heard told of as so precious; that we could not exercise something more of patience and forethought in arranging the relative claims of what our lives compelled us to make for our immediate use, and what our honour and gratitude bade us hand down from our fathers to our children. . . . These monuments, so precious a possession of this country, do bear with them a certain responsibility: we must either . . . deal with them carefully and patiently, or neglect the duty which cultivation and civilisation has imposed upon us as descendants of those who built them."

"I have one last word to say," continues Morris, in the above-quoted lecture, "on the before-mentioned restless vanity that so often mars the gift our fathers have given us. Its results have a technical name now, and are called 'restoration.' . . . My plea against it is very simple, . . . but it seems to me . . . unanswerable. . . . I love art and I love history; but it is living art and living history that I love. . . . It is in the interest of living art and living history that I oppose 'restoration.' What history can there be in a building bedaubed with ornament, which cannot at the best be anything but a hopeless and lifeless imitation of the hope and vigour of the earlier world? . . . A strange folly it seems to me for us who live among these bricken masses of hideousness, to waste the energies of our short lives in feebly trying to add new beauty to what is already beautiful. . . . Don't let us vex ourselves to cure the antepenultimate blunders of the world, but fall to on our own blunders. Let us leave the dead alone, and, ourselves living, build for the living and those that shall live." "Meantime, my plea for our Society is this: that since it is disputed whether restoration be good or not, and since we are confessedly living in a time when architecture has come on the one hand to jerry-building, and on the other to experimental designing, . . . let us take breath and wait; let us sedulously repair our ancient buildings, and watch every stone of them as if they were built of jewels (as indeed they are), but otherwise let the dispute rest till we have once more learned architecture, till we have once more among us a reasonable, noble, and universally used style. Then let the dispute be settled. I am not afraid of the issue. If that day ever comes, we shall know what beauty, romance, and history mean, and the technical meaning of the word 'restoration' will be forgotten. Is not this a reasonable plea? It means prudence. If the buildings are not worth anything they are not worth restoring; if they *are* worth anything, they are at least worth treating with common sense and prudence. Come now," the lecturer concludes, "I invite you to support the most prudent society in all England."

Again, the remains of our native art, says William Morris, in his lecture on "The Lesser Arts," are "growing scarcer year by year, not only through greedy destruction . . . but also through the attacks of another foe, called now-a-days 'restoration.' . . . Thus the matter stands: these old buildings have been altered and added to century after century, often beautifully, always historically; their very value, a great part of it, lay in that: they have suffered almost always from neglect also, often from violence, . . . but ordinary obvious mending would almost always have kept them standing, pieces of nature and of history. But of late years a great uprising of ecclesiastical zeal, coinciding with a great increase of study, and consequently of knowledge of mediæval architecture, has driven people into spending their money on these buildings, not merely with the purpose of repairing them, of keeping them safe, clean, and wind and water-tight, but also of 'restoring' them to some ideal state of perfection; sweeping away if possible all signs of what has befallen them at least since the Reformation, and often since dates much earlier: this has sometimes been done with much disregard of art and entirely from ecclesiastical zeal, but oftener it has been well meant enough as regards art: yet . . . from my point of view this restoration must be as impossible to bring about as the attempt at it is destructive to the buildings so dealt with: I scarcely like to think what a great part of them have been made nearly useless to students of art and history: . . . terrible damage has been done by that dangerous 'little knowledge' in this matter: . . . it is easy to be understood, that to deal recklessly with valuable (and national) monuments which, when once gone, can never be replaced by any splendour of modern art, is doing a very sorry service to the State."

Once again, in the lecture on "The Beauty of Life," Morris says: "Many and many a beautiful and ancient building is being destroyed all over civilized Europe as well as in England, because it is supposed to interfere with the convenience of the citizens, while a little forethought might save it without trenching on that convenience; but even apart from that, I say that if we are not prepared to put up with a little inconvenience in our lifetimes for the sake of preserving a monument of art which will elevate and educate not only ourselves, but our sons, and our sons' sons, it is vain and idle for us to talk about art—or education either. . . . The same thing may be said about enlarging, or otherwise altering for convenience sake, old buildings still in use for something like their original purposes: in almost all such cases it is really nothing more than a question of a little money for a new site: and then a new building can be built exactly fitted for the uses it is needed for, . . . while the old monument is left to tell its tale of change and progress, to hold out example and warning to us in the practice of the arts: and thus the convenience of the public, the progress of modern art, and the cause of education, are all furthered at once at the cost of a little money. Surely . . . it is worth while spending a little care, forethought, and money in preserving the art of bygone ages, of which (woe worth the while!) so little is left, and of which we can never have any more, whatever good-hap the world may attain to. No man who consents to the destruction or the mutilation of an ancient building has any right to pretend that he cares about art; or has any excuse to plead in defence of his crime against civilization and progress, save sheer brutal ignorance. But . . . I must say a word or two about the curious invention of our own days called 'restoration,' a method of dealing with works of bygone days which, though not so degrading in its spirit as downright destruction, is nevertheless little better in its results on the condition of those works of art. . . . Ancient buildings being both works of art and monuments of history must obviously be treated with great care and delicacy: . . . the imitative art of to-day is not, and cannot be the same thing as ancient art, and cannot replace it; and . . . therefore if we superimpose this work on the old, we destroy it both as art and as a record of history; lastly, . . . the natural weathering of the surface of a building is beautiful and its loss disastrous. Now the restorers hold the exact contrary of all this: they think that any clever architect to-day can deal off-hand successfully with the ancient work; that while all things else have changed about us since (say) the thirteenth century, art has not changed, and that our workmen can turn out work identical with that of the thirteenth century; and, lastly, that the weather-beaten surface of an ancient building is worthless, and to be got rid of wherever possible. . . . The question is difficult to argue, because there seem to be no common grounds between the restorers and the anti-restorers. I appeal therefore to the public, and bid them note that though our opinion may be wrong, the action we advise is not rash: . . . if, as we are always pressing on people, due care be taken of these monuments, so that they shall not fall into disrepair, they will be always there to 'restore' whenever people think proper, and when we are proved wrong; but if it should turn out that we are right, how can the 'restored' buildings be restored? . . . Therefore . . . let the question be shelved till art has so advanced among us that we can deal authoritatively with it, till there is no longer any doubt about the matter. Surely these monuments of our art and history, which . . . belong . . . to the nation at large, are worth this delay: surely the last relics of the life of the 'famous men and our fathers that begat us' may justly claim of us the exercise of a little patience."

Morris presided, and gave an address, at the annual meeting of the Society for the Protection of Ancient Buildings, on June 4th, 1885. On this occasion he informed the Society that he had himself attended twice to give evidence before the Commission of the Select Committee that sat on the subject of Mr. Pearson's plan for altering and rebuilding parts of the exterior of Westminster Hall, but that he (Morris) feared that the Hall was doomed, in spite of all that had been done to preserve it intact. Mr. Morris took also an active part at this time in opposing the mischievous scheme for demolishing, or allowing to fall into decay, certain of the ancient churches of York. He visited that city at the end of May, 1885, and addressed an enthusiastic meeting which was held there to protest against the proposed monstrosity, as he described it. "It was not our business to interfere," he said, "with ecclesiastical arrangements. All we wanted was that in carrying out the scheme the churches should not be destroyed. . . . Altogether it was a very successful meeting." Morris gave an address at the Society's annual meeting on July 3rd, 1889. In the autumn of 1890, at Trinity College, Cambridge, thanks to the energy of Dr. Cunningham, who both proposed it and carried it to a satisfactory issue, a meeting was held in support of the aims of the Society, the Master of Peterhouse in the chair. There was a numerous attendance, and the audïence listened with sympathetic attention to the arguments which were put forward by Mr. Morris and the other speakers, including Mr. Cobden-Sanderson and Mr. Micklethwaite, on behalf of the religious as well as the artistic value of the genuineness of ancient buildings, in contrast to the sham presentment of the modern restorer.

In an article, already mentioned, in "The Nineteenth Century," of March, 1889, on "Westminster Abbey and its Monuments," Mr. Morris opposed the scheme for providing for additional interments and the erection of fresh memorials in the Abbey Church. He wrote another paper on the same subject, published officially by the Society (n.d. 1894), entitled "Concerning Westminster Abbey." In this pamphlet Morris traces the various misfortunes that have successively defaced and degraded the great church from "the two Puritan upheavals," and through the "long series of blunders" of the architects, one after another, into whose hands it has fallen, from the days of Wren down to the present day. The result of Mr. Pearson's new work, and particularly his conjectural restoration of the façade of the north transept, Mr. Morris pronounces to be "most unsatisfactory." It is, "as it was bound to be," under the circumstances, but "another example of the dead-alive office work of the modern restoring architect, overflowing with surface knowledge of the mediæval work in every detail, but devoid of historic sympathy and true historical knowledge, and with no other aim in view than imitating the inimitable. But this example of the error is made more palpable and absurd by the fact that it is an imitation of very ornate thirteenth century work, including abundance of figure sculpture." Morris then proceeds to explain, in a remarkably lucid and instructive passage, the essential differences, and the cause of those differences, between the work of the olden sculptors and the new. The former were men who expressed "their own conceptions with their own hands, . . . they belonged to no inferior rank of artists . . . but were the leaders of their art; there were no artists above them doing work more intellectual and educated. Their productions, therefore, were always works of art, whatever their relative merits might be. Nor is that all; they were working under the full influence of traditions unbroken since the very first beginnings of art on this planet; they were entirely unable to feign themselves other than they were, artists of their own day." This "bond of tradition" was of the greatest advantage to them, and "was so far from being a fetter, that it left them truly free to give form to their thought according to their own wishes. Their works still speak for them, and show us what a great body of artists of the highest skill and sense of beauty was at work amidst the scanty populations of mediæval Europe." Whereas nowadays an entirely opposite state of things prevails, and is the cause of the failure of modern carved work. "There are undoubtedly many clever sculptors, (or modellers, rather, . . .) in civilized countries, but the capacity for designing and executing the subsidiary forms of carved ornament has completely departed from those countries, . . . while . . . the sculptors aforesaid are divorced from architectural or ornamental work. . . . This is so obvious to the architects in need of carved work for their imitative restorations that they never even attempt to employ *artists* on their work; but a supply has sprung up to meet the demand, and workmen are employed to produce imitative Gothic sculpture in which they have no interest, and of the spirit of whose prototypes they have no understanding; the tangible result of this being what is called ecclesiastical sculpture—so utterly without life or interest that nobody who passes under the portal of the church on which it is plastered, treats it as a work of art" at all. "The restoring architect, therefore, is in this dilemma, that what there is of skilful and original sculpture is not fit for his purpose, and will not make ornament; and that what he can have, and which professes to be ornament, has no artistic value. What is to be done in such a case? . . . He is met by the difficulty that he has set out to make a scientific imitation of, say, a French portal of the thirteenth century, and such portals always had sculpture of such and such subjects on them, so that his restoration will not be *thorough* unless he has the due amount of quasi-ornament to show. Therefore, in the teeth of reason and logic, he is *compelled* to accept the makeshift for the real thing, and as a consequence to leave his work *bedizened* rather than *ornamented*. That this has necessarily been the case with the new front of the north transept at Westminster must be obvious to anyone who understands art. . . . If any . . . person doubts this, let him compare the new imagery of the porches with the angels high up in the transept within; . . . and he will surely see in every line of the first the vigour and pleasure of the hand of the workman, and in the other a joyless putty-like imitation that had better have been a plaster cast." Mr. Morris was much disturbed, as might be expected, by the rumour that a "thorough restoration" of the interior of the Abbey Church was in contemplation, and finished by protesting, in the name of the Society, against the attempt to carry out so futile and presumptuous a project. The building "was the work," he says, "of the inseparable will of a body of men, who worked as they lived, because they could do no otherwise, and unless you can bring those men back from the dead, you cannot 'restore' one verse of their epic. Re-write the lost trilogies of Æschylus, put a beginning and an end to the fight at Finsbury, finish the Squire's tale for Chaucer, . . . and if you can succeed in that, you may then 'restore' Westminster Abbey. But though you cannot restore it you can preserve it. And . . . to do less than that is to involve yourselves in a great national stupidity, a national crime. . . . If we are asked what should be done, our reply is very simple. We believe that one architect, however distinguished and learned, is too heavily burdened by having the sole charge of the Abbey in his hands. We think that a consultation should be called of the best practical architects, builders, and engineers, and that they should report as to the stability of the fabric, and what means should be taken to render it thoroughly secure. . . . We are also sure that such a scheme should disclaim most emphatically any intention of meddling with the ornamental features of the building. . . . Let bygones be bygones, but do not let us enter on a second series of alterations and improvements, which will deprive us at last of all that is now left us of our most beautiful building."

Should the foregoing extracts seem excessive, it must be remembered that Morris considered the church of Westminster to be a typical building, and that the principles, therefore, which he enunciated in respect of this one in particular, are the same which he applied to other monuments of antiquity in their degree. Never relaxing the assiduity of his zeal for the cause, again and again, as secretary of the Society for the Protection of Ancient Buildings, did Mr. Morris write to "The Times," "The Pall Mall Gazette," "The Daily Chronicle," and other papers, to plead for the integrity of this or that venerable monument, menaced with peril of scathe or demolition. Thus, besides his advocacy in defence of the buildings already named, may be mentioned the City churches, the Trinity Almshouses, Canterbury and Chichester Cathedrals, St. Alban's and Peterborough, as well as Stratford-on-Avon Church, and the Hanseatic Museum at Bergen. With regard to the scheme of rebuilding the north-west tower of Chichester Cathedral, Morris said that such an undertaking must involve in addition the pulling down of much of the remains of old work, and moreover excavating fresh foundations to sustain the weight of the new structure; that the risk of doing so would be great, and such that could not possibly be confined to one spot. It was "scarcely too much to say that a wound inflicted on any part of such a building as one of our old cathedrals, is felt throughout its whole body, and may have a most prejudicial effect in disturbing its equilibrium." As for certain proposed changes at the metropolitan cathedral, they could only result, as Morris warned the public, in the building becoming "confused and falsified by the usual mass of ecclesiastical trumpery and coarse daubing that all true lovers of art and history dread so sorely; that, in short, the choir of Canterbury will go the way of Ely, St Cross, and Salisbury. Elsewhere he deplored "the destruction of all interest and beauty . . . in such examples as Worcester and Lichfield." Concerning a new reredos to be erected in Stratford-on-Avon Church, Morris wrote: "Will not every fresh piece of modern work make 'the old place' (the church, I mean,) look less old and more like a nineteenth century mediæval furniture-dealer's warehouse? . . . Once for all I protest against the trick which clergymen and restoration committees have of using an illustrious name as a bait wherewith to catch subscriptions. Shakespeare's memory is best honoured by reading his works intelligently; and it is no honour to him to spend money in loading the handsome mediæval church which contains his monument with trash which can claim none of the respect due to either an ancient or a modern work of art." Again Morris writes: "In these days, when history is studied so keenly through genuine original documents and has thereby gained a vitality which makes it such a contrast to the dull, and not too veracious accounts of kings and nobles that used to do duty for history, it seems pitiable indeed that the most important documents of all, the ancient buildings of the Middle Ages, the work of the associated labour and thought of the *people*, the result of a chain of tradition unbroken from the earliest ages of art, should be falsified by an uneasy desire to do something, a vulgar craving for formal completeness, which is almost essentially impossible in a building that has *grown* from decade to decade, and century to century."

"Again, the special beauty of mediæval buildings which, after a long period of neglect and ignorance, has forced itself on the attention of our time, should surely by now be recognized by all intelligent persons as the outcome of the conditions of the society of that epoch, a thing impossible of reproduction under the modern system of capitalist and wage-earner; . . . the whole surface of a mediæval building shows intelligent, free, and therefore pleasurable work on the part of the actual workman, while that of a modern building has nothing in it more than toil done against the grain under the threat of starvation." Elsewhere Morris says that the modern architect is but a superintendent of masons, who could not by any possibility have any real feeling in them for the spirit of old builders. It may be objected that there are plenty of precedents throughout the Middle Ages of the transformation of earlier buildings. This is true enough. But then the reconstruction of any ancient building by modern hands differs radically from, and is not to be compared with, such as was wrought by men like Edington or Wykeham, for instance; and we know that it is so. "We are perfectly conscious that when they took away something they left us a living thing in its place. . . . Tradition compelled them to set the mason and the carpenter to work on the buildings, according to *their* traditions. But as for us, the tradition of our times forbids us to pretend to do this. . . . We could not do so with a clear conscience; we should be masquerading in the past-master's clothes." The old tradition is dead, and with it has passed away the habit and the method of old work. "Such an ordinary thing as a wall, ashlar or rubble, *cannot* at the present day be built in the same way as a mediæval wall was. . . . The unconscious habit of working the stone in a certain way cannot be supplied artificially, and in such habits lies the very life of the buildings. . . . You can have but a diagram of it. . . . Here is the point, how can you patch that 'old' with this 'new'? It is quite impossible, it is preposterous. . . . All the knowledge and mastery over nature, which modern civilization has given us, cannot change the executant, whom our system forces to be a machine, into being (for the occasion) a free artist directed by necessary tradition."

Common sense, then, must recognize this primary fact, that old work is a reality, a vivid creation; new work at best an artificial and lifeless reproduction. The original, traditional life of a building is what the Society's aim is to cherish and save; whereas the nineteenth century "restorer" would rather destroy and stamp it out for ever. He takes the ancient building to pieces and substitutes for it that which is no genuine invention at all, but a stereotyped copy, a mere worthless counterfeit. The great, yet indefinable, charm which belongs to an old building is that air of venerableness which is the first thing to disappear under renovation; and therefore the value of any monument of antiquity depends not on what modern 'restorers' have been able to spend on it, but on what they have been able to leave alone. An old picture repainted is no longer authentic; an ancient manuscript rewritten, with any unfinished or perished parts in it filled in by a modern scribe, if it dare claim to be original, is a forgery. But what is true of paint and canvas, of ink and parchment, holds good no less in the case of wood and stone. A historic building re-fashioned implies the annihilation of all its associations, lost finally, never again to be recovered; the replacing of the evidence of time, of art, of human thought and human strivings, by something as blank as the newest villa or the newest conventicle in the newest suburb. It has become a spurious antique, a *pastiche;* while the process by which it has been converted into so base a sham can earn nothing other than the opprobrium of Alexandrinism. There is no such thing as restoration in the literal sense of the word; for though the student of antiquity may discipline himself according to the temper of the time he most admires, and may, to a certain extent, live in the past, "there is always his other self, the product of the time in which he works, and there is always the influence upon himself and his work of the modern world, strong enough to give the stamp of modernity to his most cunning 'revivals.' Archæological studies are delightful, but they are of no use to the artist, except to show him that the art he studies has always been one, that its manifestations only have changed, and that *the changes are essential conditions of its existence*, since they represent the relations of his art to the ever-changing conditions of life." The "restorer," ignoring all this, thinks to suppress his own time; yet "the irrepressible present is always with him," and the consequence is that, for all his vaunted lore, his work is but an inane cast of the borrowed forms of an art that as "the outcome of a whole environment," as a force organically developing, has long since vanished. In the state in which we received them, the buildings of our forefathers "represent an epoch of English art which is closed, which is absolutely *ancient;* which has no thread of tradition to connect it with the art of the present time; and therefore . . . it is impossible to treat these buildings as living things, to be altered, enlarged, and adapted as they were in the days when the art that produced them was alive and progressive. . . . They are documents of a wholly past condition of things, documents which to alter or correct is, in fact, to falsify and render worthless." "So long as these are allowed to remain and to retain their original character, unfalsified by restoration, they are at once among the most attractive and instructive of its chronicles. In them we have communion with the life and times in which they arose. They bring the dead world back again more vividly than books of history. The past in them is palpable and tangible; not only are these substantial records the liveliest incentives to the study of history, they are themselves among the most genuine and trustworthy materials for the prosecution of that study." "There is no kind of historical evidence," said Professor Bryce, "which is so precious, so certain, so incontrovertible, as that supplied by an ancient building; traditions may err, chronicles may be spoiled by partiality, and documents may be falsified, but a building—at least until restoration set in some thirty years ago"—(these words were spoken at the Society's general meeting in 1879) "was a history, and its historical evidence could not deceive." In fine, every old building is to be regarded as a bequest of the art of the past, a bequest which we owe to the art of the future. It is not our own property absolutely. We are only custodians and trustees, with a life interest in it: we should take care lest we be fraudulent trustees; we cannot be too guarded in our treatment of it; our bounden duty is to hand on unimpaired to posterity the priceless heritage as we received it.

Such are the principles which it is the Society's office to uphold. Nor is its action a negative one merely, as some of its detractors have alleged. On the contrary, the Society maintains a very definite policy on the question of proper repairs to ancient buildings; and that not simply by formulating a set of rules for general guidance, but by entering into minute particulars in each separate case that comes before its notice. The Society's enumeration of the things to be studiously avoided in churches includes the following: varnished pine, cathedral glass, encaustic tiles, repointing in black or red cement, and the removal of plaster. "Innovations of this kind have been found disagreeably obtrusive and infinitely destructive to the quiet effect which the ancient architects so successfully attained." Indeed, the Society's strenuous opposition to the pernicious practice of scraping and pointing, processes "which must infallibly destroy all ancient character," is answerable for its familiar designation of "Anti-Scrape" Society. "Because, in the benighted days of a century ago they had a craze for plastering *everything*, many architects have jumped to the conclusion that all plaster is modern and bad. Whereas it is certain that where they had large and highly-finished blocks of stone the ancient builders left them bare," but that where, on the other hand, "they had merely rubble masonry, they never exposed it—at any rate in the case of a church—but always" covered it, within and without, "with a uniform coat of plaster, thereby obtaining a quiet surface, restful to the eye, and leaving any carved work uncompeted with." The old plaster, then, is an essential part of the ancient beauty of a building, and helps to give it that air of distinction which is one of the charms of genuine antiquity as opposed to the parvenu and the sham, and it should therefore invariably be left. When it is removed it exposes the rough stones and the big, honest mortar joints of the ancient work. This, however, does not present a sight pleasing to the eye of the "restorer," who must needs cut away the stones to make them level, and then erect between each "a sham, raised joint, professing to be what it is not, . . . thus destroying all dignity and breadth of effect." But this is not the worst evil that results from stripping old plaster from the surface of exterior rubble work. It is to be condemned on the more practical ground that the stonework, deprived of its original protection, is sure to split and crumble by the action of wet and frost.

Again, it ought to be more generally understood that fine details and beautiful ornament will not of themselves make a beautiful building, and that architecture depends upon proportion and a right relation to surrounding objects. It seldom seems to occur to a clergyman or his architect that a fine church may be spoilt by having a vestry or an organ chamber tacked on to it, and, provided no ancient feature is to be destroyed, they consider no harm can be done." Another subject to which far too little heed is accustomed to be paid, is yet of very great importance, viz., "The External Coverings of Roofs." Under this title Mr. Morris wrote a pamphlet (anonymous and undated), which is published officially by the Society for the Protection of Ancient Buildings. The author begins by drawing attention to the fact that the roof of a building adapted to the climate of a northern country like ours always shows, to speak broadly, above the walls. It is a feature, therefore, which cannot fail to contribute largely to the sightliness or unsightliness of the view, whether it be in towns where the buildings are many, or in the country where only one incongruous-looking roof may spoil the whole landscape. "Now in the Middle Ages (or, indeed, down to the end of the eighteenth century), all roof coverings were more or less good." The materials that were used until comparatively modern times "made it almost impossible for a roof to be really ugly, and more often insured its being actually beautiful." Morris then names instances to illustrate his position, and appeals to architects and guardians of old buildings "to consider what a great stretch of material, good or bad, a high-pitched roof makes, and what a difference there is between" the two, the bad "a perpetual eyesore," . . . "the good of itself beautiful, and furthermore harmonious with the ancient walls and gables." On the last leaf of the pamphlet is given, for the sake of clearness, in parallel columns, a list of good roof-coverings side by side with the bad, it being premised "always that if any regard is to be had to the general beauty of the landscape, the *natural* material of the special country-side should be used instead of *imported* material."

In his lecture on "The Prospects of Architecture in Civilization," Morris incidentally showed his sympathy for some other societies whose objects are to a great extent in harmony with the last-named. "Though I ask your earnest support for such associations as the Kyrle and the Commons Preservation Societies, and though I feel sure that they have begun at the right end; . . . though we are bound to wait for nobody's help than our own in dealing with the devouring hideousness and squalor of our great towns, and especially of London, for which the whole country is responsible; yet it would be idle not to acknowledge that the difficulties in our way are far too huge and wide-spreading to be grappled by private or semi-private efforts only. All we can do in this way we must look on not as palliatives of an unendurable state of things, but as tokens of what we desire; which is, in short, the giving back to our country of the natural beauty of the earth, which we are so ashamed of having taken away from it: and our chief duty herein will be to quicken this shame and the pain that comes from it in the hearts of our fellows: this, I say, is one of the chief duties of all those who have any right to the title of cultivated men."

On March 11th, 1884, in the board-room of the Charing Cross Hotel, was founded the Art Workers' Guild. This Society had grown out of the St. George's Art Society, founded in 1883, and composed in the main of pupils of Mr. Norman Shaw. The members were thus necessarily architects; but the idea of trying to bring together the sundered branches of Art being mooted, in the autumn of the Society's first year, led to certain meetings and discussions with other artists. The result was the formation of a society "to consist of Handicraftsmen and Designers in the Arts" under the title of the Art Workers' Guild. This body absorbed into itself practically the St. George's Art Society and another society named "The Fifteen," a band of artists who used to meet monthly at one another's houses for the reading and discussing of papers on decorative art, their first gathering having taken place under the roof of Mr. Lewis F. Day. The Art Workers' Guild grew and increased rapidly; among its objects being the practical exposition of different art methods; social gatherings for conversation and discussion, with a paper occasionally read by a member, or some eminent authority, on any art topic; and the holding of small exhibitions of old and modern objects of beautiful workmanship, as well as of pictures and drawings. The Guild, "whose present place of meeting is the hall of Clifford's Inn, "includes, besides the principal designers in decoration, painters, architects, sculptors, wood-carvers, metal-workers, engravers, and representatives of various other crafts." Mr. William Morris became a member in November, 1888. He read before the Guild a paper on "The Influence of Building Materials upon Architecture." He was elected Master for the year 1892, and afterwards ranked as Past-Master of the Guild.

Morris took a much more active part in the conduct of the Arts and Crafts Exhibition Society, although neither in this case was he the actual originator. However, he very soon became drawn into it, and readily lent it his influential support soon after the scheme of it had been formulated. Thus he may be accounted as a co-founder of the Society, whose existence he recognized as "one of the tokens" of the revival of decorative art in our day. It was "in the summer of 1886," according to Mr. Walter Crane, the first President of the Society, that "the smouldering discontent which always exists among artists in regard to the Royal Academy, threatened to burst into something like a flame." A letter signed by Messrs. George Clausen, W. Holman Hunt and Walter Crane, "appeared in the leading dailies proposing the establishment of a really national exhibition of the arts, which should include not only painting, sculpture, and architecture, but also the arts of design generally. . . . The idea of such a comprehensive exhibition was an exciting one, and large and enthusiastic meetings were held of artists." But the great stir that had promised so much began to dwindle into inanity. It was soon disclosed that the motive of the picture-painters was not the developing of the arts at all, but only the pressing of certain changes in the election of the hanging committee of the Academy. "The decorative artists . . . perceiving their vision of a really representative exhibition of contemporary work in the arts fading away and the whole force of the movement being wasted in the forlorn hope of forcing reforms upon the Academy, left the agitators in a body," and took counsel together, with the immediate result that the Arts and Crafts Exhibition Society came into being. Most of the members of the new Society already belonged to the Art Workers' Guild. They desired to illustrate and emphasize the importance of the industrial arts as distinguished from the art of picture-painting, or, to quote Mr. Crane once more, "to assert the claims of the decorative designer and craftsman to the position of artist, and give every one responsible in any way for the artistic character of a work full individual credit, by giving his name in the catalogue, whether the work was exhibited by a firm or not. They also desired to bring the worker and the public together." There being great risk of pecuniary loss attending an exhibition of this kind, a certain number of gentlemen came forward and made themselves answerable as guarantors in the event of a deficit. Among the number Mr. Morris, who was on the committee, generously guaranteed a considerable sum. His action in the matter was the more noteworthy on account of its perfect disinterestedness. Morris himself had, as it is scarcely necessary to point out, nothing to gain, either for himself personally or for his firm, by an exhibition. His own artistic reputation had been established long since; and the only possible consequence to him, apart from the satisfaction he would naturally feel in the general advancement and popularizing of the arts, would be that he might have helped to advertise other and younger workers in the same field, and thereby have equipped them to enter the more easily into competition with himself on his own ground. The first exhibition was held in the autumn of 1888 at the New Gallery, in Regent Street. It comprised not merely designs for work, but the actual work itself, executed in wood-carving and furniture; embroidery, tapestry, and other textiles; glass and pottery; wall-papers; leather and metal work and jewellery; as well as book decoration, printing and binding, all selected for their artistic and decorative quality alone; "and undoubtedly included some of the best contemporary work which had been produced in England up to that time." This sort of exhibition was quite a new departure and created a precedent which has since been followed in many places, not only in the United Kingdom, but also on the Continent and in America. Four subsequent exhibitions of the Arts and Crafts Society have been held in London, at the New Gallery, in the years 1889, 1890, 1893, and 1896 respectively. Mr. William Morris was elected President of the Society at their annual general meeting in January, 1891, which office he continued to discharge until his death. Mr. Morris himself and his family, as well as the firm of Morris and Co., have contributed numerous objects of art work to the several exhibitions of the Society. Moreover, a series of lectures in connection

with the exhibitions (saving the third one) having been organized for the purpose of setting out the aims of the Society, and, by demonstration and otherwise, of directing attention to the processes employed in the arts and crafts, and so laying a foundation for the just appreciation both of the processes themselves and of their importance as methods in design, Morris delivered three lectures: viz., on "Tapestry and Carpet Weaving" during the first exhibition; on "Gothic Architecture" during the second; and "On the Printing of Books" during the third. Prefixed to the catalogues of the first three exhibitions of the Society were various essays on special arts and crafts written by different members. Morris was one of the contributors, and when the essays were collected and published together in 1893, he wrote a preface to the volume. In fact, as the whole movement owed its being to him, so were his interest and guidance the inspiration and mainstay of the Society throughout. It may be added that the choice of the Society could not have fallen upon a worthier representative living to carry on the traditions of their late President than Morris's friend and colleague, Walter Crane.

Mr. Morris belonged also to the Bibliographical Society. A preliminary meeting of those interested in the formation of such a society was held on July 15th, 1892, at the offices of the Library Association. Mr. W. A. Copinger set forth the aims of the proposed Society, which are as follows: the acquisition of information upon subjects connected with bibliography; the promotion and encouragement of bibliographical studies and researches; the printing and publishing of works connected with bibliography; and the formation of a bibliographical library at the headquarters at 20, Hanover Square. Resolutions to the above effect were carried, and a provisional committee and honorary secretary appointed to draw up rules based on the resolutions. On November 21st, 1892, the Society was inaugurated formally with an address by its first President, Mr. Copinger, who concluded with these words: "The objects of the Society are broad, and the

sphere of labour great—success depends mainly on united effort. The formation of the Society should mark an epoch in the literature of this country. It should raise the standard of excellence, and should labour with steady growth until bibliography is established as an exact science, and occupies that proper position in the realm of literature from which it has been so long by ignorance excluded." The Society meets from time to time for the purpose of hearing some paper or papers upon matters connected with the objects of the Society, it being within the discretion of the Council to print such papers among the Society's Transactions. William Morris contributed a valuable paper entitled "The Ideal Book."

On June 7th, 1894, Mr. Morris was elected a Fellow of the Society of Antiquaries of London, and admitted formally on November 22nd. To the Exhibition of English Mediæval Paintings and Illuminated MSS., organized by the Society at their apartments in Burlington House, in June, 1896, Mr. Morris contributed a valuable and important selection from his own library; viz., a Bestiary on vellum, given to the Church of SS. Mary and Cuthbert at Radeford (*i.e.*, Worksop Priory), in the year 1187; a Latin Psalter of the twelfth century, on vellum, with illuminated initials, with forty pages with pictures of biblical subjects and martyrdoms of saints; four leaves from a Latin Psalter, date *circa* 1260; a Book of Hours, with two full-page miniatures, and richly illuminated initials and ornamentation throughout, executed *circa* 1300; a Sarum Missal, with historiated initials and a great number of other ornaments; and another Sarum Missal, illuminated, of the fourteenth century.

The same collection of MSS., belonging to Mr. Morris, which had been on loan at Burlington House, after the exhibition there was over, was transferred temporarily to the South Kensington Museum, where they remained on view for about a fortnight, during their owner's absence abroad. However, before Mr. Morris's death occurred, they had been duly returned to Kelmscott House.

CHAPTER TWELVE: SOCIALISM.

THE notices which appeared in the public press at the time of Morris's death were many and varied. But, to sum them up, the several writers, according to the different attitudes they assumed, might, with certain notable exceptions, be divided into two main classes, viz., those who, for hatred of his Socialism, would not allow William Morris any particular credit, but affected a high disdain of the man and his work in general; and those, on the other hand, who out of deference to dominant prejudices, kept the unpalatable fact as far as they could in the background, referring to it as a mere episode, or at most as a weakness to which he unfortunately succumbed, through excess of benevolence, who was otherwise a very excellent and gifted man. Both, of course, were wrong in their estimate, hardly more so they that would disparage Morris altogether, than they that would disparage any single branch of his work, particularly one which he deemed so important and so inseparable a portion of it as this. His art and his Socialism were, to Morris's mind, associated integrally with one another; or rather they were but two aspects of the same thing. Those well-meaning apologists, then, who try to explain away William Morris's share in the movement are not doing him a real service, nor such for which he would have thanked them. For, as he himself remarked, when the plan of the present book was proposed to him, and he heard that it was desired, as far as might be, to avoid polemics, no account could be considered satisfactory or complete which should omit to notice and give due prominence to his attitude in respect of things political and social. But since it is so difficult as to be wellnigh impossible to treat the subject with any approach to that full and clear statement of Mr. Morris's views which fairness requires, and at the same time to manage to wound no one's susceptibilities, those who cannot trust themselves not to take offence will perhaps do wisely to skip this chapter.

Now it is sometimes asked: was Mr. Morris always a Socialist, and, if not always, when did he become one? To this question it must be answered, that Morris did undergo a change of mind; but that it is quite certain he was unconscious of any save a gradual and logical expansion of ideas into that settled shape which eventually caused him, when he had come to realize its import, to avow himself a Socialist. From documentary evidence it may be inferred that there was a period when Morris saw no objection to the monarchical principle. Thus, in 1856 (in the essay on "Ruskin and 'The Quarterly,'" in "The Oxford and Cambridge Magazine"), he wrote: "People will have a king, a leader of some sort, after all; wherein they are surely right, only I wish they would not choose king critic-mob." Neither does there appear to be any passage at variance with this loyalist sentiment among his published utterances prior to "The Earthly Paradise;" and although, in the light of after events, it is easy enough to recognize in that great work the tokens of disaffection, they seem to have escaped observation at the time, and not to have excited against their author any suspicion of revolutionary tendencies. Else what a weapon they might have furnished to the writer of the attack on "The Fleshly School of Poetry!"—a weapon which he could scarcely have failed to turn upon William Morris, had it presented itself to him. For in those days of the early seventies, when the opinions of this country were less advanced and less tolerant than they are now, a hostile critic, for the purpose of prejudicing the British public against a young poet whom he designed to crush, could have wanted no means more telling (not even excepted the insinuation of doubtful morals) than the reproach of unsound views on politics. Yet this charge was not brought; presumably because, if it occurred to "Thomas Maitland" or any other adversary to bring it, such proofs as might have been adduced were too few and too unsubstantial to warrant the attempt being made with reasonable probability of success. So time went on; and although Morris's attitude, already alluded to, with regard to the Bulgarian atrocities and the Russo-Turkish war, did not necessarily imply his having arrived at any further stage of development than that of thorough-going Liberalism, it was, nevertheless, an index that showed along what line he was moving, and might be expected to advance.

Meanwhile there was one great influence actively exerting itself upon him; and that was the study of John Ruskin. This influence is manifest and may be traced perceptibly in the series of lectures which Morris began to deliver in 1878, continued at intervals until 1891, and eventually collected and published under the title "Hopes and Fears for Art." In one of these the disciple explicitly acknowledges his indebtedness to his illustrious master, "because," as he says to his audience, "I should be ashamed of letting you think that I forget their labours on which mine are founded. I know," he continues, "that the pith of what I am saying . . . was set forth years ago, and for the first time, by Mr. Ruskin in that chapter of 'The Stones of Venice,' which is entitled 'On the Nature of Gothic,' in words more clear and eloquent than any man else now living could use. So important do they seem to me, that to my mind they should be posted up in every school of art throughout the country; nay, in every association of English-speaking people which professes in any way to further the culture of mankind. But I am sorry to have to say it, . . . they have been less heeded than most things which Mr. Ruskin has said: I suppose because people have been afraid of them, lest they should find the truth they express sticking so fast in their minds that it would either compel them to act on it or confess themselves slothful and cowardly. Nor can I pretend to wonder at that: for if people were once to accept it as true, that it is nothing but just and fair that every man's work should have some hope and pleasure always present in it, they must try to bring the change about that would make it so." Later on Morris formulated the distinct proposition thus: "'*It is right and necessary that all men should have work to do which shall be worth doing, and be of itself pleasant to do; and which should be done under such conditions as would make it neither over-wearisome nor over-anxious.*' I have looked at this claim," says he, "by the light of history and my own conscience, and it seems to me, so looked at, to be a most just claim, and that resistance to it means nothing short of a denial of the hope of civilization. . . . Turn" it "about as I may, think of it as long as I can, I cannot find that it is an exorbitant claim; yet . . . I say if Society would or could admit it, the face of the world would be changed; discontent and strife and dishonesty would be ended. To feel that we were doing work useful to others and pleasant to ourselves, and that such work and its due reward *could* not fail us! What serious harm could happen to us then? And the price to be paid for so making the world happy is Revolution." Therefore, whether or not Ruskin repudiate responsibility in the matter, there can be no doubting that it was he who both laid the foundations upon which, and supplied the materials out of which, Morris framed the fabric of his Socialism. It is in fact impossible for any, even the most casual reader of Ruskin's writings upon art to escape the dissertations with which they abound on ethical and social questions, or the author's ever-recurring tirades against the recognized order and ways of modern civilization. Now, Morris was no unsympathetic nor inapt disciple. He not only studied Ruskin, but studied him profoundly; from that great teacher he acquired both a vivid perception of existing evils and an insight into the causes that underlie them. But to anything much beyond this knowledge Ruskin does not help. He is scarcely a constructive philosopher; or, if he provides an ideal, he provides no practical scheme for the realization of it. Anyhow Morris was not to be contented to stay still at the point where Ruskin stayed. Ruskin preached and denounced; he showed the way, but did not pursue it. Morris, on the other hand, with Ruskin's premisses to start from, carried the gospel of Ruskin's discontent to its logical outcome, and placed himself in the van of the advance movement of the day.

On a memorable occasion Morris addressed an Oxford audience in a lecture that immediately provoked an orthodox protestation on the part of the Master of the College within whose walls it had been delivered. Ruskin, too, was there, heard the lecture (whose significance he must have understood as clearly as anyone present), and, when his own turn came to speak, had the opportunity, if he had so chosen, of expressing, like Dr. Bright, his disapproval of William Morris's opinions. But Ruskin was pleased to do nothing of the kind; and, if he did not endorse, word for word, everything that the lecturer had said, spoke in a strain so far similar as to convey the impression that he did not dissent. However, this occurrence was an isolated one; nor is it safe to infer from it too much; for Ruskin certainly cannot be suspected of sympathy with Revolution. He has all a Tory's horror of Socialism as it was understood by Morris and his friends; nevertheless, it must be asserted again, paradoxical though it may seem, when Ruskin himself continues no more than a querulous reactionary, that his teaching was what operated as the most powerful factor in inducing William Morris to accept the creed of Socialism. Possibly it is a matter of the difference of temperaments in the two men; or it may be attributable to the difference of their several occupations—Ruskin's wholly intellectual work, Morris exercising hand and arm as well as brain. A man, busily engaged in the arts, repulsion to pessimism was, as indeed he felt it to be, but natural in him and inevitable. His very activity compelled him to look forward to a positive change for the better; compelled him "once to hope that the ugly disgraces of civilization might be got rid of by the conscious will of intelligent persons: yet as I strove," he says, "to stir up people to this reform, I found that the causes of the vulgarities of civilization lay deeper than I had thought, and little by little I was driven to the conclusion that all these uglinesses are but the outward expression of the innate moral baseness into which we are forced by our present form of Society, and that it is futile to attempt to deal with them from the outside. Whatever I have written, or spoken on the platform, on these social subjects, is the result of the truths of Socialism meeting my earlier impulse, and giving it a definite and more serious aim; and

I can only hope . . . that any . . . who have found themselves hard-pressed by the sordidness of civilization, and have not known where to turn for encouragement, may receive the same enlightenment as I have."

Now as to what this hope of his was, and what this enlightenment, which brought to William Morris such joy in its first outpouring that he did not wait to measure it nor to calculate either the exact date when it might be accomplished or the exact means by which that accomplishment was to change the face of Society, it is best to give an account of it in his own words. "First, I will say," he writes, in 1894, in answer to the request of the Editor of "Justice," "what I mean by being a Socialist, since I am told that the word no longer expresses definitely and with certainty what it did ten years ago. Well, what I mean by Socialism is a condition of Society in which there should be neither rich nor poor, neither master nor master's man, neither idle nor overworked, neither brain-sick brain workers, nor heart-sick hand workers, in a word, in which all men would be living in equality of condition, and would manage their affairs unwastefully, and with the full consciousness that harm to one would mean harm to all—the realization at last of the meaning of the word COMMONWEALTH."

"Now this view of Socialism, which I hold to-day," says Morris, "and hope to die holding, is what I began with; I had no transitional period, unless you may call such a brief period of political radicalism during which I saw my ideal clear enough, but had no hope of any realization of it. That came to an end some months before I joined the (then) Democratic Federation, and the meaning of my joining that body was, that I had conceived a hope of the realization of my ideal."

In recalling the stages of development through which he passed to his final profession of Socialism, Morris stated that he was sensible of the fact that, in his "position of a well-to-do man not suffering from the disabilities which oppress a working man at every step, he might never have been drawn into the practical side of the question if an ideal had not forced" him "to seek towards it. For," he continues, "politics as politics, *i.e.*, not regarded as a necessary if cumbersome and disgustful means to an end, would never have attracted me, nor, when I had become conscious of the wrongs of Society as it now is, and the oppression of poor people, could I have ever believed in the possibility of a *partial* setting right of these wrongs. In other words, I could never have been such a fool as to believe in the happy and 'respectable' poor. If, therefore, my ideal forced me to look for practical Socialism, what was it that forced me to conceive of an ideal? . . . Before the uprising of *modern* Socialism almost all intelligent people either were, or professed themselves to be, quite contented with the civilization of this country . . . and saw nothing to do," the majority of them, "but to perfect the said civilization by getting rid of a few ridiculous survivals of the barbarous ages." This was, as Morris conceived it, the typical "*Whig* frame of mind." But "there were a few who were in open rebellion against the said Whiggery—a few, say two, Carlyle and Ruskin. The latter, before my days of practical Socialism, was my master," writes Morris, "towards the ideal aforesaid, and, looking backward, I cannot help saying, by the way, how deadly dull the world would have been twenty years ago but for Ruskin! It was through him that I learned to give form to my discontent, which I must say was not by any means vague. Apart from the desire to produce beautiful things, the leading passion of my life has been and is hatred of modern civilization. What shall I say of it now, when the words are put into my mouth, my hope of its destruction—what shall I say of its supplanting by Socialism? What shall I say concerning its mastery of and its waste of mechanical power, its commonwealth so poor, its enemies of the commonwealth so rich, its stupendous organization—for the misery of life? Its contempt of simple pleasures which everyone could enjoy but for its folly? Its eyeless vulgarity which has destroyed art, the one certain solace of labour? All this I felt then as now, but I did not know why it was so. The hope of the past times was gone, the struggles of mankind for many ages had produced nothing but this sordid, aimless, ugly confusion; the immediate future seemed to me likely to intensify all the present evils by sweeping away the last survivals of the days before the dull squalor of civilization had settled down on the world. This was a bad look-out indeed, and . . . especially so to a man of my disposition, careless of metaphysics and religion, as well as of scientific analysis, but with a deep love of the earth and the life on it, and a passion for the history of the past of mankind. Think of it! Was it all to end in a counting-house on the top of a cinder heap, . . . the pleasure of the eyes . . . gone from the world, and the place of Homer . . . taken by Huxley? Yet believe me, in my heart when I really forced myself to look towards the future, that was what I saw in it, and, as far as I could tell, scarce anyone seemed to think it worth while to struggle against such a consummation of civilization." Nor had life, under such circumstances, any other than a pessimistic prospect for Morris, until it somehow dawned upon him that amidst all the tangled, odious mass "of civilization the seeds of a great change, what we others call Social Revolution, were beginning to germinate. The whole face of things was changed to me by that discovery, and all I had to do then in order to become a Socialist was to" attach himself to the practical movement, which he proceeded to do. "To sum up then, the study of history," says Morris, "and the love and practice of art forced me into a hatred of the civilization, which, if things were to stop as they are, would turn history into inconsequent nonsense, and make art a collection of the curiosities of the past, which would have no serious relation to the life of the present." But "it is the province of art to set the true ideal before" the workman, "a life to which the perception and creation of beauty, the enjoyment of real pleasure that is, shall be felt to be as necessary to man as his daily bread, and that no man, and no set of men can be deprived of this except by mere oppression, which should be resisted to the utmost." "The consciousness of revolution stirring amidst our hateful modern Society prevented me, luckier than many others of artistic perceptions, from crystallizing into a mere railer against 'progress' on the one hand, and on the other from wasting time and energy in any of the numerous schemes by which the quasi-artistic of the middle classes hope to make art grow when it has no longer any root, and thus I became a practical Socialist." "For the rest, when I took that step I was blankly ignorant of economics; I had never so much as opened Adam Smith, or heard of Ricardo, or of Karl Marx. Oddly enough I *had* read some of Mill, to wit, those posthumous papers of his . . . in which he attacks Socialism in its Fourierist guise. In those papers he put the arguments, as far as they go, clearly and honestly, and the result, so far as I was concerned, was to convince me that Socialism was a necessary change, and that it was possible to bring it about in our own days. These papers put the finishing touch to my conversion to Socialism."

William Morris, as it has been said truly, "never did things by halves. He hated shams, and in whatever he undertook he was thorough." Having, then, become convinced that the doctrines of Socialism were right, he could not hang back, but must declare himself without delay. The only question that remained for him to determine was what existing association, if any, set forth faithfully his ideal?

Now here it is necessary to pause a little, and trace the origin of the body to which Morris allied himself. One need not go farther back in the history of the movement than the collapse of Chartism, at which date it might have seemed as though the hope of the labouring class had been extinguished altogether. But, in spite of all discouragements, "Socialism was making great strides," says Mr. Morris in "Socialism, its Growth and Outcome," "and developing a new and scientific phase, which at last resulted in the establishment of the International Association, whose aim was to unite the workers of the world in an organization which should consciously oppose itself to the domination of capitalism." The International Association "was inaugurated in England in 1864, at a meeting held in St. Martin's Hall, London, at which Professor Beesly took the chair," Messrs. Marx and Odger also having a leading part in the proceedings. This Association "made considerable progress among the trades unions, and produced a great impression . . . on the arbitrary governments of Europe." "In 1869, at the Congress of Basel, Marx drew it into the compass of Socialism; and though in England it still remained an indefinite labour body, on the Continent it became at once decidedly Socialistic and revolutionary, and its influence was very considerable." Thus the Central Committee, during the Paris Commune of 1871, was "largely composed of members of the International." But the fall of the Commune naturally involved that of the International; and the latter did not long survive. "Internal dissensions, also, were at work within the International, and at the Congress of the Hague in 1872 it was broken up; for though it still existed as a name for the next year or two, the remaining fragments of it did nothing worth speaking of." "Once more, for several years, all proletarian influence was dormant in England, except for what activity was possible among the foreign refugees living there, with whom some few of the English working men had relations."

"In the year 1881 an attempt was made to federate the various Radical clubs of London under the name of the Democratic Federation. Part of the heterogeneous elements, mainly the mere political radicals, of which this was composed, withdrew from it in 1883; but other elements, connected with the literary and intellectual side of Socialism, joined it, and, soon after, the body declared for unqualified Socialism, and took the name of the Social Democratic Federation. This was the first appearance of modern or scientific Socialism in England, and on these grounds excited considerable public attention, though the movement, being then almost wholly intellectual and literary, had not at that time reached the masses." The most prominent figure at this stage of the movement was Mr. H. M. Hyndman. The earliest meeting between him and Mr. Morris had taken place in 1879, and found them in opposite camps. "Morris had been," says Hyndman, "more active than perhaps anybody else against the Turks. I, as it chanced, though having no love for the Turks, had worked hard on the other side against Russia." Hyndman having also "written some articles on India in 'The Nineteenth Century' which had made a little stir," was invited by Mr. Henry Broadhurst to deliver an address on the same subject at 19, Buckingham Street, Strand, at that time the headquarters of the National Liberal League and of the Trades Union Congress Parliamentary Committee, in whose deliberations Morris used to join. Thus, then, the two first encountered one another. But "not until the end of 1882, or the beginning of 1883," writes Hyndman, "did I see Morris again. Then . . . the Democratic Federation was holding a series of meetings on 'Practical Remedies for Pressing Needs,' in the large hall at Westminster Palace Chambers. The subjects were the now familiar Eight Hours Law, Free Meals for Children, Nationalization of Railways, and so on. Morris came to the first discussion and forthwith joined the body." "Morris's adhesion," says another writer, "was a chief victory to them, because of his known worth and name," a fact which is fully borne out by Mr. Hyndman's own testimony: "It is difficult perhaps for men who have come into the movement of late years to understand how we welcomed capable recruits in those days of very small things. True" they reckoned among their number certain able and active individuals, "but, even so, we were few and Socialism was new. Morris, with his great reputation and high character, doubled our strength at a stroke by giving in his adhesion."

"Well," says Morris, "having joined a Socialist body (for the Federation soon became definitely Socialist), I put some conscience into trying to learn the economical side of Socialism, and even tackled Marx, though I must confess that, whereas I thoroughly enjoyed the historical part of 'Capital,' I suffered agonies of confusion of brain over reading the pure economics of that great work. Anyhow, I read what I could, and will hope that some information stuck to me from my reading; but more, I must think, from continuous conversation with such friends as Bax, and Hyndman, and Scheu, and the brisk course of propaganda meetings which were going on at the time, and in which I took my share. Such finish to what of education in practical Socialism I am capable of I received afterwards from some of my Anarchist friends, from whom I learned, quite against their intention, that Anarchism was impossible, much as I learned from Mill, against *his* intention, that Socialism was necessary." But this experience of Anarchism did not befall him until some years later. Meanwhile, Hyndman bears witness how hard his new ally worked. Morris, he says, "was as ready to do anything as the youngest and least known among us. In fact he resented attempts being made to keep him back from doing things which he really ought not to have done. Writing, speaking in and out of doors, conferring, full of zeal and brimming over with good humour and suggestion—it all seems but yesterday." Mr. Bernard Shaw recalls how, at this time, he met Mr. Morris in company with Mr. Hyndman; how those were "days of bad trade, desperate poverty, and newly-awakened social compunction," when "there seemed . . . nothing for it but to break with commercialism, with its pretensions, its respectability, and its law and order altogether, and to stand aloof from it, shame it, and support every attempt to overturn it;" and how greatly he was struck by hearing Morris modestly confess "that he had no pretensions to be able to lead, or organize, or manage things politically, but that he was ready to do what he was told and go where he was led,"—a remark characteristic not less of Morris's docility as a neophyte than of his habitual sincerity and unselfconsciousness.

Having set to work with a will upon studying the economic aspect of his subject, and having become sufficiently master of its dry details to be able to expound to others, Morris produced, in conjunction with Hyndman, a small handbook of some sixty pages and more, entitled "A Summary of the Principles of Socialism." This work, which appeared in the winter of 1883-4, was described as a pamphlet that "takes a wide and scientific survey of the industrial development of the past, states in detail the causes of the world-wide industrial distress of the present, and makes Proposals both for the immediate and ultimate application of Socialism in the industrial organization of the future." It was published with the official approbation of the entire Executive Committee of the Democratic Federation—not yet differentiated, it is worth observing, with the prefix "Social." The list of signatures appended shows that Hyndman occupied the position of Chairman, while Morris was Honorary Treasurer. The latter discharged also the by no means sinecure office of collector for the Propaganda Fund of the Federation. Now, hitherto, the body had lacked an official mouthpiece, but this was not a state of things that could continue unless the work was to be seriously handicapped. It was indispensable to have a journal, not only for the exposition of their views, but also for the publication of notices of lectures, meetings, &c. Edward Carpenter found the requisite funds, and on January 19th, 1884, appeared the first number of "Justice," a weekly paper, bearing the sub-title, which it retains to this day: "The organ of the Social Democracy." It was advertised as being "entirely independent of plutocratic support," and "one of its distinctive features is the weekly summary of the foreign revolutionary movements. It also contains articles on the economical theories of the Social Democrats, and a complete record of the Socialist meetings and propaganda." Morris threw himself into the enterprise "with vigour, and wrote frequently;" his contributions beginning with the first issue, and in the shape chiefly of articles and verses, continuing until December 20th in the same year. The objects of the Federation, as stated in the first number of the paper, were: "To unite the various Associations of Democrats and Workers throughout Great Britain and Ireland, for the purpose of securing equal rights for all, and forming a permanent centre of organization: to agitate for the ultimate adoption of the Programme of the Federation: to aid all Social and Political movements in the direction of these reforms." The programme of the Democratic Federation was thus set forth:

1. Adult Suffrage.

2. Annual Parliaments.

3. Proportional Representation.

4. Payment of Members; and of Official Expenses of Elections out of the Rates.

5. Bribery, Treating, and Corrupt Practices at Elections to be made acts of Felony.

6. Abolition of the House of Lords and of all Hereditary Authorities.

7. Legislative Independence for Ireland.

8. National and Federal Parliaments, including representation of Colonies and Dependencies.

9. Nationalization of the Land.

10. Free Justice.

11. Disestablishment and Disendowment of all State Churches.

12. The power of Declaring War, Making Peace or Ratifying Treaties, to be vested in the Direct Representatives of the People.

To the above articles, as an exposition of the working methods of Socialism, Morris subscribed. But, however they might serve as a provisional scheme, it could hardly have been supposed that he bound himself to accept them as final. On the face of them they bore too much the stamp of having been elaborated, so to speak, from the outlines of State Socialism as sketched in the class-books of political economists of the mediocre Liberal School, to be able to correspond with his growing aspirations. They partook too much of an attempt to evolve a new State out of existing things; to construct a fresh Society out of a patchwork of the rags of the old. In some respects, indeed, the horizon of the policy they laid down was narrower in extent than that of the defunct International. Thus, even in 1870, the sense of the brotherhood of humanity was sufficiently developed for the Socialists of Germany to defy the Jingoism of the Prussian patriotic party, and to issue a corporate protest against the iniquity of going to war with France. Whereas, in 1884, the twelfth section of the programme of the Democratic

Federation provided for the event of war; and the eighth recognized the separate existence of the nation with its Colonial possessions, and the Dependencies under its protection—in fact, all the aggregate of the British Empire. But the day was not far ahead when Morris would laugh at the idea of the territorial delimitation of mankind into separate and antagonistic communities, and of the arbitrary distinction between blood and blood that the word "nation" conveys. As to Section 10, did he not deem that in the ideal State the "Administration of *Justice*," so-called, should be relegated to the domain of Icelandic snakes, *i.e.*, nowhither? And, again, as to Section 7, it is doubtful whether he continued long to imagine that the claims of equity would be satisfied by the concession of merely "*Legislative* Independence" to Ireland. But all this is to anticipate.

In "Justice" of April 5th, 1884, appeared another official statement of the Democratic Federation. The means whereby its objects were to be carried out were the holding of "public meetings, lectures, the publication and circulation of literature, the formation of branches, and such other methods as the Executive may consider advisable." And, "as measures called for to remedy the evils of our existing Society the . . . Federation" urged the following for immediate adoption:

The Compulsory Construction of healthy artisans' and agricultural labourers' dwellings in proportion to the population, such dwellings to be let at rents to cover the cost of construction and maintenance alone.

Free Compulsory Education for all classes, together with the provision of at least one wholesome meal a day in each school.

Eight Hours or less to be the normal Working day in all trades.

Cumulative Taxation upon all incomes above a fixed minimum not exceeding £300 a year.

State Appropriation of Railways, with or without compensation.

The Establishment of National Banks, which shall

absorb all private institutions that derive a profit from operations in money or credit.

Rapid Extinction of the National Debt.

Nationalization of the Land, and organization of agricultural and industrial armies under State control on Co-operative principles.

Anent the last item may be mentioned two statements of Mr. Morris's about this time with reference to his own business. The first was at Cambridge, in February, 1884, on the occasion of a debate on Socialism, when one of those present asked Mr. Morris to justify his position as head of a mercantile house; who replied that under existing things it was inevitable, but that he was ready to resign as soon as ever the State was prepared to take over his business. Until then, however, he was convinced of the "utter hopelessness of merely handing over capital to another capitalist while the certainty of its being used for the exploitation of labour remained unassailed." Morris has often been taunted with inconsistency for making costly articles for the use of the wealthy classes. But if it was so, it was none of his choosing. He had no more desire to minister to the luxury of the rich than to deprive the poor of that enjoyment which he held to be theirs by right as human beings. But if the poor lacked both the money to buy, and the taste to appreciate the beautiful things he was constrained to make, surely Morris was not to blame. The second statement is contained in a letter, dated April 21st, to Miss Emma Lazarus, in which Morris explained that in his business only a partial system of profit-sharing prevailed. When he (Morris) had begun to turn his attention to the subject, although he had little faith in profit-sharing as a solution of the labour and capital question, he "thought it might advance that solution somewhat, in the absence of any distinct attempt towards universal co-operation, *i.e.* Socialism;" and he had hoped to be able to put his whole establishment on a profit-sharing basis. But now that he saw more clearly, he was no longer tempted "to try to advance a movement which, in its incompleteness, would rather injure than help the cause of labour," and that because it could "do nothing towards the extinction of *competition*, which lies at the root of the evils of to-day;" for, granted the establishment of various co-operative societies, each one of them would only "compete for its corporate advantage with other societies, would, in fact, so far be nothing but a joint-stock company." It could only "create a body of small capitalists, who would exploit the labour of those underneath them quite as implacably as bigger capitalists do." Moreover, the increase to which it would tend of over-work on the part of the industrious "would practically mean putting the screw on all wage-earners, and intensifying the contrast between the well-to-do and the mere unskilled," so that the general result would only be "increase of work done . . increase of luxury, increase of poverty." In his own business he had "tried to produce goods which should be genuine as far as their mere substances" were "concerned," but it had "been, chiefly because of the social difficulties, almost impossible to do more than to insure the *designer*" (mostly Morris himself) "some pleasure in his art by getting him to understand the qualities of materials, and the happy chances of processes. Except with a small part of the more artistic side of the work," he continues, "I could not do anything (or at least but little) to give this pleasure to the workmen, because I should have had to change the method of work so utterly that I should have disqualified them from earning their living elsewhere. You see I have got to understand thoroughly the manner of work under which the art of the Middle Ages was done, and that that is the *only* manner of work which can turn out popular art, only to discover that it is impossible to work in that manner in this profit-grinding society. So on all sides I am driven towards revolution as the only hope, and am growing clearer and clearer on the speedy advent of it in a very obvious form." Three articles from Morris's pen on "A Factory as it might be," and "Work in a Factory as it might be," appeared in "Justice" in May and June.

On August 4th, 1884, at its fourth annual conference,

the Federation adopted formally the title of the Social Democratic Federation.

On September 29th, Mr. Morris wrote an Introduction to Mr. J. Sketchley's book, "A Review of European Society, with an Exposition and Vindication of the Principles of Social Democracy." As the work of an old Chartist, and therefore as forming a connecting link between the popular movements of the past and the Scientific Socialism of the present, Morris considered it to be specially interesting and valuable. To see the sleeping cause re-awakened in such wise, was a source of no small encouragement, as Morris pointed out. The book appeared in the following November.

It happened that a paper called "The Mediæval and the Modern Craftsman," an address delivered before the Society for the Protection of Ancient Buildings when that body had completed the seventh year of its existence, was printed in "Merry England" for October, 1884. The version so published never received Mr. Morris's *imprimatur*, and therefore it is unsafe to quote from it: although, to judge by the general tenour of the article, it does not seem to misrepresent his views to any material extent. Neither is it probable that Morris would have taken any notice of it, had not a leading article, by way of a criticism upon Morris's opinions as expressed in the said address, appeared in "The Echo" of October 1st. In the course of this leader, the writer remarks that W. Morris "has allied himself with a body with the aims of which, we must charitably suppose, he is only in imperfect sympathy." Very naturally Morris resented the suggestion that he was acting in bad faith, and wrote a letter of remonstrance which was published in "The Echo" of October 7th, 1884. After pointing out one or two minor misconceptions, Morris continues: "What is, I think, of more importance, is the assumption in the article that I care only for Art, and not for the other sides of the the Social Questions I have been writing about, and also that I do not go all lengths with my colleagues of the Social Democratic Federation. Against these assumptions I must protest. Much as I love art and ornament, I value it chiefly as a token of the happiness of the people, and I would rather it were all swept away from the world than that the mass of the people should suffer oppression; at the same time, Sir, I will beg you earnestly to consider if my contention is not true, that genuine Art is always an expression of pleasure in Labour. As to my connection with the Social Democratic Federation, I have had my full share in every step it has taken since I joined it, and I fully sympathise with its aims." He then expresses his utter disbelief in the sanctity of class privilege, and says that he cannot shut his "eyes to the fact that, whatever position any portion of the working-classes now holds, it has gained by the exercise of force at the expense of the moneyed class, land-holding or capitalist, and that it is only by continued and energetic antagonism to that class, by what you have named social revolt, that the working class can either keep its gains or add to them, and that this antagonism will be continued till all classes are abolished, and a new form of society is built up." At the same time, lest the above should not appear in "The Echo," Morris wrote a short letter to the like effect to the editor of "Justice," although he knew, as he said, that to most of his comrades of the Social Democratic Federation, an assurance on his own part that he was in full sympathy with them would not seem necessary. And also to provide against possible misunderstandings that might ensue from any future piracy, he announced his determination "not to contribute articles to any capitalist paper whatsoever." This resolution, however, happily for literature, Morris so far modified as to write, at subsequent dates, for the "Fortnightly," and "Nineteenth Century" Reviews, and for "The Magazine of Art."

Morris's letter to "The Echo" incidentally affords the explanation of a difficulty which has sometimes been felt. People have been at a loss to reconcile the two seemingly contradictory phenomena, viz., Morris's rigidly conservative measures with regard to the preservation of Ancient Buildings, and his throwing in his lot with the Socialists.

Yet the very fact of his conservatism in the one case should avail to acquit him from any possible accusation of having acted in the other from want of reflection or from capricious lust of unsettlement. On the contrary, it ought to suggest to every thoughtful mind the existence of some simple key to the problem; and that, after all, the course Morris adopted in either respect may have been determined by one common motive, one rational and consistent method of action throughout. And such indeed was the case.

Being oppressed with a painful sense of the utter incongruity between new work and the old in architecture, Morris set himself conscientiously to inquire into the essential qualities of the two things; of the old, which was a delight to him, and of the new, which was an offence. And having been led to the discovery of the truth, in the first place, as has been shown, by the aid of Ruskin on "The Nature of Gothic," and, in the second, by observing in his own experience that things worsened, instead of mending, with the increase of commercial prosperity and the progress of science and civilization so-called, he could not evade the intellectual conviction that a people, whose greed was continually prompting it to destroy what all its wealth was impotent to replace, must be in such sorry plight and altogether so corrupt that no remedy was to be found short of an entire reconstruction of society from the root up.

Morris was constantly harping upon the theme of the unhappy condition of the modern workmen as compared with that of the workman of the past. "Now," says Morris, "they work consciously for a livelihood and blindly for a mere abstraction of a world-market which they do not know of, but with no thought of the work passing through their hands. Then, they worked to produce wares, and to earn their livelihood by means of them, and their only market they had close at hand and they knew it well," and it knew them. "Now, the result of their work passes through the hands of half a dozen middlemen. Then, they worked directly for their neighbours, understanding their wants, and with no one coming between them. Huckstering, which was then illegal, has now become the main business of life, and, of course, those who practise it most successfully are better rewarded than anyone else in the community. Now, people work under the direction of an absolute master whose power is restrained by a trade's union, in absolute hostility to that master. Then, they worked under the direction of their own collective wills by means of trade guilds. Now, the factory hand, the townsman, is a different animal from the countryman. Then, every man was interested in agriculture, and lived with the green fields coming close to his own doors. In short, the difference between the two may be told very much in these words: In those days, daily life, as a whole, was pleasant, although its accidents might be rough and tragic. Now, daily life is dreary, stupid, and wooden, and the only pleasure is in excitement, even if that pleasure should be more or less painful or terrible. Surely the vile and disgraceful heaps of misery and fatuity that should not be called buildings, which curse our towns and curse the history of the country, are truly and properly the expression of our life, which is lived in and round about them, just as those which it is our business to preserve" —(these words were addressed to the Society for the Protection of Ancient Buildings)—"and those which have been destroyed . . . were in their beauty and manliness the expression of the life which was lived then." Again, it was the old system which believed, in its simplicity, that commerce was made for man, that produced the Art of the Middle Ages; whereas our modern system, founded on the assumption that man is made for commerce, that he is not an intelligent being, but a machine or part of a machine, yields but one result, "the degradation of the external surroundings of life,—or, simply and plainly, unhappiness."

"I confess," says Morris again, "that it is with a strange emotion that I recall these times and try to realize the life of our forefathers, men who were named like ourselves, spoke nearly the same tongue, lived on the very same spots of the earth, and therewithal were as different from us in manners, habits, ways of life and thought, as though they lived in another planet: . . . Not seldom I please myself with trying to realize the face of mediæval England, . . . and when I think of this it quickens my hope of what may be." In the Middle Ages there was literally "no such thing," says Morris, "as a piece of handicraft being ugly; everything made had a due and befitting form; most commonly, however ordinary its use might be, it was elaborately ornamented, and such ornament was always both beautiful and inventive, and the mind of the workman was allowed full play and freedom in producing it." Indeed, the element of association in the life of the mediæval workman was in a fair way to develop into an ideal society; which somehow, however, it did stop short of forming, since such a society can have no foundation but the equality of labour. "The Middle Ages, so to say, saw the promised land of Socialism from afar, like the Israelites, and like them had to turn back again into the desert;" for the associations became too exclusive, the upper classes were for aggrandizing themselves with perpetual war, and so opened the door to the advance of the evil thing, bureaucracy. But, "commerce, in our sense of the word, there was none; capitalistic manufacture, capitalistic exchange was unknown: to buy goods cheap that you might sell them dear was" in the fifteenth century a misdemeanour, called forestalling and was punishable by law: "to buy goods in the market in the morning and to sell them in the afternoon in the same place was forbidden under the name of regrating: . . . the holidays of the church were holidays in the modern sense of the word, downright play-days, and there were ninety-six obligatory ones" in the year. At any rate, "it is clear," says Morris, "that such misery as existed in the Middle Ages was different in essence from that of our own times; one piece of evidence alone forces this conclusion upon us: the Middle Ages were essentially the epoch of *popular* art, the art of the people; whatever were the conditions of the life of the time, they produced an enormous volume of visible and tangible beauty, even taken *per se*, and still more extraordinary when considered beside the sparse population of those ages. The 'Misery' from amidst of which it came, whatever it was, must have been something totally unlike, and surely far less degrading than the misery of modern Whitechapel, from which not even the faintest scintilla of art can be struck, in spite of the idealizing of slum life by the modern philanthropic sentimentalist and his allies, the impressionist novelist and painter." Morris certainly scorned the idea of any permanent good coming from patronizing the poor with People's Palaces and Picture Shows, without undertaking to abolish the present economical system. He was not so foolish as to deny that beside "plenty of unnecessary labour which is merely painful," "there is some necessary labour even which is not pleasant in itself." He maintained that "if machinery had been used for minimising such labour, the utmost ingenuity would scarcely have been wasted on it," for the right and proper object for the invention of machinery is the alleviation of human toil and suffering. But Morris questioned whether the so-called "labour-saving" machinery of modern times had lightened one whit the daily work of one labourer. And as to competitive commerce, it means at the best pursuing one's "own advantage at the cost of some one else's loss." Unlike association, which is "human," Morris considered "the condition of competition between man and man . . . bestial only." It is nothing less than an "implacable war," whose whole energy and organized precision "is employed in one thing, the wrenching the means of living from others."

From the outset until his severance from the Federation, Morris was continually going about on Lecturing tours (sometimes in company with Hyndman, to support the latter, as at the meeting at the Clarendon Rooms at Oxford, and at the Debate at Cambridge), but more usually by himself. The Federation drew up and advertised in the pages of "Justice" a list of Lecturers and the subjects on which they were prepared to speak, on application. William Morris had four addresses: "Useful work *versus* useless Toil;" "Art and Labour;" "Misery and the way out;" and "How we live and How we might live;"

which he delivered on numerous occasions. Beside lecturing in various parts of London and the suburbs, *e.g.*, Clerkenwell and Bethnal Green, Southwark and Hammersmith, Hampstead, Merton Abbey and Woolwich, Morris visited for the same purpose many of the principal towns in the provinces, *e.g.*, Ancoats (Manchester), Bradford, Leeds, Preston, and Sheffield. His lecture at University College, Oxford, has been mentioned above. Another lecture, delivered at Leicester, on January 23rd, 1884, was published under the title of "Art and Socialism;" and on three occasions in 1884 alone, viz., in March, November, and again in December he lectured in Edinburgh.

It is of interest to note the growth of a spirit of formularizing and, in a sense, of constitutionalizing in the Federation; a growth that can clearly be traced in the different shapes in which its aims and principles were set forth successively from that in the first number of "Justice" to that which appeared on October 25th, 1884. As then stated, their object, deduced from the maxim that "Labour is the source of all wealth; therefore, all wealth belongs to Labour," was "The establishment of a Free Condition of Society based on the principle of Political Equality, with Equal Social Rights for all and the complete Emancipation of Labour;" the programme being drawn up as follows:

1. All officers or Administrators to be elected by Equal Adult Suffrage, and to be paid by the community.

2. Legislation by the People, in such wise that no project of Law shall become legally binding till accepted by the Majority of the People.

3. The Abolition of a Standing Army, and the Establishment of a National Citizen Force; the people to decide on Peace or War.

4. All Education, higher no less than elementary, to be Free, Compulsory, Secular, and Industrial for all alike.

5. The Administration of Justice to be Free and Gratuitous for all Members of Society.

6. The Land with all the Mines, Railways, and other Means of Transit, to be declared and treated as Collective or Common Property.

7. Ireland and all other parts of the Empire to have Legislative Independence.

8. The Production of Wealth to be regulated by Society in the common interest of all its Members.

9. The Means of Production, Distribution, and Exchange to be declared and treated as Collective or Common Property.

But this was not all. In November, 1884, the Executive Committee of the Social Democratic Federation began to agitate for the State organization of unemployed labour, as though the task-mastership of the State were likely to press otherwise than hardly upon those whom the cruel competitive system, which is of the essence of its existence, had made outcasts.

In the first blush of enthusiasm for the cause "We then thought and said," writes Mr. Hyndman, "that we should all work on together in harmony to the end. Alas! that was not to be." In the autumn of 1884 the "little rift" appeared which ended by splitting the organization in twain; nor does it seem to have been a very great while before some inkling of dissensions in the Socialist ranks began to get abroad, and William Morris's name to be mentioned in this connection. Now, although it was quite true that the latter was in perfect accord with his comrades of the Federation as to fundamental principles, yet a disagreement as to the right method of propagating and of fulfilling those principles undoubtedly existed, and was fomenting for some time before the actual catastrophe occurred. In the meantime, the circulation of such reports was calculated to do no good. Rather it must tend to precipitate matters; an event plainly most undesirable, so long as any likelihood yet survived of a settlement being arrived at that would obviate the scandal of an open rupture. And so Morris continued to write in "Justice," and to go about lecturing and organizing for the Federation up to the very last. Notwithstanding, his position, holding as he did a prominent place in the body, was becoming daily more and more insupportable. "The Socialism of the Social Democratic Federation rapidly took on a dogmatic and sectarian colouring," says Mr. Kenworthy. According to this writer it was their narrow shibboleths, and the fact that "they less and less admitted . . . a Socialist might live and work outside their association" that alienated the support of a broad-minded man like Morris, ay, and of many another beside. To Morris, "Marx's analysis and demonstration were only one, and that a not interesting, but academic, arithmetical way of stating the truth about 'the social problem.' Political agitation and parliamentary action, to which the Social Democratic Federation became committed, upon the failure of their first wild, violent, revolutionary outbreak, had become to Morris utterly impossible directions of work and hope. For he saw deeper. His insight and purpose went far beyond anything that statistics can prove and Acts of Parliament effect." It was perhaps inevitable that Morris's early submissiveness should give place to that self-reliance which completer knowledge of his subject brought with it, when he had learned to think independently for himself. Moreover his was a nature that chafed against the imposing of formal definitions. Thus, on one occasion, when some fresh regulations were being adopted at a meeting of the Arts and Crafts Exhibition Society, William Morris, who occupied the chair as President, while assenting to the proposals which had commended themselves to the majority of the Society, remarked, at the same time, that personally he should much prefer to do without rules altogether.

Anyhow the time arrived at last when "differences of opinion, chiefly on points of temporary tactics," were such that could no longer be composed, and some decisive action had to be taken. What then occurred was a schism in the Social Democratic Federation. Morris was the most important and influential figure among the seceders, who, being met together at 27, Farringdon Street, on December 30th, 1884, formed themselves into the Socialist League. A provisional council was named, including Morris in the capacity of Treasurer; and as the first thing to be done was to start an organ of their own, he was appointed also, on January 6th, to act as editor, with Edward Aveling for sub-editor. The purpose for which the League was founded, as Mr. Morris said, was the spread of Revolutionary International Socialism. The intention of the founders was to carry through the doctrine purely, unmixed with opportunism; for they deprecated "all meddling with parliamentary methods of reform." The first number of "The Commonweal. The official Journal of the Socialist League," was dated February, 1885, and contained the text of the manifesto which had been drawn up and signed by the whole body of the Provisional Council of the League, on the day of its foundation. Under their control "The Commonweal" was immediately placed. It began, and continued for the first fifteen months of its existence, as a monthly paper. The first number had the heading in plain capitals, but the second and subsequent numbers appeared with the words "The Commonweal" upon a light under-pattern of willow leaves, designed by Mr. Morris. The first issue opened with an Introductory column, written and signed by William Morris, in which he observed: "It is our duty to attack unsparingly the miserable system which would make all civilization end in a society of rich and poor, of slaves and slave-owners;" and again: "We assume as a matter of course that a government of privileged persons, hereditary and commercial, cannot act usefully towards the community; their position forbids it; their arrangements for the distribution of the plunder of the workers, their struggles for the national share of the exploitation of barbarous peoples are nothing to us, except so far as they may give us an opportunity of instilling Socialism into men's minds." The manifesto, which occupied as it were, with the Socialist League the corresponding position to the programme of the Federation, made no direct reference to that body, but by the very way in which its paragraphs were worded its policy was lifted at once on to a higher and broader platform than that of the Social Democratic Federation. The object of the League was stated to be to destroy all "distinctions of classes and nationalities." And whereas "the workers, although they produce all the wealth of Society, have no control over its production or distribution," the League proposed to alter all this "from the foundation: the land, the capital, the machinery, factories, workshops, stores, means of transit, mines, banking, all means of production and distribution of wealth, must be declared and treated as the common property of all." And further, "as to mere politics, Absolutism, Constitutionalism, Republicanism, have all been tried in our day and under our present social system, and all alike have failed in dealing with the real evils of life. Nor . . . will certain incomplete schemes of social reform . . . solve the question. Co-operation so-called—that is, competitive co-operation for profit" will not do; neither will "nationalization of the land alone. . . . No better solution would be that of State Socialism. . . . No number of merely administrative changes, until the workers are in possession of all political power, would make any real approach to Socialism. The Socialist League therefore aims at the realization of complete Revolutionary Socialism, and well knows that this can never happen in any one country without the help of the workers of all civilization. For us," proceeds the manifesto, "neither geographical boundaries, political history, race, nor creed makes rivals or enemies; for us there are no nations, but only varied masses of workers and friends, whose mutual sympathies are checked or perverted by groups of masters and fleecers whose interest it is to stir up rivalries and hatreds between the dwellers in different lands." The manifesto, from which space does not permit of more extracts to be made, received the formal ratification of the Socialist League at the first general meeting, which was held at 13, Farringdon Road, on July 5th, 1885. Mr. Morris, who was voted to the chair, explained the origin and intentions of the League; an executive council of twenty members and the officers were chosen; an annual conference of delegates from all the branches of the League was decided upon; and the report was read of the proceedings of the executive body up to date. From this document it was shown that out of twenty-eight council meetings Morris had attended all but four, and those he had missed only through being on duty elsewhere on the business of the League. All this is evidence of Morris's indefatigable earnestness for the cause. If he had worked hard for the Federation, his exertions were more than doubled by the responsibilities which came upon him with the birth of the Socialist League. The same round of lecturing as heretofore was kept up with unabated energy. Nor did these meetings always pass off smoothly. Thus, on February 25th, 1885, when Mr. Morris, supported by Mr. Faulkner, Fellow of University College, and Dr. Aveling, was conducting a Socialist meeting in Holywell, Oxford, some bigoted opponents of fair play caused the assemblage to break up in something very near disorder. However, Morris's zeal was not to be subdued by sulphuretted hydrogen, and, understanding the undergraduate better than the Prince of Wales's policemen do, he took the incident, as far as he might, in good part. In the first number of "The Commonweal" it was announced that Morris was prepared to lecture, and that lectures could accordingly be arranged, on four subjects—the same practically on which he had been in the habit of speaking for the Federation. The wear and tear, physical and mental, entailed by this propaganda was terrific, and the marvel is that Morris managed to bear the strain so long as he did. On April 24th he lectured at Glasgow; next day he went to Edinburgh for the same purpose; he was back again at Glasgow on 26th, and two days later was lecturing at Chesterfield. It is a relief to find he was back at Hammersmith, where he lectured on May 10th on the subject "How shall we Help?" and, on June 14th, on "The Hopes of Civilization." It is not possible, however, to follow in detail the long course of Morris's labours in this department. Suffice it to say that the work of the Socialist League now fairly set afoot went on apace. The new Society, though a rival, in no way interfered with the older, "both societies carrying on an active Socialist propaganda, and in process of time often acting in concert. The West End riots on Monday February 8th, 1886, and the consequent trial of four members of the Social Democratic Federation, brought the two organizations much together. A good many branches, both of the Federation," says Morris, "and the League, were founded and carried on with various fortunes." But this is to anticipate.

At the Social Entertainment of the League at the South Place Institute on June 11th, 1885, the prologue spoken was a poem by Morris entitled "Socialists at Play." Another time he wrote a Socialist interlude called "The Tables Turned; or, Nupkins awakened," which was performed at the Hall of the Socialist League on October 15th, 1887. On this occasion, as appears from the list of the original cast, Morris himself played the astounding *rôle* of the Archbishop of Canterbury. Mr. Bernard Shaw, who was present, asserts his belief that "there has been no other such successful first night within living memory." Again "later, at one of the annual festivities of the Hammersmith Socialist Society," Morris played a part "in a short piece," not from his own pen, called "The Duchess of Bayswater." But such amusements as these were rare exceptions amid the serious work he had undertaken.

On Morris fell the greater share of the League's expenses, and he also it was who financed "The Commonweal." Most arduous of all his labours were those entailed in the management of that periodical, which after fifteen monthly parts was then issued weekly, from May 1st, 1886, and continued to be so as long as Morris had anything to do with it, *i.e.*, until near the end of the year 1890. Thus, although as a matter of fact "The Commonweal" "contained less and less of Morris's work towards the close," some 250 successive issues passed through his hands, a prodigious amount of work for him to have accomplished seeing that he did not stay quietly in the office but was going about for the more part of the time organizing meetings, and lecturing for the furtherance of the movement up and down the country,—and all this in addition to his previous occupations and responsibilities, from which of course he could not free himself, even if he would. At first, and for a long time, an enormous proportion of the contents of each number Morris furnished with his own pen. "In almost every issue," says Mr. Temple Scott, "he contributed editorial notes, with the headings . . . 'Notes on News,' 'Political Notes,' 'Notes on Passing Events,' &c. These were sometimes signed with his full name, but oftener with the initials W. M. Scattered here and there throughout the issues are minor notes all initialled W. M. Occasionally, during or after a lecturing tour, he would send on notes or impressions. These appear under" their several headings: *e.g.*, "Socialism in Dublin and Yorkshire," as well as letters from Manchester and Scotland. "Mr. Morris's more important contributions to 'The Commonweal' consist of political and social leaders, poems, stories, and articles on art. In conjunction with Dr. Aveling, E. Belfort Bax, and H. Halliday Sparling, he signed several editorials and special pronouncements of the Socialist League." On May 4th, 1889, was published a "Statement of Principles," in which it was declared that the League would abide by the old motto of Liberty, Fraternity, and Equality, adding to it, however, St. Simon's maxim: "From each according to his capacity, to each according to his needs." But the Socialist League pledged itself to no specific programme. And herein, if, in one sense, its strength, lay also a fruitful source of weakness. For while the absence of a formula left the Society comprehensive, unrestricted, and with power to modify or to develop itself as occasion might arise, on the other hand it furnished no sort of test by which insubordinate members could be brought to account, nor dissentients expelled. Beneath such a state of things were latent discord's seeds from which there could not fail, sooner or later, to be matured disruption. The very diversity of fortune among the various members of the Socialist body was of itself a bar against their continuing always to act in concert, unless indeed the poorer were to become permanent pensioners of the more wealthy. William Morris, living, as he himself said, in comparative comfort, might afford to await with patience the accomplishment of the ideal he had ever before him—an ideal so exalted that, attained, it would mean nothing short of the millennium inaugurated—and meanwhile to reject temporary measures of relief as unworthy and inefficient compromises. But what of the rest? the very poor, the downtrodden, the starving? Were they all in a position to wait likewise, with practical needs pressing upon them day by day, and demanding to be satisfied? If they went empty, and lacking the bare means of subsistence, could the sentiment of maintaining the integrity of an ideal be expected to check them from being driven by force of hunger to desperation? Was it not more than flesh and blood could endure for them to be content with the proclamation of goodwill and fellowship? Must not such words sound but an empty mockery in their ears? To reconcile these conflicting claims, to apply the principles of an ideal to the appeasing of the instant distress of the necessitous, this is the problem which has never yet been solved satisfactorily. It was a problem, however, which Morris did not shrink from facing.

Now, as it has been inferred already, the position Morris took up with regard to these matters was very far removed from being that of a mere onlooker, or extern prompter. He was not the man to shirk the responsibility and the consequences of his own acts, to sit at home in comfortable security and leave it to others to bear the rough brunt of the campaign he himself was helping to instigate. From the first he plunged into the thick of the agitation. He sold Socialist literature in public, he spoke at street corners, he marched in procession along with the most rampant of malcontents, he braved imprisonment in support of the cause. Twice he actually became embroiled to the extent of arraignment in the police court. The Dod Street affair, and that which arose out of it, have been alluded to in the opening pages of this work. It was then that "a policeman, whose helmet-strap had been broken and whose temper was worn out, suddenly seized the nearest victim," who happened to be Morris, "and charged him forthwith with assault." The sequel has been related already. "On the only subsequent occasion," continues Mr. Bernard Shaw, "when he" (Morris) "appeared in court as a prisoner—for speaking, in defiance of an attempt to put down open-air meetings, at a " certain level space of ground "near the Edgware Road—counsel for the Crown, appalled by the eminence of his prisoner, loaded him with compliments, and appealed to him to overlook the formality of a shilling fine." For a man of Morris's temperament "the agonies of nervous discomfort and apprehension " entailed by experiences of this sort cannot easily be overrated.

The real meaning of all the petty persecution of open-air meetings was at length made clear, says Morris, culminating as it did in "the shameful day of November 13th" (1887), "and the still more shameful scenes in the police and law courts which followed it. This time the Socialists found themselves in alliance with the extreme Radicals, as in the affair of Dod Street." In these well-remembered events, too, Morris took part. In view of the intended gathering in Trafalgar Square, Sir Charles Warren had prohibited by proclamation any meeting being held in the Square itself; and not only this, he gave instructions that no organized procession should be permitted to approach the Square. It was held by many, however, that he was exceeding his lawful powers in issuing such orders, and it was resolved accordingly to disregard and resist them. As has been said, the determination formed was not that of one party alone, but of certain Radical clubs and the Irish National League, augmented by a branch of the Social Democratic Federation and the Socialist League. They agreed to assemble at various centres and, marching westward, to join at Trafalgar Square. William Morris attached himself to the Clerkenwell contingent. "At about two o'clock, or shortly after that time," says the "Times" report, a number of persons crossed the Green and ascended a cart, from which they soon proceeded to address the people. "Among those in the cart were Mr. William Morris and Mrs. Besant, both of whom delivered speeches of a determined character. Mr. William Morris began his speech by expressing sympathy with Mr. O'Brien. He then proceeded to say that wherever free speech was attempted to be put down, it was their bounden duty to resist the attempt by every means in their power. He thought their business was to get to the Square by some means or other, and he intended to do his best to get there, whatever the consequences might be. They must press on to the Square like orderly people and like good citizens. . . . At about half-past three," the account continues, "the procession started from Clerkenwell Green," with banners flying and bands playing, up Theobald's Road, through Hart Street, Bloomsbury, and into Bloomsbury Street. "When the procession reached the Bloomsbury end of St. Martin's Lane, the police began to disperse it. So far the people had gone quietly and rather exultantly on their way towards Trafalgar Square; but at this point matters took a serious turn. The police, mounted and on foot, charged in among the people, striking indiscriminately in all directions, and causing complete disorder in the ranks of the processionists. I witnessed," says the writer, "several cases of injury to men who had been struck on the head and face by the police. The blood, in most instances, was flowing freely from the wound, and the spectacle was indeed a sickening one. The struggle at this point did not last long; here and there the men attempted to rally and face the police; but the unrestricted use which the police made of their *bâtons* overcame all resistance, and in a short time the bands were dispersed and the police had captured the remnants of the banners, which were torn and destroyed, and carried them off as trophies of the encounter. The action of the police in this struggle was received with yells of execration, and with groaning and hooting from the mob. When the people saw there was no hope of re-forming the procession, a great number of them mixed with the crowd and wended their way towards Trafalgar Square, and so disappeared what but a short time before had been the Clerkenwell contingent." "When the procession was formed," says Mr. Bernard Shaw, who was also present, "he" (Morris) "took his place beside me for some time, and then, realizing that the column had grown a good deal in front of us, went to the head, where he saw the rout at its most striking moment." "It was all over in a few moments," writes Morris. Mr. Bernard Shaw says: "If the men who had had the presumption to call themselves his" (Morris's) "'comrades' and 'brothers' had been in earnest about cleaning and beautifying human society as he was in earnest about it, he would have been justified in believing that there was a great revolutionary force beginning to move in society. Trafalgar Square cured him and many others of that illusion." To resume Morris's own account of the affair: "Our comrades fought valiantly, but they had not learned how to stand and turn their columns into a line, or to march on to the front. Those in the front turned and faced their rear, not to run away, but to join in the fray if opportunity served. . . . The band instruments were" seized, the "flags destroyed; there was no rallying point and no possibility of rallying, and all that the people composing our once strong column could do was to straggle into the Square as helpless units. I confess I was astounded at the rapidity of the thing and the ease with which military organization got its victory. I could see that numbers were of no avail unless led by a band of men acting in concert, and each knowing his own part. . . . Once in the Square we were, as I said, helpless units." Had the mass of demonstrators succeeded in reaching the Square "the result would probably have been a far bloodier massacre than Peterloo." As it was, "the police, horse and foot," were completely "masters of the situation." The reading of the Riot Act followed; and the Life Guards, and, shortly after them, the Foot Guards, with fixed bayonets, making their appearance, "completed the triumph of law and order." Nevertheless, it was scarcely an exaggeration to describe London at the time as "in a state of siege." "In fact," wrote Morris, while the impression was still fresh, the "affair, as far as it has gone, has been an ominous flash from the smouldering volcano of class war which underlies modern sham-society." A panic set in similar to that "caused by the last great demonstration of waning Chartism in 1848;" and on this occasion also a large number of special constables were sworn in, and ordered to hold themselves in readiness for fear of future disturbances, and in particular lest any attempt should be made to hold a meeting of protest on the following Sunday in Hyde Park; nor did the enrolment close for several weeks to come. And the net result of it all? Three hundred or so arrested, many sent to prison, several condemned to penal servitude, and three men killed. The first victim of the disorders of "Bloody Sunday," as the day came to be called, was Alfred Linnell, killed on November 20th. His funeral took place in Bow Cemetery. Morris was present, and made a speech at the grave, where there was sung also a death-song written by him, containing the following stanzas:

"We asked them for a life of toilsome earning,
They bade us bide their leisure for our bread,
We craved to speak to tell our woeful learning,
We came back speechless, bearing back our dead.

* * * * * *

"Here lies the sign that we shall break our prison;
Amidst the storm he won a prisoner's rest;
But in the cloudy dawn the sun arisen
Brings us our day of work to win the best."

In "News from Nowhere" occurs a reference to the painful affair. Morris fancies himself therein visiting many old familiar *places* under *Utopian* circumstances. In the course of this paradoxical journey he comes to Trafalgar Square, and makes one of his characters remark, on the scarcely recognizable spot, "'I have read a muddled account in a book . . . of a fight which took place here in or about the year 1887. . . . Some people, says this story, were going to hold a ward-mote here, or some such thing, and the Government of London, or the Council, or the Commission, or what not other barbarous . . . body of fools, fell upon these citizens . . . with the armed hand. . . . According to this version of the story, nothing came of it.' . . . 'It *is* true; except that there was no fighting, merely unarmed and peaceable people attacked by ruffians armed with bludgeons.'" They "'*had* to put up with it';" they "'could not help it.' . . . 'This came of it . . . that a good many people were sent to prison because of it.'"

Their tactics changed once more, the Socialists with the unemployed—strange freak on their part—took to attending, in a body, Sunday services at various places of worship in the metropolis, being willing to submit to the infliction of hearing sermons, so their presence there in numbers might help to advertize their claims. It was on a certain wet, wintry day during this period that a striking scene occurred, which Mr. Joseph Pennell has described. "I remember," he says, "seeing William Morris . . . one Sunday afternoon walking up Parliament Street. A meeting was being held in the Square— . . . the people holding it had made up their minds to march to Westminster Abbey, with a vague idea probably that when they got there they might do something. Suddenly an enormous crowd began to pour out of the Square down Parliament Street. . . . On they came, with a sort of irresistible force, . . . and right in front—among the red flags, singing with all his might the 'Marseillaise'—was William Morris. He had the face of a Crusader, and he marched . . . as the Crusaders must have marched. One turned round and went with the crowd, which, when it got to the Abbey, seemed half inclined to smash the windows; but those at the head of it were switched off, and passed into Poets' Corner, there to sit down and be preached to, while the others, who could not get in, were addressed by Canon Rawlinson outside. But what was so curious was to find this artist . . . leading a crowd who really did not know what they wanted to do. However, had this crowd determined to destroy, to tear down even a stone of the Abbey, or to break a window, I think, instead of William Morris leading them a step further, that they would only have taken that step over his body." So "The Daily Graphic" says: "He bailed out offenders who got into trouble by asserting the right of free speech, and helped their families when they were finally convicted, . . . and he has been seen at the head of a procession of the 'workless workers' of Hammersmith, tramping through the rain to interview the Guardians of the Poor." Thus in all weathers, in season and out of season, did he champion the cause of the friendless and the suffering, who alone know, unskilled though they be in the power to express, what a friend in need and in deed they have lost in the person of William Morris. It is not forgotten how, in September, 1884, he intervened on behalf of the costermongers of Hammersmith, when some tyrannical vestry—or whatever authority it be that controls such matters—decided to banish these poor folk from the thoroughfare, where they had hitherto plied their none too lucrative trade, to some out-of-the-way street, and was issuing coercive summonses against them right and left.

But to return to the subject of Mr. Morris's Socialistic writings. And firstly of poetry. While yet a member of the Democratic Federation he had begun to bring out a series of "Chants for Socialists." The first, "The Day is coming," was issued separately; the second, third and fourth, "The Voice of Toil," "All for the Cause," and "No Master," appeared in "Justice," after which the series was continued in "The Commonweal," viz., "The March of the Workers," and "The Message of the March Wind." The latter was made the first of a new series, entitled "The Pilgrims of Hope," which included "The Bridge and the Street," "Sending to the War," "Mother and Son," "The New Birth," "The New Proletarian," "In Prison—and at Home," "The Half of Life Gone," "A New Friend," "Ready to Depart," "A Glimpse of the Coming Day," "Meeting the War Machine," and "The Story's Ending." All of the above were reprinted in some form or other, one edition of "Chants for Socialists" including an additional poem entitled "Down among the Dead Men."

And next of prose. Under this head must be included first a number of pamphlets, and lectures, &c. Among the former may be named "The Reward of Labour," "True and False Society," and "Monopoly; or, How Labour is Robbed." Mr. Morris collaborated with two other writers in a pamphlet on "The Commune of Paris." A lecture by Morris on "Socialism," delivered under the auspices of the Norwich Branch of the Sociailst League on March 8th, 1886, appeared in "Daylight," and was subsequently reprinted in pamphlet form. Shortly after the formation of the first Socialist Society in Aberdeen, the new community was visited by William Morris. A course of lectures on various aspects of the Labour Problem being organized and delivered by several different lecturers in Scotland in the summer of 1886, Mr. Morris spoke on "The Labour Question from the Socialist Standpoint." His lecture was included with the others in the volume called "The Claims of Labour," published at Edinburgh in 1886.

To "The Principles of Socialism made plain," by Frank Fairman, Morris wrote a preface, dated December 5th, 1887, notwithstanding he was bound to own in it that he differed from the author "as to the method of bringing about the change set forth by him in the ninth chapter" of the work. "It seems to me," said Morris, "that the constitutional or parliamentary method which he advocates would involve loss of energy, disappointment, and discouragement; . . . and, judging by the signs of the times, I cannot help thinking that the necessities of the miserable, ever increasing as the old system gets closer to its inevitable ruin, will outrun the slow process of converting parliament from a mere committee of the landlords and capitalists into a popular body representing the best aspirations of the workers. . . . I venture to state that my own hope lies in converting the associated workmen to Socialism, and in their organizing a great inclusive body, which would feel itself consciously at strife with the proprietary class, and its organ Parliament; which would regulate labour in the interest of the workers as well as might be under the present system till the time was ripe for the general assertion of the principles of Socialism and for the beginning of their practice, when Parliament might be used mechanically for the setting forth of a few enactments . . . so as to allow freed, but organized labour to take its due place, and throw off the mere encumbrances" dealt with in Mr. Fairman's book.

A collection of seven lectures, two of which had been previously printed as pamphlets, while three others were reprints from "The Commonweal," was published under the title of "Signs of Change," the preface bearing date March, 1888.

Four letters on "Socialism," addressed by Mr. Morris from Kelmscott House, Hammersmith, to Rev. George Bainton, of Coventry, in 1888, on April 2nd, 4th, and 10th, and May 6th respectively, were printed for private circulation only, in a limited impression of thirty-four copies, with a facsimile of the second letter, upon Japanese vellum. A note states that these letters, in the possession of the addressee, are printed with the author's permission, though not upon his initiative; the volume bears date 1894. The letters form a particularly simple and lucid exposition of Mr. Morris's views on the subject. In one of them he says that what he requires is "an ethical or religious sense of the responsibility of each man to each and all of his fellows." And again he says, "Socialism aims . . . at realizing equality of condition as its economical goal, and the habitual love of humanity as its rule of ethics."

To "The New Review" of January, 1891, Morris contributed an article on "The Socialist Ideal: Art." Next must be mentioned three historical tales which appeared in "The Commonweal." "An Old Story Retold," which was published in number 36, was afterwards reprinted with the new title of "A King's Lesson." The tale is one related of Matthias Corvinus, King of Hungary. A longer story, taken from Froissart, "The Revolt of Ghent," which ran through seven numbers, from July 7th, 1888, to August 18th inclusive, has not been republished. But the most important, and such that it would be difficult to conceive a more exquisite romance of its kind, was "A Dream of John Ball," which extended from number 44 to 55 inclusive. It was reprinted as a separate volume, together with "A King's Lesson," in April, 1888. Morris's highest vision and "deepest word," says Mr. Kenworthy, "are in" his "Dream of John Ball." "Infinitely better than in any history, Morris has here restored the thought, speech, and deed of the English Parish Priest, the Communist and rebel, and has given them the setting of his own thought and belief. . . . To his John Ball, the Church of Christ means Human Good-fellowship; the Communion of Saints means Communism in practice; the sinners are the selfish, oppressors, and lustful; the flock Christ would save is the labouring poor; the king, the lawyer, and the soldier are worst foes; the lordship to be desired is that of 'the King's Son from Heaven.' The question that Morris turned in his mind as he wrote this book is, why should a man struggle for the right, if only to fail and to die, and lose even what he might have had of this lovely life of earth? His John Ball . . . and the other rebels, some fighting, some slain, are true human lives—poeticized, but still true—in whom this problem of sacrifice is wrought out." ("I pondered on all these things," says Morris, "and how men fight and lose the battle, and the thing they fought for comes about in spite of their defeat, and when it comes it turns out not to be what they meant, and other men have to fight for what they meant under another name.") "In the talk, John Ball speaks of his own hope in a Christian Fellowship in the Heavens."

In 1889 there appeared in England a work which had already been published in the United States of America, viz., "Looking Backward," written by Dr. Edward Bellamy. The book sold by tens of thousands; and was translated into several languages, versions of it being circulated in French and Italian, in German, Dutch and Portuguese. "It purported to give us," says Mr. Lionel Johnson, "an insight into the perfected society of the future; and what we saw was a nightmare spectacle of machinery dominating the world." Morris deemed "Looking Backward" of sufficient importance to write a long criticism upon it in "The Commonweal," in which he reckons the book unhesitatingly among the signs of the times. "The pessimistic revolt," he says, "of the latter end of this century, led by John Ruskin against the philistinism of the triumphant bourgeois, halting and stumbling as it necessarily was, shows that the change in the life of civilization had begun, before anyone seriously believed in the possibility of altering its machinery." Morris then proceeds to point out certain dangers attending a work of this kind. It may mislead unless the reader bear in mind that "the only safe way of reading a Utopia is to consider it as the expression of the temperament of its author"—a remark which, by the way, is equally applicable to Morris's own Utopian romance. "So looked at," he continues, "Mr. Bellamy's Utopia must be . . . called very interesting, as it is constructed with due economical knowledge, and with much adroitness." In whatever way Dr. Bellamy imagined that his Utopia was to be brought about, it would seem that he regarded with complacency the greater part of modern life and civilization. In fact his ideal was nothing other than that of State Socialism after all. To his mind the growth of large private monopolies was tending towards the desired climax, when all of them should be absorbed in one vast monopoly—the State itself. "This hope of the development of the trusts and rings to which the competition for privilege has driven commerce, especially in America, is the distinctive part of Mr. Bellamy's book;" but it was not a hope that Morris was able to share. "The economical semi-fatalism of some Socialists is a deadening and discouraging view. . . . In short, a machine-life is the best which Mr. Bellamy can imagine for us on all sides." For his own part, Morris said, "I believe that . . . the multiplication of machinery will just —multiply machinery; I believe that the ideal of the future does not point to the lessening of man's energy by the reduction of *labour* to a minimum, but rather to the reduction of *pain in labour* to a minimum, so small that it will cease to be pain; a gain to humanity which can only be dreamed of till men are more completely equal than Mr. Bellamy's Utopia would allow them to be, but which will most assuredly come about when men are really equal in condition; although it is probable that much of our so-called 'refinement,' our luxury—in short, our civilization—will have to be sacrificed to it." Dr. Bellamy was at pains to discover some incentive to labour in his ideal State, whereas Morris held that the necessary incentive would be found nowhere else than in the pleasure afforded by the work itself. He did not believe in the individual repudiating personal responsibility and transferring "the business of life onto the shoulders of an abstraction called the State;" but that "all men must deal with it in conscious association with each other." A final caution needed to be given, that although, for many reasons, "Looking Backward" might be considered seriously, at the same time it must on no account be taken "as the Socialist Bible of reconstruction."

In some sort, then, as a counterpoise to and a corrective of possible errors to which "Looking Backward" might lead the unwary, Morris undertook to embody *his* views in a fresh work, somewhat on the same lines. On January 11th, 1890, appeared the first instalment of Morris's own Utopian romance, "News from Nowhere; or, An Epoch of Rest," which ran as a serial through thirty-nine numbers of "The Commonweal," until it was concluded on October 4th. The work appeared in separate book-form in 1891. Morris affords us no details of the period of transition, but goes straight to the ultimate outcome in this "delightful romance, in which," says Mr. Frederic Myers, "he has described earthly life led happily, with no thought of life beyond. What to retain, what to relinquish, has here been carefully thought out. Religion and philosophy disappear altogether; science and poetry are in the background; but we are left with the decorative arts, open-air exercise, and an abundance of beautiful and innocent girls." "In imagining a Utopia, as in everything else," remarks "The Athenæum," Morris "could not help being original. While the other inventors of ideal states of society depict a people that is at least abreast of the knowledge of its time, Mr. Morris paints a people that has forgotten nine-tenths of what the world has been laboriously learning. For instance, while the very first thing promised by every other Utopia is a universal education, the absence of all education is a fundamental part of Mr. Morris's scheme." There are no laws nor lawyers; no judges; no government. In short Morris aims at escaping altogether from the complex conditions of modern life, and seeks to find a more primal and elementary state of simplicity. He shows, to quote Mr. Lionel Johnson once again, a "loving and personal regard for the very earth itself, . . . that sense of the motherhood of the earth, which makes a man love the smell of the fields after rain, or the look of running water." The two chief tenets the author strives to impress upon the reader are that "pleasure in work is the secret of art and of content," and that "delight in physical life upon earth is the natural state of man."

As delegate of the Socialist League, and being also on the committee, Morris attended and spoke at the Paris Socialist Congress in the summer of 1889. Edward Carpenter has given thus his reminiscence of the scene: "After the glib oratorical periods of Jules Guesde and others, what a contrast to see Morris . . . fighting furiously there on the platform with his own words . . . hacking and hewing the stubborn English phrases out. . . . The effect was remarkable. Something in the solid English way of looking at things, the common sense and practical outlook on the world, the earnestness and tenacity" of the speaker, "made that speech one of the most effective in the session." Morris's own "Impressions of the Paris Congress" he contributed to the columns of "The Commonweal." There were upwards of four hundred delegates present representing different countries, twenty-one of the number hailing from England. In the early part of the proceedings much time was wasted in fruitless discussions and attempts to bring about a fusion between the "Possibilists" and the "Genuine Socialists." From the first Morris was adverse to the scheme. The breach between the two parties was too deep to be healed over by the empty formality of a nominal reconciliation—for that there could never be more than that he was convinced, and so he stated when he had to declare his opinion on the subject. There followed speeches, in the form of reports, from the several representatives of different countries; all which speeches were interpreted, one by one, and thereby much time was lost. Whereas Morris considered it would have been better, since the reports were all going to be published, for the assembly to treat them as read, thus reducing the formal business to as short a compass as possible, and allowing plenty of opportunity for practical discussion and exchange of ideas. Such he deemed to be the proper function of a Congress, whereas under the circumstances it was too much inclined to be turned into a mere demonstration. Such was the impression he formed even after M. Jules Guesde's speech, which, though *the* speech of the session and "certainly splendid oratory," had nevertheless "too strong a flavour of electioneering." By the time his own turn came to speak of the work in England, Morris was obliged to curtail his speech within twenty minutes or so. Subsequently he wished to put a resolution which should pledge the meeting definitely to Socialism; but as no agreement seemed likely to be arrived at on the point, he left, several days before the formal conclusion of the Congress, for the more congenial atmosphere of his beloved Rouen, on the way home. It was far more to his mind to philosophize "under an elm tree" in the quiet country-side than to be plunged into the disheartening turmoil of, so to speak, civil, internecine controversy. But unfortunately it was not possible for him to avoid it.

For meanwhile—nay, even before this, things had been working towards a crisis in the Socialist League. On April 13th, 1889, James Blackwell started in "The Commonweal" the correspondence which was destined to bring matters to a head. The writer proposed the establishment, after a foreign model, of a "Free Tribune" for the freer discussion of Socialism in the columns of the organ of the League, and that especially in view, so he said, of the "recent decided tendency of the Socialist League toward Communist-Anarchism," and also in view of certain clauses recently adopted at the Anarchist Congress at Valentia. On May 18th appeared a letter from Morris on the subject, and the correspondence was then taken up by others. After considerable delay, for which he excused himself mainly on account of his "journey to the Paris Congress, and business necessary to be done before and after that event," Morris wrote a second letter in reply, which appeared in "The Commonweal" of August 17th, 1889. "I will begin," writes Morris, "by saying that I call myself a Communist, and have no wish to qualify that word by joining any other to it. The aim of Communism seems to me to be the complete equality of condition for all people; and anything in a Socialist direction which stops short of this is merely a compromise with the present condition of society, a halting-place on the road to the goal. . . . From these two things, the equality of condition and the recognition of the cause and effect of material nature, will grow all Communistic life. So far I think I can see clearly; but when I try to picture to myself the forms which that life will take, I confess I am at fault, and I think we must all be so. . . . All genuine Socialists admit that Communism is the necessary development of Socialism; but I repeat, further than this all must be speculative." And here was where Morris joined issue with the Anarchists. There *must* be authority, a common bond, in the shape of "the conscience of the association, voluntarily accepted in the first instance." By all means "let us have the least possible exercise of authority," said he, but there must be a social or "*public conscience* as a rule of action." The second letter of Morris's was a re-affirmation of what he had said in the first, and an answer, moreover, to the various objections that had been raised on the other side. One correspondent "appears," says Morris, "to meet my commonplace 'that you have a right to do as you like so long as you don't interfere with your neighbour's right to do as he likes' with a negative; which he cannot mean to do. Anyhow, I assert it again, and also assert that the *social* conscience, which being social is common to every man, will forbid such individual interference, and use coercion if other means fail: and also that without that there can be no society; and further, that man without society is not only impossible, but inconceivable." Another "misunderstands my use of the word Communist in supposing me to use it as the Owenites did, as implying life in separate communities, whether those communities were mere scattered accidents amidst a capitalistic society or not; whereas I use it as a more accurate term for Socialism, as implying equality of condition and consequently abolition of private property. In this sense, of course, you could not live communistically until the present society of capitalism or contract is at an end. . . . As to the matter of majority-rule, let us look at the matter again. All rule must be . . . majority-rule —*i.e.*, of the *effective* majority. If at any time the minority rules, it is because they are better organized, better armed, less stupid, more energetic, than the mere" numerical "majority: this effective majority, therefore, coerces the minority; and as long as it *can* coerce it, it *will*. The time may come, and I hope it will, when the social conscience will be so highly developed that coercion will be impossible, even on the part of the community: but then in those days the community will be composed of men who so thoroughly realize Communism that there will be no chance of any of them attacking his neighbour in any way."

"But," says Morris, "I do not consider myself a pessimist because I am driven to admit that such a condition of things is a long way ahead. And what can we do in the meantime?" Surely all must allow that, "as long as the individual acts unsocially, in that case he has no right against the society which *he himself* has cast off." As to the question of association, "where all men are equal, I believe 'the give and take' would have such influence over men's minds, that 'the authority of compulsory representative institutions,' or whatever took their place, would be so completely at one with the social conscience that there would be no dispute about it as to principle, that in detail . . . the few would have to give way to the many; I should hope without any rancour. . . . As for me," concludes Morris, "I can only say that whatever will give us equality, with whatever drawbacks, will content me, and I find that at bottom this is the ideal of all Socialists. So I think the fewer party-names and distinctions we can have the better, leaving plenty of scope for the inevitable differences between persons of different temperaments, so that various opinions may not make serious quarrels."

The above letters are of importance as determining Morris's attitude at this time with regard to Anarchism. He might try to allay differences between himself and his "comrades," to persuade them that the question was rather one of verbal expression than of essentially diverse principles. But it was of no use. The upshot of the whole matter was that a certain number of the League, and those by no means only the most inconspicuous members of it, were at variance with Morris on several vital issues. It is significant, then, that thenceforward, until the appearance of his final letter, towards the end of 1890, the greater proportion of Morris's contributions to "The Commonweal" was comprised in "News from Nowhere," which, as altogether an ideal romance, scarcely admitted the raising of any controverted points.

"The Commonweal" of November 15th, 1890, contained Morris's last contribution to that paper, to wit, an article by way of a review of the situation at the close of seven years' existence of the Socialist movement. Entitled "Where are we now?' it was taken, as no doubt it was intended to be, for a farewell declaration on the part of the writer. "To some," he says, the term of seven years "will seem long, so many hopes and disappointments have been crowded into them." He continues: "For what was it which we set out to accomplish? To change the system of society on which the stupendous fabric of civilization is founded, and which has been built up by centuries of conflict with older and dying systems. . . . Could seven years make any visible impression on such a tremendous undertaking as this? . . . It cannot be said that great unexpected talent for administration and conduct of affairs has been developed amongst us, nor any vast amount of foresight either. We have been what we seemed to be (to our friends, I hope)—and that was no great things. We have between us made about as many mistakes as any other party in a similar space of time. Quarrels more than enough we have had; and sometimes also weak assent, for fear of quarrels, to what we did not agree with. . . . When I first joined the movement I hoped that some working-man leader, or rather leaders, would turn up, who would push aside all middle-class help, and become great historical figures. I might still hope for that, if it seemed likely to happen, for indeed I long for it enough; but, to speak plainly, it does not so seem at present." True, there was much encouragement in the spectacle of what had already been attained in the spread of progressive principles. "But are there not some of us disappointed in spite of the change of the way in which Socialism is looked on generally? It is but natural that we should be. When we first began to work together there was little said about anything save the great ideals of Socialism, and so far off did we seem from the realization of these that we could hardly think of any means for their realization." But "with the great extension of Socialism this is also changed. Our very success has dimmed the great ideals that first led us on." It was but natural that through longing to realize in their own lifetime the objects for which they had striven, they should be tempted to clutch with eagerness at any methods which presented themselves with a plausible prospect of attainment. Now, these methods Morris divided into two classes: the one, the method of palliation or compromise, by the acceptance of half-measures that did not go to the root of the evils they professed to remedy; the other, "the method of partial, necessarily futile, inconsequent revolt, or riot rather, against the authorities, who are our absolute masters, and can easily put it down. With both these methods," he said emphatically, "I disagree; and that the more because the palliatives have to be clamoured for, and the riots carried out by, men who do not know what Socialism is"—aided by the roughs, who are always waiting and ready to join any movement that seems to afford them a chance for rowdyism, and a sharing of plunder at other folks' expense, such men, in fact, as bring discredit on the best of causes—"and have no idea what their next step is to be, if, contrary to all calculation, it should happen to be successful. Therefore, at the best, our masters would be our masters still, because there would be nothing to take their place. *We are not ready for such a change as that!* The authorities might be a little shaken perhaps, a little more inclined to yield something to the clamours of their slaves, but there would be slaves still, *as all men must be who are not prepared to manage their own business themselves.* Nay, as to the partial violent means, I believe that the occurrence of these would not shake the authorities at all, but would strengthen them rather, because they would draw to them the timid of all classes," a common danger making even opposite parties unite for the common cause of self-protection. For his part, Morris neither believed in State Socialism as desirable in itself, nor did he think it possible as a complete scheme. However, he apprehended that some sort of approach to it was sure to be tried. "The success of Mr. Bellamy's Utopian book, deadly dull as it is, is a straw to show which way the wind blows. The general attention paid to our clever friends the Fabian lecturers and pamphleteers is not altogether due to their literary ability; people have really got their heads turned more or less in their direction."

As to "Trades Unionists, disturbance-breeders, or what not," let them go their way and do what they could, but for those who were "complete Socialists—or let us call them Communists"—for them the only rational, practical business at present is to make converts by spreading "the simple principles of Socialism, regardless of the policy of the passing hour;" to convince "people that Socialism is good for them and is possible. When we have enough people of that way of thinking, they will find out what action is necessary for putting their principles in practice. Until we have that mass of opinion, action for a general change that will benefit the whole people is *impossible.* Have we that body of opinion or anything like it? Surely not." Only when the whole body of the people should have become educated up to Socialist principles could any successful move take place;

till then any partial uprising was foolish and premature, and, as such, doomed to failure. It is impossible to force reforms on a people who are not prepared to receive them, who do not know what it is they want. Whereas too many persons yet believed in the practicability, by means of combinations, strikes, and the like, of compelling their masters to treat them better; as yet only a very small minority were really prepared *to do without masters.* When that minority has become a general majority, then, and then only, will Socialism be realized; "but nothing can push it on a day in advance of that time."

This letter of Morris's, expressed as it was in terms studiously moderate, was accepted on the part of his "comrades" as a definite challenge. His language, clear enough to be understood by those to whom he addressed himself, had refrained from going into details, for the information of the world at large, of the particular methods he disapproved. But the rejoinders which appeared in "The Commonweal" a fortnight later threw caution to the winds, and disclosed the nature of some, at least, of the measures against which Morris protested. One writer said: "Even the ordinary criminal is an unconscious revolutionist, and is doing good work for us;" while another openly and specifically advocated the use of dynamite. *Corruptio optimi pessima.* Alas! that the columns of the very paper that had given to the world the sublime utterances of John Ball, words which might have fallen direct from the lips of the seraphic Francis himself, should ever have been sullied in this fashion. No better vindication of the wisdom and uprightness of Morris's course could be wanted than this circumstance, which showed, full unmistakably, whither affairs were tending among the extremists of the Socialist body. Gradually the League had been drifting further and further, until it had got quite beyond Morris's control. But when it would fain drag him along with it and commit him too, as it had already committed itself, to wild extravagances, he stood firm. Though it should mean breaking with some whilom friends and associates, the wrench must be borne if need be. With

Morris no private nor personal considerations must be allowed to outweigh principle. At any sacrifice he must be true to *that*. The only way left to him was to withdraw; and so he did. "Morris's entire rejection of militant Anarchism," writes Mr. Kenworthy, "and of what is called 'Individualist Anarchism,' caused schism in the Socialist League. Without protest, without resistance, Morris permitted certain 'comrades' to appropriate the League's resources, including the type, plant, and copyright of 'The Commonweal,' that journal which for years Morris produced at his own cost and partly wrote. He had that great wisdom which prevented him from seeking to hold to a false position." After this the downfall of the League was a foregone conclusion. "The Commonweal" of November 29th, 1890, was the last issue to bear the original sub-title of "The Official Journal of the Socialist League." It became once more a monthly paper, the December part being described as "A Journal of Revolutionary Socialism." In February, 1891, a notice informed the readers of "The Commonweal" that it had now become the property of the newly constituted London Socialist League. The climax was all but reached when the May number appeared, printed upon red paper, and being described in the sub-title as "A Revolutionary Journal of Anarchist Communism." But worse was yet to come. On November 28th, 1891, "The Commonweal" admitted a letter signed J. Creaghe, which was undisguisedly a denunciation of the attitude of Mr. Morris, his name being coupled with that of Edward Carpenter, an object of especial disfavour on the writer's part. And the vehicle used for this purpose was Morris's own paper! On April 9th following "The Commonweal" published an article so flagrantly intemperate as to lead to C. W. Mowbray and D. J. Nicholl, as proprietor and publisher of the paper, being prosecuted by the Treasury and charged at Bow Street with inciting to murder and Anarchism. It happened that Mowbray's wife died just at this time, and was to be buried on April 23rd. Mowbray applied to be released in order to attend the funeral. Permission was refused, and he must have had to remain in prison had not William Morris been generous enough to attend the Court in person and become surety for the offender for the occasion in the sum of five hundred pounds. The prisoners were shortly afterwards committed for trial. The plant of "The Commonweal" was confiscated, and the paper itself, having "lived by fits and starts as a monthly," in a year or two finally became extinct.

For Morris the break-up of the League did not imply so great a change of life as might have been supposed. He had worked at Socialist propaganda on every possible occasion in public, until he had become convinced that the inevitable conflicts with the police which ensued were damaging rather than forwarding the movement. Thenceforward "he began to extricate himself from an impossible position as best he could;" he gradually abandoned a plan of public campaign for less openly aggressive, but not less thorough and effective methods of work for the cause. "He remained unchanged in his Socialism," writes Mr. Bernard Shaw, "but he practically adopted the views of the Fabian Society as to how the change would come about. . . . His latest important act in the Socialist movement was to try to unite all the Socialist Societies into a single party. He did not initiate the plan, but he did his best to carry it out; and he was certainly the best man for the purpose, since" the societies were all agreed in having "a deep regard and respect for him. Mr. Hyndman, on behalf of the Social Democratic Federation, and I, on behalf of the Fabian Society, had some . . . conferences at his house, where we talked about the past and the future rather than the present." But Morris did not succeed in effecting the proposed union, near though the project was to his heart. A rapprochement, then, with Mr. Hyndman had come about, although Morris never regained the Federation. "For many years past," writes the former immediately after Morris's death, "the relations of the Social Democratic Federation and all its branches with William Morris were as cordial as they ever had been before. Again he wrote poems for 'Justice,'" *e.g.*, for

May Day, 1892, a poem of ten stanzas, the first verse of which begins: "O earth, once again cometh Spring to deliver;" and for May Day, 1894, a poem of nine stanzas, beginning: "Clad is the year in all her best," "again he lectured for our branches, and kindly contributed to our funds. He spoke, also, most vigorously and generously in support of our Parliamentary candidates in Burnley and Walworth; and his last appearance on a public platform was at our New Year's Meeting in the Holborn Town Hall in January last" (1896). "He then met with a reception from the crowded audience so hearty and so enthusiastic that I know, from what he said afterwards, that he felt that his work for the cause was fully understood and appreciated by the men whom he was endeavouring to serve. . . . None who were present will ever forget the touching appeal that he then made, or the words of counsel and good cheer that he then spoke."

Meanwhile, upon the wreck of the Socialist League, Morris had gathered round him the small band of faithful survivors, and formed them into the Hammersmith Socialist Society. This body was directly an off-shoot of the League, being the local branch that "had grown up . . . during the secretaryship of his friend Mr. Emery Walker." They had for headquarters a building which, almost from the beginning of his Socialist days, Morris had placed at the service of the cause, viz., the hall attached to his own house on the Upper Mall. "Quaint, rough and ready," this hall has been described, "with strong uncushioned chairs and rough wooden benches for seats," with a piano on the platform, a book-stall at one end of the room, and a few pictures on the walls,—scantily furnished, and yet enshrining withal many cherished memories. There every Sunday evening for thirteen years or more past, until February, 1897, when it was publicly announced that the hall was closed, it had not failed that a Socialist meeting had been held. And now such gatherings were to take place no more! "Of late years," says "The Pall Mall Gazette," "the Sunday evenings at Kelmscott Hall have been nearly equally divided between socialistic and artistic, historic or literary subjects. . . . The Hammersmith Socialist party was full of artists and literary men who were able to stand before a meeting and deliver an address of sound sense and rich in the results of patient research, and the evenings on which such" recreations "were announced to be given were popular with outsiders." The favourite speaker "was Morris himself, . . . honest, . . . brusque of address, . . . picturesque and capable. On evenings when he was announced to speak . . . people were packed into the hall, . . . and as his addresses usually dealt with arts and crafts in some long-past age, they were not interesting merely but . . . efforts of value. . . . Altogether the hall and its 'entertainments' were patches of bright colour in the great drab, dreary, dull, dirty Hammersmith, and many people who paid little or no heed to Socialistic teachings and tenets have heard with sorrow of the closing of the Kelmscott Hall doors."

Mr. Morris's last and most mature and, as such, perhaps also his most important work on the subject of Socialism, was one which he wrote in conjunction with Mr. Belfort Bax. The book was published in 1893, with the title "Socialism, its Growth and Outcome." It was for all intents and purposes a re-casting of a series of twenty-four papers by the same authors, which had first seen the light under the description of "Socialism from the Root up" in "The Commonweal" in 1886. "The work," say the authors, "has been in the true sense of the word a *collaboration*, each sentence having been carefully considered by both the authors in common, although now one, now the other, has had more to do with initial suggestions in different portions of the work." The main part of the book deals with the "subject from the historical point of view," but it "also necessarily deals with the aspirations of Socialists now living towards the society of the future." In the last chapter, which is headed "Socialism Triumphant," is reaffirmed once more Morris's theory about the relation of art to labour. "It is no wonder," he says, "that almost all modern economists (who seldom study history, and never art), judging from what is going on before their eyes, assume that labour generally must be repulsive, and that hence coercion must always be employed on the necessarily lazy majority. . . . We have seen that the divorce of the workman from pleasure in his labour has only taken place in modern times, for we assert that, however it may be with artless labour, art of any kind can never be produced without pleasure. In this case, then, as in others, we believe that the New Society will revert to the old method, though in a higher plane." The conditions under which "with very few exceptions . . . all labour could be made pleasurable . . . are, briefly: freedom from anxiety as to livelihood; shortness of hours in proportion to the stress of the work; variety of occupation if the work is of its nature monotonous; *due* use of machinery, *i.e.*, the use of it in labour which is essentially oppressive if done by the hand; opportunity for everyone to choose the occupation suitable to his capacity and idiosyncrasy; and, lastly, the solacing of labour by the introduction of ornament, the making of which is enjoyable to the labourer." In "The Daily Chronicle" of November 10th, 1893, appeared a letter by Morris, entitled "The Deeper Meaning of the Struggle," wherein he states his opinion on the future of the fine arts and their necessary connection with the new order.

Now, loyally, bravely, and untiringly as William Morris laboured for his Socialist ideal,—laboured for it hand in hand with the Socialist body, it cannot be denied that his connection with the latter brought him a long and bitter series of disappointments and disillusionments, from the events which led to the schism in the Social Democratic Federation at the end of 1884, down to his severance from the management of "The Commonweal" six years later. The interval had witnessed the ignominious failure of the several popular risings from which great things had been expected, notably of the Trafalgar Square demonstration, the defeat of which made a deep impression upon him; the discord of the Paris Congress; and the eventual alienation of the Socialist League from the high standard of the opening of their career. It was a cruel mortification, while the Federation, from which he had originally sundered himself, continued to hold its own, for Morris to see the association he had founded and maintained and directed with fatherly care, degenerate and dwindle and dissolve. Many of its members had been admitted without reserve to his immediate friendship and confidence—to William Morris's, that would never so much as hurt wittingly a hair of any man's head—and yet among them were some who proved they had appreciated so little and profited so ill by his example and teaching as to recommend the dastardly and execrable engines of tigerish savagery fit only for fiends and men possessed of fiends. And then there had followed the attacks to which he was subjected in the very pages of "The Commonweal." The last was the hardest blow of all. To have to bear with the scoffs and misrepresentations of the outside world which had never properly understood his motives was comparatively easy, nay, it was only what Morris might expect; but it was quite another thing when those who had known him intimately and who should therefore have no excuse for want of appreciating, turned round upon him and began to reproach with cowardice, with selfishly enjoying his own culture and disregarding the sufferings and wrongs of others. They seemed quite to have forgotten all that Morris had done hitherto, how he had been ready, in espousing the non-respectable cause of Socialism, to forfeit his own great reputation; whereas they were men who had nothing to lose, and could therefore afford to go to any lengths of extravagance with impunity. Younger men, most of them, than himself, they should have remembered that the experience which they lacked, and which he had purchased—ay, and that dearly enough, too!—entitled him to every consideration at their hands. For he was not a very young man—on the contrary, he was nigh on fifty years old at the time he joined the Democratic Federation. But his was an ardent nature; and when there offered a short road to the regeneration and happiness of the whole human race, his exultation knew no bounds. He was fairly dazzled with the radiant prospect. It was as though an inspired revelation had been vouchsafed him. Could he do otherwise than embrace Socialism with eagerness, when the way looked so clear and straight before him that the goal appeared almost within reach? Whereas it was, and yet is, a very great way off, and the road that lies between not only long and wearisome, but also beset with snares and pitfalls. The solution of the social problem which had baffled him hitherto, the clue which all his life he had been striving to unravel, groping for it through years of perplexity and ineffectual opposition to the ugliness and squalor of nineteenth century surroundings, seemed at length to have been found! Lo, on a sudden he held in the palm of his hand the key, which only waited to be applied, to open the door of universal good-fellowship. *But the key refused to turn in the lock.* The wards had rusted through ages and ages of disuse; and it must take ages still for so long-established a defect to be remedied. Such was the painful, the unwelcome lesson that had to be brought home to William Morris. It was a very bitter awakening. Yet the stubborn fact was there, and not to be naysaid, that the accumulated wrongs of centuries cannot be set right in a lifetime; that the evolution of human happiness cannot be otherwise than very gradual. The tragedy of Morris's hopes of presently realizing his great ideal befell at Trafalgar Square, when, seeing the pitiful rout of the thousands on whose resolution he had counted, the fact was forced upon him of the utter instability of the masses. It was ever so, from the days, ay, and before the days, when the same crowd that cried "Hosanna" joined, a brief space after, in the shout of "Crucify," down to the present day, when the voices of the populace who have marched, as it were, but yesterday under the banners of "Free Speech" and "No Master," go to swell the chorus at a royalist jubilee. From that hour Morris was convinced of the futility of premature revolution. So long as the people is in a state of unpreparedness for such a change, any attempt to compel it must be abortive, and, more than that, must recoil upon those who take part in it. Some of them, and those maybe not the most responsible, but the most defenceless, are sure to be made scapegoats, and the sum total result only be more suffering, more despair. Whereas the very certainty of one's belief in the advent of the good time should forbid one to presume to force it forward ere the race be ready to receive it.

What, then, it may be asked, did William Morris accomplish if, after all, he had to content himself with inculcating abstention; for that is what it amounts to practically? Was it nothing that he succeeded in maintaining unsullied from beginning to end his splendid ideal; that he never lent himself to anything paltry or dishonourable in order to gain a temporary victory; that over and over again in defence of principle he submitted to the loss of friends and of money outlays, because in him the moral and the political conscience were one? Surely this *was* something, nay, a very great deal. Of how many statesmen at the present day can the like be affirmed? "Outwardly and to outsiders," says Mr. Kenworthy, the last years of Morris's life might indeed seem years of disappointment. "He fretted and strove against the ruts in which he, with his later knowledge of life and purpose in life, found himself sunk; . . . a warm, energetic, . . . great soul, going about in the world," and yearning, "out of the great passion for humanity" that was in him, for response, for sympathy; but yearning and appealing too often in vain. And yet "to-day it is a fact that, while the outward form of the League broke in the hand and left Morris apparently adrift, isolated, his purpose of, and work for, 'fraternity' survive and grow—the largest idea and greatest vitality in the Socialist movement." But to what extent and in what sense is it true to say that Morris idealized Socialism? Now, if by idealizing it is meant that he looked upon it through a fanciful aureole of poetry and romance, which, because he never properly grasped the full import of the subject, he allowed to colour his whole conception of it, this is altogether false. Neither was he led away by the philanthropic aspect of the question, as some have affirmed. He was quite definite and unequivocal on the point. With him it was a perfectly rational and necessary system. He was a poet, an artist, and had the poet's and the artist's point of view. Yes, but in his eyes art was indissolubly bound up with Socialism, and derived from that very connection a higher purpose than he had ever imagined for it before. Morris's, then, was no nominal adhesion; far from it. He had all his wits about him, he knew quite well what he was doing when he joined the Socialist body. Neither did he ever regret having taken the step. But even had it been otherwise he had ample opportunities offered, any one of which he might have availed himself of to renounce Socialism altogether if he had believed himself to have been mistaken. But he did nothing of the kind. Through good and evil report he clung to his ideal, and shrank from none of the difficulties and hardships, however distasteful, which met him in the way. No task, however uncongenial or irksome, but he performed it cheerfully, esteeming nothing too humiliating or too far beneath him, if only it might avail for the good of his fellows. Indeed, it makes one sad to reflect, with Mr. Bernard Shaw, how much fruitful energy and valuable time of Morris's was squandered on an unthankful public's interests "which might very well have been cared for by citizens of less importance." There is no manner of doubt that Morris's almost superhuman exertions for the cause, sustained during many years without respite, overtaxed his strength and carried him off when scarcely past the prime of his natural life. What, then, did he succeed in doing? That he did cannot be reckoned, not because it was too little, but because it was too great a thing to be represented in words or in arithmetical figures. One very tangible legacy, at any rate, he left behind in the shape of the works with which he enriched the literature of Socialism, and that to an extent that, had he never written upon any other subject, his name were worthy to live through his contributions to this subject alone, or even through the merit of a single work, "A Dream of John Ball." And now recurs the question, how can Morris be said to have idealized Socialism? The sort of idealization he achieved was the making Socialism first known and then palatable to a large mass of people who, but for the fact that he, with his unimpeachable honesty of purpose, lent his support to the cause, would have turned away shuddering from the bare idea of any such thing. His eloquence overcame prejudices, his advocacy reconciled many who, had the social revolution been proclaimed by any other than the poet's lips, would have scorned and scouted anything so abnormal and extreme. It was difficult when brought face to face with so winning an exponent of the subject as Morris was to resist the power of his persuasiveness. Thus ennobling the whole theme, he made it seem quite reasonable to refer his own exultant words to the now no longer unfamiliar movement and doctrines of Socialism : " Have you not heard how it has gone with many a cause before now? First, few men heed it; next, most men contemn it; lastly, all men accept it—and the cause is won."

CHAPTER THIRTEEN: ROMANCES.

THE year 1888 marks the beginning of Morris's last period in literary art. It was signalized by the appearance of the first of the cycle of prose romances, with which it cannot be said that Morris did less than inaugurate "a new thing in literature;" a series in the production of which he was occupied almost to the very day of his death. In the introduction to the Saga Library are set forth the dominant characteristics of Norse stories, the same standard which it cannot be rash to assume that Morris had before him as his ideal in the writing of his own prose tales. This is what he says: "After all, the impression that dramatic events make upon us is not measured by the mere count of heads of those who took part in them. *I*, *thou*, and *the other one* . . . are enough to make a drama, as Greek tragedy knew. Only the actors must be alive, and convince us . . . that they are so. For this quality the Icelandic Sagas are super-eminent; granted the desirability of telling what they tell, *the method* of telling it is the best possible. Realism is the one rule of the Saga-man: no detail is spared in impressing the reader with a sense of the reality of the event; but no word is wasted in the process of giving the detail. There is nothing didactic and nothing rhetorical in these stories; the reader is left to make his own commentary on the events, and to divine the motives and feelings of the actors in them without any help from the story-teller. In short, the simplest and purest form of epical narration is the style of these works." The above should form surely the best introduction to the study of Morris's own romances.

The first of these, entitled "A Tale of the House of the Wolfings and all the kindreds of the Mark written in prose and in verse," appeared in December, 1888. The period when the events of this wonderful myth-story are supposed to take place is that "when the long struggle between the Romans and the Gothic people was reaching its culmination." The hero is Thiodolf of the Wolfings; the heroine his daughter, a mysterious prophetess called the Hall-Sun, born to him of the Wood-Sun, an equally mysterious being, child of the gods, and one of the Choosers of the Slain. Provided with a magical hauberk, the gift of the latter, Thiodolf, who has been elected war-duke over his own people for the occasion, wages war against the Romans. The hauberk, however, while it secures to its wearer immunity from death, nevertheless acts as a curse upon the people and the cause he has espoused, until finally the heroic Hall-Sun persuades her father to give over wearing it. The interest of the story turns on the daughter's devotion, who sets the interests of her people before the more personal ones of her family, and on Thiodolf's splendid renunciation of the talisman which would have kept his own life safe to the ruin of his country. And so he falls on behalf of his people, their triumph obtained by the sacrifice of their leader's life. In this work "The Athenæum" remarks that Mr. Morris has invented "a form of art so new that new canons of criticism have to be formulated and applied to it. Without going so far as to affirm that this book is the most important contribution to pure literature that has appeared in our time, we may without hesitation affirm it to be one of the most remarkable. . . . Every now and then . . . we come in this volume upon touches that show the extraordinary vividness of the imagination at work." The peculiar quality of the book "lies in the texture of the prose style. . . . The fact is that . . . Mr. Morris has here enriched contemporary literature with a poetic prose of his own, a prose that has all the qualities of poetry except metre. . . . The few archaisms introduced . . . lend a *naïveté* to a style such as only one living man can ever hope to write. So poetic, indeed, is the prose in this fascinating volume that even the verse, fine as it is, seems to fade in the midst of it, as the linnet's voice fades when the black-cap or the nightingale begins." The work is, in short, a "superb epic," and such that "will be a delight to those who in literature are alone worth delighting, the cultivated students of all that is sweet and high and noble in literary art."

In 1890 was published a longer work, of the same

class as the last, called "The Roots of the Mountains wherein is told somewhat of the Lives of the men of Burgdale their friends their neighbours their foemen and their fellows in arms." The book had been announced at first as "Under the Roots of the Mountains." The plot of the story is briefly as follows: Gold-mane, a noble chieftain of the men of Burgdale, a people of German blood, is betrothed to a damsel of the same clan, a damsel who is called on account of the relationship that exists between them "The Bride." Matters thus go well for a time, until, very early one morning, Gold-mane steals away, not knowing what secret force impels him, through the woods to the Shadowy Vale. It is a magic spell which has brought him thither, and leads him to meet there a daughter of the kindred of the Wolf, named the Sunbeam. He becomes desperately enamoured of her, so much so that, though he returns to Burgdale, his old love for the Bride is dead thenceforward. An alliance is formed between the men of Burgdale and the kindred of the Wolf, for the purpose of attacking their common enemy, the Dusky men, who are of Mongol or Hunnish race. Meanwhile the Sunbeam's brother, Folk-might, out of compassion at first, and afterwards from deeper feelings, is drawn to fall in love with the Bride, who has now joined the band of warrior maidens that form part of the allied forces. The latter, with the help of these Amazons, under their valorous leader, Bow-may, surprise and attack the Dusky men at Silverstead—the account being "one of the most splendid battle-pieces in all poetry." "The felons are massacred, and peace returns to the desolated valleys." The kindreds become one folk "for better or worse, in peace and in war, in waning and waxing." "Few of those who have read it," says "The Daily News," "will forget the impression produced on them by that picture of a little northern settlement among the roots of the mountains, connected with the outer world by the travelling merchant, or by the return of a wanderer who has spent some years in the service of the cities. And when danger falls on them from some tribe of the

Huns, we follow their fortunes breathlessly, till the great fight and day of deliverance comes, and the tale draws to its close with the happy leading home of the bride through the garden-pleasaunce of love." Whereas the important speeches in "The House of the Wolfings" are given in metre, in "The Roots of the Mountains" a different plan is followed. "The dramatic action is rendered entirely in prose; and nothing is given in verse save such matter as is purely lyrical" in character. The author is said to have been most proud of this one, of all his prose stories. Mr. Steele describes it as "perhaps the finest story of primitive Northern life ever written. In this romance the poet touched the high-water mark of his prose style: its archaisms, if such there be, are exactly necessary for the expression of his thought, and the narrative itself is exciting and well-planned."

"The Story of the Glittering Plain, which has been also called the Land of Living Men or the Acre of the Undying, written by William Morris," appeared first in serial form in Macmillan's "English Illustrated Magazine" in the year 1890. The sentiment and setting of the tale are thoroughly Norse. The state of society depicted is patriarchal; the chief in his old age lying in a "shut-bed" in the great hall which is the headquarters for the assembling of the clan. The story tells of a lovely man and so fair that he put all other men to shame; of how his betrothed was carried off by sea-robbers, and of all the adventures that befell him before he won her back. Of the prose romances of Morris's later years, "The Morning Post" says "The Glittering Plain" is "a fascinating example, simple, noble in sentiment, and attractive alike to old and young." Another writer remarks that it tells of "the search for immortality, for the land of life, . . . how at the last a man was found who refused immortality and beauty for love's sake; and how love rewarded him."

The next romance, "News from Nowhere," was of a totally different order from the preceding. Its object was not merely to tell a pleasant tale. It had a definite political intention, and has therefore been dealt with under another head.

"The Wood Beyond the World," which bears date May, 1894, is an unadulterated fairy-tale. It relates how one Walter, son of a merchant of Langton, a seaport of no particular locality in mediæval Christendom,—it might as well be located in Flanders as elsewhere—sails in one of his father's trading vessels to foreign lands; how before he starts he has seen a mirage of a Queenly Lady, accompanied by a thrall-maid and a hideous dwarf; how these three appear to him twice again and then mysteriously disappear; how at last Walter comes to an unknown land, disembarks, and, stealing away from his companions, wanders across the country until he arrives at the Wood beyond the World, and there encounters once more the three he had seen and missed and so long sought. The tale tells then of the various strange adventures that befall him in that land of guile, and of his escape thence with the maid after the death of the lady-sorceress; of the passage of the two through the Bear-folk's territory, and how in the end Walter is made king of an ancient city, the maid becomes his queen, and they two together the founders of a long line of royal descendants. "This last exquisite story of his," says "The Athenæum," "must be held to surpass the best of its predecessors in poetical feeling and poetical colour, and to equal them in poetical substance. Here more than ever we get that marvellously youthful way of confronting the universe which is the special feature of Mr. Morris's genius." His purpose in writing this story having been misunderstood, however, in some quarters, Mr. Morris felt called upon to depart from his usual custom, and addressed a short letter of explanation to "The Spectator," July 20th, 1895. "I had not the least intention," he writes, "of thrusting an allegory into 'The Wood beyond the World'; it is meant for a tale pure and simple, with nothing didactic about it. If I have to write or speak on social problems, I always try to be as direct as I possibly can. On the other hand, I consider it bad art in anyone writing an allegory not to make it clear from the first that this was his intention, and not to take care throughout that the allegory and the story should interpenetrate, as does the great master of allegory, Bunyan."

The next romance, in two small volumes, entitled "Of Child Christopher and Goldilind the Fair," is "a variant," says Mr. Steele, "of the Havelock the Dane legend." It is dated July, 1895; and was succeeded a year later by "The Well at the World's End," the last work that Morris published before death overtook him. This tale, which is longer than any of its predecessors, is divided into four books, as follows:

I. The Road unto Love (24 chapters).
II. The Road unto Trouble (41 chapters).
III. The Road to the Well at the World's End (22 chapters).
IV. The Road Home (32 chapters).

As to the title of the book, Mr. Morris told Mr. Mackenzie Bell that "there was an old Scottish ballad called by that name, and though he had never read the ballad he had heard the title, and took a fancy to it." The hero of the story is one Ralph of Upmeads, a king's son, who is endowed with the gift of winning the goodwill of every woman he meets. There are two heroines, both of whom Ralph encounters in a day's journey. One of them is an innkeeper's daughter, the other a lady of the land, who, having drunk of the Well at the World's End, is possessed of certain powers denied to ordinary mortals. Ralph wins her love, after having rescued her from the hands of her enemies; yet she is slain by them on the eve of the wedding. Ralph now seeks consolation in adventure. He has heard obscure hints as to the life-giving properties of the wonderful well, and, after sundry perils and escapes, is brought to the Castle of Abundance, where in a book he obtains further information about the well. The "sweet poison" enters into his heart and impels him to persevere in the quest of the water of whose virtues he has read. On the way through the wood under the mountain he falls in with the maiden who had already befriended him

Discovering that they are both bound for the same object, they journey along together, the maiden telling him her name Ursula, by which she is known thenceforward. Various fortunes befall them. At the house of sorcery they obtain from an elder yet more precise information, which enables them to find the Well at the World's End, of whose waters they both drink. The rest of the book is occupied with the story of their return home, whither in the end Ralph brings Ursula—whom meanwhile he has come to love—as his wife; and they dwell together long and happily, until they die and are buried beside his ancestors in the choir of St. Laurence Church at Upmeads. "The task of portraying the change of affections from one love to another," says the reviewer in "The Daily News," "is one that has been often undertaken, but we know of no book in which the result is so completely successful. . . . Truly, we have no man left to paint us the sweetness and bitterness of love as the poet who has 'changed his life' has done. . . . He alone gives us the picture of the days when love and life were young—a picture sweet even to bitterness. . . . All that those who know the poet will look for in his work they will find here. The tender love scenes of 'Ralph meets with Love in the Wilderness' and elsewhere, the beautiful descriptions of scenery, reminiscent or imaginative, the breath of morning in the woods, the chill horror of desolation, hope and success will be remembered. But, above all, the crowning glory of the work is that Mr. Morris has made these folk become something more than mortal, and has led them back, man and wife, through 200 pages, without our ever losing this impression, that they are to us as the gods come among men. Other men can write adventure, others know the secret of love, a few that of simplicity and strength; but no man alive can tell us what like a mortal would be and how he would act when he had put on something of immortality without losing his humanity." The above appeared ten days after Mr. Morris's death. A few other criticisms of these romances are worth recording. Mr. George Saintsbury writes: "In 'The House of the Wolfings'

. . . and in 'The Roots of the Mountains,' and most of all in 'The Glittering Plain,' we have what, before Mr. Morris, even Kingsley never quite achieved, true Sagas, not in the least mosaics or *pastiches* from the Sagas proper, but 'sets' or 'cuttings' from them, instinct with genuine life, and reproducing with due variation the character of the parent stock." "Mr. Morris's prose romances," writes Mr. Le Gallienne in "The Idler," "have not yet been adequately appreciated, their deliberately archaised English being a stumbling-block to many readers—though there are others who consider it, and, I think, rightly, an admirable and often beautiful medium for the stories Mr. Morris had to tell. It is to be found at its best in 'The Wood beyond the World,' and in 'News from Nowhere,' two of the loveliest fairy-tales ever written." A writer in "The Athenæum" says: "It is an extremely interesting fact that Mr. Morris in exercising his rare poetical gift has so often of late turned from metrical to unmetrical forms. Though his romances must needs be taken as being in some measure the outcome of his studies in Saga literature, they hold, in conception no less than in execution, a place of their own. If the name 'metreless poem' can properly be given to any form of imaginative literature, these romances are more fully entitled to that name than anything that has gone before. . . . In Mr. Morris's romances the form of imaginative literature is imbued throughout with poetical colour rendered in a perfectly concrete diction, . . . the sentences (built on the simple method of poetry and not in the complex method of prose) have a cadence in which *recognized* metrical law has been abandoned, a cadence whose movement is born of the emotions which the words embody. . . . Intensely poetic and intensely dramatic, moreover, as are the Icelandic Sagas, they are lacking in one of the most delightful qualities of the unmetrical poems of Mr. Morris . . .—that delicate sense of beauty in which the author of 'The Earthly Paradise' has had no superior, even in the epoch which has inaugurated the neo-romantic movement."

A word as to the alleged archaisms of language which

have given offence to some readers of Morris's prose romances; for there has been not a little misconception on this point. The archaisms have been treated as though they were arbitrary and wilful affectations of extinct phraseology on Morris's part; whereas no greater mistake as to his intention could be made. True, the language is not that of the colloquial, no, nor even that of the written, English of the day. But then Morris was not writing for the present generation alone. There is nothing about these romances which should localize them within the limits of this nineteenth century of ours, or render them out of date or less interesting for any other time than now. The author certainly believed that generations yet to come would read his stories; and he must have been conscious (though, of course, he was too modest to express it in words) that he might have some share in moulding the English that unborn lips should learn to speak. And, if so, he could not fail to be sensible of the responsibility resting upon him; he could not fail to wish all the weight of his influence to be on the side of a purer and nobler form of speech than that which we employ to-day. It was not, then, with an eye to the dead past, to the antiquity of the thing for mere antiquity's sake, that Morris phrased his romances as he did. His prose is not the language of Wardour Street or Walter Scott; it is not imitative of any known dialects, as is the Scotch of Barrie or Crockett or Maclaren; no, but it is an idealized English such as Morris deemed worthy to serve as model for the living style of the future.

William Morris left behind him two unpublished romances, of which one, entitled "The Water of the Wondrous Isles," was already in the press before the date of the author's death; while the other, "The Sundering Flood," was finished only just in time. It is of about double the length of "The Wood beyond the World," but, unlike that romance, has lyrics interspersed. Mr. Morris was engaged upon it nearly up to the last. Ere he had reached the end of it he had become too ill to write any more with his own hand, and the concluding chapters, therefore, had to be written at his dictation. It is said that he was not able to revise the MS., and, moreover, that he had to leave the chapter headings wanting to be supplied. However, the romance, which Mr. Theodore Watts-Dunton foretold would "be found to be finer than any hitherto published" by the author, was so far perfected as to admit of no question as to the feasibility of publishing it in due course.

CHAPTER FOURTEEN: BOOK DECORATION AND THE KELMSCOTT PRESS.

IT may, perhaps, be asked, how did William Morris come to devote his latter years to the art of printing? What motive induced him, whose heart was wholly set on the earlier Gothic periods, to take up with the most mechanical and the latest of all the arts of the Middle Ages, with such that came into being only at a time when those Ages, as surely he believed, had long since passed their zenith and were already far advanced in decadence? The answer to such a question is to be sought in Morris's own words: "The only work of art which surpasses a complete mediæval book is a complete mediæval building." At an early date in his career Morris experienced the obstacles in the way of any building at the present time being raised worthy to compare with mediæval buildings; he discovered that the root of the whole matter lay in the adverse circumstances under which the modern workman is compelled to labour, deprived of pleasure in the work of his hands; and accordingly set about to remedy the defect, to restore his lost pleasure to the worker. In a word, despairing of beautiful architecture under existing economical conditions, Morris became a Socialist. But when his hopes of effecting any beneficial reforms in that direction were postponed indefinitely, he was thrown back again upon his own resources to produce at least some perfect and lasting monument before he should die and pass away. The establishment of his printing press, then, coincides with his withdrawal from a more aggressive share in Socialist propaganda. The main fact that favoured the production of beautiful books was that "they were self-contained," as distinguished from architectural buildings. Indeed, there were not "the same difficulties with a book as with many other articles of commerce." This, therefore, was the means that Morris adopted as the readiest in his power towards the fulfilment of his purpose. It must be recorded, however, that books and the beautifying of books in some form or other were no new fancy of Morris's. He began in the early sixties by taking up wood-engraving. The process he learnt in the first instance by copying for practice some of Albert Dürer's woodcuts. Mr. Faulkner also learnt the art; and it was he who engraved, after D. G. Rossetti's design, the frontispiece for Miss Christina Rossetti's "Goblin Market," which was published in 1862. The initials M. M. F. and Co., in the corner of the picture, identified it as having been executed on the part of the firm of Messrs. Morris, Marshall, Faulkner and Co.

About 1865 Mr. Morris was full of the project of the great poem of "The Earthly Paradise," for which work he purposed an elaborate scheme of illustrations, to be engraved after Burne-Jones's drawings. The first of these were a set founded upon Apuleius's story of Cupid and Psyche. Mr. Fairfax Murray is the owner of the original studies, tracings of which by the artist's hand, to the number of forty-three, outlined partly in pencil and partly in ink upon tracing paper, for the purpose of transferring to the wood-blocks, are now preserved in the Ruskin School, beneath the University Galleries, in the building of the Taylorian Institution at Oxford. Among these drawings one at least, viz., that of Pan and Psyche, was developed into an oil painting (1874). Morris used to work on his own account upon the engraving of these designs in the evenings after business hours. Eight or nine were cut by others—the Misses Faulkner (one of whom had learnt the technique of the process at Messrs. Smith and Linton's), Miss Burden, Messrs. Wardle and Campfield; but the majority of the engravings were the work of Morris's own hand. A few impressions only were printed, of which a limited number of sets are yet extant in private possession. They are now very scarce and valuable, never having been published. Other designs for the same work were made by Burne-Jones to illustrate the stories of "Pygmalion and the Image," "The Ring given to Venus," and Tännhauser; but the undertaking was discontinued before very long. The collaboration of the two artists has been mentioned already in these pages. So, also, Morris made verses for Burne-Jones's set of pictures of Pygmalion and Galatea, Day, Night, the Seasons, and "The Briar Rose"—the last-named series being completed in 1890. Morris, moreover, engraved with his own hand the small square block designed by Burne-Jones for the title-page of "The Earthly Paradise"; which block, however, was used only in the first edition of that work, having been accidentally burnt in a fire at Strangeways' printing office, Castle Street, Leicester Square. The block for the second and subsequent editions was re-engraved for Mr. Morris by George Campfield. A larger wood-block, designed, for another purpose, by Morris himself, and representing St. Catherine, was likewise destroyed in the fire.

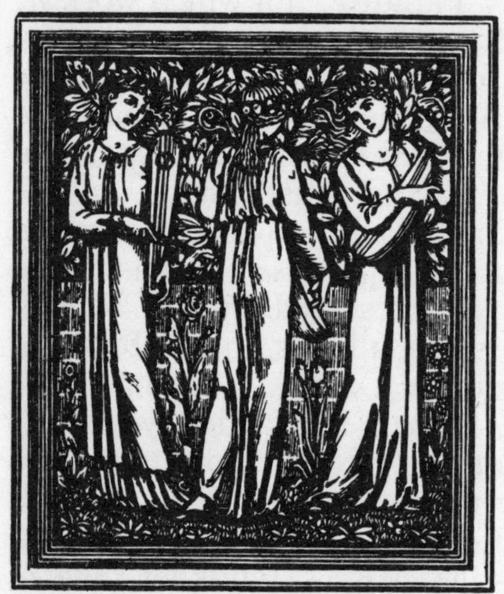

FACSIMILE OF BLOCK ENGRAVED BY WILLIAM MORRIS FOR THE TITLE-PAGE OF "THE EARTHLY PARADISE."

In 1871 Morris was preparing to issue as a decorative volume his poem "Love is Enough." He himself designed and engraved blocks for initials, borders, and other ornaments for it, including a small amount of figure-work. The first page was set up in type and printed, but the work went no further. Burne-Jones, however, in 1872 made a set of drawings to illustrate the poem, as well as a frontispiece. The latter was not finished until after the idea of the publication had been abandoned. By that time the drawing had passed into the hands of Fairfax Murray, and it was for him that Burne-Jones eventually completed the design.

About 1870 Morris had cut from his designs a set of punches for the hand-tooling of leather bindings. These punches were unfortunately lost—not, however, before they had been turned to practical account in the ornamentation,

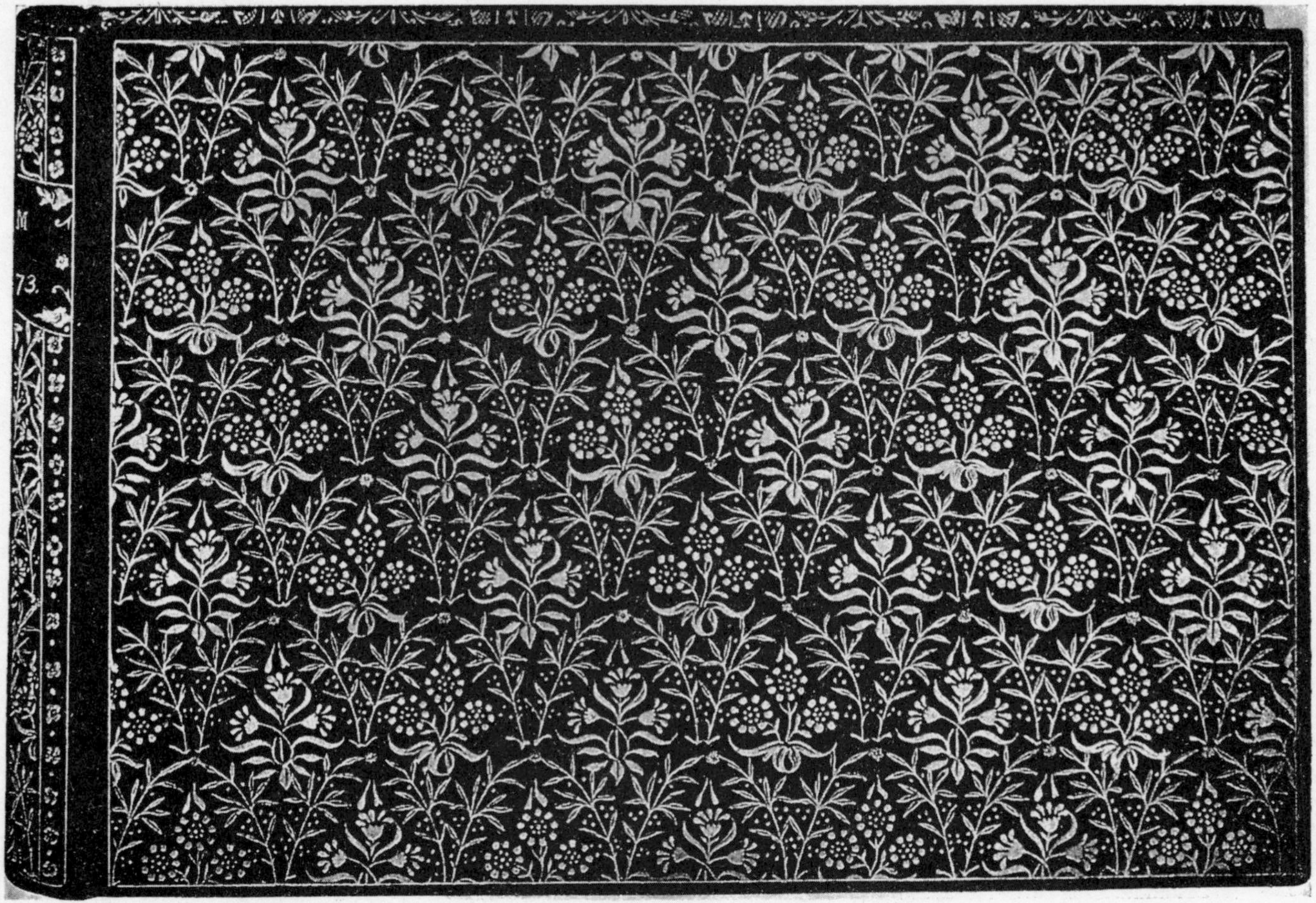

GOLD-TOOLED LEATHER BINDING,
MR. FAIRFAX MURRAY'S SKETCH-BOOK.

DESIGN BY WILLIAM MORRIS.

in floral diaper pattern, of at least two book covers, which belong respectively to Lady Burne-Jones and to Mr. Fairfax Murray.

Although it cannot be claimed that Morris was actually the first to whom the idea occurred to deal with the cloth cover as an object susceptible of artistic adornment (seeing that, as far back as 1845, attempts were made which were considered highly satisfactory at the time to introduce improvements in this direction), at any rate he was not far behindhand. Perhaps the earliest design produced for this class of work that can make serious pretension to artistic merit is the cloth binding of "Recollections of A. N. Welby Pugin, and his father, Augustus Pugin," by Benjamin Ferrey, published in 1861. This is a semi-heraldic design with martlets, and the motto "En Avant" running across in diagonal bands. The next may be said to be Rossetti's design for the cover of his sister's poems in 1862. Although neither was the next design from Morris's pencil, yet it was made at his instance for the cover of his and Magnússon's translation of "The Story of the Volsungs and Niblungs." The pattern on the side consists of flowers and flying birds on an arabesque ground; while that on the back, with conventional birds and rabbits, may be taken, from the severely decorative point of view, to mark the highest point of the designer, Mr. Philip Webb's capacity in this line. There were twelve large paper copies of the book, the title-page in some few instances, of which one was Mr. F. S. Ellis's copy, being ornamented with colour-decorations by Morris's own hand. His first design for a cloth cover was the graceful pattern of foliage, made in 1872, to be printed in gold on the cover of his poem "Love is Enough"; his second for the edition of "The Earthly Paradise," complete in one volume (1890)—a beautiful design of willow leaves for the back, and a device of somewhat oriental outline on the side of the book. He also provided the design, consisting of simple willow sprays, for the back of the cover of the Saga Library.

Morris had always a strong feeling in favour of the art of illumination, as may be gathered from the words which he puts into the mouth of "A Good Knight in Prison" in "The Defence of Guenevere." The captive declares that the worst misfortunes that threaten fail to strike terror into him:

> "Why, all these things I hold them just
> Like dragons in a missal book,
> Wherein, whenever we may look
> We see no horror, yea, delight
> We have, the colours are so bright;
> Likewise we note the specks of white,
> And the great plates of burnish'd gold."

At the time that he resided in Queen Square, Morris used to occupy himself on his own account, that is to say, independently of the firm, with transcribing and illuminating. The Odes of Horace, the heads in the angles of the first page from designs by Burne-Jones, but otherwise without pictures, and transcribed and ornamented entirely by his own hand, he retained in his own possession; but the greater part of the fruits of his immense industry in this branch of art he gave away. Lady Burne-Jones is the owner of four of these works, the particulars of which are as follows:

No. 1. A Book of Verse, by William Morris, written in London, 1870. Bound MS. on paper. 4to. 51 numbered pages. The title-page is illuminated and contains a medallion portrait head of the author to left, inscribed William Morris MDCCCLXX. C. F. Murray pinx. The table of contents:

The Two Sides of the River.
The Shows of May.
The Fears of June.
The Hopes of October.
The Weariness of November.
Love Fulfilled.
Rest from Seeking.
Missing.
Prologue to the Volsung Tale.
Love and Death.
Guileful Love.
Summer Night.

Hope Dieth, Love Liveth.
Love Alone.
Meeting in Winter.
A Garden by the Sea.
The Ballad of Christine.
To Grettir Asmundson.
The Son's Sorrow.
The Lapse of the Year.
Sundering Summer.
To the Muse of the North.
Lonely Love and Loveless Death.
Birth of June.
Praise of Venus.

The second, third, fourth and fifth poems in this list were published among the poems of the months in "The Earthly Paradise" for May, July, October, and November respectively. The majority of the remaining poems appeared in "Poems by the Way." The headpiece above the commencement of the first poem was executed by the hand of Burne-Jones. An inscription at the end of the book details by whom the various parts of the work were carried out: "As to those who have had a hand in making this book, Edward Burne-Jones painted the picture on page 1. The other pictures were all painted by Charles F. Murray, but the minstrel figures on the title-page and the figures of Spring, Summer, and Autumn on page 40, he did from my drawings. As to the pattern work, George Wardle drew in all the ornaments in the first ten pages, and I coloured it; he also did all the coloured letters both big and little; the rest of the ornament I did, together with all the writing. Also I made all the verses; but two poems, 'The Ballad of Christine' and 'The Son's Sorrow' I translated out of the Icelandic. (Signed) William Morris, 26 Queen Sq., Bloomsbury. London. August 26th, 1870."

No. 2. The Story of the Dwellers in Eyr. Bound MS. on Whatman's paper. Folio. 239 numbered pages, exclusive of the index. The work begins with a Prologue, in four-foot measure, consisting of two stanzas of fourteen lines each, and concludes with an Epilogue, in the same measure, of 19 and 9 lines in rhymed couplets. There are sixty-five chapters, and the whole is written in a set script, the headlines, Prologue and Epilogue in brown ink, the rest in black. The first page is elaborately illuminated in gold. "Here beginneth the story of the Dwellers at Eyr: And this first chapter telleth of Ketil Flatneb: and of how he won the South Isles;" and similarly, at the end of the text, is illuminated in gold: "And thus endeth the story of the men of Thorsness, the Dwellers of Eyr, and those who dwelt by Swanfirth." This is followed by an index of names of people, in double columns, 6 pages.

The floral ornament throughout the book is outlined in brown ink, delicately tinted in with pale greens and blue greens, and embellished more richly in parts with gold and silver. A note at the end of the book in Morris's ordinary handwriting says: "I translated this book out of the Icelandic with the help of my master in that tongue, Eiríkr Magnússon, sometime of Heydalr in the East Firths of Iceland; it was the first Icelandic book I read with him. I wrote it all out myself, and did all the ornament throughout the book myself, except the laying on of the gold leaf on pp. 1, 230, and 239, which was done by a man named Wilday, a workman of ours. (Signed) William Morris, 26 Queen Square, Bloomsbury, London. April 19th, 1871."

No. 3. The Story of Hen Thorir, The Story of the Banded Men, The Story of Haward the Halt. Translated and engrossed by William Morris. Bound MS. on paper. Small 4to. 244 numbered pages. There is an illuminated title and a large capital letter at the beginning of each story. The work, which has no date nor note, concludes with: A Gloss in Rhyme on the story of Haward by William Morris, consisting of 58 lines of heroic couplets. The transcript is in black, with headlines and also the gloss in brown ink. On the first page are illuminated the owner's initials, G. B. J.

No. 4. The Rubáiyát of Omar Khayyám. Bound in leather with gold stamped ornament. 23 pages of fine vellum, covered with text and ornament, with only the very narrowest margins left plain. At the back of the last page is written: "I finished my work on this book on the sixteenth of October, 1872. (Signed) William Morris."

This last surpasses the others in the minute elaboration and richness of its gold and coloured ornament; in respect of which generally, as in the other books, should be noted the extraordinary power displayed in the treatment of natural forms—such naturalness that each kind of flower or fruit may be recognized clearly, at the same time that the effect is perfectly decorative: and so far from being in any sense a reproduction or copy of old work, it seems rather, by carrying on the art in accordance with old traditions, to bring it to a stage of evolution of style in advance of anything it ever attained before.

A larger and, on that account, more ambitious project than any of the foregoing was Virgil's "Aeneid," which Morris proposed to transcribe entirely with his own hand, and to adorn with storied initials and other ornaments. The pictures at the head of each book, and the figure subjects within the initials were designed by Burne-Jones, and executed partly by Morris, partly by Fairfax Murray. The Latin text is written, in very antique style of writing, upon folio sheets of the finest vellum, imported expressly from Italy. This work, begun in the early seventies, was never finished. The leaves which comprise the existing fragment of it belong to Mr. Fairfax Murray, who, subsequently to Mr. Morris's death, entered into an arrangement with Mr. W. H. Cowlishaw that the latter should complete it; a task which his illuminations, shown at the Arts and Crafts Exhibition in 1896, seemed to point him out as being an artist fully competent to undertake. Mr. Murray is the owner also of a folio book of the Story of Frithiof, transcribed by Morris in somewhat similar script to the last, and adorned with illuminations by the same hand. Few only of these ornaments were ever completed. They consist of floral sprays executed with exquisite delicacy of design and colouring; but for the most part the outline only of the ornament has been roughed in in pencil.

Thus from early times the germs of his printing press, itself the logical and necessary outcome of ornamenting books by hand, were present with Morris; although pressure of other work intervening, postponed their fruition for a season.

In November, 1890, on the eve of the establishing of the Kelmscott Press, Morris caused to be printed for himself at the Chiswick Press, in octavo size, "The Story of Gunnlaug Worm-tongue," in Caxton type, blank spaces being left for the initials, that they might be rubricated. This task, however, was never accomplished; and consequently the edition, which consisted of three copies on vellum, intended for private circulation, and seventy-five on handmade paper, for sale, was not issued at all; in fact, most of the sheets remained stored away, unbound.

Already the Chiswick Press had produced, under Mr. Morris's direction, in December, 1888, "The House of the Wolfings," with its striking title-page—striking, that is, at the time; for the thing is done commonly enough now, once the way has been shown of making a title-page "a thing of beauty, and not the mere artless statement of a fact." But in 1888 it could only be done by setting at naught all the received conventions of the printing trade. "In every other book," says Mr. Joseph Pennell, "the aim of the printer was, at that time, to get in as many opposing styles as possible," and to drop them down upon "the page in the most absurd and inharmonious fashion." "In Morris's book," on the contrary, "there is a perfect unity in the type itself, there is perfect beauty in the way it is put on the page, and yet only one character is used." He repeated his experiment in "The Roots of the Mountains," in 1890.

Although, according to Mr. Herbert Horne, it was as far back as 1883 or 1884 that Morris had serious thoughts of setting up a printing press of his own, "it was not until the year 1890, when he bought a copy of Wynkyn de Worde's edition of the 'Golden Legend' that his intention took a practical form in the determination to reprint that famous work." From this time to the day of his death Morris concentrated his best energies on the craft of printing. "With the help of his friend Mr. Emery Walker, he set about to design and" get punches cut for "a new fount of type; and to this end he bought whatever *incunabula* he was able to procure, causing a number of examples of the type, with which they were printed, to be enlarged by photography to five times their original size. In this way he studied not only their original forms, but the causes also of the effect to which those separate letters contributed in the composition of the page. . . . His invariable practice in reviving any craft was to go back to the time when it was last exercised in its highest perfection, to examine its processes in the best examples, and then to apply them to existing needs and circumstances, so far as that was compatible with good taste and good workmanship." Having then compared and analyzed and studied the various founts of type until he had mastered, with his usual thoroughness, the ideal form and the underlying principles that constitute the beauty of every letter of the alphabet, Morris began to fashion his own type. Each single letter was designed by his own hand; on a larger scale at first, lest any blemish of line or proportion might escape notice in little. He then had them reduced by photography to the required working size, and again submitted to him for final revision before being handed to the typecutter. It may be mentioned here that Morris caused the type to be cut under his immediate direction, and cast by Sir Charles Reed and Sons. Those only who themselves have tried to design letters, and who, in the process, have learnt how slight a modification goes to the making or marring of the perfect form, will appreciate the labour and patience involved in designing two whole founts of type in upper and lower-case—two, for although Morris had nominally three founts, the Golden, the Troy, and the Chaucer, the last two practically do not differ from one another except in scale, the Troy type being larger than the other one. They are both Gothic in style, as distinct from the Golden type, which is roman. To consider first, then, the latter, since it was designed first. In his paper on "The Ideal Book" Morris goes into details with regard to the correct formation of roman letters—details which may be quoted here, as they embody some of the principal points which he observed in the designing of his own type. For instance, "the full-sized lower-case letters 'a,' 'b,' 'd,' and 'c' should be designed on something like a square to get good results: otherwise one may fairly say that there is not room enough for the design; furthermore each letter should have its due characteristic drawing; the thickening out for a 'b,' 'e,' 'g' should not be of the same kind as that for a 'd'; a 'u' should not merely be an 'n' turned upside down; the dot of the 'i' should not be a circle drawn with compasses but a delicately drawn diamond, and so on. To be short, the letters should be designed by an artist, and not an engineer." The founts in general use at the present day are less the products of a deteriorated tradition than of sheer commercial economy, the object being to crowd as much printed matter as may be into a given space. Thus the ordinary letters are of a narrow and pinched appearance, as compared with Morris's, which, as in the case of the "m" and "n" for instance, are remarkably broad and strong. In fact a general sense of breadth and squareness characterizes his letters. His "o" does not follow the commonly received oval outline, but is nearly a circle, with an oblique instead of the usual vertical opening. In the head of his letter "c" he has got rid of the usual ugly pear-shaped enlargement. The ceriphs, which in ordinary type are either all thin throughout, or sliced off to very near a point at the ends, are, it should be noted, in Morris's letters strong and broad. It is also to be noted, as significant of his unconscious bias towards Gothic forms, that the ceriphs of his roman type are set, many of them, diagonally, whereas they are horizontal in Jenson's letters, which Morris took for his model.

But to continue with his remarks on "The Ideal Book," he says that the hideous "Bodoni letter," with its "clumsy thickening and vulgar thinning of the lines," is "the most illegible type that was ever cut," and it "has been mostly relegated to works that do not profess anything but the baldest utilitarianism. . . . It is rather unlucky . . . that a somewhat low standard of excellence has been accepted for the design of modern roman type at its best, the comparatively poor and wiry letter of Plantin, and the Elzevirs, having served for the model, rather than the generous and logical designs of the fifteenth century Venetian printers, at the head of whom stands Nicholas Jenson; when it is so obvious that this is the best and clearest roman type yet struck, it seems a pity that we should make our starting point for a possible new departure at any worse period than the best." Jenson was the first Frenchman who brought the roman letter to perfection. Morris then goes on to say that "except where books smaller than an ordinary octavo are wanted" he would oppose "anything smaller than pica." As to black letter, the kind introduced from Holland and used in this country since the days of Wynkyn de Worde, "though a handsome and stately letter, is not very easy reading. It is too much compressed, too spiky, and, so to say, too prepensely Gothic. But there are many types which are of a transitional character and of all degrees of transition, from those which do little more than take in just a little of the crisp floweriness of the Gothic, like some of the Mentelin, or quasi-Mentelin, ones (which, indeed, are models of beautiful simplicity), or, say, like the letter of the Ulm Ptolemy, . . . to the splendid Maintz type, of which, I suppose, the finest example is the Schœffer Bible of 1462." In another place Morris says: "The Middle Ages brought caligraphy to perfection, and it was natural therefore that the forms of printed letters should follow more or less closely those of the written character, and they followed them very closely." He was also of opinion that "the capitals are the strong side of roman, and the lower-case of Gothic letter." The difficulty of constructing upper-case Gothic letters is one which Morris himself seems scarcely to have been quite successful in overcoming. His M and N do not harmonize with the pronouncedly Gothic aspect of the F, the L, the S, and the

V; while the other letters, for the most part, incline rather to the Lombardic style. His Arabic numerals, however, are altogether excellent, both for clearness and for beauty. This is the place to point out the fact of Morris's entire freedom from affectation of archaism when archaism, no matter howso overwhelmingly strong a precedent it might show, would have meant endangering the legibility of the work. For instance, he did not adopt the long form of the lower-case "s," because it is liable to be confounded with an "f": he employed tied letters but sparingly; and as to the abbreviations, which constitute the main difficulty of reading mediæval books, he discarded them altogether. He did not even print the catchword at the foot of the page.

As regards the aspect of the book, the "matter" in every case will necessarily "limit us somewhat" says Morris. "A work on differential calculus, a medical work, a dictionary, a collection of a statesman's speeches, or a treatise on manures, such books, though they might be handsomely and well printed, would scarcely receive ornament with the same exuberance as a volume of lyrical poems, or a standard classic, or suchlike. A work *on* Art, I think, bears less of ornament than any other kind of book (*non bis in idem* is a good motto); again, a book that *must* have *illustrations*, more or less utilitarian, should, I think, have no actual *ornament* at all, because the ornament and the illustration must almost certainly fight. Still, whatever the subject matter of the book may be, and however bare it may be of decoration, it can still be a work of art, if the type be good, and attention be paid to its general arrangement. . . . Well, I lay it down that a book quite unornamented can look actually and positively beautiful . . . if it be, so to say, architecturally good. . . . Now, then, let us see what this architectural arrangement claims of us. *First*, the pages must be clear and easy to read; which they can hardly be unless, *Secondly*, the type is well designed; and *Thirdly*, whether the margins be small or big, they must be in due proportion to the page of letter." There should be small whites between letters: what tends to illegibility is not this sort of compression, but the lateral compression of the letters themselves. A consideration, indeed, of great importance in the making of a beautiful page, is "the lateral spacing of the words. . . . No more white should be" left "between the words than just clearly cuts them off from one another; if the whites are bigger than this it both tends to illegibility and makes the page ugly. . . . If you want a legible book, the white should be clear and the black black. . . . You may depend upon it that a grey page is very trying to the eyes." As to the "position of the page of print on the paper . . . the hinder edge (that which is bound in) must be the smallest member of the margins, the head margin must be larger than this, the fore larger still, and the tail largest of all." These are the proper proportions, for the simple reason that the unit of the book is not one page by itself but the two corresponding pages of an open book, regarded together. Morris then goes on to say that he is not in favour of large paper copies, "though I have sinned a good deal in that way myself, but that was in the days of ignorance." "Making a large paper copy out of the small one" leads to a dilemma, that, "if the margins are right for the smaller book, they must be wrong for the larger, and you have to offer the public the worse book at the bigger price: if they are right for the large paper they are wrong for the small, and thus *spoil* it, . . . and that seems scarcely fair to the general public." The logic of this reasoning is unanswerable. Morris would prefer, in every case where there are two prices, to make some material difference in the work itself, so that the two issues should not correspond so far as to rival one another, nor occasion any dissatisfaction in the minds of those who had purchased on the higher or the lower scale. Then, as to the ornament, it "must form as much a part of the page as the type itself, or it will miss its mark, and in order to succeed, and to be ornament, it must submit to certain limitations, and become *architectural*." Morris puts the matter thus in his Arts and Crafts essay: "The essential point to be remembered is that the ornament, whatever it is, whether picture or pattern-work, should form *part of the page*, should be a part of the whole scheme of the book. Simple as this proposition is, it is necessary to be stated, because the modern practice is to disregard the relation between the printing and the ornament altogether, so that if the two are helpful to one another it is a mere matter of accident." To resume, "The picture-book is not, perhaps, absolutely necessary to man's life, but it gives such endless pleasure, and is so intimately connected with the other absolutely necessary art of imaginative literature, that it must remain one of the very worthiest things towards the production of which reasonable men should strive."

With the exception of the figure-subject illustrations, Mr. Morris designed with his own hand every ornament for the Kelmscott publications, from the minute leaves and flowers, forming a sort of "glorified full-stop," to which exception has been taken by some, to the large borders and titles for folio-size pages. Although it is true that the same borders and initials do sometimes recur in one and the same work (recur indeed too often to please certain of the artist's critics) in many, perhaps in the majority of instances, the ornaments were designed, one by one, as occasion demanded, for any given page, and moreover with a view to each one's position on the page. The artist would be provided with a sheet of paper from the Press, ready set out with ruled lines, showing the exact place and space that was required to be occupied by initial, border or what not, and he would fill accordingly. Morris designed the ornaments, not with a pen, but with a brush. It was most usual during the last few years of his life, on calling, to find him thus engaged, with his Indian ink and Chinese white in little saucers before him upon the table, its boards bare of any cloth covering, but littered with books and papers and sheets of MS. He did not place any value on the original drawings, regarding them as just temporary instruments, only fit, as soon as engraved, to be thrown away. Many an exquisite design of this sort has been rescued from the waste-paper basket by Morris's friend, Emery Walker. Morris used to keep what he called a "log-book" of the Press, *i.e.*, a book with a printed specimen, by way of reference and record, of every ornament he had ever designed for the Kelmscott Press. He included in the collection those designs which, though executed, were not eventually used; whether it was because an ornament in any given case had proved unsuitable for the page for which it was originally intended, or because the artist adjudged it, after all, to fall short of the high standard he exacted. For, as to the time and trouble and expense wasted, these considerations counted nothing with Morris; if the result itself was unsatisfactory in his eyes, he would not allow it to be used at all. The principal designs were engraved on wood, under Morris's own supervision, by W. H. Hooper; the less important ornaments by C. E. Keates, W. Spielmeyer, and a small number by G. Campfield.

Since no detail was overlooked that might contribute to make the books of the Kelmscott Press as perfect as possible, Morris paid particular heed to the kind of paper he used. He was no advocate of thick paper, least of all in small books, but that it should be of the first quality was an indispensable condition. He disapproved strongly of machine-made papers of every sort, from the frankly mechanical paper, with shiny, calendered surface, to that which is made in such wise as to imitate handwork. He was never tired of foretelling that the modern machine-made papers of wood pulp and clay will perish, and the books made of it ere long be no more. It is essential, then, that paper should be genuine handmade material. But "at the time Morris first set up the Press . . ." says Mr. Herbert Horne, "there was no paper in the market so well suited to the purposes of printing, of so fine a quality, and of so beautiful a colour and texture, as that employed by the early printers; as the paper, for example, which was ordinarily used by Aldus. To produce paper which should equal that was Morris's first care; but this was only to be done by reverting to the plain and honest methods of the old paper-makers; by using unbleached linen rags, and by employing a mould, in which the wires have not been woven with the mechanical accuracy that gives to modern handmade paper its uninteresting character. The paper which Morris succeeded in" getting was made expressly for him by Mr. Batchelor, at Little Chart, near Ashford, and "resembles the paper of the early printers in all its best qualities: it is thin, very tough, and somewhat transparent; pleasing not only to the eye, but to the hand also; having something of the clean, crisp quality of a new banknote." Even so minute a detail as the pattern of the water-marks was the object of Morris's careful attention. He himself designed the three he used for paper of different sizes, viz., the apple, the daisy, and the perch with a spray in its mouth, each of these devices being accompanied by the initials W. M.

The quality of the ink was again a consideration that caused Morris much anxiety; the greyness of ordinary inks being a serious defect in his eyes. The home-manufactured ink he used first not being found black enough, he had to procure ink from abroad for the later publications of the Press; ink composed of pure linseed oil and lampblack, and such that has excellent drying properties. Morris purposed to mix his own inks, and there is no doubt that, had he lived, he would have added this undertaking to that of the printer's craft. The ink at the Kelmscott Press was applied by hand in the old way, with pelt-balls; a process which insures a more perfect covering of the surface of the type, and consequently a richer and heavier black impression, than inking the type by mechanical means. In this connection "it must be remembered . . . that most modern printing is done by machinery on soft paper, and not by the hand-press, and . . . somewhat wiry letters are suitable for the machine process, which would not do justice to letters of more generous design."

Mr. Colebrook remarks, in his lecture printed in "The Printing Times and Lithographer" (November, 1896), that "the proper damping of sheets is a most important feature of the Kelmscott printing. The paper used is extremely sensitive. Each sheet is placed between two damping papers." Morris employed the hand-press alone at the Kelmscott Press, as it is hardly necessary to state, the old method being also, in his opinion, the best for insuring an equable pressure of the paper upon the inked type. The damping of the paper and the enormous pressure exerted by the Albion hand-press necessarily reproduced a feature of old books, to wit embossing, which sometimes gives pronounced evidence of the page having been printed on the reverse side. The proper damping of the vellum sheets was a matter of special difficulty; and, in spite of the increased cost and greater durability of the vellum copies, it may be questioned whether the paper copies, with their rougher texture, are not superior in æsthetic appearance. For it is impossible, on account of the somewhat greasy surface of the vellum, to insure the ink always adhering and giving a uniformly black impression throughout the printed page.

As regards the binding of the Kelmscott books, Morris selected Leighton for this purpose. Some books are bound in half-holland, with grey paper-covered millboard sides, while others are in white vellum with silk ties. It must be confessed that, picturesque though it be in appearance, a vellum-bound book, if of any bulk and weight, on account of the limpness of its cover, is difficult to hold in such a way that one may be able to read it, unless it is supported in both hands. For his own use, whereas the majority of copies are bound in white, Morris preferred vellum of a brownish tint.

The first book proposed to be issued from the Kelmscott Press was "The Golden Legend," but by some accident the paper intended for that work proved unsuitable for the purpose, and Morris having to utilize it somehow, it occurred to him to print a small edition of two hundred copies of his "Story of the Glittering Plain." This book then was the first that Morris printed. The first page was set up, according to Mr. Herbert Horne, on January 31st, 1891, which marks practically the date of the foundation of the Kelmscott Press. This was at No. 16, Upper Mall, Hammersmith, in the immediate neighbourhood of

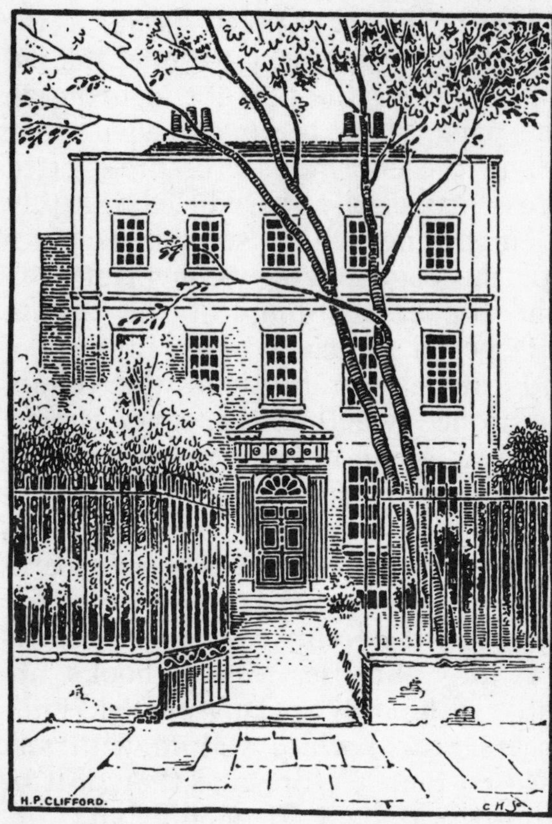

EXTERIOR OF HOUSE OCCUPIED IN PART BY THE KELMSCOTT PRESS.

Kelmscott House, and next door to the house No. 14, in which the Press was subsequently established. "The Story of the Glittering Plain" was finished on April 4th. It was a plain edition, with only one border and no illustrations, but its successful reception showed Morris at once the opening there was for books of the kind. Nearly three years later Morris produced, in Troy type, another edition of the same work enriched with twenty-three pictures designed by Walter Crane, very beautiful in themselves, but perhaps not quite free enough from the suspicion of Renaissance influence to be altogether in keeping with the Gothic character of the surrounding borders and other ornaments in whose company they were set.

The second book that issued from the Kelmscott Press was another of Morris's own works, "Poems by the Way," finished in September, 1891. This volume is printed in black and red. It contains the earliest of the ornamental borders designed by Morris, and betokens that he had not as yet developed his own peculiar Gothic style for this sort of work. It has the unmistakable character about it of Italian book ornaments of the fifteenth century, a remarkable style, because it seems to point to a recurrence—

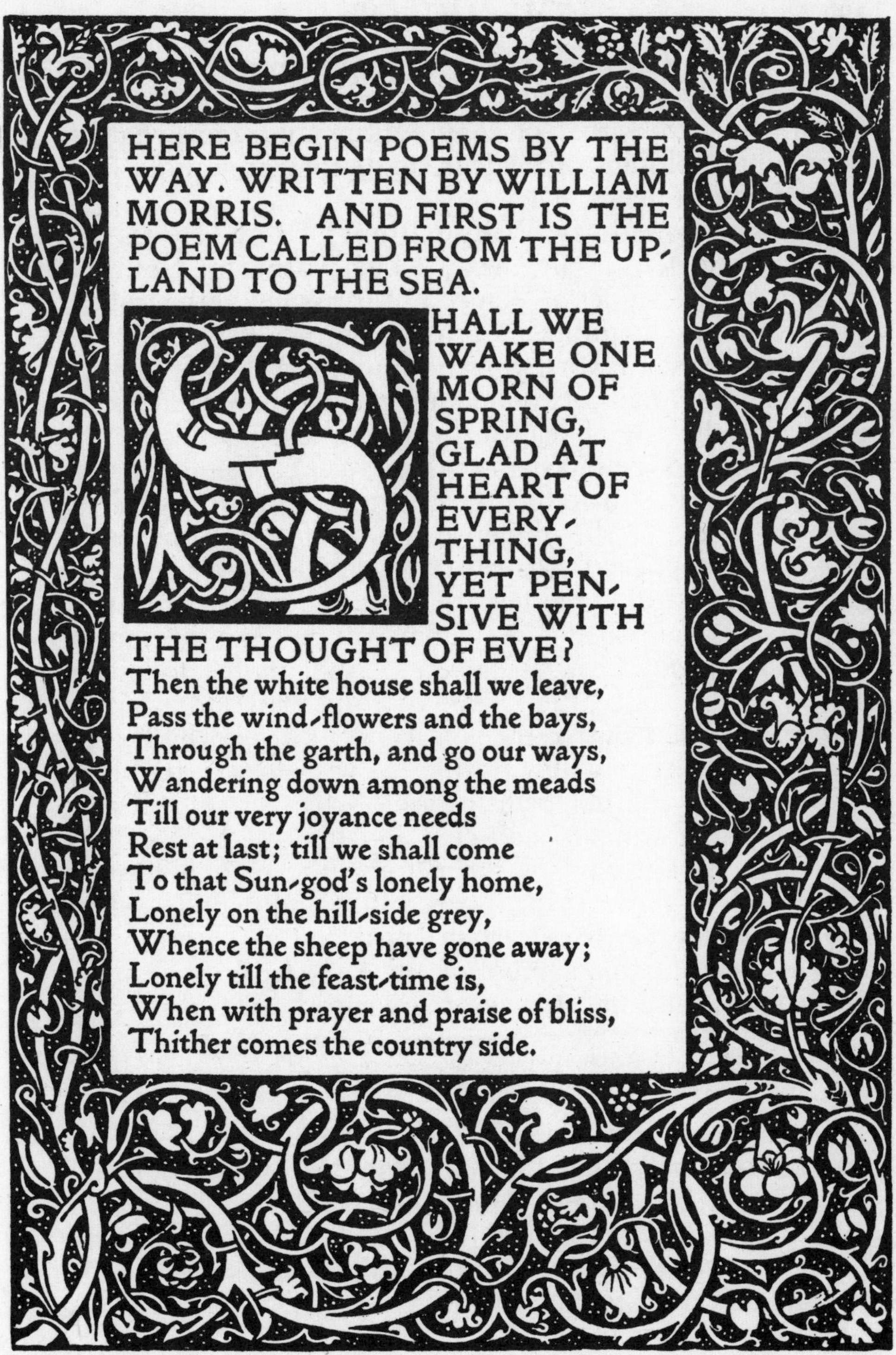

HERE BEGIN POEMS BY THE WAY. WRITTEN BY WILLIAM MORRIS. AND FIRST IS THE POEM CALLED FROM THE UPLAND TO THE SEA.

SHALL WE WAKE ONE MORN OF SPRING, GLAD AT HEART OF EVERYTHING, YET PENSIVE WITH THE THOUGHT OF EVE?
Then the white house shall we leave,
Pass the wind-flowers and the bays,
Through the garth, and go our ways,
Wandering down among the meads
Till our very joyance needs
Rest at last; till we shall come
To that Sun-god's lonely home,
Lonely on the hill-side grey,
Whence the sheep have gone away;
Lonely till the feast-time is,
When with prayer and praise of bliss,
Thither comes the country side.

FIRST PAGE OF "POEMS BY THE WAY." KELMSCOTT PRESS.

whether intentional or not it is impossible to say—to a kind of early Romanesque ornament, of which the main feature consists rather of convolutions and somewhat intricate intertwinings of tendrils, as distinct from bold lines or masses of foliage.

There followed Mr. Wilfrid Blunt's "Love Lyrics and Songs of Proteus;" and next, "The Nature of Gothic, a Chapter of the Stones of Venice." Morris felt very strongly that Ruskin's magnificent prose English had never yet been presented in worthy garb; and the selection of this book therefore had a twofold aim, viz., to show what might be done in the way of beautiful printing of Ruskin's works; in addition to emphasizing Morris's deep sense, as he explained in the introduction he wrote and printed along with the book, of the immense importance he attached to this, which represents the very kernel of Ruskin's teaching on the subject of Architecture. Next, finished in April, 1892, was published the Kelmscott Press edition of Morris's "Defence of Guenevere;" and, in the following month, his romance, "A Dream of John Ball and a King's Lesson." The frontispiece is a woodcut design by Burne-Jones, appropriately illustrating a passage in the text, descriptive of the democratic priest's banner: "a picture of a man and woman, half-clad in skins of beasts, seen against a background of green trees, the man holding a spade and the woman a distaff and spindle, rudely done enough, but yet with a certain spirit and much meaning; and underneath this symbol of the early world and man's first contest with nature were the written words:

> "'When Adam delved and Eve span,
> Who was then the gentleman.'"

This fact is worth noticing, since it has been asserted, quite erroneously, that the conception was due to a panel, one of ten, by Jacopo della Quercia, that decorate the pilasters of the western portal of San Petronio, in Bologna. Burne-Jones afterwards re-drew this composition and it appeared as a cartoon, entitled "Labour," in "The Daily Chronicle," February 11th, 1895.

At length there appeared, seventh in order of publication, the work which had long been preparing, "The Golden Legend of Master William Caxton, done anew," completed on September 12th, 1892. This was the largest and most important work that had hitherto been undertaken at the Kelmscott Press. It is of large quarto size, in three volumes, the pages numbered consecutively to 1286. The last thirty-nine pages, after the lives of the Saints, comprise, first, "The Noble Historye of thexposicion of the Masse," and "the Twelve articles of our feythe;" then a list of some obsolete or little used words, and, lastly, four pages of "Memoranda, Bibliographical and Explanatory, concerning the Legenda Aurea of Jacobus de Voragine, and some of the translations of it," from the pen of Mr. F. S. Ellis, editor of the Kelmscott edition. A note at the end states that "no change from the original" has been made in this edition, "except for correction of errors of the press, and some few other amendments thought necessary for the understanding of the text." It is printed in Mr. Morris's Golden type, in black only. Beside the initial letters, borders, ornaments, and the title-page in handsome black letter, on a background of delicate arabesque outlines, all of which designs exhibit Mr. Morris's matured Gothic style of book-decoration, there are two woodcuts after Burne-Jones. The first, facing the beginning of "The Storye of the Byble," is Adam and Eve standing with an angel within the enclosure of Eden; the second, facing the first of "The Legendes of Saynctes," is the Redeemed (whom, by some strange caprice, the artist has chosen to represent as exclusively of the fair sex, save one ambiguous being in the right-hand corner) being welcomed by Angels into Paradise. It may be mentioned, perhaps, as a singular circumstance, that in no part of the book is there any intimation of the authorship of these two illustrations. True, the advertisements of the work announced the fact; and, moreover, Burne-Jones's style is sufficiently familiar to all contemporary connoisseurs to be unmistakable. But is it certain that anyone who comes across a copy of this edition, say a hundred years hence, or later still, will know by intuition—and that more particularly when at the corners of both these illustrations is to be seen none other than the identical signature which is appended to many of Mr. Morris's own designs in the publications of the Kelmscott Press? It should be noted that Mr. Morris never signed his designs; the device in question bearing the mark, W. H. H., of the engraver, Mr. Hooper. For the purpose of achieving the utmost possible accuracy in the Kelmscott edition, Morris, on giving his bond for a large sum as security, obtained from the syndics of the University Library at Cambridge the loan of their valuable copy of the first edition printed by Caxton in 1483. The whole of this work was transcribed for the Press by the editor's daughter, Mrs. Paine, an immense labour, and one that was performed with such care as to reduce the number of necessary proof-corrections to a minimum; while the copy for the other Caxton reprints, all but "The Order of Chivalry," was type-written by Mrs. Peddie, at the British Museum.

The next work, in two volumes, large quarto, was a reprint of the first book printed in English, viz., "The Recuyell of the Historyes of Troy," done after the first edition of Caxton. For this book a fairly large size of black letter was used for the first time, and hence was named by Morris the Troy type. The work is dated October 14th, 1892. In the same month was finished Mr. Mackail's "Biblia Innocentium;" and on 22nd of the following month, William Morris's "News from Nowhere," printed in black and red, with a woodcut frontispiece, drawn by Mr. C. M. Gere, of the Birmingham School of Art, being a representation of the entrance-front of Kelmscott Manor House. A reprint of Caxton's edition (1481) of "The Historye of Reynard the Foxe," printed in Troy type, was finished in December, 1892. "The Poems of William Shakespeare, printed after the original copies of Venus and Adonis, 1593. The Rape of Lucrece, 1594. Sonnets, 1609. The Lover's Complaint," edited by Mr. F. S. Ellis, and finished on January 17th, 1893, preceded "The Order of Chivalry," translated by Caxton, together with "The Ordination of Knighthood," a translation by Morris, in octosyllabic verse, of a twelfth century French poem, entitled "L'Ordene de Chevalerie," the text of which is also included in the volume. The work of transcribing for the press was done by Mr. Ellis, who has inserted six lines at the bottom of page 33, a passage which, though omitted in Caxton's version, is necessary to the

And whyle they were besy in fyghtyng, they that were embusshed shold sodenly breke and come by hynde on them and fyght, and so shold they be enclosed bytwene them within and them withoute, in suche wyse that none shold escape.

THEY that herd thise lettres & thyse messagers doubted them moche of our peple, wherfor they acorded gladly to this counseyl. They assembled them of Hallape, them of Cezayre, them of Haman, and of other cytees about, tyl they were a grete nombre of peple, and this dyde they the moost secretely they myght, as was to them commaunded, and began to departe and approuche Anthyoche. And cam to a castel named Harant, whiche is fro thens a xiiij myle, there they lodged; and thought on the morne, as sone as the scarmuche shold be bytwene the pylgryms and

PART OF PAGE OF "GODEFREY OF BOLOYNE." KELMSCOTT PRESS.

sense. Mr. Ellis translated them from the text of the French MS. in the Royal Library at the British Museum. Finished on February 24th, 1893, and printed in the small Gothic called the Chaucer type, the book is enriched with a woodcut frontispiece designed by Burne-Jones.

Next in order was George Cavendish's "Life of Cardinal Wolsey," transcribed by Mr. Ellis from the autograph manuscript of the author, now in the British Museum.

The Kelmscott edition was finished on March 30th, 1893. It was followed by "The history of Godefrey of Boloyne and of the conquest of Iherusalem," in large quarto size, done after Caxton's first edition; printed in Troy type in black and red, and having a decorative title designed by W. Morris in similar style to the title of "The Golden Legend."

On August 4th, 1893, was finished the reprint, in black and red, of Ralph Robinson's English translation from the Latin of Sir Thomas More's "Utopia." Of the 300 copies issued, 40 had been ordered in advance by an Eton master, with the intention of distributing them as prizes among the boys of the college, but when the work appeared with a compromisingly Socialistic introduction by Morris, the order, from motives of prudence, had to be cancelled. However, the copies were all disposed of before a year was out, so Morris did not suffer any loss.

In August, 1893, also was finished Tennyson's "Maud;" and on September 15th "Sidonia the Sorceress," translated from the German of William Meinhold by Lady Wilde. The author was "a man so steeped in the history and social life of his country during the period" of which he wrote, "that he might almost be said," remarked Morris, "to have been living in it rather than in his own, the early part of the present century. The result of his life and literary genius was the production of two books: 'The Amber Witch,' and 'Sidonia the Sorceress,' both of which, but, in my judgment, especially 'Sidonia,' are almost faultless reproductions of the life of the past; not mere antiquarian studies, but presentations of events, often tragic, the actors in which are really alive, though under conditions so different from those of the present day. In short, 'Sidonia' is a masterpiece of its kind, and without a rival of its kind. . . . The present edition of the book will answer satisfactorily" the "many questions" which the two drawings of Burne-Jones, shown at the exhibition of his works in the early part of 1893, caused to be asked. "Lady Wilde's translation, which was the one," continues Morris, "through which we made acquaintance with Meinhold's genius, is a good, simple, and sympathetic one." The Kelmscott edition is in large quarto, with beautiful borders or half-borders at the beginning of the several books, with initials and other ornaments, in the margins, but it lacks the attraction of an ornamental title-page. The work was certainly less of a success than any publication that had preceded it from the Kelmscott Press. But a generation that delights in introspective fiction, spiced with theological debate, and the discussion of problems dealing with the relations of the sexes; a generation whose popular authors are Mrs. Humphry Ward, Sarah Grand, and Marie Corelli, could scarcely be expected to find an old-world, objective romance of the type of "Sidonia the Sorceress" congenial to its taste. No wonder then that the sale was slow.

A small work, the first in 16mo, entitled "Gothic Architecture," a lecture by W. Morris, spoken at the New Gallery for the Arts and Crafts Exhibition Society in 1889, was printed in one of the Kelmscott presses, to demonstrate the practical method of hand-printing, at the New Gallery during the Society's Exhibition there in the autumn of 1893.

"Ballads and Narrative Poems" by Dante Gabriel Rossetti, with a title in roman letters on an arabesque ground within a vine border, was finished in October, 1893; and on December 16th, the first of a series of translations of French tales of the thirteenth century, to wit, "Of King Florus and the Fair Jehane," in black letter with decorative title. It may be not uninteresting to record that this one was selected by Mr. and Mrs. Tregaskis, the well-known antiquarian booksellers, as a typical and appropriate volume for the exercise of the binder's craft. For the purpose, one work only was taken, identity of subject and uniformity of size (in this case 16mo), insuring obviously the readiest unit of comparison of different modes of binding. A century of copies, more or less, were bought up and sent to all parts of the globe, without conditions as to the kind of binding, save the general recommendation that each binder should adopt whatever style was most characteristic of his own locality, and of the materials at his disposal. In due course, the copies came back again, bound in the fashion

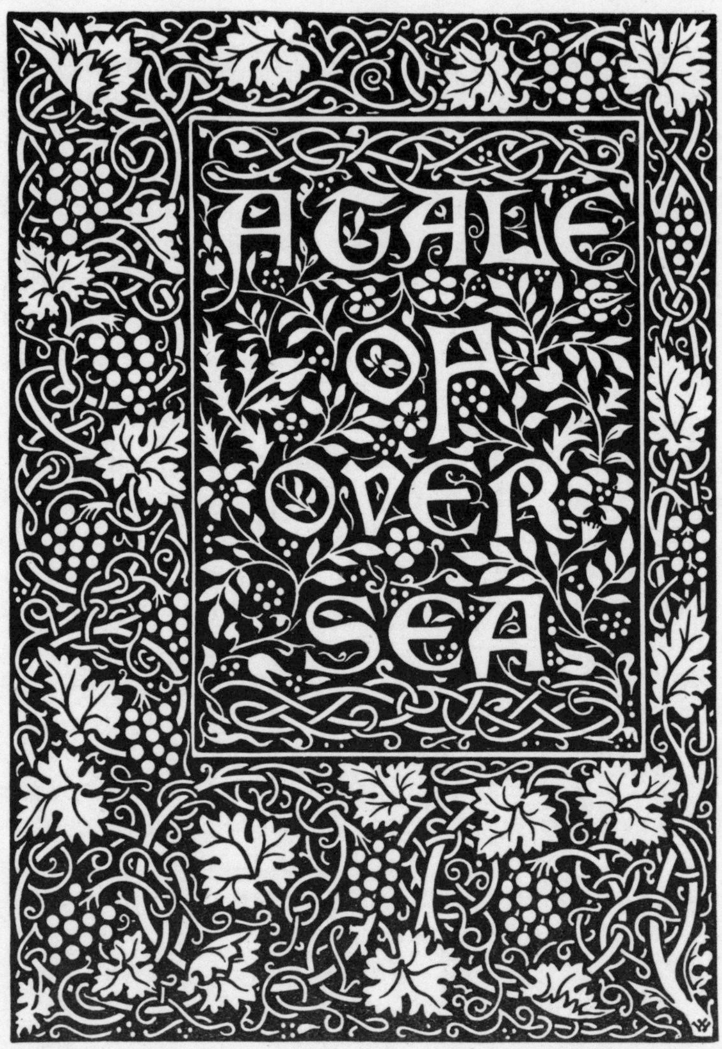

TITLE-PAGE OF "A TALE OF OVER SEA." KELMSCOTT PRESS.

peculiar to divers countries and peoples, and were shown at the International Bookbinding Exhibition held at the Caxton Head, Holborn, in 1894. The seventy-five specimens thus gathered together attracted no little attention; they were taken by Royal command to be inspected by the Queen at Windsor; and eventually Mrs. Rylands purchased this unique collection *en bloc*, thus saving it from the fate of dispersion.

The companion volumes to "King Florus" appeared at intervals, one being entitled "Of the Friendship of Amis and Amile;" the other "The Tale of the Emperor Constans and of Over Sea"—two romances in one volume, with each its own title-page. The four completed Mr. Morris's repertory of this particular collection of stories. They were reprinted in 1896 by Mr. George Allen, in one volume, under the title "Old French Romances. Done into English by William Morris, with an introduction by Joseph Jacobs," who, however, has not put them in Mr. Morris's order, but has made the first and third tales change places. From the introduction it appears that the source whence Morris derived the romances was "Nouvelles Françaises en prose du XIIIième Siècle," by MM. L. Moland and C. D'Hericault, published in Paris in 1856, and that they could be traced back to a remote origin in old Byzantium.

On February 20th, 1894, was finished a companion volume to the "Ballads and Narrative Poems" of Rossetti, viz., his "Sonnets and Lyrical Poems," with a similar title-page, only that in the latter case the border was darker and more solid than in the first. "The Poems of John Keats," with ornamental title, was finished in March, 1894; and in May a large quarto edition of "Atalanta in Calydon, a Tragedy made by Algernon Charles Swinburne," with an ornamental title. The Greek characters used in the opening verses are those designed for Messrs. Macmillan and Co. by Mr. Selwyn Image. They are uncials only. For Sigma the most antique form C is adopted. There are not any accents nor aspirates; thus it is a little puzzling at first sight, when, for example, the word ΤΕ or ΔΕ is elided, to find the Tau or Delta standing by itself without the usual mark of elision. But the general effect of the page is wonderfully beautiful. It would have been of course in the highest degree incongruous in this sumptuous volume to have employed the ugly modern type of Greek used in school books and in Hellenic newspapers of the present day.

On May 30th, 1894, was finished the printing of a new romance of Morris's, called "The Wood beyond the World," in his Chaucer type, in black and red, with a woodcut frontispiece designed by Burne-Jones. This work having been pirated in America, Morris brought out a cheaper edition, published by Messrs. Lawrence and Bullen, in 1895.

On Michaelmas Day was finished "The Book of Wisdom and Lies," a collection, made in the eighteenth century, of Georgian traditional stories, translated into English, with notes, by Oliver Wardrop. In the decorated title of this work, in roman characters in white upon a black ground, with a vine border, is introduced an escutcheon with the arms of Georgia, in Asia. This is noteworthy as being the sole instance of a heraldic device among the *published* designs of William Morris. Indeed, it is a very remarkable fact that, with the strong predilection he had for mediæval ornament, one of its most familiar elements should, nevertheless, be almost entirely absent from the artist's decorative work. It is further to be observed that, having chosen to make use of a shield in his composition, he should have taken, not the immature spade-form, like an early English arch inverted, technically called Roman or Heater shape, maintained by heralds to be the most correct, but a later one, viz., the fifteenth century elaborate, decorative shape, with incurved edges or arrises like the section of a Doric column, and *à bouche*, *i.e.* hollowed out in the dexter chief to make a lance-rest.

In November, 1894, was printed a rhymed version of the Penitential Psalms, found in a manuscript of the Hours of our Lady, written at Gloucester about the year 1440. This work, transcribed and edited by Mr. Ellis, with the title "Psalmi Penitentiales," had been advertised, in the previous April, as "A Fifteenth Century English Hymn Book, being a paraphrase in verse of the Seven Penitential Psalms, written in Gloucester about A.D. 1420." About the same time was finished a letter in Italian, by Savonarola, on Contempt of the World, printed for Mr. Fairfax

Murray, the owner of the autograph letter, and the designer of the frontispiece.

Next followed, at intervals, in three volumes, "The Poems of Percy Bysshe Shelley," with a title to the first volume.

On January 10th, 1895, was finished "The Tale of Beowulf, sometime King of the folk of the Weder Geats," done out of the old English tongue by William Morris and A. J. Wyatt, in large quarto size, with an ornamental title-page, of Gothic lettering on arabesques, within a beautiful border.

On February 16th, 1895, was finished the reprint of "Syr Percyvelle of Gales," after the edition printed by J. O. Halliwell, from the MS. in the Library of Lincoln Cathedral. The Kelmscott edition of this poem is printed in black and red, in the Chaucer type, with a woodcut frontispiece, designed by Burne-Jones. Morris's "Life and Death of Jason" was reprinted on May 25th, 1895, with two woodcuts after Burne-Jones, and in July another work by Morris—in prose this, and published now for the first time—a romance, in two 16mo volumes, with decorative title, named, "Of Child Christopher and Fair Goldilind."

On October 25th, 1895, was finished at the Kelmscott Press, for Messrs. Way and Williams, of Chicago, Rossetti's "Hand and Soul," a reprint, in small size, from "The Germ," with a roman-letter title on light arabesque ground with an ornamental border.

On November 21st, was finished "Poems Chosen out of the Works of Robert Herrick," with ornamental title, and edited from the text of the edition put forth by the author in 1648. A uniform edition of "Christabel and other Poems of Samuel Taylor Coleridge," was issued also from the Kelmscott Press.

On March 2nd, 1896, was finished a new romance of Morris's, entitled "The Well at the World's End," with four woodcuts designed by Sir Edward Burne-Jones. The work is printed in Chaucer type, and is the first to exhibit a new feature in Kelmscott books, viz., double columns with ornament between them. Moreover, the opening words, instead of the initials only, at the heading of the several divisions of the work are treated in an ornamental design.

The last-named feature appears again in the Kelmscott edition of Chaucer, in folio size, printed in black and red,

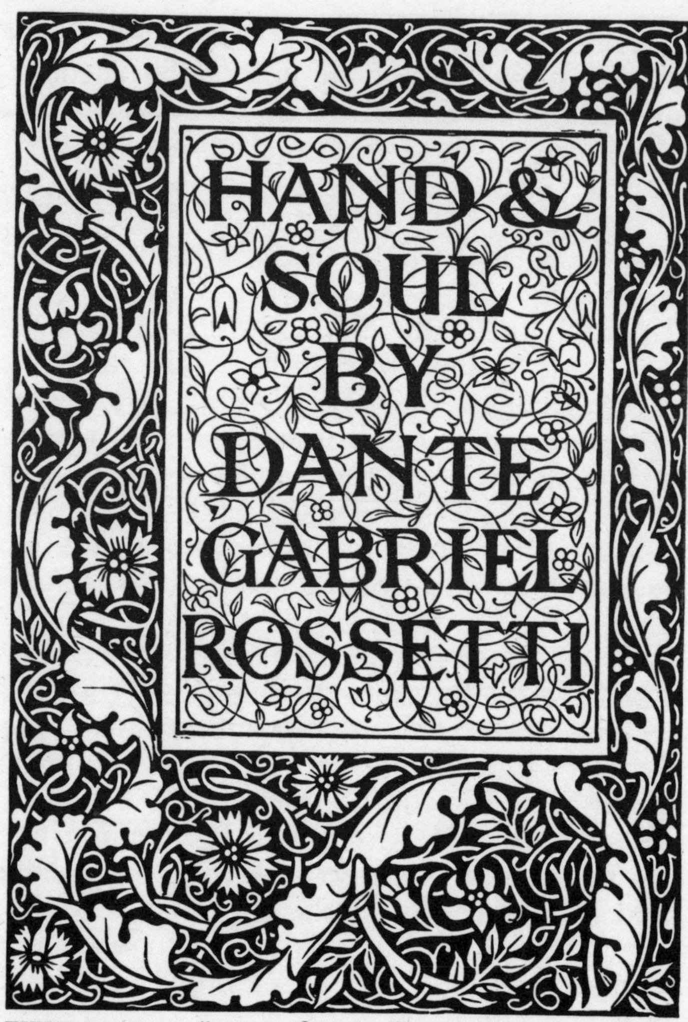

TITLE-PAGE OF "HAND & SOUL." KELMSCOTT PRESS.

with double columns. This work, as Morris wrote to inform the editor of "The Daily Chronicle," in July, 1894, was "advancing rapidly," and he hoped to be able to issue it about the middle of the following year. However, it was not completed until the month of May, 1896; one

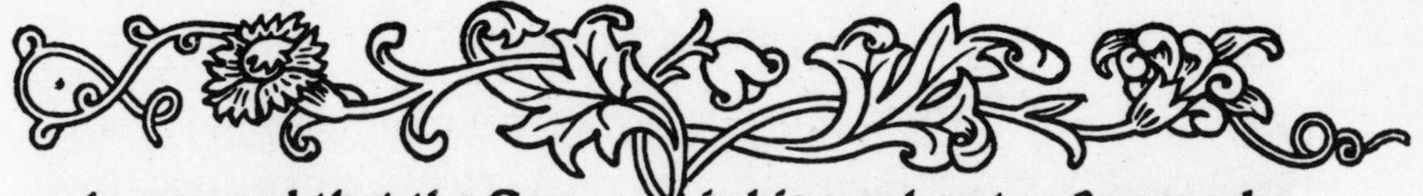

en in war, and that the Companions who had conquered it were looking for chapmen to cheapen their booty, and that he was the first, or nearly the first, to come who had will and money to buy, and the Companions, who were eager to depart, had sold him thieves' penny-worths: wherefore his share of the Upmeads treasure had gone far; and thence he had gone to another good town where he had the best of markets for his newly cheapened wares, and had bought more there, such as he deemed handy to sell, and so had gone from town to town, and had ever thriven, and had got much wealth: and so at last having heard tell of Whitwall as better for chaffer than all he had yet seen, he and other chapmen had armed them, & waged men-at-arms to defend them, and so tried the adventure of the wildwoods, and come safe through.

THEN at last came the question to Ralph concerning his adventures, and he enforced himself to speak, and told all as truly as he might, without telling of the Lady and her woeful ending. Thus they gave & took in talk, and Ralph did what he might to seem like other folk, that he might nurse his grief in his own heart as far asunder from other men as might be. So they rode on till it was even, and came to Whitwall before the shutting of the gates and rode into the street, and found it a fair and great town, well defensible, with high and new walls, and men-at-arms good store to garnish them. Ralph rode with his brother to the hostel of the chapmen, & there they were well lodged.

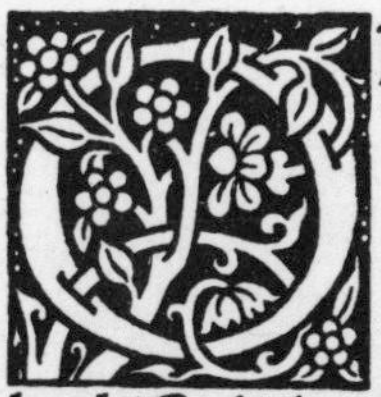

ON the morrow Blaise went to his chaffer and to visit the men of the Port at the Guildhall: he bade Ralph come with him, but he would not, but abode in the hall of the hostel and sat pondering sadly while men came and went; but he heard no word spoken of the Well at the World's End. In like wise passed the next day and the next, save that Richard was among those who came into the hall, and he talked long with Ralph at whiles; that is to say that he spake, & Ralph made semblance of listening.

NOW as is aforesaid Richard was old & wise, & he loved Ralph much

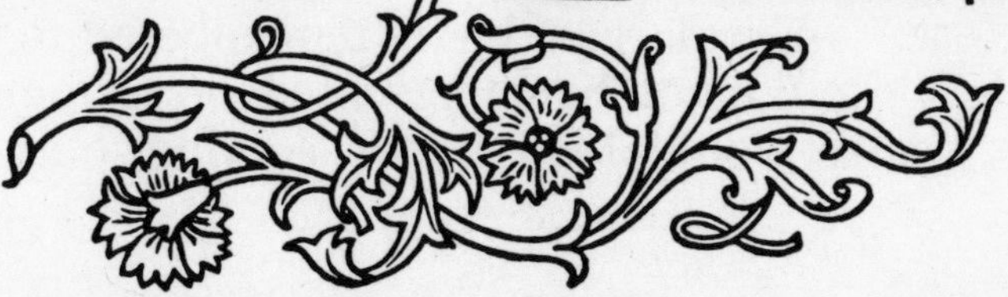

PAGE FROM "THE WELL AT THE WORLD'S END." KELMSCOTT PRESS.

press at first, and subsequently two, being employed to produce it. No folio work had hitherto been printed by Morris, and this large volume is altogether the most elaborate and most important that he issued from his Press. It contains eighty-seven pictures (the number of which was estimated originally at about sixty), designed by Sir Edward Burne-Jones, and engraved on wood by Mr. W. H. Hooper. The title-page is from Mr. Morris's own design, the drawing of which occupied him a fortnight. It is worded: "the works of Geoffrey Chaucer now newly imprinted," in large Gothic lower-case letters, shown up strongly in white against a black background, broken by delicate white floral ornament. The initials G and C are, however, of a fantastic form, so out of harmony with the rest of the lettering that it is difficult to conceive how the designer himself was satisfied with the effect of this page. The word "Kelmscott," in beautiful Gothic letters, is introduced in the ornament of the last page in a different manner from any previous work of the Press; being enclosed within the border, whereas in the other books the printer's mark forms, as it were, a detached colophon at the end of everything. The work is further enriched with magnificent borders of Morris's design. He also made fourteen designs forming a sort of inner framework to the picture illustrations. It has been declared by some critics that Mr. Morris went to great trouble to make each of his ornamental borders in perfect harmony with the subject matter of the page. At any rate, in the Chaucer this is conspicuously not the case. Thus, in the very first page of the Prologue to "The Canterbury Tales," which open with lines descriptive of April, we find a border of vines and ripe grapes. Another designer belike would have been solicitous to fashion a seasonable device out of catkins or primroses. But not so Morris; he was even vexed with someone who supposed that the rose borders in the Kelmscott Chaucer had been made specially for the "Romaunt of the Rose." A remark of his is remembered to the effect that fishes should not be represented on a fountain, for that the water would look better coming out of lions' mouths. In fact he disliked altogether the principle of seeking to have "appropriate" ornament. The decorative instinct in him was so supreme that whatever occurred most spontaneously to the artist's hand to design at the moment, that he did. He could not be hampered with the restriction of observing times and seasons and symbolic significations; nor had he a mind for anything else save alone the æsthetic effect of the page. And so entirely did this one countervail—nay, override—every other consideration, that quite reasonable claims sometimes were disregarded for the sake of it, *e.g.*, in the opening page of "Poems by the Way," of "Jason," or of Tennyson's "Maud," in the Kelmscott editions. For it must be owned, as a critic in "The Edinburgh Review" has pointed out, that the practice "of printing poetry in continuous lines, as if it were prose, instead of in verses, in order to fill up the page in a more decorative manner . . . is putting the make-up of the page before the matter," and is only too likely to confuse the reader. "Poetry is literary expression in verse," and one feels inclined to challenge the right of the printer to transform it into "the semblance of prose." This objection applies in a degree even to Morris's masterpiece, the Kelmscott Chaucer. Yet still, "when criticism has done its best," says "The Printing Times and Lithographer," "the work is an admitted marvel. To have produced this book were, of itself, enough for fame." It is, indeed, a monument. It has been described by different writers as "the noblest book ever printed;" "the finest book ever issued;" and "the greatest triumph of English typography." In short, William Morris may be regarded as "the Caxton of our day, who, with a fine confidence unshaken by the grave pecuniary risks, carried the manufacture of books back to its original condition of one of the fine arts. Price was not to signify—the book was to be made . . . as beautiful in print, in paper, in binding, as it could be made." For those persons who might desire something costlier and more lasting than the ultra-simple cover in which the volume was issued to the public, Mr. Morris made a special design for a binding, to be executed at the Doves Bindery under the direction of his friend Mr. Cobden-Sanderson. The intention was to have it of white stamped pig-skin mounted upon a pair of wooden boards, after the old manner. The design consists of a central panel, trellissed in a diaper of lozenges, charged each with a Tudor rose spray; framed within a border of vine branches, leaves and grapes. Labels run above and below, bearing, in Gothic letter, the one the legend "Geoffrey Chaucer," the other "Kelmscott." The remaining spaces are occupied by patterns of conventional foliage.

On August 21st, 1896, was finished "The Flowre and the Leafe and the Boke of Cupide, God of Love, or the Cuckow and the Nightingale." This work was published as a supplementary volume, it having been determined by competent scholars that the poems, generally attributed to Chaucer, are not really his work. Rev. Professor Skeat, indeed, has gone so far as to produce what looks like conclusive evidence that the author of the latter was Sir Thomas Clanvoye; while the former was the work of a late fifteenth century poetess.

On May 7th, 1896, was finished the first volume of a re-issue, to be completed in eight volumes, of "The Earthly Paradise," with a title-page, new borders (occurring at the beginning of each story), and special marginal ornaments to the poems of the months. This work, advertised to appear, one volume at a time, at intervals of about three months, was still in progress at the time of Morris's death, the first volume having been published in July, 1896.

On July 7th, 1896, was finished "Laudes Beatæ Mariæ Virginis," Latin poems taken from a Psalter written in England about A.D. 1220. This is remarkable as the first Kelmscott Press book printed in three colours, black, red and blue—the latter colour being a new experiment of Morris's. Rev. E. S. Dewick has pointed out the interesting fact "that these poems were printed in 1579, in a 16mo. volume, with the title Psalterium Divæ Virginis Mariæ, &c. . . . This Tegernsee edition contains a Conclusio of four verses in the same metre as the Aves, but the text is otherwise inferior to that printed by William Morris. The ascription of the authorship to Stephen Langton is doubly interesting, as the manuscript transcribed for the Kelmscott Press was probably written before his death in 1228."

On October 14th, 1896, was finished Spenser's "The Shepheardes Calender: conteyning twelve Æglogues proportionable to the twelve monethes." In Golden type, with ornamental initials, but no borders, this edition is embellished with twelve full-page designs. Some, if not all, of these illustrations are zinco-process reproductions. The preliminary announcement of this work mentioned the names both of the author of the poem and also of the artist who drew the pictures, but—unaccountable omission—the book, as published, contains no intimation of either. Those who know will, without difficulty, recognize the initials A. J. G. in the corner of each illustration as those of Mr. Gaskin, of the Birmingham School; but for the information of posterity there is no record.

Within less than a week of the death of its illustrious founder, that the Kelmscott Press was about to close was bruited abroad. The statement, once having found its way into print, was copied, with variations and added details more or less inaccurate, by one newspaper after another, and was for some weeks allowed to circulate unchallenged. Those of the public who were sympathetic awaited—some of them with almost breathless anxiety—an authoritative confirmation of the report, dreading, and yet unwilling to believe, that the days of the Kelmscott Press were definitely numbered. Anyhow it was obvious that the full programme of the Press could not now be carried out, and that some modifications had become inevitable upon the removal of him who had been the life and genius of the undertaking, and who had given it all along his close and immediate attention. At last, after an interval of some five weeks, there came an official notice from headquarters; it bore date November 12th, 1896. Ostensibly an order form for "The Shepheardes Calender," more important significance lay in the fact that it announced some few works, already advertised, as shortly to be issued, others as abandoned, and thus seemed to set aside all uncertainty as to the approaching end of the Press. An article, indeed, to that effect appeared in "The Academy" of December 12th. Then, and not till then, was it elicited, in the shape of a letter addressed to "The Academy" by the late Mr. Morris's secretary, that the future of the Kelmscott Press was still under consideration on the part of the trustees. However, the greatest loss, and one which book-lovers must never cease to regret, is the definite abandonment of the folio editions of Froissart and of "Sigurd the Volsung." On the latter, as the one of which its author was most proud among all his poetical works, he had intended to lavish the choicest decoration. However, not much progress had been made with it. It was to have been embellished with forty woodcuts designed by Sir Edward Burne-Jones, in addition to new borders and other ornaments by Mr. Morris himself. The first announcement of this work had been made in November, 1895, when the number of woodcuts proposed was set down at about five-and-twenty. A later circular, dated February 16th, 1897, announced a small folio edition of this work, with two woodcuts only, designed by Burne-Jones. For "The Cronycles of Syr John Froissart" Mr. Morris had elected to reprint Lord Berners's translation from Pynson's edition of 1523 and 1525. This work had been advertised as in preparation in August, 1893, and as in the press in April, 1894—although, in subsequent notices, it is true, it was referred to only as in preparation. The fact of its having reached, by the time of Mr. Morris's death, a fairly advanced stage, makes its withdrawal all the more to be deplored. It was to have appeared in two volumes, with double columns and ornaments, the latter designed by Morris in a manner that recalls fourteenth century illuminations. The borders included shields with the armorial bearings of the various personages named in the course of the chronicle. The tinctures were to be in plain black and white, according to the most ancient system of representation. For it would have been an obvious anachronism to indicate them by dots and lines, hatchings, and so on, as our modern practice is to do, which cannot be traced back farther, at the very earliest, than the last quarter of the sixteenth century. Two specimen pages, on vellum, are all that the Directors of the Press could undertake to issue of this important work.

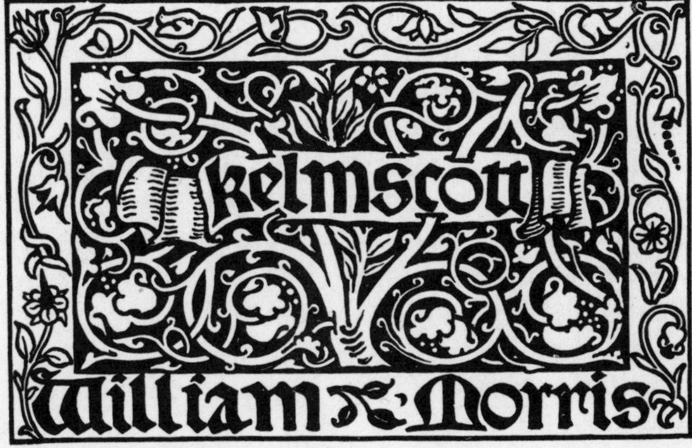

KELMSCOTT PRESS MARK.

A more recent circular announced as nearly ready the Kelmscott edition of "Sire Degravaunt," an ancient English metrical romance from the Thornton MS. at Lincoln, with a woodcut designed by Burne-Jones. The preparation of this work, which is uniform with the "Syr Percyvelle," from first to last has spread over a considerable time. "Sire Isumbras," uniform with the above, and from the same source, was advertised to follow; also a romance of Mr. Morris's, "The Water of the Wondrous Isles," ready at the end of July, 1897, uniform with "The Well at the World's End;" and a still more recent one, in fact, the last he ever wrote, the very name of which, viz., "The Sundering Flood," did not transpire until after the author's death. A circular dated July 28th, 1897, announced a second work, printed in three colours, viz., Morris's poem "Love is Enough," in quarto size, with a woodcut designed by Burne-Jones.

Among the other works which have at various times been announced as in contemplation or in preparation at the Kelmscott Press, although they have not made their appearance, may be named a collection of Poems by Mr. Theodore Watts-Dunton; "The Tragedies, Histories and Comedies of William Shakespeare," in three folio volumes, a text in the original orthography, arranged by F. J. Furnivall from the earliest edition, taking the first folio as the basis; and "Vitas Patrum," being St. Jerome's Lives of the Fathers of the Desert, translated into English by William Caxton during the last years of his life, and printed at Wynkyn de Worde's press in 1495. This work, which has never hitherto been reprinted, was to have formed two large quarto volumes, uniform with the "Golden Legend." "Amongst other editions which he (Morris) hoped to have printed," says "The Saturday Review," "was a volume of musical compositions by King Henry VIII. and the English composers contemporary with him. The project originated with Sir Edward Burne-Jones, who was to have designed the woodcuts; and the music, which was to have consisted of the contents of two MSS. in the British Museum, Add. MSS. 31,922 and 5,665, was to have been edited by Mr. Arnold Dolmetsch. The project was carried so far that the photographing of the MS. was actually commenced." It is impossible to say what books Morris might have produced besides, had not death interrupted his work; but it is believed that he had some intention of reprinting a collection of old English Ballads, "Gesta Romanorum" and Malory's "Morte d'Arthur."

There was also in preparation "A Catalogue of the Collection of Woodcut Books, Early Printed Books and Manuscripts at Kelmscott House, with Notes by William Morris," and upwards of 50 illustrations, being reproductions selected from the typical works in Mr. Morris's library. For this book, which should have been especially interesting and remarkable, a number of specimen pages and blocks had been prepared; and he had spared neither trouble nor expense to obtain the finest reproductions. Some of the contents of Mr. Morris's library, in the shape of mediæval MSS. have been enumerated in a previous chapter. As an instance of the almost romantic vicissitudes which befall art treasures, and of the responsibilities which sometimes attend the collector, the following may be related here. The details are given by Mr. Temple Scott, to whom Mr. Morris showed the MS. in question and narrated the circumstances. He had added to his collection a remarkably fine Book of Hours, of the thirteenth century, gorgeous "in its exquisite penmanship and painted initials shining with burnished gold." But the book, when Morris bought it, "was not perfect—it wanted two leaves. . . . Some time after I had acquired it," said Morris, "a friend who knew of my manuscript, and who also knew that it wanted two leaves, told me that he had seen, framed and hung up in the Fitzwilliam Museum at Cambridge, the very leaves that were originally in my book. I hastened down to Cambridge, and, sure enough, my friend was right. I there and then offered to buy them, but the authorities had no power to sell. Instead of selling me their property, they offered to buy mine, and to this I consented, on condition that I was allowed to keep the perfect work so long as I lived. And it is now in my possession for me to use, but to be given up to the Fitzwilliam Museum at my death. Of course I am responsible for its loss, but it was a pleasure to me to be able to bring together the separated parts." They "who worked at these illuminated books must have been wonderful fellows. It seems now as if they could not do anything wrong; every detail is so perfect, and in such absolute taste."

It is no exaggeration to say that Mr. Morris's expert knowledge and discrimination had enabled him, during the few years he had been practically interested with printing, to gather together a library in artistic, if not in pecuniary value, second to no private collection in the land. He did not seek for rare specimens, but for beautiful; and, having obtained, he treated them with loving, and something near akin to reverential, care; and, as they had been the constant companions amongst which the later years of his life were spent, so he passed away, surrounded by books to the end.

By the terms of Mr. Morris's will it was left to his trustees to dispose of his books as a collection, or, failing this, in separate lots, should they think fit. The fate of this magnificent library, which was indeed a matter of public interest, was decided, after a period of uncertainty, by the whole collection being sold about six months after Morris's death. Even then the destination of his books was kept secret for a time, and afforded a subject of much speculation for the curious.

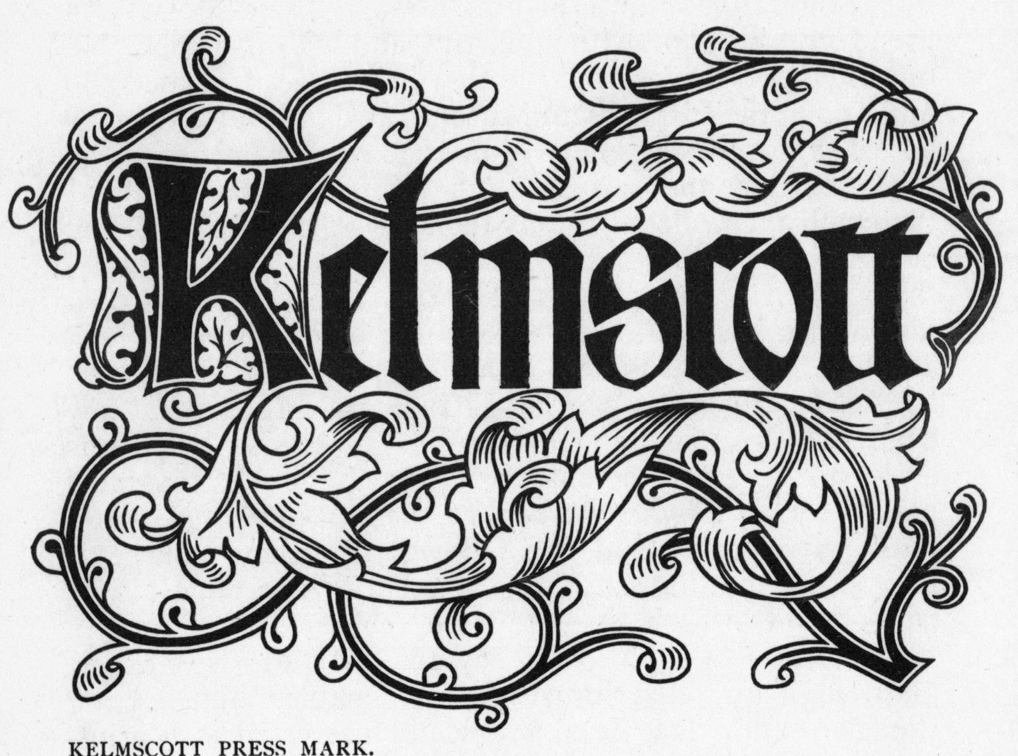

KELMSCOTT PRESS MARK.

CHAPTER FIFTEEN: THE ENDING OF DAYS.

IT may not be out of place, before concluding, to set down certain further characteristics of William Morris's not yet given in these pages. And first as to his literary judgments and preferences. On this subject there exists a tolerably complete register in the shape of the letter written by Mr. Morris at the instance of Mr. Stead, and included in the "Pall Mall Gazette Extra" (1886), on "The Best Hundred Books by the Best Judges." Morris prefaces his list by saying that he does "not pretend to prescribe reading for other people: the list I give you is of books which have profoundly impressed myself: I hope I shall be acquitted of egotism or conceit for having ventured to add a few notes to the list; in some cases I felt explanation was necessary; in all, it seemed to me that my opinion would be of no value unless it were given quite frankly; so I ask your readers to accept my list and notes as a confession such as might chance to fall from me in friendly conversation. . . . My list seems a short one, but it includes a huge mass of reading. . . . There is a kind of book which I think might be excluded in such lists, or at least put in a quite separate one. Such books are rather tools than books: one reads them for a definite purpose, for extracting information from them of some special kind. Among such books I should include works on philosophy, economics, and modern or critical history. I by no means . . . undervalue such works, but they are not, to my mind, works of art; their manner may be . . . even excellent, but it is not essential to them; their matter is a question of fact, not of taste. My list comprises only what I consider works of art. . . . I should note that I have by no means intended to put down these books in their order of merit or importance, even in their own divisions." The list commences with books which "are of the kind . . . Mazzini calls 'Bibles'; they cannot always be measured by a literary standard, but to me," says Morris, "are far more important than any literature. They are in no sense the work of individuals, but have grown up from the very hearts of the *people*. Some other books further down share in the nature of these 'Bibles,'" *e.g.*, Herodotus, some Norse and Icelandic tales and legends, the "Nibelungenlied," Danish and Border Ballads, Malory, and the "Arabian Nights." The following come under the first head: The "Hebrew Bible (excluding some twice done parts and some pieces of mere Jewish ecclesiasticism), Homer, Hesiod, 'The Edda' (including some of the other early old Norse romantic genealogical poems), 'Beowulf,' 'Kalevala,' 'Shahnameh,' 'Mahabharata,' Collections of folk tales, headed by Grimm and the Norse ones, Irish and Welsh traditional poems." The omission of the New Testament from the above list will doubtless be remarked. Morris thought very highly of "Beowulf." Indeed he considered it the finest poem surviving in the English language. Its lyrical qualities, according to him, are admirable, although its epical qualities, in the present fragmentary state in which the poem has come down to us, are impaired. The whole work would be less obscure if all the stories to which references are made in the course of the poem were extant. The list follows on with "*real* ancient imaginative works: Herodotus, Plato, Æschylus, Sophocles, Aristophanes, Theocritus, Lucretius, Catullus," others being omitted of which Morris confesses that he knows "little or nothing. The greater part of the Latins," says he, "I should call *sham* classics. I suppose that they have some good literary qualities; but I cannot help thinking that it is difficult to find out how much. I suspect superstition and authority have influenced our estimate of them till it has become a mere matter of convention. Of course I admit the archæological value of some of them, especially Virgil and Ovid." Morris's study of the Verrine orations at Oxford failed to convert him to any particular regard for Cicero; and yet, if he seems to underrate the merits of the ancient Latin writers, it was hardly from any animosity to the classics as such. For no man would think it worth while to transcribe, as Morris undertook to do, a long poem like the "Æneid"—much less to translate it—if he disliked it altogether. It is not pretended that he had a very active admiration for writers like Virgil and Horace, for example; but his attitude in this regard is to be attributed more than to anything else to his jealousy for the credit of the works of Anglo-Saxon and Scandinavian authors, whom we, in an excess of zeal for the classics, too commonly ignore. Again, notwithstanding his love for Homer, Morris held strongly to the opinion that rhyme was one of the requisites of poetry; therefore to the works of classical Latin poets he much preferred the late Latin hymns of Prudentius or Adam of St. Victor. And so, when at the close of 1895, Mr. Stead was canvassing celebrities for their opinions as to "Hymns that have helped me," the results being published in "The Review of Reviews," Mr. Morris gave a characteristic reply, which showed him, by the way, to be on this point in accord with the Catholic Archbishop, Dr. Walsh. "Mr. Morris says he knows no good English hymns; the only hymns which appeal to him are some hymns of the Middle Ages, which are in Latin." Morris then enumerates "uncritical or traditional histories: 'Plutarch's Lives,' 'Heimskringla,' . . . some half-dozen of the best Icelandic Sagas, the Anglo-Saxon Chronicle, William of Malmesbury, Froissart. Almost all these books are admirable pieces of tale-telling: some of them rise into the dignity of prose epics, so to say, especially in parts. Note, for instance, the last battle of Olaf Tryggvason in 'Heimskringla,' and the great rally of the rebels of Ghent in Froissart." It has been shown above how Morris related the last-named story in the pages of "The Commonweal." He proceeds next to "mediæval poetry," under which head he includes "Anglo-Saxon lyrical pieces (like the 'Ruin' and the 'Exile'), Dante, Chaucer, 'Piers Plowman,' 'Nibelungenlied,' the Danish and Scotch-English Border Ballads, 'Omar Khayyám' (though I don't know how much of the charm of this lovely poem is due to Fitzgerald, the translator), other Arab and Persian poetry, 'Renard the Fox,' a few of the best rhymed romances." Now, touching Chaucer, to whom it is obvious that Morris owed much, the poet begins the seventeenth book of his

"Jason" with the pious invocation, "Would that I," he says, "had but some portion of that mastery that . . . through these five hundred years such songs have sent to us, who, . . . love them yet."

"And thou, O Master!—Yea, my Master still,
Whatever feet have scaled Parnassus' hill,
Since like thy measures, clear and sweet and strong
Thames' stream scarce fettered drave the dace along
Unto the bastioned bridge, his only chain,—
O Master pardon me if yet in vain
Thou art my Master, and I fail to bring
Before men's eyes the image of the thing
My heart is filled with."

Morris speaks in still more fervent terms in L'Envoi of "The Earthly Paradise," when he addresses his book, ere discharging it forth into the world, the heart hot within it

"To reach the land of matters unforgot."

"Hast thou heard," he asks it:

"That therein I believe I have a friend,
Of whom for love I may not be afeard?
It is to him, indeed, I bid thee wend;
Yea, he perchance may meet thee ere thou end,
Dying so far off from the hedge of bay,
Thou idle singer of an empty day!

"Well, think of him, I bid thee, on the road,
And if it hap that midst of thy defeat,
Fainting beneath thy follies' heavy load,
My master, Geoffrey Chaucer, thou do meet,
Then shalt thou win a space of rest full sweet."

He then instructs the book in what words to speak to Chaucer in his name:

"'O master, O thou great of heart and tongue,
. . . Of thy gentleness draw thou anear
And then the heart of one who held thee dear
May'st thou behold! . . . .
. . . . who sent me forth
To seek a place amid thy company.

* * * * * *

Thou, keen-eyed, reading me, mayst read him through.

* * * * * *

Children we twain are, saith he, late made wise
In love, ...
O master, if thine heart could love us yet,
Spite of things left undone, and wrongly done,
Some place in loving hearts then should we get,
For thou, sweet-souled, didst never stand alone,
But knew'st the joy and woe of many an one—
By lovers dead, who live through thee we pray,
Help thou us singers of an empty day!'

"Fearest thou, Book, what answer thou mayst gain
Lest he should scorn thee, and thereof thou die?
Nay it shall not be.—Thou mayst toil in vain,
And never draw the House of Fame anigh;
Yet he and his shall know whereof we cry,
Shall call it not ill done to strive to lay
The ghosts that crowd about life's empty day."

Some later utterances, however, notably in the lecture on "Feudal England," in "Signs of Change" (1888), show a decided falling off in Morris's esteem for him whom he now describes as "the Court poet, the gentleman, Chaucer, with his Italianizing metres, and his formal recognition of the classical stories on which, indeed, he builds a superstructure of the quaintest and most unadulterated mediævalism, as gay and bright as the architecture which his eyes beheld and his pen pictured for us, so clear, defined, and elegant it is. . . . A kindly and human muse is Chaucer's, nevertheless, interested in and amused by all life, but of her very nature devoid of strong aspirations for the future; and that all the more, since . . . the habit of looking on this life as part of another yet remained: the world is fair and full of adventure; . . . when" it "is over we shall still go on living in another which is a part of this. . . . Note all and live in all, and be as merry as you may, never forgetting that you are alive and that it is good to live. That is the spirit of Chaucer's poetry; but alongside of it existed yet the ballad poetry of the people, wholly untouched by courtly elegance and classical pedantry; rude in art, but never coarse, true to the backbone; instinct with indignation against wrong, and thereby expressing the hope that was in it; a protest of the poor against the rich, especially in those songs of the Foresters, which have been called the mediæval epic of revolt; no more gloomy than the gentleman's poetry, yet cheerful from courage, and not content. . . . He who, when he has mastered the slight differences of language from our own speech, is not moved by it, does not understand what true poetry means, nor what its aim is. There is a third element in the literature of this time which you may call Lollard poetry, the great example of which is William Langland's 'Piers Plowman.' It is no bad corrective to Chaucer, and in *form* at least belongs wholly to the popular side." Morris has been heard to remark that, by the introduction of French words, Chaucer corrupted our language, whereas it should rather have gone on developing somewhat in the lines of the English of "Piers Plowman." But if he brought himself to write and to speak thus disparagingly of his master in the art of song, Morris surely made amends in the astounding diligence with which he prepared his unique reprint of Chaucer's works, and in the loving prodigality with which he adorned the pages of that work.

But to return from this digression to Morris's selected list again. Next in order he mentions "mediæval story books," among which he names Malory's "Morte d'Arthur," "The Thousand and One Nights," Boccaccio's "Decameron," and the "Mabinogion." "I know," he says of the first named, "that this is an ill-digested collection of fragments, but some of the best of the books it is made from ('Lancelot' is the best of them) are so long and so cumbered with unnecessary matter that one is thankful to Malory after all." Then follow "modern poets," of whom Morris would have it observed that he has not attempted to deal with any of "those of this generation, whether dead or alive." He names "Shakspeare, Blake (the part of him which a mortal can understand), Coleridge, Shelley, Keats, Byron." To refer back to the poetry of an earlier period, Morris regrets his inability to "read even *old* German" save "with great difficulty and labour; so I miss much good mediæval poetry—Hans Sachs, for instance." As for the later writers, "Goethe and Heine I cannot read, since I don't know German, and they cannot be translated." The

Germans, said Morris, dissatisfied with their language at the close of the mediæval period, spoilt it by introducing into it a syntax, with the pedantic device of making it more like Julius Cæsar's tongue. As for English poets, the absence from Morris's list may be remarked of Spencer, to whom oftentimes, nor that from every point of view unjustly, Morris himself has been compared. For the rest Morris rather dreads the consequences of the resentment of his countrymen for his having left out Milton, "but the union in his works of cold classicalism with Puritanism (the two things which I hate most in the world) repels me so that I *cannot* read him." Modern fiction is the next item on the list, and under this head Morris includes Bunyan's "Pilgrim's Progress," which, as he remarks elsewhere, "shines out, though a religious romance, amidst the dulness of the literature of the time," "Defoe's 'Robinson Crusoe,' 'Moll Flanders,' 'Colonel Jack,' 'Captain Singleton,' 'Voyage round the World,' Scott's novels (except the one or two which he wrote when he was hardly alive), Dumas, the elder (his good novels)"—though which of them all he approves as such Morris does not specify—"Victor Hugo (his novels), Dickens, George Borrow ('Lavengro' and 'Romany Rye')." With regard to the second writer named in this category, Morris observes elsewhere that the assumption "that the wealth of a country consists in the amount of the precious metals which it can retain . . . is curiously exemplified in the half-commercial, half-buccaneering romances of Defoe." Morris's supreme admiration for Sir Walter Scott has been recorded in an early chapter of the present work. A few words more of his on the same subject must suffice. "With that literature in which romance, that is to say humanity, was re-born, there sprang up also a feeling for the romance of external nature, which is surely strong in us now, joined with a longing to know something real of the lives of those who have gone before us; of these feelings united you will find the broadest expression in the pages of Walter Scott." A statement of Rossetti's may also be mentioned here, viz., that he frequently heard

Morris recommend "St. Ronan's Well" as being, in the latter's opinion, one of Scott's best. "Of the novelists of our generation," says Morris, "to my mind . . . Dickens is immeasurably ahead." Again, in one of his published lectures, lest possibly a certain allusion of his might be misunderstood, Morris was careful to append a note to explain: "I do not mean any disrespect to Dickens, of whom I am a humble worshipper." Morris's list concludes with several works which he does not know, he says, how to class, viz., Sir Thomas More's "Utopia," "Ruskin's works (especially the ethical and politico-economical parts of them), Thomas Carlyle's works, and, lastly, Grimm's "Teutonic Mythology," which, though it "is of the nature of the 'tools' above mentioned, . . . is so crammed with the material for imagination, and has in itself such a flavour of imagination, that I feel bound to put it down." Morris's opinion concerning certain writers not comprehended in the above list is worth recording. Thus he writes elsewhere: "The first part of the eighteenth century . . . finds England" with "a literature produced by a few word-spinning essayists and prosaic versifiers, like Addison and Pope, priding themselves on a well-bred contempt for whatever was manly or passionate or elevating in the past of their own language; while their devotion to the classical times, derived from the genuine and powerful enthusiasm of the Renaissance, had sunk to nothing but a genteel habit of expression." As to Dante Gabriel Rossetti, his long and close friendship with Morris, and the latter's enthusiasm for his poetical and artistic work, reference to the subject has already been made in these pages. Writing in "The Oxford and Cambridge Magazine" of March, 1856, Morris concludes an appreciative notice of "Men and Women" with the words: "I suppose, reader, that you see whereabouts among the poets I place Robert Browning; high among the poets of all time, and I scarce know whether first, or second, in our own: and it is a bitter thing to me to see the way in which he has been received by almost everybody; many having formed a certain theory of their own about him from reading, I suppose, some of the least finished poems among the 'Dramatic Lyrics,' make all facts bend to this theory . . : they think him, or say they think him, a careless man, writing down anyhow anything that comes into his head." In refutation of this view Morris adduces "the soft flow" of the poem "By the Fireside," and the "wonderful rhythm, . . . tender sadness" and "noble thoughts" of "Paracelsus." As to the charge of obscurity brought against Browning, Morris cannot combat *that*, but "I assert fearlessly," says he, "that this obscurity is seldom so prominent as to make his poems hard to understand on this ground: . . . it results from depth of thought and greatness of subject on the poet's part." If, however, instead of being "merely a department of 'light literature'" poetry "is rather one of the very grandest of all God's gifts to men, we must not think it hard if we have sometimes to exercise thought over a great poem, nay, even sometimes the utmost straining of all our thoughts, an agony almost equal to that of the poet who created the poem. However, this accusation against Browning of carelessness and consequent roughness in rhythm, and obscurity in language and thought, has come to be pretty generally believed; and people, as a rule, do not read him, . . . many are kept from reading . . . who, if they did read, would sympathize with him thoroughly. But it was always so; it was so with Tennyson when he first published his poems: it was so last year with 'Maud'; it is so with Ruskin; they petted him, indeed, at first, his wonderful eloquence having some effect even upon the critics; but as his circle grew larger and larger, embracing more and more the truth, they more and more fell off from him; his firm faith in right they call arrogance and conceit now; his eager fighting with falsehood and wrong they call unfairness." Morris's indecision expressed in the above passage as to whether Browning or Tennyson were the greater poet, vanished before long, and "in after years," says Mr. Herbert Horne, "the qualities which Morris found and admired in Tennyson appealed to him more and more—qualities of purely poetical and almost abstract beauty;" while his original high estimate of Browning underwent considerable modification. Nay, the poetry of the latter, with its "abrupt, formless methods," its obscurity, its theology, its subtle, introspective psychology, and "its constant dwelling on sin and probing of the secrets of the hearts," were in truth so essentially at variance with Morris's whole temperament that, spite of his earlier verdict, he came to entertain for it, in the end, a feeling near akin to dislike.

So much for Mr. Morris's opinions of other writers. And now as to his own position in literature. This is the tribute paid to him some years ago by another poet, and Oxford man, in "The Garden of Eros":

"Spirit of Beauty! tarry with us still,
It is not quenched the torch of poesy,
* * * * * * * *
O tarry with us still! for through the long and common night

Morris, our sweet and simple Chaucer's child,
Dear heritor of Spenser's tuneful reed,
With soft and sylvan pipe has oft beguiled
The weary soul of man in troublous need,
And from the far and flowerless fields of ice
Has brought fair flowers to make an earthly paradise.

"We know them all, Gudrun the strong men's bride,
Aslaug and Olafson we know them all,
How giant Grettir fought and Sigurd died,
And what enchantment held the king in thrall
When lonely Brynhild wrestled with the powers
That war against all passion, ah! how oft through summer hours
* * * * * * * *
Have I lain poring on the dreamy tales his fancy weaves,

And through their unreal woes and mimic pain
Wept for myself, and so was purified
And in their simple mirth grew glad again;
For as I sailed upon that pictured tide
The strength and splendour of the storm was mine
Without the storm's red ruin, for the singer is divine.

"The little laugh of water falling down
Is not so musical, the clammy gold
Close hoarded in the tiny waxen town
Has less of sweetness in it, and the old
Half-withered reeds that waved in Arcady
Touched by his lips break forth again to fresher harmony."

More recently a writer in "The Athenæum" says: "For something like three hundred years have Euphuism, the love of being didactic, and prose rhetoric been eating into English poetry. . . . As to the didactic element, the idea that the primary function of poetry was the enunciation of thoughts was at the bottom of the aridity of the eighteenth century; and even the great Romantic revival did not fully cure English poetry of this tendency. The love of preaching ate into the wings of Shelley. It threatened even Keats at the outset of his career. It made of Wordsworth a writer of quintessential prose who could occasionally take a glorious spring into poetry. It could not, of course, ruin Coleridge, but its effect upon him was so disastrous that his truly precious work is confined to about half a dozen poems. . . . It was left to our own time to produce the one poet of the nineteenth century upon whom Euphuism, the didactic spirit and rhetoric have exercised no influence whatever; that is to say, the one poet whose work is poetry and nothing else. Of all our writers Mr. Morris is, save in his . . . polemical chants, the most purely romantic. . . . That the two leading poets of the world are Englishmen—Mr. Swinburne and Mr. Morris—is recognised by all criticism that is worthy of the name."

On the death of Lord Tennyson the name of William Morris was freely mentioned in connection with the vacant Laureateship; and further it was asserted that he had been indirectly approached and sounded on behalf of the authorities as to whether he would be willing to accept the post in the event of its being offered to him officially. From the first, of course, Morris's holding such an office was out of the question. For that Laureate's would be an utterly anomalous position who must have remained for ever silent on the subject of the toings and froings, the matrimonial unions, the child-bearings, the bereavements, and such like domestic episodes in the fortunes of the reigning house. And, moreover, Morris made no secret of his conviction that the appointment to the Laureateship was on a par with that to any other office in the Royal household. It was not a question of poetical merit, but, on the contrary, a personal concern which rested solely with the sovereign's individual choice. Nevertheless, though it was inconceivable that Morris could ever have consented to occupy the post, his friends and admirers will gratify themselves with the thought of his having had that much recognition that the laurel wreath was placed within his reach if he had chosen to open his hand and take it; and that in any case the honour was assigned him in the consensus of a very large number of his fellow-countrymen. When he died the suggestion in various public ways was made that the Poets' Corner in Westminster Abbey was the most appropriate place for his remains to be laid in; nor, perhaps, the pomps and vanities of this world over, crowned heads and his un-laurelled head alike stricken low by the universal leveller Death, would William Morris, Socialist as he was, have disdained for his own dust to mingle with the dust of kings, within the walls of that hallowed shrine for whose inviolable preservation he had, in his lifetime, pleaded again and again. But it was not to be.

Several persons who professed to know have taken upon themselves to assure the public that William Morris was not musical. Now, although superficially the statement might be true, in its fullest sense nothing could be more false and misleading. With the graphic arts indeed—with all those which appeal to the eye, Morris had a closer affinity than with the art, or science, rather, which appeals to the ear; and, as may be noted, it came naturally to him in describing a musical performance, to borrow an image of his own craft. Thus the metaphor of the loom is used for harp-playing in the poem of "Sigurd the Volsung":

> "She ceased, and no voice made answer save the voice of smitten harps,
> As the hand of the music-weavers went o'er their golden warps."

In one of his earliest published utterances, "A Night in a Cathedral," (1856), Morris dwelt with passionate earnestness on the exquisite delight afforded him by ancient music as heard in some venerable cathedral of the old faith. Nor, albeit later years had brought revision of

Thenceforward Morris acted upon the advice, which was indeed that of a specialist. To have his MSS. bound was a simple matter, as his custom was to write on sheets of paper of uniform folio size; and Morris found himself taking quite an interest in these additions to his library. Among the volumes of his works which he preserved in this way were "Love is Enough," the translations of the "Æneids" and "Odyssey," together with his prose romances—"The Story of the Glittering Plain," "Child Christopher," and "The Well at the World's End."

Morris rarely cared to let himself be drawn into controversies in the newspapers. It has been mentioned already that he took no notice of Mr. Buchanan's attack upon him in the article on "The Fleshly School." All sorts of falsehoods about him used constantly to be appearing in print, but as a rule Morris chose to let them pass in dignified silence. He knew very well that, if he wrote and contradicted anything untrue which had been published concerning himself, the mere fact of his having corrected it would keep the affair open the longer by supplying the public with material for further discussion. People might talk for a few days of what they had read about him, but only until something more novel and more exciting should have occurred to divert their attention; and then the former subject would drop. So Morris's wisdom was generally to leave things alone, on the principle that the less said the sooner forgotten. For the most part it is doubtful whether Morris troubled his head with the numerous notices, etc., that were written concerning him. A friend of his once took a Frenchman who, to do him credit, was much impressed by the art-movement in this country, to be introduced to William Morris. The Frenchman previously announced his intention of asking Morris to name what he considered the most satisfactory account in English which had been published of himself and of his work. The foreigner was forewarned by the other, to whom Morris was no stranger, that it would be futile to put such a question, for that the latter was a man of absolutely single purpose, a man who, having a definite aim in view, pursued unswervingly his own way of obtaining it; was unconscious of other people's criticisms, and that, even if he did happen to read or hear of them, he would not be influenced in the smallest degree by the advice the officious might choose to tender him, being independent alike of the world's praise as of its censure. The Frenchman argued differently. Surely no man, he urged, can be so wholly indifferent as all that to the advancement of the cause he has at heart; surely no one can help caring and looking with interest for evidences of his principles gaining acceptance, of his work becoming appreciated; and in order to do this he *must* inform himself as to what the press says of him. It was a natural enough view to take, perhaps, and in the case of any other man than Morris it might have been the correct one. The sequel proved which was right, for the Frenchman persisting in disregard of the other's assurances, could scarcely conceal his disappointment at the result of the interview; his cross-questioning having failed, of course, to elicit the information he wanted from Morris. The fact was Mr. Morris was, before all things, a worker rather than a talker, at any rate when the subject of conversation was himself and his own achievements.

Mr. Bernard Shaw, in "The Saturday Review," writes thus of certain other traits of Morris's: "Now, when Morris would not take an interest in anything, and would not talk about it—and his capacity for this sort of resistance, both passive and active, was remarkably obstinate—it generally meant that he had made up his mind, on good grounds, that it was not worth talking about. A man's mouth may be shut and his mind closed much more effectually by his knowing all about a subject than by his knowing nothing about it; and whenever Morris suddenly developed a downright mulishness about anything, it was a sure sign that he knew it through and through and had quarrelled with it. Thus, when an enthusiast for some fashionable movement or reaction in art would force it into the conversation, he would often behave so as to convey an impression of invincible prejudice and intolerable ignorance, and so get rid of it. But later on he would let slip something that showed, in a flash, that he he had taken in the whole movement at its very first demonstration, and had neither prejudices nor illusions about it. When you knew the subject yourself, and could see beyond it and around it, putting it in its proper place and accepting its limits, he would talk fast enough about it; but it did not amuse him to allow novices to break a lance with him, because he had no special facility for brilliant critical demonstration, and required too much patience for his work to waste any of it on idle discussions. Consequently there was a certain intellectual roguery about him of which his intimate friends were very well aware; so that if a subject was thrust on him, the aggressor was sure to be ridiculously taken in if he did not calculate on Morris's knowing much more about it than he pretended to." Withal Morris was a wonderfully shrewd man, and it was not his wont to hazard an opinion on any subject unless he had thought it out first and arrived at some definite decision one way or the other. But, once satisfied in his own mind concerning it, he would remain fixed and unmovable in his conviction. And more than that, he would be extraordinarily downright in the expression of his views upon it; so much so that one hesitated sometimes to believe that he meant himself to be taken quite seriously. Still, no matter how startling his conclusions might appear, one would be tolerably certain to discover in the end that he had more sound and substantial reason on his side than his almost extravagant statement of the case might have inclined one to suspect. Take, for instance, the sweeping assertion as to the absence of any serious art in Japan. What a revelation is this to those who took their ideas of æstheticism from the pages of "Punch," from the silly gibes of "The Colonel," or the more elaborate but not less futile buffoonery of Gilbert's musical farce, "Patience!" All art—so Morris argued—must be related to architecture. Now architecture, which is the art of beautiful building, cannot in its noblest forms exist in any place where there is no security, but that buildings constructed otherwise than of wood are liable to

poem or tale. Once I heard him say anyone ought to be able to write a novel in six weeks, and that then it ought either to be so good or so bad that no subsequent revision could alter it materially. He said much more to the same purport, and it is mentioned here as an evidence that, in his judgment, the value of a literary product depended on the original inspiration, not on subsequent revision. His own activity in letters knew no abatement, and it was easier for him to begin writing on a fresh theme than to labour with patience at revising what he had written already." The absence, indeed, of what Cicero in one of his letters calls *limæ labor*, a process that is apt to take the life and soul out of a man's work and leave it a mere piece of dead academicalism, is one of the most striking of Morris's characteristics. His touch has the quality of being swift and firm and unfaltering; therefore, prodigious as was the amount of the work accomplished by Morris's brain and hand, it never seems jaded, never conveys the painful impression of having cost its author much anxious or prolonged effort to produce. And this was the result not by any means of carelessness and indifference, but rather of a faculty of mental absorption which, for the time being, enabled him to project his whole intelligence on one single object to the exclusion of all else. As Mr. Watts-Dunton has truly observed: "Whatever chanced to be Morris's goal of the moment was pursued by him with as much intensity as though the universe contained no other possible goal, and then, when the moment was passed, another goal received all his attention." This versatility of Morris's, this capacity for passing, from having been completely engrossed in one thing, as readily and unreservedly to another, is to be reckoned as one of the secrets of his success in his art. Indeed, as has been seen already, he laid down change of occupation as an essential condition. The worker "must be allowed" not only "to think of what he is doing," but also "to vary his work as the circumstances of it vary and his own moods." There is no surer way to preserve his buoyancy and spontaneity, to insure him from sinking into the dull insensibility of an automaton. Again, just as Mr. Pater says of Denys l'Auxerrois in "Imaginary Portraits:" "And that unrivalled fairness and freshness of aspect—how did he alone preserve it untouched through the wind and heat?", so, too, may it be asked concerning William Morris; what was the secret of his unflagging vigour and freshness? and much the same answer must be given: "by a natural simplicity of living," by a love of and a conformity, as far as might be, to elemental nature. For his part Morris was distinguished, in his own habits and surroundings, by the same frugality he enjoined upon others. To abstain "from multiplying our material wants unnecessarily . . . and, as far as we can, to see to it that" the articles we do use "are the work of free men and not of slaves; these two seem to me," says Morris, "to be the main duties to be fulfilled by those who wish to live a life at once free and refined, serviceable to others and pleasant to themselves." "Apart," however, "from the morality of the matter, . . . let me tell you," says Morris in one of his lectures, "that though simplicity in art may be costly as well as uncostly, at least it is not wasteful, and nothing is more destructive to art than the want of it. I have never been in any rich man's house which would not have looked the better for having a bonfire made outside of it of nine-tenths of all that it held. Indeed, our sacrifice on the side of luxury will, it seems to me, be little or nothing; for, as far as I can make out, what people usually mean by it is either a gathering of possessions which are sheer vexations to the owner, or a chain of pompous circumstance, which checks and annoys the rich man at every step. Yes, luxury cannot exist without slavery of some kind or other, and its abolition will be blessed like the abolition of other slaveries, by the freeing both of the slaves and of their masters." Again: "Simplicity is the one thing needful in furnishing, of that I am certain." "If only our houses were built as they should be, we should want such a little furniture, and be so happy in that scantiness. Even as it is, we should at all events take as our maxim the less the better: excess of furniture destroys the repose of a lazy man, and is in the way of an industrious one; and besides, if we really care for art we shall always feel inclined to save on superfluities, that we may have wherewithal to spend on works of art." "Believe me, . . . we must clear our houses of troublesome superfluities that are for ever in our way: conventional comforts that are no real comforts, and do but make work for servants and doctors: if you want a golden rule that will fit everybody this is it: '*Have nothing in your houses that you do not know to be useful, or believe to be beautiful.*'" Morris's opinion, the exact opposite to that which is commonly received, was that luxury is the curse instead of being the promoting cause and mainstay of the arts. For them to flourish wholesomely no Mæcenas is needed. Once again says Morris: "No room of the richest man should look grand enough to make a simple man shrink in it, or luxurious enough to make a thoughtful man ashamed in it; it will not do so if art be at home there, for she has no foes so deadly as insolence and waste. Indeed, I fear that at present the decoration of rich men's houses is mostly wrought out at the bidding of grandeur and luxury, and that art has been mostly cowed or shamed out of them. . . . Art was not born in the palace; rather she fell sick there, and it will take more bracing air than that of rich men's houses to heal her again. If she is ever to be strong enough to help mankind once more, she must gather strength in simple places; the refuge from wind and weather to which the goodman comes home from field or hill-side; the well-tidied space into which the craftsman withdraws from the litter of loom and smithy and bench; the scholar's island in the sea of books; the artist's clearing in the canvas-grove; it is from these places that Art must come if she is ever to be enthroned" again supreme amongst mankind.

Though not actually the latest, among the latest published of Mr. Morris's verses are some which appeared in the Catalogue of the Arts and Crafts Exhibition of the winter of 1893. They consist of one stanza of eight lines and two stanzas of ten lines each. They were written for the text to be embroidered by his daughter's hand on the hangings of the old tester bed on which Morris used to sleep at Kelmscott Manor. The poem itself, which begins "The wind 's on the wold," is in praise of rest, and as such has come to have a melancholy interest, and seems almost like a premonition of the poet's end. Another passage in the latest romance of his which Morris lived to see issued, has a similarly pathetic significance. One, speaking in the name of those who, having no very lofty aspirations, have already attained all their hearts' desire, says: "So have the gods given us the gift of Death lest we weary of Life." But such contentment was not meant for all. There were some who had a further mission to fulfil, who must go in quest of the life-giving waters. To such it was said: "Ye do but right to seek the Well at the World's End, that ye may the better accomplish that which behoveth you, and that ye may serve your fellows and deliver them from the thraldom of those that be strong and unwise and unkind." Nevertheless some should perish or ever they attained unto the object of their striving: "Ye must depart and leave undone things which ye deem ye were born to do, which to all men is grievous." Here then is the motive of living, to benefit one's fellow men, and the reason also why Morris should have felt an overwhelming sorrow at the prospect of dying ere yet his work had been fully accomplished. A more direct statement of his ideas on the subject of death may be gathered from "A Dream of John Ball," in the speech that passes between Morris himself and the aforesaid priest while they are supposed to be standing together beside the bier of one slain in a tumult. "'What sayest thou, scholar?'" asks John Ball, "'feelest thou sorrow of heart when thou lookest on this, either for the man himself, or for thyself and the time when thou shalt be as he is?' . . . 'Nay, I feel no sorrow for this; for the man is not here: this is an empty house, and the master has gone from it. Forsooth, this to me is but as a waxen image of a man; nay, not even that, for if it were an image it would be an image of the man as he was when alive. But here is no life, nor semblance of life. . . . I am more moved by the man's clothes and

APPENDIX I. CHRONOLOGICAL LIST OF THE PRINTED WORKS OF WILLIAM MORRIS.

"The Oxford and Cambridge Magazine," Contributions to, in Prose and Verse (*see* pp. 21 and 22 of this work). Bell and Daldy, Jan. to Dec., 1856.

Sir Galahad, a Christmas Mystery. Bell and Daldy, 1858.

The Defence of Guenevere, and other Poems. Bell and Daldy, 1858.

The Life and Death of Jason: a Poem (in seventeen books). 1867.

The God of the Poor: a Poem. "The Fortnightly Review," Aug., 1868.

The Two Sides of the River: a Poem. "The Fortnightly Review," Oct., 1868.

The Earthly Paradise (a poem in four parts, in three vols.). 1868-1870.

The Saga of Gunnlaug the Worm-tongue and Rafn the Skald (translation with E. Magnússon). "The Fortnightly Review," Jan., 1869. (Included in "Three Northern Love Stories," 1875).

Hapless Love: a Poem. "Good Words," April, 1869.

On the Edge of the Wilderness: a Poem. "The Fortnightly Review," April, 1869.

Grettis Saga. The Story of Grettir the Strong (translation with E. Magnússon). F. S. Ellis, 1869.

Poems by Dante Gabriel Rossetti: a Review. "The Academy," May 14, 1870.

Völsunga Saga. The Story of the Volsungs and Niblungs, with Certain Songs from the Elder Edda (translation with E. Magnússon) F. S. Ellis, 1870.

The Dark Wood: a Poem. "The Fortnightly Review" (reprinted in "Poems by the Way," 1891, under the title "Error and Loss"). Feb. 1, 1871.

The Seasons: Verses. "The Academy" (reprinted, with a variant for the last stanza, in "Poems by the Way," 1891). Feb. 1, 1871.

The Story of Frithiof the Bold (translation). "The Dark Blue," Vol. I., Mar. and Aug., 1871. (Included in "Three Northern Love Stories, 1875.)

Love is Enough, or the Fleeing of Pharamond: a Morality. Ellis and White, 1873.

Three Northern Love Stories, and other Tales (translation with E. Magnússon). Ellis and White, 1875.

The Æneids of Virgil done into English verse (dated 1876). Ellis and White, 1875.

England and the Turks. A letter to the Editor of "The Daily News." (Dated Oct. 24) Oct. 26, 1876.

The Two Sides of the River, Hapless Love, and The First Foray of Aristomenes (three poems, of which the first was reprinted in "Poems by the Way," 1891) Printed privately, 1876.

The Story of Sigurd the Volsung, and the Fall of the Niblungs. Poem in four books. Ellis and White, 1877.

On Canterbury Cathedral. Two letters to "The Times." June 4 and July 7, 1877.

The Principles of the Society for the Protection of Ancient Buildings. Broadside issued officially by the Society. (Reprinted 1891) 1877.

"Wake, London Lads," &c. Verses on a broadside for distribution at Exeter Hall. Jan. 16, 1878.

Destruction of City Churches. Letter to "The Times." April 17, 1878.

On St. Albans Abbey. Letter to "The Times." Aug. 2, 1878.

The Decorative Arts, their Relation to Modern Life and Progress. An Address. (Reprinted with the title "The Lesser Arts" in "Hopes and Fears for Art.") 1878.

An Address delivered at Birmingham on 19 February. (Reprinted with the title "The Art of the People" in "Hopes and Fears for Art.") 1879.

Quatrain for four paintings by E. Burne-Jones. Catalogue of the Summer Exhibition at the Grosvenor Gallery. 1879.

Speech on June 28, printed in the Annual Report of the Society for the Protection of Ancient Buildings. 1879.

On the Restoration of St. Mark's, at Venice. Two letters to "The Times." Nov. 28 and 29, 1879.

Labour and Pleasure *versus* Labour and Sorrow, an address at Birmingham. (Reprinted with the title "The Beauty of Life." in "Hopes and Fears for Art.") Feb. 19, 1880.

Vandalism in Italy. Letter to "The Times." April 12, 1882.

Hopes and Fears for Art. Five Lectures. 1882.

"The History of Pattern Designing" and "The Lesser Arts of Life," two lectures included in "Lectures on Art," delivered in support of the Society for the Protection of Ancient Buildings by various authors. 1882.

A Summary of the Principles of Socialism, written for the Democratic Federation, with H. M. Hyndman as joint-author. 1883-4.

Report of Royal Commission on Technical Education, Vol. III., Mr. Morris's evidence, March 17, 1882. Published in 1884.

Mural Decoration, illustrated article, with Professor Middleton as joint-author, in "Encyclopædia Britannica," Vol. XVII., ninth edition. 1884.

The Three Seekers: a Poem, in "To-Day." Jan., 1884.

"Justice, the Organ of the Social Democracy," Contributions to, from Jan. 19, 1884, to Dec. 20, 1884.

Art and Socialism: a Statement of the Aims and Ideals of the English Socialists of To-Day. A Lecture at Leicester, Jan. 23, 1884.

Art under Plutocracy. A lecture delivered at Oxford, Nov. 14, 1883. "To-Day," Feb. and Mar., 1884.

Meeting in Winter: a Poem. "The English Illustrated Magazine," Mar., 1884.

The Exhibition of the Royal Academy by a Rare Visitor. "To-Day," July, 1884.

Textile Fabrics: a Lecture at the International Health Exhibition. July 11, 1884.

The Mediæval and the Modern Craftsman. An address published (without authorization) in "Merry England." Oct., 1884.

Mr. William Morris and Socialism. A letter (dated Oct. 4) to the Editor of "The Echo." Oct. 7, 1884.

Introduction, dated Sept. 29, to J. Sketchley's "A Review of European Society with an Exposition and Vindication of the Principles of the Social Democracy." November, 1884.

Chants for Socialists, No. I., "The Day is Coming." 1884.

The Voice of Toil: All for the Cause. Two Chants for Socialists. Reprinted from "Justice," 1884.

For whom shall we Vote? Addressed to the Working-men Electors of Great Britain. 1884.

What Socialists Want (leaflet). 1884.

The Manifesto of the Socialist League. Dec. 30, 1884.

"The Commonweal," the Official Journal of the Socialist League, Contributions to. From Feb. 1885, to Nov. 15, 1890.

Address on June 4, printed in the Annual Report of the Society for the Protection of Ancient Buildings. 1885.

Socialists at Play. Prologue at the Entertainment of the Socialist League. June 11, 1885.

The Manifesto of the Socialist League, a new edition annotated by William Morris and E. Belfort Bax. 1885.

Chants for Socialists (six poems); another edition with an additional poem. 1885.

Useful Work *v.* Useless Toil; pamphlet (editorial note bears signature of W. Morris and E. B. Bax). 1885.

A Short Account of the Commune of Paris; pamphlet, with two others as joint-authors. 1886.

Socialism, a Lecture at Norwich on March 8. Printed in "Daylight," 1886.

On Profit Sharing. Extracts from a letter, dated April 21, 1884, published at the end of an article "A Day in Surrey with William Morris," by Emma Lazarus, in "The Century Magazine." July, 1886.

The Labour Question from the Socialist Standpoint. Claims of Labour Lectures, No. 5. 1886.

The Best Hundred Books. "Pall Mall Gazette" (extra), No. 24, 1886.

The Pilgrims of Hope: a poem in thirteen books, brought together from "The Commonweal." (Privately printed), 1886.

The Aims of Art (republished in "Signs of Change"). 1887.

The Tables Turned; or, Nupkins Awakened. A Socialist Interlude performed Oct. 15, 1887.

Alfred Linnell (Nov. 20): A Death Song. 1887.

Christmas Song. Boston, U.S.A., 1887.

The Odyssey of Homer done into English verse. 2 vols. 1887.

True and False Society. A pamphlet. 1888.

A Dream of John Ball and a King's Lesson. (Reprinted from "The Commonweal.") April, 1888.

Signs of Change. Seven Lectures delivered on various occasions. The preface is dated March, 1888.

The Revival of Architecture. "The Fortnightly Review," May, 1888.

Textiles. Essay prefixed to Arts and Crafts Exhibition Society's Catalogue. 1888.

The Revival of Handicraft. "The Fortnightly Review," Nov., 1888.

On Tapestry and Carpet Weaving. Report of Mr. Morris's Lecture. "The Times," Nov. 2, 1888.

Preface to F. Fairman's "The Principles of Socialism made Plain." 1888.

A Tale of the House of the Wolfings and all the Kindreds of the Mark. Written in prose and in verse. Dec., 1888.

Westminster Abbey and its Monuments. "The Nineteenth Century," Mar., 1889.

Address on July 3, printed in the Annual Report of the Society for the Protection of Ancient Buildings. 1889.

On Peterborough Cathedral. Letter to the "Pall Mall Gazette," Sept. 20, 1889.

Of Dyeing as an Art. Essay prefixed to the Arts and Crafts Exhibition Society's Catalogue. 1889.

Art and Industry in the Fourteenth Century. "Time," Jan., 1890.

News from Nowhere, or an Epoch of Rest: being some Chapters from a Utopian Romance.
Appeared serially in "The Commonweal" from Jan. 11 to Oct. 4, 1890.
(Published in book form 1891.)

The Hall and the Wood: a Poem. "The English Illustrated Magazine," Feb., 1890.

The Roots of the Mountains, wherein is told somewhat of the Lives of the Men of Burgdale, their Friends, their Neighbours, their Foemen and. their Fellows in Arms. 1890.

The Story of the Glittering Plain, which has been also called the Land of Living Men, or the Acre of the Undying.
Appeared first serially in "The English Illustrated Magazine, 1890.
(Published in book form 1891.)

On Stratford-on-Avon Church. Letter to "The Times," Aug. 15, 1890.

On the Hanseatic Museum at Bergen. Letter to "The Times," Sept. 10, 1890.

The Legend of the Briar Rose: 1. The Briarwood; 2. The Council Room; 3. The Garden Court; 4. The Rosebower. Verses for picture painted by E. Burne-Jones, exhibited at Thos. Agnew and Sons' Galleries. 1890.

The Day of Days: a Poem. "Time," Nov., 1890.

Monopoly: or, How Labour is Robbed. A pamphlet. 1890.

The Socialist Ideal. I. Art. "The New Review," Jan., 1891.

On Westminster Abbey. Letter to "The Times," Feb. 11, 1891.

Under an Elm Tree; or, Thoughts in the Country Side. Pamphlet reprinted from "The Commonweal." 1891.

Poems by the Way. 1891.

Address on the Collection of Paintings of the English Pre-Raphaelite School. Delivered at Birmingham Oct. 2, 1891.

The Saga Library, with Maps. Done into English out of the Icelandic with E. Magnússon:—

- Vol. I. The Story of Howard the Halt. The Story of the Banded Men. The Story of Hen Thorir. 1891.
- Vol. II. The Story of the Eve-Dwellers with the Story of the Heath-Slayings. 1892.
- Vols. III., IV., V. and VI. The Stories of the Kings of Norway, called the Round World (Heimskringla). (*In progress*) 1893 *sqq.*

Two letters to W. Bell Scott, dated May 6, 1875 and April 27, 1882, printed in "Autobiographical Notes of the Life of W. Bell Scott." 2 vols. 1892.

The Influence of Building Materials upon Architecture (by permission of the Art Workers' Guild). "The Century Guild Hobby Horse," Jan., 1892.

On the External Coverings of Roofs. Leaflet issued by the Society for the Protection of Ancient Buildings. N. D.

The Woodcuts of Gothic Books. A paper read before the Society of Arts. Jan. 26. "Journal of the Society of Arts," Feb. 12, 1892.
Preface to J. Ruskin's "The Nature of Gothic." Dated Feb. 15, 1892.
May Day: a Poem. "Justice," April 30, 1892.
The Ordination of Knighthood, verse translation from old French, included in "The Order of Chivalry." Nov., 1892.
Preface to Medieval Lore, an Epitome of the Science, Geography, Animal and Plant Folk-Lore and Myth of the Middle Age: being Classified Gleanings from the Encyclopedia of Bartholomew Anglicus on the "Properties of Things." Edited by Robert Steele. 1893.
Prospectus for the Kelmscott edition of "Sidonia the Sorceress." 1893.
The Ideal Book; a paper read on June 19, published in the Transactions of the Bibliographical Society. 1893.
Preface to Arts and Crafts Essays. Dated July, 1893.
In this work are reprinted Mr. Morris's Essays on Textiles and of Dyeing as an Art, and his name also appears as joint-author of the re-cast Essay on Printing, which, in its original form, had been issued in the name of Emery Walker alone.
Foreword to Sir Thomas More's "Utopia." Aug., 1893.
"The Wind's on the Wold," etc., verses for embroidery. Arts and Crafts Exhibition Society's Catalogue of the Fourth Exhibition. 1893.
The Printing of Books. Report of Mr. Morris's Lecture. "The Times," Nov. 6, 1893.
Help for the Miners: the Deeper Meaning of the Struggle. A letter to "The Daily Chronicle." Nov. 10, 1893.
Gothic Architecture. A Lecture for the Arts and Crafts Exhibition Society; delivered 1889, and printed. 1893.
Socialism, its Growth and Outcome. With E. Belfort Bax as joint author. 1893.
The Reward of Labour: a Dialogue. Reprinted from "The Commonweal," N.D.
Of King Florus and the Fair Jehane. Translation from old French romance. Dec., 1893.
Some Notes on the Illuminated Books of the Middle Ages (Illustrated). "Magazine of Art," Jan., 1894.
Early England. Report of Mr. Morris's Lecture. "The Daily Chronicle," Jan. 15, 1894.
The Proposed Addition to Westminster Abbey. Letter to "The Daily Chronicle," Feb. 27, 1894.
Of the Friendship of Amis and Amile. Translation from old French romance. Mar., 1894.
May Day, 1894: a Poem. "Justice," May 5, 1894.
The Wood Beyond the World. May, 1894.
How I became a Socialist. "Justice," June 16, 1894.
Mr. Morris's Chaucer. Letter to "The Daily Chronicle," July 24, 1894.
The Tale of the Emperor Coustans and of Over Sea. Translations from old French romances. Aug., 1894.
Introductory Note, dated Sept., 1894, to A. J. Gaskin's illustrated edition of Dr. J. M. Neale's carol "Good King Wenceslas." Birmingham, antedated 1895.
Concerning Westminster Abbey. Pamphlet issued by the Society for the Protection of Ancient Buildings. 1894.

Letters on Socialism, four, addressed to Rev. G. Bainton.
Privately printed, 1894.
Communism. A pamphlet. 1894.
The Tale of Beowulf, done out of the old English tongue, with A. J. Wyatt as joint translator. Jan., 1895.
Peterborough Cathedral, letter to the Daily Papers. April 2, 1895.
Tree-Felling in Epping Forest, letter to "The Daily Chronicle."
April 23, 1895.
Change of Position—not Change of Condition.
"Justice," May Day special number, 1895.
Epping Forest, Mr. Morris's Report on.
"The Daily Chronicle," May 9, 1895.
On the Royal Tombs in Westminster Abbey.
Letter to "The Times," June 1, 1895.
On "The Wood beyond the World."
Letter to "The Spectator," July 20, 1895.
Of Child Christopher and Fair Goldilind. July, 1895.
Rouen Cathedral. Letter to "The Daily Chronicle," Oct. 12, 1895.
Gossip about an Old House on the Upper Thames (Illustrated). Dated Oct., 25. "The Quest," Birmingham, Nov., 1895.
Trinity Almhouses. Letter to "The Daily Chronicle," Nov. 26, 1895.
Peterborough Cathedral. Letter to "The Daily Chronicle," Dec. 5, 1895.
Chichester Cathedral. Letter to "The Times," Dec. 14, 1895.
On the Artistic Qualities of the Woodcut Books of Ulm and Augsburg in the Fifteenth Century (Illustrated). "Bibliographica," Vol. I., 1895.
The Well at the World's End. March, 1896.
The Water of the Wondrous Isles. Published July, 1897.
The Sundering Flood. (*In the press.*)

APPENDIX II. PUBLICATIONS OF THE KELMSCOTT PRESS.

The Story of the Glittering Plain, by William Morris. April 4, 1891.
Poems by the Way, written by William Morris. Sept. 24, 1891.
The Love Lyrics and Songs of Proteus, by Wilfrid Scawen Blunt. Jan. 26, 1892.
The Nature of Gothic: a Chapter of the "Stones of Venice," by John Ruskin. Feb., 15, 1892.
The Defence of Guenevere and other Poems, by William Morris. April 2, 1892.
A Dream of John Ball and a King's Lesson, by William Morris. May 13, 1892.
The Golden Legend of Master William Caxton done anew. 3 vols. Sept. 12, 1892.
The Recuyell of the Historyes of Troy, new edition of William Caxton's. Oct. 14, 1892.
Biblia Innocentium: being the Story of God's Chosen People before the Coming of Our Lord Jesus Christ upon Earth, written anew for children by J. W. Mackail. Oct. 22, 1892.
News from Nowhere: or An Epoch of Rest, being some Chapters from a Utopian Romance, by William Morris. Nov. 22, 1892.
The History of Reynard the Foxe, done into English out of the Dutch. Dec. 15, 1892.
The Poems of William Shakespeare: printed after the original copies of Venus and Adonis, 1593; The Rape of Lucrece, 1594; Sonnets, 1609; The Lover's Complaint, Jan. 17, 1893.
The Order of Chivalry, translated from the French by William Caxton, finished Nov. 10, 1892; and The Ordination of Knighthood. Feb. 24, 1893.
The Life of Thomas Wolsey, Cardinal, Archbishop of York, written by George Cavendish. Mar. 30, 1893.
The History of Godefrey of Boloyne and of the Conquest of Iherusalem, new edition of William Caxton's. April 27, 1893.
Utopia, written by Sir Thomas More. Aug. 4, 1893.
Maud: a Mono-Drama, by Alfred Lord Tennyson. Aug. 11, 1893.
Sidonia the Sorceress, by William Meinhold; translated by Francesca Speranza Lady Wilde. Sep. 15, 1893.
Gothic Architecture; a Lecture for the Arts and Crafts Exhibition Society, by William Morris, printed by the Kelmscott Press during the Arts and Crafts Exhibition at the New Gallery, Regent Street, London. 1893.
Ballads and Narrative Poems, by Dante Gabriel Rossetti. Oct. 14, 1893.
Of King Florus and the fair Jehane. Dec. 16, 1893.
The Story of the Glittering Plain: or The Land of Living Men, by William Morris, ornamented with 23 pictures by Walter Crane. Jan. 13, 1894.
Sonnets and Lyrical Poems, by Dante Gabriel Rossetti. Feb. 20, 1894.
The Poems of John Keats. Mar. 7, 1894.
Of the Friendship of Amis and Amile, done out of the ancient French into English by William Morris. Mar. 13, 1894.
Atalanta in Calydon: a Tragedy, made by Algernon Charles Swinburne. May 4, 1894.
The Wood beyond the World, by William Morris. May 30, 1894.

The Tale of the Emperor Coustans and of Over Sea. Aug. 30, 1894.

The Book of Wisdom and Lies, a Georgian Story-book of the Eighteenth Century, by Sulkhan-Saba Orbeliani; translated, with notes, by Oliver Wardrop. Sept. 29, 1894.

Psalmi Penitentiales: an ancient rhymed version. Nov. 15, 1894.

Epistola de Contemptu Mundi di Frate Hieronymo da Ferrara dellordine de frati predicatori la quale mada ad Elena Buonaccorsi sua madre, per consolarla della morte del fratello suo Zio. Nov., 1894.

The Poetical Works of Percy Bysshe Shelley. 3 vols. Aug. 21, 1895.

The Tale of Beowulf sometime King of the Folk of the Weder Geats, done out of the Old English tongue by William Morris and A. J. Wyatt. Jan. 10, 1895.

Syr Percyvelle of Gales. Feb. 16, 1895.

The Life and Death of Jason: a Poem, by William Morris. May 25, 1895.

Of Child Christopher and fair Goldilind, by William Morris. 2 vols. July 25, 1895.

Hand and Soul, by Dante Gabriel Rossetti. Oct. 24, 1895.

Poems chosen out of the Works of Robert Herrick. Nov. 21, 1895.

Poems chosen out of the Works of Samuel Taylor Coleridge. Feb. 5, 1896.

The Well at the World's End, by William Morris. Mar. 2, 1896.

The Earthly Paradise, by William Morris. Vol. I. Finished May 7, 1896.
(To be completed in eight volumes; in progress.)

The Works of Geoffrey Chaucer, ornamented with pictures by Sir Edward Burne-Jones. May 8, 1896.

Laudes Beatæ Mariæ Virginis: early thirteenth century poem. July 7, 1896.

The Floure and the Leafe, and the Boke of Cupide, God of Love, or the Cuckow and the Nightingale. Aug. 21, 1896.

The Shepheardes Calendar: conteyning Twelve Æglogues, proportionable to the Twelve Monethes. With twelve illustrations by A. J. Gaskin. Oct. 14, 1896.

The Water of the Wondrous Isles, a new romance by William Morris. Ready July 28, 1897.

THE FOLLOWING IN THE PRESS:

Sire Degravaunt.

Sire Isumbras.

Sigurd the Volsung and the Fall of the Niblungs, by William Morris. Small folio.

The Sundering Flood, the last romance written by William Morris.

Two Specimen Pages of Froissart's Works, with the special armorial border and ornaments designed for this book by William Morris. Folio.

Love is Enough, by William Morris.

INDEX.

PUBLIC SECTOR LABOR RELATIONS: ANALYSIS AND READINGS